COLLI

COMPI

MEDITERRANEAN
WILDLIFE

PHOTOGUIDE

PAUL STERRY

John & Margaret
Oubridge

HarperCollins*Publishers*

HarperCollins*Publishers* Ltd
77-85 Fulham Palace Road
London W6 8JB

The HarperCollins website address is www.**fire**and**water**.com

I am grateful for the shared enthusiasm and knowledge of a number of
people who have helped with the preparation of this book over the past
few years. In particular, I would like to thank Andrew Cleave, whose
advice on the subject of Mediterranean wildlife has been invaluable.
I am also indebted to Lee Morgan, Michael Foord, Gary and Debbie
Day, and Mark and Jane Bolton for their company and various
expertises and to Michael Chinery for his help with the
identification of invertebrates.

First published 2000

1 3 5 7 9 8 6 4 2

00 02 04 05 03 01

Collins is a registered trademark of HarperCollins*Publishers* Ltd.

ISBN 0 00 220161 5

Colour reproduction by Colourscan, Singapore
Printed and bound by Rotolito Lombarda SpA, Milan, Italy

CONTENTS

INTRODUCTION

The last 50 years has seen an explosion in the number of visitors travelling to the Mediterranean and today the region is Europe's premier holiday destination. Resort developments have sprung up in almost every country with a coastal boundary and there are comparatively few areas now that cannot be reached with ease from almost anywhere further north in Europe or indeed from elsewhere in the world.

As a naturalist contemplating a first time visit to the region, the prospect of rubbing shoulders with thousands of sun-seeking tourists against a backdrop of towering hotel developments may seem a bit off-putting. However, as any seasoned visitor will tell you, the vast majority of tourists concentrate around the resorts themselves and seldom venture further afield during their stays. Consequently, the majority of sites with wildlife interest remain comparatively deserted for much of the time and you can have thrilling encounters with birds and discover spectacular displays of flowers with nothing more the buzzing of insects for company.

With each passing year, it would seem that the proportion of visitors to the Mediterranean whose primary interest is natural history increases. Some are happy just to enjoy the plants and animals that they encounter for their own sakes but the majority of these naturalists is keen enough to want to put names to new species they encounter. Therein lies something of a problem. Naturalists from northern Europe are spoilt for choice when it comes to field guides for their region and there are few subject areas of their natural world that are not covered to some degree. Expect the same of the Mediterranean region and you are likely to be frustrated. Certainly botanists and birdwatchers will find a number of excellent and comprehensive guides to their fields of interest but other groups are poorly covered. In part, *Complete Mediterranean Wildlife* was

Mallorca's Formentor Peninsula boasts breathtaking coastal views.

born of this frustration and within the constraints of a book of modest proportions it tries to cater for those with an all-round interest in natural history. It is aimed at people whose visit to the Mediterranean lasts perhaps not much longer than two or three weeks but who are willing, on a daily basis, to travel for a few hours in search of the region's wonderful wildlife.

THE REGION COVERED BY THIS BOOK

Study a map of the Mediterranean region and you will discover it to be centred around the almost land-locked Mediterranean Sea, which stretches from Strait of Gibraltar in the west to the coasts of Syria and Israel in the east. This book has been designed to provide general wildlife coverage for the whole of this region although emphasis has been given to species likely to be encountered at sites easily accessible to, and regularly visited by, tourists. This has meant focusing mainly on the northern shores of the sea, from Spain to Turkey.

For the short-term visitor, the bulk of the Mediterranean's wildlife interest is concentrated along the coastal strip that extends usually some 100 miles or so inland. All of the central Mediterranean islands are important wildlife sites and, being a favoured holiday destination, Cyprus has also been included too. The influence of the Mediterranean climate is far-reaching and extends along the Algarve coast of Portugal, strictly speaking not in the Mediterranean, and across much of the southern half of the Iberian Peninsula, almost the whole of Italy, as well as Greece and the Balkans. The book's coverage extends to these areas as well.

Much of the Mediterranean coast is low-lying but in some parts of the region the land rises steeply inland and you only have to travel comparatively short distances to reach considerable altitudes. Thus on Cyprus for example a journey of less than two hours can take you from sun-baked maquis near the sea to areas where snow still lies in April. Although some of the species found here

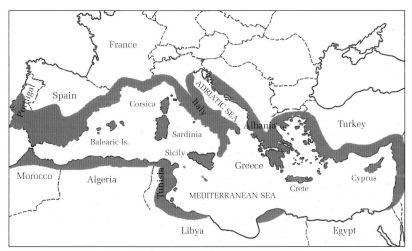

Regions that experience a Mediterranean climate

might not be Mediterranean flora and fauna in the strict sense, they are part of many people's holiday experience when visiting the region and hence some of them are included in this book. Truly alpine plants and animals are, however, not covered.

HOW TO USE THIS BOOK

This book has been designed so that the text and photographs for each species are on facing pages. An easy to use series of grids, placed next to each species description, clearly identifies which photograph corresponds to the appropriate text. The text has been written to complement the information conveyed by the photographs.

At the start of each species description the most commonly used and current English name is given – where one exists – followed by the scientific name of the plant or animal in question: this comprises the species' genus name first followed by its specific name. There then follows some measure of the species' size. In the case of mammals, and many birds, this is often the length but in the case of birds or insects usually seen in flight or with their wings spread, wingspan was felt to be a more useful indicator of absolute and relative size. With other animals, the most appropriate dimension, be that height, length or width has been used, this being clearly indicated alongside the dimension itself. Similarly with the plants, overall height, or sometimes flower length or width, has been employed as appropriate.

The text has been written in a condensed manner so that as much information as possible could be included. It begins with a description of the species in question. With some groups, for example, birds, this is broadened to cover male, female and juvenile, and summer or winter plumages, where necessary. For insects, stages in the life cycle not illustrated are sometimes mentioned when these are conspicuous and distinctive.

With the exception of some bird species, the animals covered in the book are essentially resident. Where a bird is migratory, however, an indication is given of the months or seasons during which it is likely to be present in the region; many migrants are present during the breeding season only while a few are strictly non-breeding winter visitors. In the case of plants, the flowering season is given and for seasonal invertebrates, the main months of appearance are stated. For all the plants and animals covered in the book, an indication is given as to their favoured habitats. The range over which they occur is conveyed by a variety of means. If the species in question has a restricted distribution then specific countries or islands are sometimes mentioned. If it is widespread then this is stated. Sub-divisions of the region are also used on occasions: W Mediterranean covers an area roughly from Italy westwards; C Mediterranean covers an area from Italy to Greece and their respective associated islands; E Mediterranean covers an area from Greece eastwards. An idea of relative abundance or scarcity is also given; use of the term widespread implies not only that a species occurs widely throughout the region but also that it is at least locally common.

THE CHOICE OF SPECIES

Because the Mediterranean region harbours such a rich and diverse variety of wildlife, the selection of species for inclusion in this book was always going to be difficult. The choice was influenced strongly by the interests of the numerous wildlife enthusiasts whom I have encountered in the Mediterranean over the past few years. I have tried to include all of the characteristic and distinctive plants and animals that the visitor might hope to encounter on a two-week visit to the region and for which there is a reasonable prospect of determining identity. However, since the primary interests of most visitors appear to be birds, butterflies and flowers – and in particular·orchids – these areas have been particularly thoroughly covered. The emphasis among the species has been on plants and animals that will be encountered on land. Species that may be found while scouring the seashores or snorkelling in the shallows are also included but no attempt has been made to cover those that will be found only by diving in deeper water or far from land.

Colourful bee-eaters are present in the region from May to September.

THE CHOICE OF PHOTOGRAPHS

Foremost on my mind when choosing the photographs for this book was their role as identification aids. Thus I tried to select pictures that illustrated clearly the most characteristic features of any given species. In certain subject areas, space only permitted the inclusion of a single photograph for species that occur in several different forms. For example, among birds, some species may be encountered in several different states of plumage, determined for example by the sex of the individual, its age and the time of year. Where it was possible to include just a single photograph, it was chosen to illustrate the most distinctive plumage or the one most usually encountered in the Mediterranean; this is not always one and the same thing. Generally this means that the photograph is of a male but other plumages are clearly detailed in the text with reference to the picture used. In most cases, the photographs of plants show specimens in flower since this is when they are most distinctive and hence easiest to identify.

PLANT AND ANIMAL GROUPS

Scientists and naturalists divide plants and animals into groups, members of which have characters in common with one another. The species included in this book have been organised into these widely accepted groups and the accompanying notes detail their most distinctive features. The coloured symbols to the left of the page correspond to those used throughout the book as thumbnail indicators of page subjects.

VERTEBRATE ANIMALS

Animals with backbones which comprise:

 Mammals: warm-blooded animals which have hairy skins, give birth to live young which are subsequently suckled by the mother.

 Birds: warm-blooded animals whose skins are covered with feathers, these aiding heat regulation and allowing flight; all birds lay eggs.

 Reptiles: cold-blooded animals with scaly skins and which breathe air. The young develop inside eggs which, in some species, hatch within the body of the female.

 Amphibians: cold-blooded animals with soft, moist skins capable of absorbing oxygen from water; also have lungs and can breathe air. Often found on land but always breed in water, laying eggs which grow as larval tadpoles before metamorphosing into miniature adults.

 Fish: cold-blooded animals that live in water throughout their lives; all the species use gills to extract oxygen from water. In most species, the skin is covered with scales and fins facilitate swimming.

INVERTEBRATE ANIMALS

Animals without backbones which include:

Sponges: primitive, aquatic animals whose bodies have external vents and are covered in minute pores.

Coelenterates: radially symmetrical, soft-bodied creatures that include sea anemones, jellyfish and freshwater hydras.

 Molluscs: soft-bodied animals that occur on land, in freshwater and in the sea. Some molluscs protect their bodies by producing hard shells, while this feature is absent or much reduced in slugs, sea slugs and octopuses.

9

Segmented worms: examples of which occur in soil, freshwater and in the sea. The body is soft, segmented and often bears bristles to aid movements as with earthworms and marine annelid worms.

 Arthropods: the most numerous group of animals and one which is characterised by the presence of an external skeleton and paired, jointed limbs. Members include Insects, Crustaceans, Spiders and allies, Millipedes and Centipedes. Insects groups dealt with in this book include butterflies and moths, mayflies, dragonflies and damselflies, grasshoppers and crickets, earwigs, mantids, lacewings, bugs, bees, wasps, ants and beetles; Crustacean groups covered include woodlice, crabs, shrimps, prawns and barnacles; spider allies include scorpions.

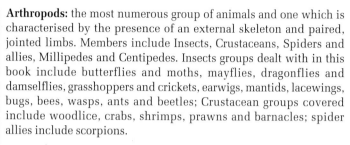 **Echinoderms:** animals which are radially symmetrical, mostly organised into five rays. Some members have bodies protected by a hard shell comprising armoured plates with spines. Included in the book are sea urchins, starfishes and brittlestars.

HIGHER PLANTS

Distinguished from animals by the presence of the green pigment chlorophyll which is used to manufacture food from sunlight energy, water and carbon dioxide; oxygen is produced as a by-product of this chemical reaction known as photosynthesis. Higher plants come in all shapes and sizes and are separated into two groups:

 Flowering Plants: plants whose reproductive structures are borne in flowers; their seeds are enclosed in structures known as fruits, a term which, for botanists, is not confined to conspicuous and edible forms. Flowering plants covered in this book include deciduous and some evergreen trees, shrubs and wildflowers. For ease of interpretation, some characteristic aquatic flowering plants are featured separately alongside aquatic lower plants.

 Grasses, rushes and sedges, all flowering plants, are grouped separately.

 Conifers: mostly sizeable, evergreen plants whose reproductive structures are borne in cones; the seeds are naked.

LOWER PLANTS

These lack the complex reproductive structures of higher plants and are generally smaller and less robust. Those included in this book include the following:

 Algae: primitive aquatic plants. Many are microscopic and not covered in this book but the larger seaweeds are included.

Mosses: primitive land plants which lack roots and whose stems bear simple leaves.

Liverworts: primitive land plants which are usually broad and flattened, anchored to the substrate by root-like structures.

Lichens: unusual organisms that exist as a symbiotic relationship between a fungus and an alga. Usually for encrustations on rock or bark.

Clubmosses: small, simple plants with upright stems which bear numerous narrow leaves. Clubmosses bearing a passing resemblance to miniature conifers.

Horsetails: perennial plants that comprise an underground stem or rhizome from which arise upright stems bearing whorls of narrow leaves.

Ferns: easily recognised during their spore-producing stages that are large and robust and have a vascular system and roots.

THE MEDITERRANEAN CLIMATE AND VEGETATION

One of the main reasons that holidaymakers are drawn to the Mediterranean region is the fact that the climate is so different from that experienced further north in Europe. In particular the prospect of almost guaranteed sunshine during the summer months is such as contrast to the fickle climate that prevails upon the Atlantic coast of the north-west Europe; invariably warm seas are also something of a novelty. Not surprisingly, the climate of the Mediterranean exerts a profound influence upon the wildlife found there and consequently the botanical habitats and their animal communities are quite distinct from those found in any other region of Europe. The precise area covered by this book on Mediterranean wildlife is in reality determined by the influence of the climate, so profound is its effect upon the region' s plants and animals.

Temperature and rainfall are generally the most significant climatic factors affecting terrestrial plant and animal life in Europe but the fact that the Mediterranean region is warmer and dryer in general terms than the rest of Europe masks more subtle seasonal influences upon wildlife. The Mediterranean climate is one of hot, dry summers and mild, wet winters. From June to August there is almost no rainfall and daily temperatures can exceed 30°C. Most rainfall occurs between November and February but temperatures seldom fall below 5°C and frosts are almost unknown in the south of the region.

The wind is a notable feature of the Mediterranean region' s climate and for the visitor it must be endured as one of life' s hardships. Compared to other parts of Europe, the winds here are more predictably seasonal and directional and have acquired all sorts of local names. A sudden improvement in the weather in early spring is often brought about by hot dusty winds blowing north from the Sahara; the commonest name by which this is known is *Sirocco*. From June to early September strong northerly winds blast the region, rushing southwards from inland upland land masses. In southern France they are called *Mistral*, in the Adriatic they are *Bora* while in the east of the region they are known as *Meltemi*.

The majority of native trees and shrubs are evergreen. Many possess adaptations that allow them to cope with minimal rainfall during the long hot summers. Typical adaptations that reduce water loss through transpiration include leaves that are waxy-coated or narrow and needle-like with tiny stomata; the production of aromatic oils is another characteristic that serves to reduce water loss from leaves. The latter character also serves to make the plant unpalatable to grazing animals as does being coated in spines, another feature of many Mediterranean plants and one not unique to evergreen species. It is also seen among some of the smaller herbaceous plants, which have adapted to the Mediterranean climate by surviving the long hot summers as underground bulbs, corms or tubers. Annual plants complete their growth and flowering from autumn to spring; their seeds survive the summer months in a dormant state.

Right: The maquis flora is profoundly influenced by the region's climate.

MEDITERRANEAN HABITATS

The Mediterranean region comprises a wonderful collection of different, wildlife-rich habitats, many of which look entirely natural. However, almost all have modified been at the very least by people and it is worthwhile considering the impact of the region's human inhabitants – both past and present – on the landscape.

As a result of many thousands of years of land use and exploitation in the form of tree-felling, burning, grazing and land cultivation, little remains of the original vegetation cover; this would have comprised evergreen forests. Although there are remnant pockets of forest that have remained untouched, the woodlands that we see today are often planted or managed by man and hence biologically less diverse than pristine native tracts.

The bulk of the Mediterranean landscape comprises a mosaic of comparatively open habitats that have colonised land denuded of its tree cover at some point in the past. Factors such as the underlying soil type, the type of cultivation to which the land was subjected, and the grazing pressure it has suffered since clearance, have influenced the nature of the vegetation found in any given location today and hence the animals that live there too. The landscape and vegetation have also been modified in more subtle ways: trees and shrubs such as olive, fig, orange, carob and grapevine, often thought of as quintessentially Mediterranean, are either introduced to the region or have had their ranges greatly expanded by cultivation. The process of introductions continues to this day.

As a complement to the terrestrial habitats, which harbour arguably the greatest diversity of accessible wildlife species, the Mediterranean has both freshwater and marine habitats to offer the visiting naturalist. Given the nature of the climate, it is hardly surprising that the former are in comparatively short supply although often this only serves to enhance their appeal to wildlife. When unspoilt and undeveloped, the latter are some of the most attractive habitats the region has to offer. Sadly, many areas are marred by coastal development.

For the naturalist, recognising the various habitats found in the Mediterranean region is more than just an academic exercise because an ability to distinguish one from another can help improve the chances of finding a particular species or identifying it correctly once discovered. This is because, while a few plants and animals are catholic in their preferences, most are more specific in their requirements and only occur in a particular habitat. In the case of animals, this may be because their behaviour, feeding requirements, structure and tolerances have evolved to suit special niches. With plants, factors such as soil type, rainfall, the degree of shade and competing species are all influential.

Although a species may be habitat-specific, it does not necessarily follow that it will be found in all examples of a particular habitat across the Mediterranean. In biological terms, the region is vast, leading to potential for geographical isolation of plants and animals. Furthermore, although the principles of the climate are consistent across the Mediterranean, subtle differences do occur

National park status ensures that Cyprus' Akamas Peninsula coast remains pristine.

from east to west and north to south. Consequently, with the plants of terrestrial habitats in particular, areas of similar habitat in the east are likely to harbour many different species from areas in the west. This is despite the fact that they may look superficially similar and hold the same floral elements. As an example, flowering maquis in southern Spain and on a Greek island will harbour both pink and white Cistus species, yellow-flowering shrubby members of the pea family and *Ophrys* orchids but the exact species will be different in each area.

THE COAST

The rocky shore at Mallorca's Cabo Salinas supports a wealth of marine life.

The coast is generally the focal point of any holiday to the Mediterranean and most visitors choose, or area obliged, to stay within a short distance of the sea. Fortunately many of the best terrestrial wildlife habitats are found along the coastal strip but the interface between sea and land is itself often an equally rich hunting ground for the naturalist.

In global terms, the Mediterranean is a comparatively small sea. Furthermore it is almost land-locked although its waters are replenished on a twice-daily basis by influxes from the Atlantic Ocean through the Strait of Gibraltar. The pull of the moon still exerts itself on the Mediterranean as it does elsewhere in the world but, because of sea' s small size, the actual tidal range is comparatively limited. Consequently, the area of exposed shoreline seen at low tide is small. So do not expect to find the same wealth of wildlife here as would do in comparable habitats elsewhere on the coastlines of major oceans. On a rocky shore in north-west Europe, for example, up to 50metres or more of shoreline might be exposed at low tide, the precise amount dependant upon the state of the tide and the slope of the shore. On a comparable shore in the Mediterranean you might only find 5metres at best. This is one of the reasons why birds such as waders that specialise in feeding on the intertidal zones are so hard to come by in the region.

Despite its modest proportions by oceanic standards, the Mediterranean is still not a sea to be trifled with. You only have to experience a sudden summer squall or a winter storm to realise that it is capable of the same elemental rage as oceans the world over. Maritime hazards such as currents and submerged reefs pose just as real a threat in the Mediterranean as elsewhere and rocky coasts throughout the region serve as graveyards for ships and mariners from antiquity to the modern day.

CLIFFS AND COASTAL LAND

Eroded by the pounding wave action of the sea, many of the Mediterranean's cliffs are precipitous and dangerous to explore and their very inaccessibility can be seen as their salvation since it effectively precludes large-scale coastal development. Fortunately, however, there are many vantage points and dramatic coastal roads throughout the region allowing the visitor to marvel at some of the most breathtaking scenery in Europe.

CHARACTER AND WILDLIFE

In many parts of the region, the land bordering the cliffs is often covered by wind-pruned and grazed shrubs, grading from low maquis to barren garrigue depending on factors such as the soil type and the degree of disturbance. With care, a rich variety of flowers can sometimes be found in the spring and if the cliffs are stepped and harbour pockets of vegetation below the observer, a small but select band of Mediterranean warblers can sometimes be located by song at the start of the nesting season.

If the cliffs are rocky and sheer but stable, good populations of geckoes and other lizards may be present, scurrying over the rocks during the heat of the day and inviting the attentions of the blue rock thrushes which favour this sort of terrain. Screaming parties of swifts are often a feature of spring and summer and pallid and Alpine swifts may even nest if suitable crevices and holes are present high up on the cliff face. Inaccessible rock ledges occasionally harbour small colonies of that most dashing of raptors, Eleonora's falcon, and on one stretch of cliffs in Cyprus, good numbers of Griffon vultures nest and roost on broad ledges.

The limestone flora at Portugal's Cape St Vincent is a true botanical wonder.

Do not expect to find Mediterranean cliffs thronged with breeding seabirds during spring and summer as would be the case in many parts of north-west Europe for example. Comparatively small colonies of yellow-legged gulls and shags are sometimes encountered but the largest concentrations are likely to be on offshore and inaccessible islands, also favoured by species such as Mediterranean and Cory's shearwaters and Audouin's gulls. Seabirds may not nest in significant concentrations on Mediterranean cliffs but the elevation they afford make them good vantage points for watching movements of these species over the sea below. As an added bonus there is always the chance of see dolphins or even whales.

WHERE TO GO
You seldom have to travel far in the Mediterranean region to find wonderful coastal cliff scenery and many of the best areas are protected to some degree by national park, nature reserve or equivalent status. Among the highlights are those on the Akamas Peninsula in western Cyprus, the Formentor Peninsula on Mallorca and Cape St Vincent in Portugal, the most south-westerly point in Europe. Spring flowers are good at all these sites and bird migration in both spring and autumn can also be spectacular.

ROCKY SHORES

Given the nature of the terrain it is not surprising that rocky shores are less popular with tourists than areas with clean sandy beaches. Consequently many stretches of rocky coastline are comparatively deserted and undisturbed. Although the tidal range is limited and the intertidal zone extends to only a modest area, there are still marine creatures such as crabs and small fish to be discovered by turning stones and searching among seaweeds. Snorkelling in the shallows can be a rewarding experience on Mediterranean rocky shores.

CHARACTER AND WILDLIFE
Immediately above the splash zone, the rocks are likely to be coated with lichens, many of which are extremely colourful and progressing up the shore a few hardy plants gain a tenuous hold on this inhospitable terrain. Widespread across the region are rock samphire, the unrelated golden samphire and members of the sea-lavender family, including the striking and clump-forming limoniastrum of the western Mediterranean. Two species of Hottentot figs are also characteristic plants of many Mediterranean coasts, both being alien to the region and introduced from South Africa. Although their colourful flowers give them a spectacular appearance, the fact that both plants often grow to the exclusion of native species makes their presence less than welcome from a wildlife perspective.

Throughout most of the Mediterranean, the tidal range – the difference in sea level between high and low tides – varies between 30cm and 50cm, compared

Warm waters invite exploration of the region's unspoilt rocky shores.

to range of some 4-5metres on the Atlantic coasts of north-west Europe during spring tides. Consequently, the intertidal zone is condensed into a small band on the seashore and the characteristic zonation of plants and animals seen elsewhere in the world is less apparent. A fascinating array of seaweeds and marine creatures can be found at this interface between land and sea but for the greatest variety of life, explore deeper rock pools or snorkel in the shallows. Although the limited tidal range may mean there are fewer discoveries to made in the intertidal zone, the fact that rocks only ankle-deep in water are likely to remain permanently submerged creates an environmental stability that allows a rich diversity of life to proliferate here.

WHERE TO GO

Almost any rocky shore is going to be worth exploring so long as you are away from the influences of coastal development and some distance from the nearest river mouth. Particularly good locations include the Cabo Salinas in the south of Mallorca and large stretches of many of the Greek Islands, notably Cephalonia, Rhodes and Crete.

SANDY SHORES, DUNES, ESTUARIES AND MUDFLATS

During the summer months, sandy beaches that are easily accessible by road or that lie close to coastal towns are largely the preserve of sun-seeking holidaymakers. However, if you are prepared to travel to more remote locations on foot you can often enjoy this habitat in comparative isolation, even at the height of the holiday season. Outside the peak summer season, sandy beaches everywhere are often deserted; this is the time to search for shells along the tideline and explore the sand dunes that form on the landward side of the beach.

The estuaries that form at the mouths of rivers where they empty into the Mediterranean are far from static environments. A continuing process of silt deposition that occurs where freshwater meets the sea ensures that banks of sand and mud are always being laid down. Consequently, the estuary grows and expands into the sea year by year while at its landward edge, colonisation by plants such as common reed and giant reed creates extensive beds leading eventually to the creation of dry land.

CHARACTER AND WILDLIFE

Given the shifting nature of the substrate, the sandy shore is an inhospitable habitat for many seashore creatures. Consequently, although a few molluscs in particular can be found on the surface of the sand in shallow water, most live buried beneath the surface, either permanently or for at least part of the time. The best way of discovering the true diversity of marine life harboured by a sandy beach's is to search the tideline after a gale. Vast numbers of empty shells of all shapes and sizes appear along with all manner of other debris.

Beaches inaccessible to cars are often deserted, even in summer.

The upper reaches of undisturbed sandy beaches are often colonised by hardy plants such as sea rocket and yellow horned-poppy but one plant in particular – marram grass – is largely responsible for the creation of stable dunes. Its tangled network of roots help bind the particles of sand together and among the clumps of grass you should discover a whole range of salt-tolerant plants such as sea-holly, cottonweed, sea medick and sea bindweed. A surprising range of invertebrates, notably beetles, are also adapted to this harsh and unforgiving environment.

Estuaries and mudflats are often colonised by specialist plants such as glasswort, shrubby glasswort, shrubby seablite and prickly saltwort. The animal inhabitants of these habitats may not be so conspicuous but are no less abundant and phenomenal densities of molluscs and crustaceans live here. Although birdlife on these estuaries during the summer months is rather limited and often just confined to little egrets and groups of loafing non-breeding gulls, at other times of the year they come into their own. Huge numbers of wildfowl and waders use the Mediterranean's estuaries as winter havens and an impressive range of birds pass through on spring and autumn migration.

WHERE TO GO

Even the smallest of estuaries can be good for wildlife but some of the larger Mediterranean sites are of global importance. These include the Ebro Delta and the Coto Doñana, both in Spain, the Camargue in southern France, the Po Delta in Italy and the Évros and Nestos Deltas in Greece.

SALTMARSHES AND SALTPANS

Brackish lagoons, and the saltmarsh community of plants that colonise their margins, are natural features of the margins of many Mediterranean estuaries as well as in the lee of extensive sand dune systems. Man has extended these habitats, however, sometimes as a consequence of building sea walls for land defence but also when creating evaporation pans for the extraction of salt. Saltpans are a familiar sight throughout the region and the age of some of the more established pans reflects the importance of salt to human society past and present.

Stunning flowers adorn sand dunes in the Camargue, southern France.

CHARACTER AND WILDLIFE

It takes a specialised plant indeed to colonise brackish conditions but those that have evolved to cope with the salt-laden soils often thrive. Typical saltmarsh community members include members of the sea-lavender family, shrubby glasswort and golden samphire; sharp rush is a characteristic plant of drier ground.

Long-lasting saltmarsh pools and flooded saltpans support only a small band of specialised invertebrates but when conditions of salinity and temperature are favourable these can be present in phenomenal numbers. Consequently, it is hardly surprising that wading birds such as black-winged stilts and avocets should be a familiar sight at these locations and huge numbers of migrant waders pause at good sites to feed during spring and autumn migration. Although fickle in their appearance, flamingos also favour these habitats and glossy ibises and spoonbills also occur regularly. Marsh terns and pratincoles, both of which feed primarily on aerial insects, also grace the pools for short periods in spring and autumn. The drying margins of the pools, decked with cracked mud and encrusted with salt, provide nesting sites for Kentish plovers while the stilts and avocets usually favour isolated islands surrounded by the saline waters for breeding.

The salt workings at Salin de Giraud in the Camargue are on a massive scale.

WHERE TO GO

All the main estuaries, including those mentioned above, have their full complement of saltmarsh communities. Salt workings can be found there too and are a familiar sight elsewhere, especially on the coasts of Spain and Greece. In particular, there are excellent saltpans at the Salinas de Levante in southern Mallorca, Salinas de Santa Pola, just south of Alicante in Spain, and on Lésvos in Greece.

Flamingos silhouetted at sunset on the Etang de Vaccares in the Camargue.

THE OPEN SEA

Since times of antiquity, the open seas of the Mediterranean have been important to the region's inhabitants both as a source of food and as a route for transportation and travel generally. The Mediterranean remains crucially important to the economies of all countries that border it and despite the fact that over-exploitation in its many guises has taken its toll on the richness of the seas, they remain extremely productive from a biological perspective. For the general naturalist, it is often difficult to appreciate the wealth of wildlife harboured by the open seas since much of it lies hidden beneath the surface.

Audouin's gulls are almost exclusive to the Mediterranean region.

CHARACTER AND WILDLIFE

Seabird enthusiasts visiting the Mediterranean for the first time are often disappointed by the distinct lack of marine species to be found there. As a general rule, gulls are at best only locally common and familiar seabirds from northern Europe are essentially absent except as occasional winter visitors. However, there are a number of speciality species that make up for this shortfall and most people should have little difficulty seeing both Cory's and Mediterranean shearwaters along with Audouin's gull, a speciality that is almost confined to the Mediterranean basin.

Ferry crossings occasionally provide encounters with dolphins but the slower pace of sailing boats is often better for seeing the Mediterranean's other surface dwelling inhabitants. Jellyfish and violet sea-snails are often encountered and ocean sunfish are by no means uncommon. If sailing in the eastern Mediterranean, turtles are occasionally sighted.

WHERE TO GO

Ferry crossings usually offer the easiest way to see the open sea although hiring a boat can also be a wonderful experience, enabling the visitor to see the region's coastline from a different perspective. The water around the Balearic Islands and the Aegean Islands are some of the richest for the naturalist to explore.

Truly pelagic seabirds can sometimes be seen surprisingly well from land under certain circumstances. Strong onshore winds often allow comparatively close views of shearwaters to be obtained, particularly if you station yourself on a rocky headland jutting into deep water.

FRESHWATER

Freshwater is at a premium in the Mediterranean and as a consequence wetland habitats are both relatively scarce and frequently altered by man. However, those that remain harbour a rich diversity of wildlife and visiting naturalists quite rightly focus much of their attention on these watery sites.

A raging torrent in winter, this river bed has dried up by early summer.

Given the annual rainfall cycle in the Mediterranean – the summers are essentially dry while most rainfall occurs during the winter months – it is hardly surprising that freshwater habitats in the region vary in appearance throughout the year. Possibly the most dramatic seasonal changes can be seen in the rivers which are often full to bursting in January and February but whose level is reduced to a mere trickle by comparison by early summer. Of course, larger watercourses invariably maintain some level of flow even during the hottest months but smaller rivers and streams are often bone dry by early June. Natural freshwater lakes are comparatively few and far between in the Mediterranean and the majority of sizeable water bodies exist where manmade dams have flooded valleys to form reservoirs. With no history of wetland vegetation in the surrounding land, colonisation of these reservoirs by freshwater species is often slow. However, after a few decades many have acquired good growths of emergent plants on their margins and are visited by a typical range of Mediterranean waterbirds. Mature reservoirs and natural lakes in the region are of greater interest to the naturalist since their margins often have vast reedbeds in the shallow water.

CHARACTER AND WILDLIFE

Study the bed of most Mediterranean rivers during the drier months and you will find that most stretches, apart from close to where the river empties into the sea, are lined with stones and boulders, some the size of small cars. The scouring effect that these have during the torrential flows of winter can be imagined easily and it is hardly surprising therefore that the beds of inland stretches of rivers themselves usually harbour little in the way of plants. Where a stony riverbed has been colonised by a stable mix of flowers, this is often a sign that the river's flow has been altered or abstracted in some way by man.

The flow of rivers diminishes in spring and before long a succession of deep pools is often all that is left of the watercourse. These are quickly occupied by breeding frogs – notably marsh frogs – whose tadpoles grow at an amazing rate.

25

Rivers, such as this one on Lésvos, are most productive in wildlife terms in spring.

Unfortunately for the frogs, this tadpole bonanza usually coincides with spring migration of birds and species such as herons, little bitterns and wood sandpipers make good use of this ready food supply before resuming their travels. Insects abound along the margins of the rivers and these provide food for migrant warblers and flycatchers in spring.

The margins of most rivers are fringed with a rich growth of shrubby plants. Brooms and other members of the pea family are common but arguably the most characteristic plant of this terrain is oleander which bursts into deep pink flower in late spring.

Reedbeds and the freshwater margins of lakes and reservoirs are among the richest habitats for naturalists visiting the Mediterranean region. During the winter months they are home to resident species and large numbers of wintering wildfowl but it is in spring when they come into their own. With marsh harriers and other raptors floating low over the ground and the reeds alive to the sound of warblers, these habitats are havens for birdwatchers in particular but and abundance of dragonflies and amphibians creates interest for any wildlife enthusiast. So long as they retain water, these wetland havens hold wildlife interest throughout the summer months and, rejuvenated by the first autumn rains, the cycle of life is replenished.

WHERE TO GO

For a wide range of freshwater habitats, visit the Coto Doñana in Spain and the Camargue in France. Open water and reedbed habitats can be found at Lake Biguglia on Corsica, the Ebro Delta and Laguna de Medina in Spain, the Albufera Marsh on Mallorca, Lake Varano in Italy, and Manyas-Kus Cenneti National Park in Turkey. Some of the Greek Islands, notably Lésvos, have rivers that attract a superb range of migrant birds and even drainage ditches there are full of terrapins and breeding frogs.

WOODLAND

Although forests would have dominated the landscape prior to man's appearance on the Mediterranean scene, the habitat is comparatively rare now and most woodland encountered by today's visiting naturalists are invariably influenced in some way by people. This is not to say, however, that they are not still valuable havens for wildlife and many of the current Mediterranean woodlands support almost as rich a diversity of breeding birds and ground flora as they would have done without man's intervention.

Evergreen trees dominate woodland that occurs in areas subject to the full rigours of the Mediterranean climate with its hot, dry summers. In cooler inland and upland areas, not subject to such climatic extremes, these are occasionally replaced by deciduous forests and the ecologists often use their presence to delineate what is known as the submediterranean zone where the flora contains elements in common with central European as well as Mediterranean habitats.

EVERGREEN FORESTS

Various species of oak are the dominant members of Mediterranean evergreen forest communities and of these the holm oak is certainly still the most widespread. In the east of the region, valonia oak and kermes oak can become dominant and in parts of the west where rainfall is comparatively high, cork oak prevails. Of course, the latter tree is often managed and exploited more systematically than other oak species although this is not necessarily to the detriment of the region's birds and insects.

Among the conifers, Aleppo pine and stone pine also form sizeable forests although the range and precise occurrence of both species is often influenced by man: both are planted as windbreaks and soil-stabilisers and the latter is the source of edible pine nuts. At higher altitudes around the Mediterranean region, the black pine, in its various subspecies guises sometimes forms large stands and several other conifer species are locally common.

The understorey layer of shrubs in pristine areas of evergreen forest – particularly coniferous ones - often comprises species such as mastic tree, turpentine tree, strawberry tree and tree heather. After the removal of tree cover, these are all shrubs that come to dominate the scene in maquis habitats. Rosemary and Cistus species are also common to both habitats and so, not surprisingly, it can sometimes be difficult to detect where woodland ends and maquis habitats begin.

CHARACTER AND WILDLIFE

For the visiting naturalist it is often a relief to enter the sanctuary of an evergreen woodland after exploring the more open, shrub-dominated Mediterranean habitats. Thanks to the shade cast by the trees, the air remains delightfully cool throughout the day and this makes the study of the woodland wildlife a pleasant rather than arduous affair. Insect life, and in particular

Evergreen woodland grading to maquis and garrigue on Mallorca.

butterflies and beetles are often plentiful especially in spring when the understorey of shrubby plants is in full flower. Migrant birds stop off in this habitat in spring and autumn and breeding birds include several species of warblers along with nightingales, golden orioles and hoopoes.

WHERE TO GO
There are many superb areas of evergreen forest on Corsica as well as in the Coto Doñana in southern Spain and the Forest of Umbra on Italy's Adriatic coast. Cork oak woodlands are widespread in central southern Iberia and coniferous evergreen forests are frequent on many stretches of the Greek mainland coast as well as on islands such as Lésvos.

DECIDUOUS WOODLAND

The deciduous forests of the Mediterranean region are reminiscent of those found further north in Europe. Although found some way inland, and usually at moderate altitude, most are easily accessible to visiting naturalists who have the use of a car. The cool shade cast by the open leaf canopy and the comparatively open ground layer make this ideal walking terrain.

Downy oak is one of the most widespread and important trees that make up this habitat but a characteristic of many deciduous woodlands, especially in the east of the region, is their mixed and varied species composition. Those with a keen eye for tree species may discover Turkey oak, oriental hornbeam, hop-hornbeam, nettle-tree, manna ash or Montpelier maple among the component species and in places sweet chestnut has been encouraged to form almost continuous stands thanks to active cultivation over the centuries.

CHARACTER AND WILDLIFE

The ground layer of herbaceous plants in deciduous woodlands in the Mediterranean is usually more diverse than would be found in similar areas of evergreen forest at lower altitudes in the region. In particular, cyclamens, peonies and orchids often thrive here; although they may have low-level counterparts in other habitats the precise species found in these deciduous woods invariably differs from those from, for example, evergreen forests or maquis.

The birdlife of Mediterranean deciduous woodlands often strikes a chord with visiting birdwatchers from northern Europe. In spring, many woods ring to the songs and calls of robins, blackbirds and nuthatches while the presence of Bonelli's warblers and honey-buzzards adds a more southerly flavour to the mixture of species.

WHERE TO GO

Some of the best areas of deciduous woodlands are to be found in the foothills of the Apennines in Italy and by driving inland from the coast in Greece and Turkey. Even comparatively small islands such as Lésvos have extensive pockets of this habitat.

Autumn forest colours near Lake Préspa in Greece.

SHRUB AND GRASSLAND HABITATS

From an ecological perspective, goats are the scourge of the Mediterranean.

Although denuded of its primary tree cover, much of the Mediterranean region still supports thriving plant communities although these are necessarily comparatively low growing and open. In some areas, the different habitats grade into one another but generally speaking each is distinct and recognisable. To a dispassionate ecologist, most of the semi-natural shrub habitats we see today are perceived as following a downhill degenerative process from evergreen forests through shrubby maquis to barren garrigue and finally bare ground with steppe-type grassland. However, visit almost all these habitat types in spring and to describe them as 'degraded' can seem perverse in the extreme since most are incredibly rich and diverse in floral terms. Nevertheless there is no doubting the profound human influences of the past that have created the current Mediterranean landscape and it takes no great perception to see the far from subtle effects that the modern generation is having on the region.

MAQUIS

The term *maquis* is generally taken to be derived from the Corsican name for the low, tangled shrub habitat that cloaks much of that Mediterranean island. This widespread and species-rich vegetation type is characterised by its composition of evergreen shrubs that range in height between 1m and 5m. Maquis predominates in areas where there is reasonable annual rainfall and so it is most widespread in the west of the Mediterranean where the climate is most moist; elsewhere it tends to occur on west- and north-facing slopes that receive the greatest precipitation. Maquis usually occurs from sea level up to about 600metres although local climatic conditions may allow its survival at altitudes up to 1,000metres. Above these elevations a type of vegetation called *pseudomaquis* often predominates; it is characterised by being composed at least partly of deciduous shrubs.

In the western Mediterranean strawberry tree and tree heath are arguably the two most characteristic maquis shrubs but the plant community usually contains other species such as wild madder, smilax, carob, Spanish broom and myrtle. In the east of the region, eastern strawberry tree, spiny broom, mastic tree, turpentine tree and joint-pine are key species. Pseudomaquis is often dominated by kermes oak, box and prickly juniper. Several species of rock-rose also occur in maquis and pseudomaquis habitats but come into their own in garrigue.

CHARACTER AND WILDLIFE

As a rule of thumb guide, a given habitat is probably maquis rather than garrigue if the exploring naturalist has to force their way between the shrubs: their dense growth usually ensures there is no space or bare ground between them. When making your way through the vegetation, two things are likely to strike you immediately. Firstly, this is an extremely fragrant habitat thanks to the aromatic oils released by many of its floral inhabitants to combat water loss.

Secondly, many of the plants are extremely spiny. The spines are often modified leaves and their shape also helps reduce desiccation. However, they serve the dual purpose of discouraging grazing by animals.

Insect life abounds in the maquis and is particularly evident in spring and early summer. Bees, wasps and allies are all well represented, as are butterflies, which visit the maquis flowers in an endless quest for nectar. *Sylvia* warblers are also common in this habitat, the precise species varying according to the geographical location, and woodchat shrikes also favour this terrain. The reptile community is well represented in the maquis but given the dense cover that characterises the habitat, the presence of snakes and lizards is seldom detected other than by hearing their rustling passage among the dry leaves at ground level.

Grey-leaved cistus in full flower.

31

WHERE TO GO

Maquis habitat is so widespread in the Mediterranean that it can be found without much difficulty in most areas. It is dominant across much of southern Spain, southern France, Corsica, coastal Italy, the Greek mainland and the larger Greek islands.

GARRIGUE

The term *garrigue* (also spelt *garigue*) is applied to a comparatively wide range of subtly different habitats all of which are characterised by comprising dwarf shrubs that do not exceed 1m in height and frequently are less than 50cm; in Greece, this habitat is often referred to as *phrygana*. It is invariably found on dry stony ground that is baked dry during the long summer months. The grazing pressure and soil erosion that has prevailed since the tree cover was originally removed has influenced its appearance and character. The plant community members themselves often form low, compact shrubs that are widely spaced with bare stony ground in between.

CHARACTER AND WILDLIFE

Given the open nature of garrigue habitat, it is usually possible for visiting naturalists to walk between the compact shrubs on bare ground although in some areas the growth of *Cistus* plants in particular is often as dense as would be found in maquis terrain. The flora contains a high proportion of species that are aromatic or have leaves that curl or drop in summer; both features are adaptations to reduce water loss. The presence of spines or unpalatable tastes both serve to discourage grazing.

It may appear bleak but garrigue habitat is a haven for the naturalist.

Although small, the flowers of the bumblebee orchid repay close scrutiny.

After the *Cistus* family, species of thyme, lavender, sage, rue and rosemary are among the most characteristic plants of the garrigue. Depending on the geographical location, large Mediterranean spurge and kermes oaks are often present along with low-growing junipers and dwarf fan palm. Spiny burnet is extremely important in the eastern Mediterranean. From the botanists' point of view, garrigue is one of the richest habitats for orchids and in particular for members of the genus *Ophrys*. These die back by early summer and persist underground, a strategy also adopted by sea squill, grape hyacinth species, *Ornithogalum* species and *Allium* species. In addition, garrigue habitats also harbour large numbers of annual species of plants that contribute to the flowering spectacle of early spring.

Being a comparatively open habitat means that its animal inhabitants are comparatively easy to see and beetles in particular are well represented. Lizards and snakes are usually found in good numbers but, despite the fact that the vegetation is low, they can be extremely difficult to relocate if they have been disturbed and have gone to cover. A few specialised *Sylvia* warblers favour this habitat and in the west of the region Thekla larks also occur here. Birds of prey, notably short-toed eagles, often hunt overhead, scanning the ground for snakes and other reptiles.

WHERE TO GO

Like maquis, garrigue habitat is extremely widespread in the region and indeed is probably the most frequently encountered form of vegetation. It is often the dominant habitat on many smaller Greek islands and is superb in floral terms on many stretches of the east coast of Mallorca.

STEPPE AND ARID GRASSLAND

The process of vegetative degeneration and soil loss that appears to be the inevitable consequence of the removal of tree cover in the Mediterranean region is often speeded up or exacerbated by other activities such as burning and grazing by animals. The final stage in the process is often stony grassland that has much in common with Asiatic steppe habitat, both in terms of appearance and in the sort of species found there. Consequently it is often referred to as steppe grassland. Its appearance is often maintained by continued grazing.

La Crau in southern France is a unique area best known for birds.

CHARACTER AND WILDLIFE

In addition to the numerous species of grasses that characterise this habitat, members of the pea family – notably medicks and clovers – are often common. A large number of herbaceous plants also occur here – these die back and persist underground in summer – along with countless annuals. Plants with qualities that deter grazing occasionally predominate and notable examples include asphodels and thistles; the former group is poisonous while the latter are spiny.

Insects are usually seasonally common in grassy habitats and hence insectivorous birds such as swallows and bee-eaters often hunt overhead. Given the lack of cover, larger creatures such as lizards and snakes are comparatively scarce. Clusters of aestivating snails are often a common sight in summer on the withered remains of plant stems.

A stunning male Cretzschmar's bunting.

WHERE TO GO

Arid grassland is a widespread habitat that can be found in many parts of the Mediterranean region. It is, however, particularly prevalent in southern Spain and on many Greek islands. One of the most extensive areas of stony plains is found at la Crau on the fringes of the Camargue in southern France; the terrain here contrasts starkly with the mosaic of wetland habitats that comprise its neighbour.

AGRICULTURAL LAND

Visitors to the region from northern Europe have got so used to associating agricultural land with a virtual absence of wildlife that it often comes as a revelation to discover that fields and orchards in the Mediterranean are often teeming with plants and animals. Of course the concept of farmland as wildlife haven is being eroded year by year due to changes in land use and the increasing use of pesticides, herbicides and fertilisers, but by and large the pace of change is much slower here than elsewhere in Europe. So you can still find arable fields and olive groves full of colourful flowers, myriad insects and other invertebrates, and a rich diversity of birdlife, in almost every corner of the Mediterranean.

An ancient olive tree towers over a carpet of crown daisies.

CHARACTER AND WILDLIFE

Without doubt the most characteristic tree of cultivation in the Mediterranean is the olive and the range over which it can be grown is often used as a rule of thumb way of defining the limits of the Mediterranean climate. Its fruits, or more precisely the oil that they produce, have underpinned the economy and lifestyle of the region for thousands of years and the tree continues to be of importance to this day.

Olive trees are usually grown in groves, often on level ground but sometimes on terraced hillsides too. From a distance these can resemble natural evergreen woodlands and indeed, in parts of the region, they fill much the same sort of niche for wildlife. Regular pruning ensures a good quantity of new growth for olive production but the trunks and larger branches are often thick and gnarled in ancient trees, covered with lichens and full of holes. Insect life usually abounds in olive groves and a wide range of bird species use them for nesting. Hoopoes, little owls, blackbirds and greenfinches are all widespread and in the east of the region further woodland flavour is added by the presence of middle spotted woodpeckers and masked shrikes.

Although the olive is arguably the most characteristic tree of agricultural land, a wide range of other species are also grown. Carob tree, fig, almond, orange and lemon are all important for the fruits they produce and when grown at sufficient density they too serve as evergreen woodlands for the region's wildlife. In spring and autumn, groves and orchards of all kinds play host to migrant birds, notably warblers and flycatchers that stop off to feed and shelter before resuming their journeys.

Where grapevines are grown commercially, the ground is usually tilled thoroughly thus preventing the build up of flowering herbaceous plants; in some areas, orchards and groves are comparatively intensely cultivated thus achieving the same botanical effect. However, by accident rather than design most agricultural land in the Mediterranean is full of flowers and incredibly colourful in spring. In olive groves and similar habitats, expect to find anemones, crown daisy, field marigold, poppies and scarlet pimpernel in abundance. Where the ground is not disturbed on a regular basis, you may even discover orchids, particularly tongue orchids and members of the genus *Ophrys*.

Even ploughed land can be amazing good for flowers if herbicides are not used. Again, poppies are often abundant but, from March to June, expect to find a succession of attractive flowers such as gladiolus species, corncockle, bladder vetch and shepherd's-needle. Red-legged partridges and corn buntings are often common in these habitats and quails are seldom found anywhere other than in these agricultural areas.

WHERE TO GO

So long as traditional farming practises are maintained, then you can expect to find agricultural land that is rich in wildlife throughout the Mediterranean for the foreseeable future.

THE URBAN ENVIRONMENT

Most visitors to the Mediterranean stay in areas of urban development, be that a timeless village or a gleaming modern resort on the coast. This man-made terrain may serve our needs well but it hardly seems like a good place to search for wildlife. Surprisingly, however, a number of animals have adapted well to towns and villages and some are seldom found anywhere else in the Mediterranean region.

A fishing village on the coast of Crete.

CHARACTER AND WILDLIFE

Visit almost any Mediterranean town in spring and early summer and one of the first things to strike anyone with an interest in the natural history will be the parties of swifts screaming overhead or flying at break-neck speed through the narrow streets. Most of their number will be common swifts but pallid and alpine swifts also occur in some areas. Typical nest sites for the swifts include church towers and the roof space of houses; house martins are found in similar locations although they build cup-shaped mud nests under eaves. In more rural districts, swallows and red-rumped swallows favour outbuildings and in southern Spain and Greece in particular white storks are often encouraged to build their large stick nests on roofs. Study these twiggy constructions for a while and you are likely to notice that house sparrows, and sometimes even Spanish sparrows, have also taken up residence.

Reptiles are seldom encountered in Mediterranean house, with the exception of geckoes. These sure-footed lizards can climb walls and ceilings with ease and are welcomed in most homes for the valuable insect-catching role they perform.

Compared to many other parts of Europe, gardening for pleasure rather than for food is comparatively uncommon in the Mediterranean and indeed the pastime would be rather challenging given the harsh nature of the climate. However, colourful displays of geraniums are common and increasingly streets and grassy parks in modern towns are planted with attractive, drought-tolerant flowers and shrubs. During the daytime these can be good for insects and in particular butterflies. After dark, hawkmoths and other large species often visit scented flowers and their presence may encourage Scops owls to take up residence in the vicinity. These cryptic birds are difficult to find although their presence can be detected by the sonar-like calls that they utter after dark.

THE MEDITERRANEAN WILDLIFE YEAR

Just as other regions in Europe experience seasonal changes in the weather throughout the year so the Mediterranean has distinct and recognisable periods of spring, summer, autumn and winter. However, the region's unique climate means that its wildlife, and in particular the plants, respond in very different ways from species that occur at more northerly latitudes. For example, summer, rather than winter, is generally a period of dormancy for many species while the main seasons for growth or activity are throughout autumn and winter. Early spring is the main flowering period and by early summer most plants have long since finished producing seeds or fruits.

SPRING

In spring, much of the Mediterranean landscape looks green with the previous winter's rains having encouraged a fresh growth of foliage in herbaceous and evergreen perennials alike and annual plants too. From March right through to early June, a succession of flowers appears in every terrestrial habitat in the region with perhaps the peak of colour occurring in late April and early May. The weather is often warm but seldom hot, and cloudy days and showers are not uncommon. The more rainfall a given area has in spring, the longer the flowering season is likely to persist.

A singing male Rüppell's warbler.

The spring is a good time of year to look for insects and reptiles. Both cold-blooded and hence in part dependent upon heat from the sun to warm up their bodies, they tend to be less active and easier to find when the weather is cool. Lizards in particular often sunbathe in spring and can sometimes be approached closely.

SPRING BIRD MIGRATION

Although a fair proportion of the Mediterranean's bird species is resident, many are migratory and only visit the region to nest. They arrive in spring along with vast numbers of birds that are passing through en route from wintering grounds, mainly in Africa, to summer nesting sites in northern Europe. These are often described as passage migrants and they comprise representatives from most European bird families. At good migration spots in the Mediterranean you can often find several migrant species together at one time but generally speaking the migration periods for each species is subtly different. Thus flycatchers and swallows tend to migrate earlier than say shrikes or marsh terns.

From the birdwatchers' perspective, no particular year is ever like another for migrant birds in the Mediterranean. The birds themselves certainly pass through the region each year but they do not always stop off at given locations to break their journey. Generally speaking it is local weather conditions that determine the numbers of migrants you are likely to find. Changeable conditions with

Migrant woodchat shrikes often perch on wires.

occasional heavy downpours of rain or strong adverse winds, particularly at night when many species are on the move, can ground large numbers of birds temporarily. The appearance of a large number of birds after such conditions is known as a 'fall' and often it involves just one or two species.

SPRING FLOWERS

Whatever your primary natural history interest, you cannot fail to be struck by the large numbers of flowers that burst into bloom in the spring. Having spent the autumn and winter putting on new growth most are stimulated by the onset of warm sunny weather in spring to produce flowers. The flowering season is brief, however, and by June much of the vegetation has shrivelled or withered in the heat.

Some species appear as early as February but the majority flower between mid-March and late May. The flowering season is generally a couple of weeks more advanced in the west of the region compared to the east and subtle differences in the climate mean that flowering in any given area is seldom consistent in terms of timing from year to year. However, if you find that you have missed a particular flower that you are keen to see at sea level, visit a similar habitat at higher elevation. Just a short rise in altitude can have a profound bearing on the flowering season and it is not uncommon for the season for flowers growing at around 500m to be delayed by a week or more compared to the same species on the coast.

Small-flowered cistus in bloom.

39

MEDITERRANEAN ORCHIDS

For many naturalists, it is the region's orchids that are its crowning glory in botanical terms. Almost every terrestrial habitat in the region has at least a few representatives of this intriguing group of plants. However, some areas of maquis and garrigue, particularly where the underlying rock is limestone, can boast what amounts to a profusion of orchids, occasionally comprising as many as ten different species in a single given location.

The orchid season begins early, often in February, with the appearance of the Mediterranean's most spectacular species, the giant orchid. Thereafter, a succession of species appears with the genera *Orchis* and *Ophrys* being particularly well represented. The latter genus – often referred to simply as 'bee orchid relatives' – is particularly prone to subtle and not-so-subtle variations in the appearance of its flowers from site to site. This fact, combined with the effects of geographical isolation and the ability of members of the genus to hybridise freely, has meant that all sorts of patterns can be found on the flower lips of members of the same species across their range. Controversy rages among orchid experts as to where the boundaries of intra-species variation and separate species status lie.

The tongue orchid group – genus *Serapias* – is one that is essentially Mediterranean in its distribution although it does have a few outlying strongholds further north in Europe. It too is prone to variability and opinions differ as to the validity of the species status of some of its members. However, for most naturalists the intriguing shape of this group's flowers is fascinating in its own right, regardless of what species is involved.

The attractive sawfly orchid.

SUMMER

During the blistering Mediterranean summer, which usually lasts from late June to early September, the landscape is parched and brown, much of the vegetation having withered away. Despite the occasional thunderstorm, the skies are usually cloudless and it is not unusual for barely a drop of rain to fall from early June to the end of September.

Plants that are evergreen survive by having evolved means of reducing water loss as their leaves transpire. Those species that are herbaceous often die back by early July and remain dormant in an underground tuber, bulb or corm. For annual plants, the annual cycle is complete by early summer. Seeds have been produced and the plants themselves die back and wither to brown stalks.

Because of the desiccating power of the sun, those invertebrates that are active at this time of year are often strictly nocturnal, hiding underground or under stones during daylight. Still more enter a dormant phase at this time of year, either underground or, in the case of many snail species, by gluing themselves to aerial plant stems, often in clusters. Temperatures drop appreciably a metre or so off the ground when

Cochlicella barbara snails aestivating.

compared to ground level. In the eastern Mediterranean in particular, some insects actually migrate to areas of relative cool and high humidity. The most notable example of this behaviour is found in the Jersey tiger moth which roosts in its tens of thousands at the shady haven of Petaloudes on Rhodes, inappropriately named the 'Valley of the Butterflies'.

Birdwatchers in the Mediterranean find the summer months frustrating since most species feed mainly at dawn and dusk and remain in cover during the day. Bee-eaters are often exceptional in this respect and can be seen flying and calling throughout the summer months. At this time of year, water becomes of prime importance to the region's birds and any permanent pools are likely to be visited by a constant succession of thirsty individuals.

Jersey tiger moths at Petaloudes on Rhodes

AUTUMN

Underpinning the Mediterranean economy, olives start maturing in the autumn.

With the arrival of autumn and its cooler airflows comes the promise of the first significant rains for several months, which usually arrive towards the end of September or early October. A few weeks after the onset of heavy downpours, the first signs of life appear in the open Mediterranean habitats as the seeds of annual plants germinate and plants that have survived the summer underground produce leaves and shoots. Of the species that favour this subterranean dormancy a select few actually flower in autumn; notable examples include sea squill, autumn snowflake and sea daffodil.

While many Mediterranean plants are putting on fresh new growth in autumn, many of the shrubs and trees produce their seasonal crop of berries, fruits and nuts at this time of year. These provide a feeding bonanza for many of the region's animals and it is a time of harvest too, with olives and grapes being particularly important. In areas of pseudomaquis and deciduous forest, the autumn fall of leaves is preceded by a change in their colour and sometimes this can be spectacular.

Thermalling white pelicans on migration.

Autumn also sees the return migration of birds passing south through the region from breeding territories in northern Europe to wintering grounds, mainly in Africa but in Asia too. Although potentially more birds are involved in autumn than in spring – the numbers of adults are swollen by young hatched that year – the season for migration is more extended and hence large concentrations of birds are less in evidence. The exception to this is found at migration hotspots such as the Strait of Gibraltar the Bosphorus in Turkey, where vast numbers of birds of prey, storks and pelicans concentrate. The birds take advantage of thermals to cross narrow stretches of open sea, migrating in the case of the former from Europe to Africa and in the latter from Europe to Asia.

Sadly, autumn is the main season when the regrettable habit of hunting birds comes into its own in the Mediterranean region. Although illegal in many areas, the senseless slaughter of species ranging in size from warblers to eagles continues unabated. This is despite the best efforts of the enthusiastic national and regional conservation bodies.

WINTER

Winters are mild and wet in the Mediterranean and consequently this is a good time for plants to grow and a lush growth of vegetation can be found in most terrestrial landscapes. Rivers and other freshwater habitats usually have their water levels rejuvenated by early January and for the next couple of months bouts of heavy rain can even lead to localised flooding.

During the winter months, the Mediterranean region plays host to birds that have migrated there from northern Europe to escape the rigours of winter. Thrushes and other songbirds are numerous, as are wildfowl and waders species on the coastal marshes; the virtual absence of frosts and the prospect of comparatively easy feeding attract these winter visitors.

Winter gales often leave beaches strewn with sea balls, the remains of Neptune grass.

CONSERVATION AND THREATS
TO MEDITERRANEAN WILDLIFE

A song thrush killed by a Mediterranean bird trap.

The plants and animals that thrive in the Mediterranean do so because they have evolved and adapted to the challenging and varied habitats that the region supports. Many of these habitats are at the very least man-influenced. They were created not by design but simply because particular management regimes or land use allowed certain species to thrive at the expense of others.

Generally speaking the best Mediterranean wildlife habitats owe their continued existence to the fact that no better use can be found for the land and so some of the best areas of maquis and garrigue for example receive little or no active wildlife conservation as such. Furthermore, although most countries that have Mediterranean coastlines or that are influenced by the region's climate have nominal statutory bodies concerned with the environment, it is probably true to say that conservation organisations do not wield the same degree of power or influence as their counterparts in northern European countries. It hardly needs saying that this makes Mediterranean habitats and their wildlife extremely vulnerable to change, often at the whim of a landowner or developer.

Some of the best Mediterranean wildlife is found on agricultural land and it should never be forgotten that this habitat remains rich in wildlife because it is cultivated less intensively – and hence less profitably in many cases – than land elsewhere in Europe. The pressure to modernise farming practises in the region is understandably going to force the pace of change. If future generations of naturalists are going to be able to enjoy the wildlife of the Mediterranean's agricultural lands then subsidies will probably have to act as disincentives to change. It is telling that many of the flowers so abundant on Mediterranean farmland were once cornfield 'weeds' in northern Europe.

It is widely repeated irony that by visiting a given place, tourists spoil the very qualities of the location that drew them there in the first place. Nowhere is this more apparent than on certain notorious stretches of the Spanish coast or on parts of many Mediterranean islands where high rise hotels mar once stunning coastal scenery and glorious sandy beaches are covered with bronze bodies in summer, as densely packed as any seal rookery. However, increased tourism has another more subtle effect upon the region, that being the increased water consumption that the visitors demand. The water has got to come from some-where and whatever its source there is an environmental impact. Abstract it locally and you run the risk of lowering the water table and hence draining nearby marshes; if abstraction occurs near the sea then increasing salinity can become a problem. Flood inland valleys to create reservoirs and not only do you destroy the habitat in question but you affect the natural, seasonal flow of water down the region's watercourses. Many Mediterranean rivers hold only a fraction of the water that once flowed through them and some are permanently dry as a result of the building of dams.

Maquis flora generally thrives without the need for active conservation measures.

As with other maritime settings, the waters of the Mediterranean, and especially coastal areas, are subject to a wide range of pollution. Of course there are elevated levels of sewage associated with the region's tourist population but pollution by industrial complexes is just as much a problem here as elsewhere in the world. However, all the problems of marine pollution are compounded by the fact that the Mediterranean is an almost land-locked sea. With comparatively little exchange in the surface waters - this is where most pollutants accumulate - with seawater from the Atlantic, contaminants are inevitably becoming more concentrated in the region.

Piles of shotgun cartridges litter many Mediterranean hillsides and cliffs and sprung bird traps are regrettably widely used. Any naturalist who discovers these artefacts, or actually witnessed bird hunting in action, is usually deeply affected by what they see. If this practise disturbs you, please write and voice your outrage to environmental departments and ministers in countries where you witness the slaughter. Many travelling naturalists boycott places such as Malta as a silent protest against the destruction and this represents an economic loss for the areas concerned. If bird hunting were completely outlawed, or better still if hunters could be educated sufficiently to stop the slaughter willingly, just imagine how much more revenue would be generated as a consequence.

LOOKING TO THE FUTURE

While it is vital to be aware of the threats that face the Mediterranean, it is equally important to put these in perspective and to emphasise the positive wildlife attractions the region has to offer. You can still find flowers in a profusion and variety almost unknown nowadays anywhere else in Europe along with stunning arrays of insects, reptiles, birds and other animals too. There is a burgeoning interest in the Mediterranean's wildlife but, thankfully, with it has come an increasing awareness of its unique nature and vulnerability, not only among those who visit for short periods but among the region's permanent national residents too. Perhaps the fact that people are willing to buy and read a book on Mediterranean natural history is in part a testament to the growing interest in, and concern for, Mediterranean wildlife in all its forms.

HEDGEHOG   *Erinaceus europaeus*   Length 16–26cm
Essentially nocturnal animal, often captured in car headlights after dark. Upper body is covered with a dense coat of spines of uniform length. Ears relatively small. Legs rather short, hence shuffling gait. Rolls into a ball when disturbed. Hibernates during winter months. Widespread throughout region, in scrub, woodland and also gardens. Western forms are generally darker than eastern animals.

LESSER WHITE-TOOTHED SHREW   *Crocidura suaveolens*   Body length 5.5–7.5cm
Active insectivorous animal, sometimes glimpsed foraging among leaf litter; close inspection usually only possible on dead animals. Has grey-brown fur on upperparts grading to paler buffish-brown on underparts; tail bears a few long, coarse hairs. Teeth white. Widespread from western France to Greece; absent from many islands.

WATER SHREW   *Neomys fodiens*   Body length 10cm
Comparatively large by shrew standards and relatively easy to watch when feeding along water margins. Fur is conspicuously bicoloured: almost black on upperparts and white on underparts; shows clear demarcation between the two along the flanks. Usually associated with water, generally streams; swims and dives well. Widespread from N Spain to N Greece; absent from most islands and arid areas.

PYGMY SHREW   *Sorex minutus*   Body length 6cm
Tiny, active animal, sometimes seen foraging on ground; can climb surprisingly well. Feeds on invertebrates. Close inspection – usually only possible with a corpse – reveals red-tipped teeth. Body colour warm brown on upperparts and pale buffish-brown on underparts. Legs relatively short and tail long. Squeals loudly when excited. Widespread from N Spain to Greece; absent from most islands.

COMMON SHREW   *Sorex araneus*   Body length 7.5cm
Similar to pygmy shrew but larger and with proportionately shorter tail. Upperparts warm brown and underparts pale, the distinction between the two more apparent than in pygmy shrew. Favours terrain with good ground cover including grassland, dense maquis and even gardens. Feeds on insects, spiders and other invertebrates. Widespread from N Spain to Greece and Turkey; absent from most islands.

MOLE   *Talpa europaea*   Body length 11–16cm
Unmistakable when seen above ground but essentially subterranean habits mean that observations are rare. Presence often detected by presence of disturbed soil as distinctive mole-hills. Has cylindrical body shape and black, velvety fur. Front legs adapted for digging. Tail short and muzzle elongate. Widespread wherever soil suitable for digging; absent from S Spain, most of Greece and many islands.

BARBARY APE   *Macaca sylvanus*   Body length 60–70cm
Unmistakable animal, size of a medium-sized dog. Walks on all fours and shows no visible tail; climbs well. The only primate – other than man – to occur wild in Europe although its origins are uncertain. Possibly introduced to its only European station – the Rock of Gibraltar – from N Africa. Generally silent although screams loudly when excited. Lives in sociable groups.

RABBIT   *Oryctolagus cuniculus*   Body length 35–40cm
Recognised by long ears, black and white tail and long legs. Fur usually grey-brown but colour variable; black forms occur. Favours sandy soil for burrowing in open, grassy country and farmland. Active mainly dawn and dusk. Original range comprised Iberian Peninsula and S France. Now widespread, including many islands.

BROWN HARE   *Lepus capensis*   Body length 60–70cm
Superficially similar to rabbit but with proportionately longer legs and black-tipped ears. Mostly solitary and lives above ground. Runs fast. Males chase one another and box in spring. Generally nocturnal. Favours open country. Widespread throughout region and found on most of the larger islands.

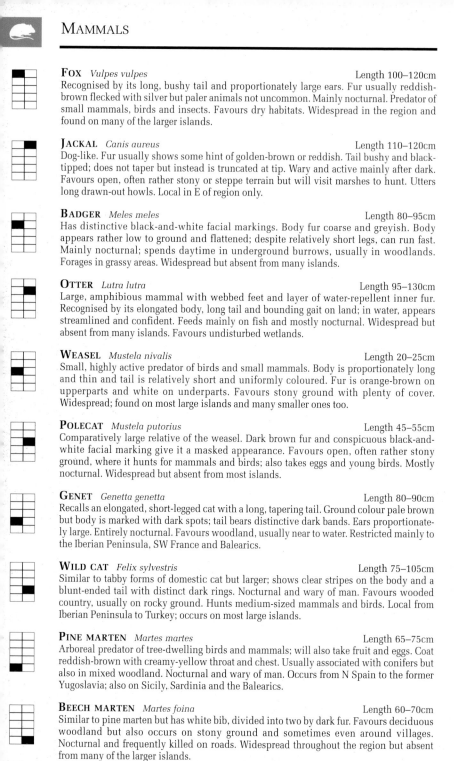

FOX   *Vulpes vulpes*   Length 100–120cm

Recognised by its long, bushy tail and proportionately large ears. Fur usually reddish-brown flecked with silver but paler animals not uncommon. Mainly nocturnal. Predator of small mammals, birds and insects. Favours dry habitats. Widespread in the region and found on many of the larger islands.

JACKAL   *Canis aureus*   Length 110–120cm

Dog-like. Fur usually shows some hint of golden-brown or reddish. Tail bushy and black-tipped; does not taper but instead is truncated at tip. Wary and active mainly after dark. Favours open, often rather stony or steppe terrain but will visit marshes to hunt. Utters long drawn-out howls. Local in E of region only.

BADGER   *Meles meles*   Length 80–95cm

Has distinctive black-and-white facial markings. Body fur coarse and greyish. Body appears rather low to ground and flattened; despite relatively short legs, can run fast. Mainly nocturnal; spends daytime in underground burrows, usually in woodlands. Forages in grassy areas. Widespread but absent from many islands.

OTTER   *Lutra lutra*   Length 95–130cm

Large, amphibious mammal with webbed feet and layer of water-repellent inner fur. Recognised by its elongated body, long tail and bounding gait on land; in water, appears streamlined and confident. Feeds mainly on fish and mostly nocturnal. Widespread but absent from many islands. Favours undisturbed wetlands.

WEASEL   *Mustela nivalis*   Length 20–25cm

Small, highly active predator of birds and small mammals. Body is proportionately long and thin and tail is relatively short and uniformly coloured. Fur is orange-brown on upperparts and white on underparts. Favours stony ground with plenty of cover. Widespread; found on most large islands and many smaller ones too.

POLECAT   *Mustela putorius*   Length 45–55cm

Comparatively large relative of the weasel. Dark brown fur and conspicuous black-and-white facial marking give it a masked appearance. Favours open, often rather stony ground, where it hunts for mammals and birds; also takes eggs and young birds. Mostly nocturnal. Widespread but absent from most islands.

GENET   *Genetta genetta*   Length 80–90cm

Recalls an elongated, short-legged cat with a long, tapering tail. Ground colour pale brown but body is marked with dark spots; tail bears distinctive dark bands. Ears proportionately large. Entirely nocturnal. Favours woodland, usually near to water. Restricted mainly to the Iberian Peninsula, SW France and Balearics.

WILD CAT   *Felix sylvestris*   Length 75–105cm

Similar to tabby forms of domestic cat but larger; shows clear stripes on the body and a blunt-ended tail with distinct dark rings. Nocturnal and wary of man. Favours wooded country, usually on rocky ground. Hunts medium-sized mammals and birds. Local from Iberian Peninsula to Turkey; occurs on most large islands.

PINE MARTEN   *Martes martes*   Length 65–75cm

Arboreal predator of tree-dwelling birds and mammals; will also take fruit and eggs. Coat reddish-brown with creamy-yellow throat and chest. Usually associated with conifers but also in mixed woodland. Nocturnal and wary of man. Occurs from N Spain to the former Yugoslavia; also on Sicily, Sardinia and the Balearics.

BEECH MARTEN   *Martes foina*   Length 60–70cm

Similar to pine marten but has white bib, divided into two by dark fur. Favours deciduous woodland but also occurs on stony ground and sometimes even around villages. Nocturnal and frequently killed on roads. Widespread throughout the region but absent from many of the larger islands.

GREATER HORSESHOE BAT *Rhinophus ferrumequinum*   Wingspan 34–39cm
Distinctive bat with horseshoe-shaped nose leaves and large, broad ears. Favours woodland in areas where caves or mines provide sites for daytime roosts and hibernation. Widespread across Mediterranean region, including most islands.

LESSER HORSESHOE BAT *Rhinolophus hipposideros*   Wingspan 22–25cm
Appreciably smaller than greater horseshoe with proportionately smaller ears; shares the same nose and ear structure. Favours woodland. Flight is fast and fluttering. Roosts and hibernates in caves and mines. Widespread throughout.

MEDITERRANEAN HORSESHOE BAT *Rhinolophus euryale*   Wingspan 25–30cm
Medium-sized bat, midway between the previous two species. Fur colour is usually pale buff. Favours woodland; roosts and hibernates in caves and mines; sociable. Flies from dusk onwards. Widespread but absent from S Iberia and smaller islands.

DAUBENTON'S BAT *Myotis daubentonii*   Wingspan 23–27cm
Medium-sized bat with proportionately short ears and tail. Fur is pale brown. Favours woodland but invariably found near water over which it often feeds on fast-beating wings. Widespread but absent from much of the E Mediterranean.

LONG-FINGERED BAT *Myotis capaccinii*   Wingspan 25–30cm
Medium-sized, hairy bat with proportionately large feet and small ears; hind legs embraced by wing membrane up to ankle. Associated with woods and olive groves but seldom far from water. Widespread from E Spain to Balkans and on many islands.

NATTERER'S BAT *Myotis nattereri*   Wingspan 25–30cm
Medium-sized bat with relatively long ears and projecting tragus. Wings pale and fur brown; fringe of hairs on wing membrane and between legs. Favours woods and olive groves; roosts in hollow trees, hibernates in caves. Found in W of region.

BECHSTEIN'S BAT *Myotis bechsteinii*   Wingspan 30–35cm
Medium-sized bat with proportionately long ears. Usually emerges late in evening; flight rather slow and laborious. Favours woodland; roosts in hollow trees but hibernates in caves. Found in N Spain, S France, Italy and Sicily.

MOUSE-EARED BAT *Myotis myotis*   Wingspan 40–50cm
Large bat with long, large ears. In flight, wings appear broad; membrane encloses hind legs to base of outer toe. Emerges late. Favours olive groves, often near houses. Flight powerful. Roosts and hibernates in caves and cellars. Widespread.

NOCTULE BAT *Nyctalus noctula*   Wingspan 32–39cm
Large bat with reddish-brown fur and broad, lobed ears. Active late afternoon onwards. Hunts over canopy of woods and olive groves. Direct flight pattern interrupted by rapid twists. Roosts and hibernates in hollow trees. Widespread.

EUROPEAN FREE-TAILED BAT *Tadarida teniotis*   Wingspan 45–60cm
Largest Mediterranean bat with bulldog-like face. Ears large and curiously shaped; touch over head. Tail long and free of wing membrane for ¼ of its length. Often near villages; roosts and hibernates in caves and buildings. Widespread.

LONG-EARED BAT *Plecotus auritus*   Wingspan 23–28cm
Small bat with fluttering flight; sometimes hovers over vegetation. Recognised by proportionately very long ears. Flies throughout night. Favours woodland. Roosts in hollow trees; winters in caves and cellars. Widespread throughout region.

PIPISTRELLE BAT *Pipistrellus pipistrellus*   Wingspan 19–25cm
Small, frequently encountered bat with reddish-brown fur and rounded muzzle. Flight fluttering and erratic. Often near villages. Roosts and hibernates in buildings, often in colonies. Widespread throughout the Mediterranean.

CRESTED PORCUPINE *Hystrix cristata*   Body length 58–68cm
Unmistakable on account of size and presence of conspicuous spines. Favours agricultural land and maquis scrub. Shakes spines and tail when threatened. Mostly nocturnal. Introduced but now established in Italy, Sicily and N Greece.

EDIBLE DORMOUSE *Glis glis*   Body length 12–15cm
Recalls a small squirrel. Has bushy tail, large, dark eyes and rounded ears. Upperparts grey and underparts white. Favours deciduous woods and orchards. Climbs well. Hibernates underground. Widespread; absent Iberia and Balearics.

DORMOUSE *Muscardinus avellanarius*   Body length 8cm
Has golden-brown fur, black, beady eyes and furry tail. Essentially nocturnal and hence difficult to observe; summer nests sometimes found. Favours deciduous woods. Hibernates. Widespread, S France to N Greece; absent from most islands.

BANK VOLE *Clethrionomys glareolus*   Body length 9–11cm
Plump vole with reddish-brown coat, short tail and clearly visible ears. Favours woods and scrub and creates shallow burrows. Mostly nocturnal. Generally silent; utters high-pitched chatters when alarmed. Occurs mainly S France and N Greece.

NORTHERN WATER VOLE *Arvicola terrestris*   Body length 18–22cm
Large, plump vole. Tail long, fur dark brown and coarse. Often associated with water; swims and dives well. In terrestrial habitats burrows in dry soil. Widespread in central and E Mediterranean; replaced in Iberia and SW France by similar southern water vole *A. sapidus*.

COMMON VOLE *Microtus arvalis*   Body length 9–12cm
Similar to bank vole but larger with grey-brown coat. Ears large and essentially hairless. Favours grassy areas including orchards. Creates burrows and shallow surface runways. Widespread but absent from most of Iberia, Italy and arid areas. Mediterranean pine vole *Pitymys duodecimostatus* is a similar sized, dumpy vole with a proportionately shorter tail and smaller ear. Coat grey-brown; reddish on back. Favours meadows and open pine woods; burrows. Mainly nocturnal. Widespread in W Mediterranean. Replaced in E by similar Savi's pine vole *P. savii*.

WOOD MOUSE *Apodemus sylvaticus*   Body length 7.5–11cm
Familiar small rodent. Upperparts yellow-brown and underparts white. Eyes are black and beady. Favours open woodland, maquis, gardens and farms. Widespread throughout the Mediterranean region and present on most islands.

BLACK RAT *Rattus rattus*   Body length 18–22cm
Fur usually blackish, grading to grey on underparts; brown forms do occur. Ears relatively larger and tail shorter than brown rat. Associated with habitation. Climbs well and visits lofts and barns. Widespread throughout, including islands.

BROWN RAT *Rattus novegicus*   Body length 22–27cm
Widespread and abundant rodent. Has brown fur, proportionately long, naked tail and relatively small ears. Mostly associated with human habitation but also found in fields and marshes. Burrows well. Widespread throughout the entire region.

HOUSE MOUSE *Mus musculus*   Body length 7.5–10cm
Distinctive grey-brown mouse. Often associated with human dwellings but survives at lower densities in most habitats, except wettest or most arid. Vocal by rodent standards. Widespread and common throughout the Mediterranean region.

HARVEST MOUSE *Micromys minutus*   Body length 6–7.5cm
One of Europe's smallest mammals. Recognised by small size, orange-brown upperparts, clean white underparts and prehensile tail, used when climbing. Favours arable fields and grassland. Occurs mainly S France and N Italy.

RED SQUIRREL *Sciurus vulgaris*   Body length 20–28cm
Has reddish-brown fur, conspicuous ear tufts and long, bushy tail. Mostly arboreal; agile climber and jumps well. Diurnal; mainly active in morning. Favours conifer woods. Does not hibernate. Widespread; absent from most islands.

PERSIAN SQUIRREL *Sciurus anomalus*   Body length 20cm
Has reddish grey upperparts, reddish-buff underparts and bushy tail. Favours rocky ground with trees. Mainly diurnal. Mainly Asiatic species found on Greek island of Lesvos.

WILD BOAR *Sus scrofa*   Body length 110–150cm
Ancestor of domestic pigs. Body of adult covered in coarse, brown hair; often masked by mud. Mature male has large tusks, used in defence and for digging. Juveniles look appealing and are pale brown and marked dark brown stripes along the length of the body. Favours deciduous woods on damp soils are damp; also found on marshes. Mostly nocturnal. Distribution patchy throughout the region.

FALLOW DEER *Dama dama*   Shoulder height 85–95cm
Medium-sized deer with relatively long tail. Wild populations often have dark coats; animals with lighter, dappled coats often selected for where herds managed by man. Male has large, palmate antlers that increase in size with each season. Favours deciduous woodland. Mostly nocturnal, resting in cover during day. Scattered populations occur across the region, mostly in large tracts of forest.

MOUFLON *Ovis musimon*   Shoulder height 65–75cm
Ancestor of domesticated sheep. Body has dark chestnut-brown hair. Males develop large, curved horns with age; in females, horns absent or small. Favours rocky ground in wooded terrain; extremely agile on rocks and cliffs. Wild mouflon occur only on Corsica, Sardinia and Cyprus; introduced elsewhere in region.

FIN WHALE *Balaenoptera physalus*   Length 20–25m
Huge marine mammal. Often first detected by the blow, shaped like an inverted cone and reaching 6m. Fast-swimming and usually encountered purely by chance on ferry crossings. Close view reveals diagnostic white right side of jaw. Body dark bluish-grey. Hooked fin seen as the animal dives. Invariably found in deep water.

SPERM WHALE *Physeter catadon*   Body length 15–18m
Body dominated by huge, bulbous head. Lower jaw comparatively long and slender; armed with two rows of large teeth. Blow projects forwards at an angle of 45 degrees and reaches 10m. When it dives, ridged back is seen before the tail stock.

COMMON DOLPHIN *Delphinus delphis*   Body length 1.8–2.5m
The dolphin species most usually seen alongside boats; swims fast and often bow-rides. Sometimes gathers in huge schools. Often leaps out of water revealing body markings: dark back, white underside and waves of colour on flanks. Widespread and fairly common throughout; usually only in deep, undisturbed waters. Striped dolphin *Stenella coeruleoalba* also occurs; similar, but colour on flanks is less intense and shows dark lateral stripe extending forwards from base of dorsal fin.

BOTTLE-NOSED DOLPHIN *Tursiops truncatus*   Body length 2.8–4m
Larger and more robust than common dolphin; has uniformly dark upperparts and flanks; underparts paler but only seen when animal jumps. Snout short and bottle-shaped. Fin proportionately tall, broad-based and curved. Usually in groups comprising five to twenty individuals. Sometimes seen close to land. Widespread.

MEDITERRANEAN MONK SEAL *Monarchus monarchus*   Body length 2.5–3.5m
The only seal species in the region. Rare and highly endangered. Looks streamlined in water with dark brown upperparts and a paler patch on the belly. Confined to inaccessible headlands and islands off Greek and Turkish coasts.

GREAT CRESTED GREBE *Podiceps cristatus* Length 46–51cm
Looks black and white at a distance; close view reveals grey-brown upperparts. In breed-ing season has orange-buff ruff, white cheeks and a black cap and crest; plumage less orna-mental at other times. Bill dagger-like and pink. Dives in search of fish. Nests on floating mound of vegetation. Found on lakes in breeding season; in winter also around coasts. Local in summer but widespread in winter.

 LITTLE GREBE *Tachybaptus ruficollis* Length 25–29cm
Tiny waterbird. In breeding plumage shows chestnut on cheeks and neck and green spot at base of bill; plumage otherwise dark brown except for white powderpuff of feathers at rear end. In winter, has brown upperparts and buff underparts. Builds floating nest of plants. Swims buoyantly and dives well. Found on lakes and slow-flowing rivers. In winter, also on sheltered coasts. Local across region.

 BLACK-NECKED GREBE *Podiceps nigricollis* Body length 28–34cm
Has diagnostic head profile comprising uptilted bill and steep forehead. In breeding sea-son, shows black head, neck and back with yellow ear tufts. In winter, looks black and white. Red eye seen at all times. In flight, all birds show white on trailing edge of inner wing. Nests on shallow lakes. In winter, also on coasts. Mainly a winter visitor; breeds locally Spain and N Greece.

 CORY'S SHEARWATER *Calonectris diomedea* Wingspan 100–125cm
Large seabird, with proportionately long, narrow wings. Upperparts pale brown, with dark wingtips and head; underparts mainly white. Black-tipped yellow bill only visible at close range. Wings usually held stiffly but slightly bowed. In windy conditions, often rises high between lengthy glides. Often seen in sizeable groups. Nests on islands and only vis-its colonies at night. Widespread.

 MEDITERRANEAN SHEARWATER *Puffinus yelkouan* Wingspan 80–89cm
Superficially similar to Cory's but smaller and with proportionately shorter wings; body is cigar-shaped. Upperparts sooty-brown. Undertail coverts are dark; otherwise underparts whitish in race *yelkouan* from E Mediterranean but dusky in race *mauretanicus* from W; these races may be separate species. Banks and glides on stiffly held wings in long lines low over water. Widespread and common.

 EUROPEAN STORM-PETREL *Hydrobates pelagicus* Wingspan 36–39cm
A tiny seabird that appears mainly dark but with diagnostic white rump. Flight pattern comprises powerful direct flight interspersed with glides and periods when feet are pat-tered on surface of sea. Breeds on isolated islands in rock crevices and burrows; only vis-its colonies after dark and so breeding status difficult to assess. Widespread, but difficult to observe.

 NORTHERN GANNET *Morus bassanus* Wingspan 165–180cm
Large seabird with cigar-shaped body and dagger-like bill. Adult has white plumage with black wingtips. Juvenile dark brown, speckled with white; acquires adult plumage over several years. Glides well, but in direct flight employs deep wingbeats. Dives from a height after fish. Winter visitor to the W Mediterranean.

 CORMORANT *Phalacrocorax carbo* Length 80–100cm
Has dark plumage and long, hook-tipped bill. At close range, back appears scaly and plumage has oily sheen. In summer, adult has white on face and thighs; in winter, thigh patch is lost and face appears grubby. Swims and dives well. Often stands on posts with wings outstretched. Breeds locally; widespread in winter.

 SHAG *Phalacrocorax aristotelis* Length 65–80cm
Similar to cormorant but smaller; plumage shows green, oily sheen. Breeding adult has crest and yellow base to bill; both features less obvious in winter. Juvenile brown above and paler below. Swims and dives well; stands on rocks with wings outstretched. Favours rocky coasts. Nests in E of region. Widespread in winter.

DALMATIAN PELICAN   *Pelecanus crispus*   Wingspan 280–290cm
Huge, pale waterbird. In good light, looks pale blue-grey. Head has shaggy mane of back-curled feathers. Bill long, with large throat sac; orange-yellow in breeding season but pinkish at other times. Seen from below in flight, adult has uniformly pale underwings; seen from above, primary feathers are black. Juvenile is uniformly grey-brown. Swims well. A superb flier, soars effortlessly. Present at breeding lakes (N Greece and Turkey) May–August.

WHITE PELICAN   *Pelecanus onocrotalus*   Wingspan 275–290cm
Huge waterbird with mainly white plumage. Bill long, with orange-yellow throat sac. Legs pinkish-orange. In flight, black flight feathers contrast with otherwise gleaming white plumage. Juvenile has brownish plumage and a yellow throat sac. Soars and glides with ease; often seen in large flocks on migration. Occurs at breeding lakes in N Greece and Turkey, May–August; winters in Africa. The commoner of the two European pelicans but still distinctly local.

NIGHT HERON   *Nycticorax nycticorax*   Length 60–65cm
Has hunch-backed appearance at rest and proportionately large head. Adult (A) has black bill, crown and back, grey wings and pale face and underparts; eyes large and red. Trailing head plumes seen in breeding season. Legs yellowish. Juvenile (B) has brown plumage, heavily marked with white spots. Often difficult to observe since mainly nocturnal and roosts in dense cover. Favours extensive wetlands. Locally common, April–September.

LITTLE BITTERN   *Ixobrychus minutus*   Length 35–38cm
Smallest heron in Europe. Adult male has greyish face, black cap, back and flight feathers and orange buff underparts. Shows wing panel that grades from orange-buff to greyish-white. Female similar but plumage subdued. Juvenile has streaked brown plumage. Breeds in extensive reedbeds and seen mainly in jerky, low-level flight. Often confiding on migration. Present April–September. Occurs locally throughout the region, wherever suitable, undisturbed habitats occur.

CATTLE EGRET   *Bubulcus ibis*   Length 48–52cm
Stocky, white heron. During breeding season, crown and back acquire a buffish tinge. Legs pinkish in breeding season but otherwise dull green. Favours dry habitats and often associated with grazing animals. At close range, has dagger-like bill and bulging throat. In flight, wings broad and round and neck is held hunched-up. Common resident in Iberia and the Camargue; occasional elsewhere.

SQUACCO HERON   *Ardeola ralloides*   Length 45–47cm
Compact, stocky heron. In breeding plumage, looks buffish-brown with streaking on crown and trailing plumes on nape; underparts white. In flight, transformed by pure white wings. Non-breeding adult and juvenile have streaked, dull brown plumage. Bill yellowish-green with black tip. Favours well-vegetated wetlands; occasionally flushed from drainage channels. Locally common, April–September.

LITTLE EGRET   *Egretta garzetta*   Length 55–65cm
Familiar white heron. Bill long and dark and legs black but with diagnostic yellow feet. Adult has trailing head plumes in breeding season. In flight, wings broad and round. Breeds locally in colonies on extensive wetlands; much more widespread during migration times and in winter. A partial migrant, most numerous March–September. Small numbers remain in region throughout the year.

GREAT EGRET   *Egretta alba*   Length 85–100cm
Large white heron. Distinguished from little egret by size and larger bill, black in breeding season but otherwise yellow. Legs yellow in breeding season but dark at other times. Local nester with colonies in the Camargue, N Italy and N Greece. Present March–September; disperses and migrates south in autumn but generally widespread in E Mediterranean in winter.

GREY HERON   *Ardea cinerea*   Length 90–98cm

Adult has dagger-like yellow bill and black crest feathers. Head, neck and underparts otherwise whitish except for black streaks on front of neck and breast. Back and wings are blue-grey. Juvenile similar to adult but markings less distinct and plumage generally grubby. In flight, wings are broad and rounded with black flight feathers; flight pattern comprises slow, flapping wingbeats. Utters loud 'frank' call. Widespread and common on wetlands and sheltered coasts. Resident in E Mediterranean; non-breeding visitor elsewhere, September–March.

PURPLE HERON   *Ardea purpurea*   Length 78–90cm

Smaller than grey heron with more slender head and neck. Adult looks mainly greyish-purple. Head and neck orange-buff with black stripe running length of neck on both sides. Shows head plumes and long, streaked breast feathers. Juvenile similar to adult but plumage more uniformly brown. In flight, wings broad and rounded; upperwing purplish-brown with dark flight feathers, underwing grey with maroon leading edge. In flight, neck held in snake-like curve and hind toe cocked upwards. Nests in reedbeds; rather secretive. Present April–August.

WHITE STORK   *Ciconia ciconia*   Length 100–115cm

Large and unmistakable bird. Plumage essentially grubby white except for black wingtips. Bill long, dagger-like and red; long legs are pinkish-red. Juvenile similar to adult but colours of bill and legs duller. In flight, all birds look white with contrasting black flight feathers; legs and neck held outstretched. Capable of sustained soaring and gliding. Often seen in large flocks on migration, rising on thermals to great heights. Nests on roofs of houses and churches. Breeds in Iberia, Greece and Turkey. Present mainly April–September.

BLACK STORK   *Ciconia nigra*   Length 95–100cm

Adult looks mostly black with contrasting white underparts. Bill long, red and dagger-like and legs long and red. A close view reveals red skin around the eye. Juvenile similar to adult but black elements of plumage have brown tinge and leg and bill colour dull. In flight, all birds look all-dark except for white belly and chest. Breeds very locally S Iberia, favouring remote wooded valleys. Widespread passage migrant seen March–April; migrating birds sometimes pause at wetlands, particularly in E Mediterranean. More wary than white stork.

SPOONBILL   *Platalea leucorodia*   Length 80–90cm

Has mainly white plumage and extraordinary bill. Bill often concealed in roosting birds. Breeding birds show yellow flush to breast and at base of bill. Legs long and black; bill long and flattened, with spoon-shaped tip. In flight, has long, bowed wings; head and neck extended, with legs trailing behind. Wings of adult white but those of juvenile are dark-tipped. Favours shallow, coastal lagoons. Breeds locally S Iberia and Greece. Widespread in E Mediterranean in winter.

GLOSSY IBIS   *Plegadis falcinellus*   Length 55–65cm

Has proportions of heron and bill shape of curlew. Plumage can seem black but in good light looks deep maroon with sheen to feathers of wings and back. Breeding bird has white lines from base of bill to eye. In flight, head and neck held outstretched with legs trailing; head looks bulbous. Favours wetlands and present April–September. Widespread passage migrant. Breeds very locally in SE Europe. Overwinters in small numbers, particularly in S Iberian Peninsula.

GREATER FLAMINGO   *Phoenicopterus ruber*   Length 125–145cm

Unmistakable. Usually seen in large flocks. Adult's pink plumage can look white in poor light. Pink, banana-shaped bill has black tip. Long neck usually held 's' shaped. Legs long and pinkish red. In flight, wings show black flight feathers and reddish-pink coverts; neck held outstretched with legs trailing. Juvenile grey brown with dull legs and bill. Favours brackish lagoons and saltpans. Nests in Camargue and S Iberia. Widespread in winter, especially in E Mediterranean.

GREYLAG GOOSE   *Anser anser*   Length 75–90cm
A large, bulky waterbird. Adult is grey-brown with barring on back and belly; has white
stern and dark, wavy feather edges on the neck. Birds seen in W have orange bills; those
from E are pink; legs pink in all birds. Juvenile similar to adult but duller and more barred.
In flight all birds show striking blue-grey panel on leading edge of inner wing. Honking
calls uttered by flocks. Locally common non-breeding visitor to extensive, undisturbed
wetland systems. Present November–March.

SHELDUCK   *Tadorna tadorna*   Length 58–65cm
Distinctive goose-sized duck. Adult has dark green head and upper neck. Plumage otherwise mostly white except for orange chest band and black on wings. Legs pinkish red and
bill bright red; male has knob at base of bill. In flight, looks very black and white. Juvenile
has white and brown plumage with pattern of adult. Coastal habitats including estuaries
and mudflats. Scarce resident breeder, mainly S France and N Greece; nests in burrows.
More widespread in winter.

RUDDY SHELDUCK   *Tadorna ferruginea*   Length 61–67cm
Adult has orange-brown body with clear demarcation from paler buff head and upper
neck. In breeding season, male has narrow black collar separating these two body colours.
Bill and eye of both sexes dark. Standing birds show black wingtips. In flight, wings look
black and white. Juvenile similar to adult but duller. Favours coastal wetlands and river
deltas in E Mediterranean; breeds very locally in N Greece and Turkey using burrows and
tree holes. More widespread in winter.

WIGEON   *Anas penelope*   Length 45–51cm
Male has orange-red head with yellow forehead, pinkish breast and otherwise finely
marked, grey plumage. Shows characteristic black and white stern and white wing patch
in flight. Female has mottled reddish brown plumage with darker feathering around the
eye; best told association with males. Widespread winter visitor, present October–March.
Favours saltmarshes and coastal grassland; forms flocks. Presence often first detected by
male's distinctive *wheeoo* call.

MALLARD   *Anas platyrhynchos*   Length 50–65cm
Male has yellow bill and green shiny head and neck separated from chestnut breast by
white collar. Plumage otherwise grey-brown except for black stern and white tail. Female
has orange bill and mottled brown plumage. In flight, both sexes have blue and white
speculum. Found on almost any unpolluted freshwater habitat; also on coasts in winter.
Widespread; commonest in winter.

GADWALL   *Anas strepera*   Length 45–56cm
Male has grey-brown plumage, finely marked with intricate dark markings, and diagnostic
black stern; bill is black. Female similar to female mallard with mottled brown plumage
and yellow bill; best told by association with males. In flight, both sexes show white on
speculum. Favours wetlands with open water. Breeds very locally S Spain and N Greece.
Widespread in winter.

PINTAIL   *Anas acuta*   Length 51–66cm
A long-bodied duck. Male has chocolate brown head and nape with white breast extending as stripe up side of head. Plumage otherwise finely marked grey but shows cream and
black at stern and long, pointed tail, often held at an angle. Female has mottled brown
plumage. Winter visitor to region and locally common on well-vegetated lakes and marshes. Present October–March.

SHOVELER   *Anas clypeata*   Length 44–52cm
Recognised by long, flattened bill seen in both sexes. Male has striking plumage comprising green head, black and white on body and reddish chestnut flanks. Female is mottled
brown and seldom seen outside the company of a male. Both sexes have green speculum
and pale blue wing panel on forewing. Best known as a non-breeding visitor, present
October–March. Widespread but local on marshes.

WHITE-HEADED DUCK   *Oxyura leucocephala*   Length 43–48cm
Male has white head, black cap and eye, and large, bright blue bill, swollen at the base; body plumage brown, darkest on neck. Female's bill similar in shape to male's but dark grey; body plumage brown and face white with dark cap and stripe. Favours well-vegetated lakes. Rare resident S Spain; winter visitor to S Turkey.

MARBLED DUCK   *Marmaronetta angustirostris*   Length 40–42cm
Sexes similar, with grey-brown ground colour marked with pale buff spots. Has dark bill, dark smudge through eye and indistinct pale patch at base of bill. In flight, wings look uniformly brown. Favours well-vegetated wetlands and keeps close to cover. Rare resident in S Spain and winter visitor to S Turkey.

RED-CRESTED POCHARD   *Netta rufina*   Length 53–57cm
Male has orange head and neck and red bill; body feathers black except for grey-brown back and white flanks. Female has pink-tipped dark bill, dark cap and nape; cheeks and throat white; body plumage brown. White wingbar and underwing seen in flight. Favours wetlands. Resident S Spain and Turkey; widespread in winter.

POCHARD   *Aythya ferina*   Length 42–49cm
Male has reddish-orange head, black breast, grey flanks and back, and black stern. Female has brown head and breast, grey-brown back and flanks and pale 'spectacle' around eye. Bill of both sexes dark with grey band near tip. Locally common winter visitor to lakes and reservoirs; breeds in small numbers.

FERRUGINOUS DUCK   *Aythya nyroca*   Length 38–42cm
Male has chocolate-brown plumage, darkest on back and chestnut on head; white stern is diagnostic. Bill grey with dark tip; eye has white iris. Female similar to male but plumage duller and eye is dark. In flight, shows striking white wingbar and underwing. Found on well-vegetated lakes, mainly September–March.

TUFTED DUCK   *Aythya fuligula*   Length 40–47cm
Male looks black and white with purple sheen to head and diagnostic tufted crest. Female has brown plumage, palest on the flanks; often shows small crest and white at base of bill. Both sexes show yellow eye and black-tipped grey bill. Winter visitor to lakes and reservoirs, September–March. Usually in small flocks.

GOLDENEYE   *Bucephala clangula*   Length 42–50cm
Male has mainly black and white plumage with large, rounded head; shows yellow eye and round white patch at base of bill. Female has grey-brown body plumage separated from dark brown head by pale neck; eye pale yellow. Winter visitor to lakes and coasts, mainly October–March. Dives frequently and for long periods.

RED-BREASTED MERGANSER   *Mergus serrator*   Length 52–58cm
Grebe-like diving duck with shaggy crest. Male has narrow red bill, green head, white neck and orange-red breast; shows grey flanks and black back. Female has red bill, dirty orange head and nape, except for pale throat; body plumage grey-buff. In flight, both sexes show white on wings. Local winter visitor to coasts.

BLACK KITE   *Milvus migrans*   Wingspan 145–165cm
Medium-sized raptor, most easily confused with female marsh harrier. Plumage dark
brown, palest on head. Has black-tipped yellow bill and yellow legs. Tail is forked but can
appear straight-ended when broadly fanned. Wings usually held flat when soaring.
Favours wooded wetlands. Sometimes scavenges at rubbish dumps. Passage migrant and
locally common breeding species. Present April–September.

RED KITE   *Milvus milvus*   Wingspan 145–165cm
Distinguished from black kite by more deeply forked tail and more colourful appearance.
Plumage mainly reddish-brown with grey head, broad pale patch near wingtip and pale
undertail. Seen from above, tail red and flight feathers dark. Soars effortlessly; manoeu-
vres by twisting tail. Favours wooded valleys and open country for feeding. Resident in
Iberia, S Italy, Corsica and Sardinia.

LAMMERGEIER   *Gypaetus barbatus*   Wingspan 265–280cm
Huge vulture. Adult has long, narrow wings and long, wedge-shaped tail. Plumage dark
except for orange-buff head and underside of body; has dark patch around eye and dark,
moustache-like feathers. All-dark juvenile recognised by its flight silhouette alone. Soars
effortlessly over cliffs and mountain tops. Feeds on carrion. Rare resident of Pyrenees,
Corsica, Crete, N Greece and Turkey.

EGYPTIAN VULTURE   *Neophron percnopterus*   Wingspand 155–180cm
Europe's smallest vulture. Seen from below in flight, adult has dirty white plumage with
black flight feathers; tail is wedge-shaped. Has bald yellow face and pinkish-yellow legs.
All-dark juvenile has flight silhouette similar to adult. Favours mountains and gorges in
warm, dry areas. Soars effortlessly. Present April–September in Iberia, S Italy, N Greece,
Turkey and S France.

BLACK VULTURE   *Aegypius monachus*   Wingspan 250–295cm
An immense raptor. Has long, broad wings that are parallel-sided and square-ended; the
primaries form distinct, splayed 'fingers'. Head looks proportionately small and tail is relatively short. In flight, appears all dark although plumage is in fact dark brown. Soars
effortlessly at immense heights over mountains. Rare, confined to S Iberia, N Greece and
Turkey; easiest to see on Majorca.

GRIFFON VULTURE   *Gyps fulvus*   Wingspan 260–280 cm
Huge raptor with brown body plumage and dark flight feathers. Head and neck bald and
pale with collar ruff of pale feathers. In flight, wings are long, broad at base but taper to fin-
ger-like primaries at tip; head looks tiny and tail short. Soars with wings in a shallow 'v'.
Perched birds look hunched up. Favours warm mountainous terrain. Resident in Iberia,
Sardinia, N Greece, Turkey and Cyprus.

MONTAGU'S HARRIER   *Circus pyrgargus*   Wingspan 105–120cm
Blue-grey male has flecked red underparts, barred tail, dark wingtips and two black wingbars. From above, note dark wing tips, single black wingbars, white rump. Brown female has
barred tail, streaked underparts and white rump. Summer visitor and passage migrant.
Common only in Iberia. Hunts over grassland.

HEN HARRIER   *Circus cyaneus*   Wingspan 100–120cm
Male pale grey with black wing tips and white rump. Brown female is streaked on underside; has barred tail and white rump. Hunts over grassland. Winter visitor,
October–March. Similar Pallid harrier *C. macrourus* occurs on migration; pale male has
small black wing tips; female almost identical to female hen harrier.

MARSH HARRIER   *Circus aeruginosus*   Wingspan 115–130cm
Often seen flying over marshes. Male reddish brown except for blue-grey head and grey
unbarred tail; in flight, has grey and brown patches on wings and black wingtips. Female
and immature birds are dark brown except for pale leading edge to wing and pale cap and
chin. Common passage migrant; breeds locally.

SPARROWHAWK   *Accipiter nisus*   Wingspan 60–75cm
Has short, rounded wings and long, barred tail. Male smaller than female with blue-grey
uppeprarts and barred reddish brown underparts. Female has grey-brown upperparts and
pale underparts with brown barring. Hunts in low-level flight for small birds. Favours
woodland and scrub. Widespread resident.

GOSHAWK   *Accipiter gentilis*   Wingspan 100–115cm
Similar to sparrowhawk but larger, especially female; has relatively bulkier body, shorter
tail and longer wings. Upperparts grey-brown with pale, dark-barred underparts. Shows
staring yellow eyes, white stripe over eyes and yellow legs. In flight, reveals fluffy white
undertail feathers. Widespread in extensive forests.

HONEY-BUZZARD   *Pernis apivorus*   Wingspan 135–150cm
Buzzard-like but paler underparts show dark barring and dark carpal patch on wings. Tail
long with two broad dark bands at base and dark terminal band. In flight, head narrow and
pale. Soars on flat wings. Favours vast forests; feeds on bee grubs. Summer visitor to N
Spain and N Italy; passage migrant elsewhere.

✓ **BUZZARD**   *Buteo buteo*   Wingspan 115–125cm
Common medium-sized raptor with broad wings and short tail, fanned when soaring.
Underwings usually pale except for dark margins and coverts; body usually dark brown
except for pale band on chest. Appears brown from above. Soars with wings in 'V' shape.
Utters mewing calls. Favours wooded areas. Widespread resident.

LONG-LEGGED BUZZARD   *Buteo rufinus*   Wingspan 130–155cm
Similar to pale buzzard but longer winged. From below, body and wing coverts are
unstreaked reddish brown, darkest on the belly; tail uniformly pale reddish and unbarred.
Pale flight feathers contrast with dark wing margin and carpal patch. Favours dry rocky
terrain and mountains. Local resident in N Greece and Turkey.

GOLDEN EAGLE   *Aquila chrysaetos*   Wingspan 190–215cm
Buzzard-like but larger, with proportionately longer tail and wings; the latter narrow at
base. Soars on parallel-sided wings held in shallow 'V'. Distant adults look dark; immatures show white at tail base and on wings. Local in mountains.

IMPERIAL EAGLE   *Aquila helica*   Wingspan 180–215cm
Similar to golden eagle but less tied to mountains. Plumage mainly dark brown. Birds
from N Greece and Turkey have golden nape and white on scapulars; S Iberian birds are
similar but with white leading edge to wings. Rare resident.

BONELLI'S EAGLE   *Hieraaetus fasciatus*   Wingspan 150–170cm
From below, has pale belly; wings show contrast between black coverts and paler flight
feathers. Tail long and grey, with dark terminal band. From above, dark with pale patch on
back. Wooded mountains, mainly Iberia, N Greece and W Turkey.

BOOTED EAGLE   *Hieraaetus pennatus*   Wingspan 100–130cm
Buzzard-like with long, splayed primaries. Pale phase has pale underparts, dark flight
feathers and tail; dark phase uniformly dark. Both show pale 'v' on back and upperwings.
Wooded hills, Iberia, Majorca, Greece and Turkey. Summer visitor.

SHORT-TOED EAGLE   *Circaetus gallicus*   Wingspan 170–185cm
Wings long, broad and pale; underparts pale and barred. Head and neck look rather dark;
tail often shows dark terminal band. Often hovers, scanning ground for snakes. Favours
open hillsides and maquis. Summer visitor, Iberia to Turkey.

OSPREY   *Pandion haliaetus*   Wingspan 145–160cm
Fish-eating raptor, usually seen near water. In flight, looks gull-like with pale underparts,
long, narrow wings, dark primaries and dark carpal patch. Upperparts brown with pale
crown. Passage migrant; small numbers winter in W or region.

KESTREL   *Falco tinnunculus*   Wingspan 65–80cm
The region's most widespread and familiar raptor. Male has spotted, orange-brown back, blue-grey head and blue-grey tail with terminal black band. Female has barred, brown plumage. Nests in trees and on cliff ledges, but also in man-made settings such as loft spaces in barns. Feeds primarily on small mammals but takes insects in summer months. Frequently hovers using head wind or updraughts for assistance. Common resident throughout the region, including most islands.

LESSER KESTREL   *Falco naumanni*   Wingspan 58–72cm
Small, elegantly proportioned falcon. Similar to kestrel but male has unspotted chestnut back, blue-grey innerwing and head, and pale grey tail with dark terminal band. Female has brown plumage marked with dark spots, dark primaries and barred tail. Usually seen in flocks and breeds colonially in old buildings or on cliffs. Hovers, but much less frequently than kestrel. Summer visitor, present from April to September. Locally common in Iberian Peninsula, Greece and Turkey; scarce and local breeding bird elsewhere but more widespread on migration.

HOBBY   *Falco subbuteo*   Wingspan 70–85cm
Small, elegant and dashing falcon. Adult has dark blue-grey upperparts and pale, dark-streaked underparts. At close range, dark moustachial markings, white cheeks and reddish orange 'trousers' are visible. In flight, has anchor-like outline with narrow, swept-back wings and proportionately long tail. In spring, often hunts dragonflies over lakes and marshes. Later in season, concentrates on the young of birds such as swallows and martins. Widespread summer visitor, present May–September; commonest in far W and E of range. Widespread on migration.

RED-FOOTED FALCON   *Falco vespertinus*   Wingspan 65–75cm
Small, elegant falcon. At a distance, can be mistaken for either kestrel or hobby. Adult male has mainly dark grey plumage with pale primaries, red vent and thighs, and red feet; red skin around eye visible at close range. Immature male is similar but has paler underparts and pale face and throat. Adult female has orange-buff crown and underparts, barred grey back and dark mask through eyes. Perches on wires but also hovers. Breeds colonially and usually seen in flocks on migration. Common passage migrant, mostly in E Mediterranean and in spring.

ELEONORA'S FALCON   *Falco eleonorae*   Wingspan 90–105cm
Similar to hobby but with longer tail and longer, more slender wings. Adults occur as two colour forms. Dark phase birds look all dark. Pale phase birds show pale cheek, dark moustachial stripe and pale underside with dark streaks; plumage otherwise dark. Specialises in catching migrant songbirds although insects are taken in spring. Breeds on sea cliffs but often hunts inland. Present May–October with scattered colonies from Majorca to Cyprus. Nests in late summer.

PEREGRINE   *Falco peregrinus*   Wingspan 95–115cm
A robust and impressive falcon. Adult has dark blue-grey upperparts and pale, barred underparts; face shows distinct dark mask. Juvenile has browner pluamge with streaked underparts. Usually seen in flight over mountains or sea cliffs. In winter, often wanders to coastal areas and marshes. Soars on bowed wings but stoops at high speed with wings swept back on prey such as pigeons. Locally common resident throughout region from Iberian Peninsula to Turkey.

LANNER   *Falco biarmicus*   Wingspan 95–115cm
An impressive falcon, similar to peregrine but slimmer and with proportionately longer tail; wings appear rather broad with rounded tips. Seen in flight, adult male has dark brown upperparts except for orange nape; underparts are pale with dark spots. Adult female is similar but nape colour is buff; underparts are more conspicuously spotted than male. Juvenile is dark brown and streaked. Favours arid, mountainous terrain and steppe habitat. Resident, occurring locally from Italy eastwards; most easily discovered in N Greece and Turkey.

GREAT BUSTARD *Otis tarda* Wingspan 190–260cm
Huge and unmistakable. Male larger than female. Both sexes have marbled brown upper-parts and white underparts. In breeding season, male displays with bulging neck and cocked-up tail; has white whisker-like feathers on face. Female and non-breeding males have grey head and neck. In flight, all birds show black and white wings. Favours grass-land and arable fields. Local in S Iberia and E Europe.

LITTLE BUSTARD *Tetrax tetrax* Wingspan 105–115cm
Has gamebird body proportions but relatively long legs and neck. Body colour marbled grey-brown above and white below. Adult male has black and white neck markings. In flight, all birds show mainly white wings with black wingtips. Favours open grassland and steppe habitat. Forms flocks outside breeding season. Locally common resident in Iberian Peninsula. Scattered populations elsewhere.

BLACK FRANCOLIN *Francolinus francolinus* Length 33–36cm
More often heard than seen: male utters incessant, grating call from cover in spring. Adult male mainly black except for white cheeks, chestnut collar and brown wings; body span-gled with white spots. Female mainly brown with paler head and chestnut collar. In flight, shows dark outer tail feathers and brown wings. Arable land and scrub. Resident and com-mon on Cyprus; local in Turkey and Tuscany.

RED-LEGGED PARTRIDGE *Alectoris rufa* Length 32–34cm
Gamebird with red bill and legs, and white throat, bordered with gorget of black spots; plumage otherwise mainly blue-grey and warm buff except for black and white barring on flanks. Found on arable land and marshes. Widespread in Iberia and S France. Male utters repetitive call. Seen in small parties outside breeding season. Replaced in N Greece, Turkey, Cyprus and Crete by chukar *A. chukar*; similar but throat and flank markings more distinct. Favours rocky ground.

QUAIL *Coturnix coturnix* Length 16–18cm
Tiny gamebird. Seldom seen, except when flushed from cover. Presence usually detected by call: male utters repetitive 'wet my lips' call. Plumage brown above and pale buff below. Male has streaked flanks and black and white head markings. In flight, wings look rounded. Widespread on arable land, April-September.

WATER RAIL *Rallus aquaticus* Length 23–28cm
Shy wetland bird, often detected by pig-like squealing calls. Has long, reddish bill, red-dish legs, mainly blue-grey underparts and reddish brown upperparts; shows black and white barring on flanks. Favours reedbeds and marshes. Local resident throughout; num-bers swollen in winter by migrants from N Europe.

LITTLE CRAKE *Porzana parva* Length 18–20cm
Tiny waterbird with disproportionately long toes. Male has mainly dark brown upperparts with pale streaks; underparts including face and blue-grey with pale streaks on flanks. Female is similar but underparts are buffish-grey. Favours marshes with dense cover. Breeds sparingly in region; seen mostly on migration.

BAILLON'S CRAKE *Porzana pusilla* Length 17–19cm
Similar to little crake but plumage generally darker, recalling that of water rail. Face, throat and breast blue grey and flanks and belly barred black and white. Upperparts dark brown with conspicuous white spots. Iris red and bill greenish. Female duller than male. Male utters frog-like croaking song. Favours marshes with dense cover. Seen occasionally on migration, mainly in spring.

SPOTTED CRAKE *Porzana porzana* Length 20–24cm
Small, dumpy waterbird. Upperparts brown, spangled with white spots. Underparts blue-grey. Plumage of male shows more contrast than that of female. All birds have stubby yel-low bill with red base and greenish legs. Favours marshes. Male utters whiplash call. Present May-September but seen mainly on migration.

✓ **MOORHEN** *Gallinula chloropus*   Length 32–35cm
Widespread waterbird. Adult has brownish wings but otherwise mainly dark grey-black
plumage. Has distinctive yellow-tipped red bill and frontal shield on head, white feathers
on sides of undertail and white line along flanks. Legs and long toes yellowish. Juvenile
has pale brown plumage. Swims with jerky movement and with tail flicking; in flight,
shows dangling legs. Tends to be rather secretive during breeding season and more likely
to feed in open in winter months. Widespread resident across much of Mediterranean but
tied to wetland habitats.

✓ **COOT** *Fulica atra*   Length 36–38cm
Recognised by all-black plumage and white bill and frontal shield to head. Has lobed toes
which facilitate swimming. Utters distinctive, loud *kwoot* call. Feeds by upending or making shallow dives in water but also grazes on waterside grass. Builds mound nest of waterplants, often in full view. Favours lakes and marshes with open water during breeding season. At other times of year, also found on reservoirs, usually in sizeable flocks. Locally
common resident throughout the region, wherever suitable habitats occur; more widespread in winter.

CRESTED COOT *Fulica cristata*   Length 38–42cm
Superficially similar to coot but larger. Adult has red knobs over white facial shield; these
are difficult to detect at a distance and in winter when colour fades. In flight, lacks white
terminal band to secondary feathers seen in coot. Found on well-vegetated lakes. Upends
for food and dives well. Calls include a peculiar 'mooing' call, usually uttered from cover.
An essentially tropical species but with a small resident population found in southern
Spain, centred on the Coto Doñana; seldom seen elsewhere.

PURPLE GALLINULE *Porphyrio porphyrio*   Length 45–50cm
Recalls an outsized moorhen in outline but colours are striking. Adult has violet-blue
plumage with blue face and red eyes, legs and bill. Undertail is white and exposed as bird
nervously flicks its tail. Juvenile is grey with pale throat and dull red legs and bill. Favours
brackish water with standing water, reedbeds and freshwater marshes. Feeds on underwater stems of waterplants. Ventures into the open mainly at dawn and dusk. A rare species
in the region; small populations in S Iberian Peninsula, Mallorca, Sardinia and Turkey.

STONE-CURLEW *Burhinus oedicnemus*   Length 41cm
A rather secretive, well camouflaged bird, mostly nocturnal but occasionally seen at dawn
and dusk. Presence often detected at night by its strange, curlew-like wailing calls. Has
sandy brown plumage, yellow legs, black-tipped yellow bill and large yellow eyes. Dark
wings and white wingbars are most apparent in flight. Favours open terrain but always a
challenge to spot. Favours areas with short vegetation. Common resident in Iberia.
Widespread in E Mediterranean in winter.

✓ **BLACK-WINGED STILT** *Himantopus himantopus*   Length 35–40cm
Unmistakable bird with black and white plumage and ridiculously long, red legs. Adult
has black wings and mantle and white underparts; head shows variable amounts of black.
Bill long, needle-like and dark. In flight, shows white on rump and lower back and long,
trailing legs. Favours coastal lagoons and shallow lakes, often where water is brackish; frequently nests beside saltpans. Locally common and widespread summer visitor to suitable habitats; a few overwinter.

AVOCET *Recurvirostra avosetta*   Length 43cm
Easily recognised by its black and white plumage, long, blue legs and long, upcurved bill,
which is swept from side-to-side through shallow water when feeding. Toes are webbed,
which aids walking on oozing substrate and facilitates swimming. Associated with shallow, coastal lagoons, saltpans and estuaries. Breeds in loose colonies and scattered breeding sites occur across the Mediterranean region wherever suitable habitats occur. Forms
flocks in winter.

COLLARED PRATINCOLE *Glareola pratincola*   Length 24–27cm

Atypical wader that recalls a long-bodied plover on the ground but a tern in flight. Adult has dark sandy brown with white belly and shows yellow throat, defined by black border. Bill is slightly hooked-tipped. Seen from above in flight, wings look dark tipped and shows white rump. Sometimes feeds on the ground but typically catches insects in flight. Favours wetlands. Breeds locally, April–September. Seen elsewhere on migration. Similar black-winged pratincole *G. nordmanni* has black, not maroon, underwing coverts. E of region only.

RINGED PLOVER *Charadrius hiaticula*   Length 19cm

Small, dumpy wader. Adult has sandy brown upperparts and white underparts with continuous black breast-band and collar. Shows black and white markings on face and white throat and nape. Legs orange-yellow and bill orange with black tip. Juvenile similar but dark markings less distinct and has dull legs and dark bill. All birds show white wingbar in flight. Associated with coastal sandy and shingle beaches in breeding season; otherwise also on estuaries. Extremely local nester.

LITTLE RINGED PLOVER *Charadrius dubius*   Length 15cm

Slightly smaller than ringed plover and with slimmer body. Has sandy brown upperparts and white underparts with black collar and breast band, and black and white markings on face. Close views of adult reveal black bill, yellow legs and characteristic yellow eyering. Juvenile similar to juvenile ringed plover but, in flight, wings lack wingbars; adults have similarly uniform wings. Widespread April–September. Breeds on dry river beds.

KENTISH PLOVER *Charadrius alexandrinus*   Length 15–17cm

Dumpy, pale-looking plover. Adult has sandy brown back separated from brown cap and nape by white collar; black markings on side of neck form incomplete collar. In breeding season, male has chestnut crown and black patch on forehead; at other times, crown becomes uniform grey-brown and similar to year-round appearance of female. Juvenile similar to female but duller. Essentially coastal, favouring saltpans, brackish lagoons and estuaries. Widespread resident in region.

GOLDEN PLOVER *Pluvialis apricaria*   Length 28cm

Large and comparatively long-legged plover. In winter plumage has spangled golden upperparts and buff, well marked underparts. In breeding plumage (seldom seen in region) acquires black belly grading to grey on face and neck; markings more distinct in male than female. In flight, all birds show white 'armpits'. Favours areas of short grass. Widespread but only locally common winter visitor.

GREY PLOVER *Pluvialis squatarola*   Length 28cm

Non-breeding visitor from high Arctic nesting grounds, usually present October–April. In winter plumage, looks mainly grey with upperparts spangled black and white and underparts whitish; juvenile is similar but usually shows buffish wash. In breeding plumage (seldom seen in region) adult acquires black underparts. All birds show black 'armpits' in flight. Favours coastal mudflats.

SPUR-WINGED PLOVER *Hoplopterus spinosus*   Length 25–27cm

Elegant, rather long-legged plover. Adult has black and white underparts and sandy brown back. In flight, upperparts look striking with black primaries separated by white panel from sandy brown mantle; rump is white and tail shows black terminal band. Underwing white, contrasting with black primaries and belly. Favours muddy saltpans and river deltas. Summer visitor to E Mediterranean.

LAPWING *Vanellus vanellus*   Length 30cm

Distinctive plover; looks black and white at a distance. In good light, shows green sheen to feathers of back; in winter, these have buffish fringes. Spiky crest of feathers visible at all times, longer in male than female; orange undertail feathers seen in all birds. In flight, has rounded, black and white wings and flapping flight. Winter visitor; favours short grassland. Forms flocks.

DUNLIN *Calidris alpina* Length 17–19cm
Widespread and locally common winter visitor. In winter plumage, adult has uniformly grey-brown upperparts and white underparts. In breeding plumage (seen occasionally in spring and autumn birds) has chestnut-brown cap and back and black belly. Juvenile has dark spots on flanks, with grey, black and chestnut on back. Call *priit*. Favours estuaries and mudflats. Seen mainly September–April.

CURLEW SANDPIPER *Calidris ferruginea* Length 19cm
Similar to dunlin but bill is markedly downcurved; shows conspicuous white rump in flight. In winter plumage has grey-brown upperparts and white underparts. In breeding plumage (seen occasionally in migrants) acquires brick red colouration. Juvenile similar to winter adult but has scaly appearance to back. Passage migrant to coastal wetlands. Overwinters in small numbers.

LITTLE STINT *Calidris minuta* Length 13cm
Tiny wader, recalling miniature, short-billed dunlin. Constant frantic activity is a clue to identity. Winter adult has grey-brown upperparts and white underparts. In breeding plumage, upperparts reddish brown with yellowish 'V' on mantle. Juvenile similar to breeding adult but paler and with white 'V' on back. Favours coastal marshes and mudflats. Passage migrant and widespread in winter.

TEMMINCK'S STINT *Calidris temminckii* Length 14cm
Similar size to little stint but legs are yellowish not black. Recalls miniature common sandpiper with short, straight bill. Adult has grey-brown upperparts and white underparts, with clear demarcation between dark breast and pale belly; in breeding plumage, has dark centres to many back feathers. Favours coastal pools and marshes. Widespread passage migrant and overwinters in small numbers.

✓ **SANDERLING** *Calidris alba* Length 20cm
Widespread and locally common winter visitor to sandy beaches, mainly September–April. Distant winter bird looks very white; at close range, shows grey upperparts, white underparts, black 'shoulder' patch, and black legs and bill. Seen in small flocks, running at great speed and feeding along edge of breaking waves. Reddish-brown breeding plumage birds sometimes seen in spring and autumn.

✓ **CURLEW** *Numenius arquata* Length 53–58cm
Distinctive large wader with long, downcurved bill. Plumage mainly grey-brown but shows white rump and wedge on lower back; tip of tail has dark, narrow barring. Seen as a wintering bird in the region, present October–April. Favours coastal wetlands, estuaries and mudflats. Uses long, blue-grey legs to wade in deep water; probes with bill for worms. Utters *curlew* call in alarm.

WHIMBREL *Numenius phaeopus* Length 41cm
Similar to curlew but smaller and with distinctive head pattern comprising two dark lateral stripes on otherwise pale crown. Presence also detected by bubbling call, usually comprising seven notes descending slightly in pitch from start to finish. Found on coasts. Widespread passage migrant. Winters in small numbers.

BLACK-TAILED GODWIT *Limosa limosa* Length 41cm
Large, long-legged wader; long, slightly upturned bill is pinkish at base. In all plumages, shows black tail, white rump and white wingbars in flight. In winter, upperparts uniformly grey-brown and underparts pale; juvenile similar but with buffish wash. Summer adult has reddish wash. Widespread in winter on estuaries.

BAR-TAILED GODWIT *Limosa lapponica* Length 38–42cm
Similar to black-tailed godwit but all birds show uniformly dark wings and white rump grading to narrow-barred tail. Juvenile and winter adult have curlew-like streaked brown plumage; darker above than below. Breeding plumage birds have reddish plumage. Widespread winter visitor to estuaries and mudflats.

REDSHANK *Tringa totanus*   Length 28cm

Easily recognised by its red legs and long, red-based bill. Plumage mostly grey-brown above and pale below with streaks and barring; plumage most heavily marked in breeding season. Presence often first detected by bird's loud, piping alarm call. Breeds very locally on wetlands in region. More widespread in winter and then usually found on coasts, favouring mudflats and brackish mashes.

SPOTTED REDSHANK *Tringa erythropus*   Length 30cm

In non-breeding plumage, similar to redshank but larger and with proportionately longer red legs and bill. Breeding plumage birds (rarely seen in region) have almost black plumage. Favours coastal marshes and often wades in comparatively deep water. In flight, wings are uniform; those or redshank show white wingbar. Widespread passage migrant. Winters in small numbers. Utters *tchlewit* call.

GREENSHANK *Tringa nebularia*   Length 30–31cm

Looks very white at a distance. In all plumages, has yellow-green legs and long, slightly upturned bill with grey base. Winter adult is pale grey above with white underparts; in breeding plumage, some feathers on back have dark centres. In flight shows uniform wings and white wedge on lower back. Flight call *tchu-tchu-tchu*. Found on coasts and marshes. Passage migrant; winters in small numbers.

WOOD SANDPIPER *Tringa glareola*   Length 20cm

Small, elegant wader with long, yellow legs; bill is slender and straight. Has brownish, spangled upperparts, brightest in juvenile birds, and pale belly. In flight, shows conspicuous white rump. White tail has narrow terminal bars, these greater in extent than on green sandpiper. Underwings mostly white. Utters *chiff-chiff-chiff* alarm call. Favours freshwater marshes. Widespread passage migrant in spring and autumn.

GREEN SANDPIPER *Tringa ochropus*   Length 23cm

Has brownish upperparts, spangled with white dots, and white underparts. Legs yellowish green and bill yellow at base. Often seen in flight, flushed from ditches or pond margins, when it looks black and white with a striking white rump; flight accompanied by yelping, trisyllabic call. Usually found beside freshwater. Distinctive bobbing gait. Widespread in winter but seldom numerous.

MARSH SANDPIPER *Tringa stagnatilis*   Length 22–25cm

Elegant wader with long legs and thin, needle-like bill. In winter plumage, has mainly grey upperparts and white underparts; dark shoulder patch usually contrasts with paler mantle. In breeding plumage, upperparts marked with black and brown feathering. Favours freshwater marshes and lake margins. Widespread passage migrant, commonest in E Mediterranean.

✓ **COMMON SANDPIPER** *Actitis hypoleucos*   Length 20cm

Small, plump-bodied wader with elongated tail end. Upperparts warm brown and underparts white showing clear demarcation between dark breast and white belly. Adopts horizontal stance and bobs body up and down. Flies on bowed, fluttering wings. Found beside freshwater. Common passage migrant. Winters in small numbers.

SNIPE *Gallinago gallinago*   Length 27cm

Has dumpy, rounded body, rather short legs and incredibly long, straight bill. Feeding method characteristic: probes vertically downwards with bill in soft mud, in manner of sewing machine. Upperparts brown, patterned with black and white lines and bars; shows dark stripes on head. Winter visitor to freshwater marshes.

TURNSTONE *Arenaria interpres*   Length 23cm

Winter adult and juvenile variably marked with black, brown and white on upperparts; shows clear demarcation between dark breast and white underparts. In breeding plumage, has orange-brown feathers on back and black and white head. Legs reddish orange. Bill stubby and triangular. Winter visitor to coasts.

MEDITERRANEAN GULL   *Larus melanocephalus*   Length 36–38cm
Superficially similar to black-headed gull but separable in all plumages with care. Most consistent features of adult are pure white wings. In winter (A), has dark smudges around eyes but in summer (B) acquires black hood, eyes defined with white 'eyelids'. Blood-red bill is stouter than that of black-headed with dark band near tip. In first winter, similar to first winter black-headed but dark streaks on head and white 'eyelids' give menacing look. Second winter similar to adult but has dark primary tips. Local breeding bird but widespread on coasts in winter. Most numerous in E Mediterranean; gathers in sizeable pre-nesting flocks.

BLACK-HEADED GULL   *Larus ridibundus*   Length 35–38cm
Plumage varies according to age and time of year but at all times easily recognised in flight by white leading edge to wings. Adult has grey back and upperwings, white underparts, red legs and reddish bill. In winter (A), has dark smudges behind eye but in summer (B) acquires chocolate brown hood. Juvenile has marbled brown and grey plumage. First winter bird has dark-tipped pink bill with grey and brown on upperwings. Scarce breeding species but widespread in winter.

SLENDER-BILLED GULL   *Larus genei*   Length 42–44cm
Elegant, rather elongated gull with a bill that is long rather than particularly slender. Adult recalls winter adult black-headed gull but lacks dark markings on head. Slightly larger than that species, with proportionately longer neck and broader wings. Adult has pale grey mantle, dark primaries and white leading edge to wings. Legs are pale orange and bill is dark orange-pink. Juvenile has dirty brown wing coverts and smudges behind eye; legs and bill pale orange. Local breeding species on coastal lagoons. Widespread but still scarce in winter.

LITTLE GULL   *Larus minutus*   Length 28cm
The world's smallest gull with buoyant, tern-like flight. Wings are relatively long and show rounded tips; those of adult have diagnostic black underside and trailing white margin. In winter, adult has dark smudges on face but in summer, acquires dark hood; legs and bill reddish at all times. Juvenile has striking black bars along wings and black-tipped tail and difficult to confuse with any other gull in the region. A winter visitor to the Mediterranean, present mainly October–April. Invariably coastal and often feeds along shoreline.

AUDOUIN'S GULL   *Larus audouinii*   Length 48–52cm
Elegant gull with relatively long wings and large bill. Adult has pale grey upperwings and mantle with white trailing edge and black-tipped primaries. Bill red but with black and yellow tip and legs black. Juvenile has grey-brown plumage, darkest on mantle, and dark bill and legs. Second winter has red bill, grey upperwing and mantle and black-tipped tail. World population of around 1,000 pairs is confined to Mediterranean. Nests on rocky islands; widespread in winter.

YELLOW-LEGGED GULL   *Larus cachinnans*   Length 55–65cm
Mediterranean counterpart of northern Europe's herring gull. Adult has dark grey mantle with white-spotted black wingtips. Bill yellow with orange spot near tip and legs yellow. Adult head pure white throughout year. Juvenile mottled grey-brown with dark bill and legs; acquires adult plumage through successive moults over subsequent two years. Local breeding species, nesting on islands. Widespread in winter when mainly coastal but also inland on fields and rubbish tips.

LESSER BLACK-BACKED GULL   *Larus fuscus*   Length 53–56cm
Similar proportions to yellow-legged gull but mantle and upperwings of adult are darker slate-grey; has similar bright yellow legs and yellow bill with orange spot near tip. Juvenile has grey-brown, mottled plumage, darker than that of juvenile yellow-legged gull; acquires adult plumage over subsequent two years. Widespread and common winter visitor to the Mediterranean, present October–March. Mainly coastal and often found far from land.

SANDWICH TERN *Sterna sandvichensis*   Length 41cm
Easily recognised in the flight by powerful, buoyant action on long, narrow wings and frequently uttered harsh *churrick* call. Back and upperwing of adult pale grey but plumage otherwise white except for dark crest; in winter plumage, sometimes seen in autumn birds, loses dark cap but retains black on nape. Legs black and bill black with yellow tip. Juvenile has scaly-looking back and dark bill. Common passage migrant, local breeding species; winters in small numbers.

GULL-BILLED TERN *Geochelidon nilotica*   Length 35–38cm
Similar to Sandwich tern but bulkier and with uniformly dark, robust bill. In breeding season, has black crown and white face and underparts; upperparts grey except for dark primary tips. Winter adult loses black cap but retains dark mask through eye. Juvenile similar to winter adult but shows brown feathering on grey upperparts. A summer visitor, present May–September. Has scattered breeding colonies across the region on coastal marshes and river deltas.

LITTLE TERN *Sterna albifrons*   Length 24cm
Smallest pale tern in the region, easily recognised by size and colour alone. At close range, black-tipped yellow bill, yellow-orange legs and white forehead of adult can be seen. Juvenile has dull legs and bill, and scaly appearance to back. Flight buoyant and frequently hovers before plunge-diving. Summer visitor to region, present April–August. Feeds on coasts, coastal lagoons and rivers. Breeds on undisturbed shingle and sandy beaches, but also beside rivers.

CASPIAN TERN *Sterna caspia*   Length 47–54cm
Large, gull-sized tern with huge, blood-red bill. In breeding season, adult has black crown and nape, grey mantle and upperwing and white underparts. In winter, dark cap is incomplete and bill colour fades. Flight powerful and buoyant. Favours sheltered coastal waters with sand banks and islets for nesting and roosting. Widespread but scarce passage migrant. Breeds very locally in E Mediterranean and winters in small numbers in W of region.

COMMON TERN *Sterna hirundo*   Length 35cm
Appearance typically tern-like with pale grey back and upperparts and otherwise white plumage. Legs are red and bill is orange-red with a black tip. Black cap present in summer adult but incomplete in winter plumage, sometimes seen in autumn birds. Juvenile has scaly appearance to back and dark leading edge to inner wing. Widespread passage migrant and breeds very locally, May–August.

BLACK TERN *Chlidonias niger*   Length 24cm
Adult in breeding plumage has black body, dark grey wings and white stern and tail. From mid-summer onwards, body plumage of adult white except for black on nape and crown. Juvenile similar to winter adult but back feathers have pale margins; tail and rump grey. Passage migrant; often seen in flocks, especially in spring. Favours coastal marshes. Breeds very locally in N central Mediterranean.

WHISKERED TERN *Chlidonias hybridus*   Length 23–25cm
Recalls common tern but much smaller and with less forked tail. Summer adult has black crown and nape and white throat; plumage otherwise smoky grey, darkest on breast and belly. Bill and legs dark red. In winter plumage, has grey upperparts and white underparts. Juvenile similar to winter adult but shows dark brown mantle and grey wings. Widespread passage migrant and breeds locally, present May–August.

WHITE-WINGED BLACK TERN *Chlidonias leucopterus*   Length 20–23cm
Striking tern in summer plumage, showing black head, neck and body, pale grey upperwings and underwings with black coverts and pale grey flight feathers. Rump, stern and tail pure white. Bill dark and legs red. Winter adult is grey above and white below; shows white collar and rump, and grey tail. Juvenile similar to adult but has dark back. Common passage migrant in E Mediterranean.

WOODPIGEON *Columba palumbus* Length 41cm

Plump, medium-sized pigeon. Plumage mainly blue-grey with pinkish maroon on breast. Has distinctive white patch on side of neck and, in flight, shows prominent, transverse white wing bars. When disturbed, flies off with loud clattering of wings. During breeding season, sings typical series of *oo-OO-oo, oo-oo* phrases. Builds twig nest on horizontal branches. Feeds on seeds and shoots. Favours areas of agricultural land but woodland essential for nesting. Widespread and common resident in W and C. Mainly a winter visitor to E.

STOCK DOVE *Columba oenas* Length 33cm

Superficially similar to woodpigeon but plumage lacks any prominent features and species recognised by uniform blue-grey upperparts and lack of white rump and white barring on neck; shows two narrow black wingbars on upper surface of inner wing. Favours open agricultural land with scattered woodland. Feeds in flocks in arable fields, sometimes with woodpigeons. Nests in tree holes and, during breeding season, utters diagnostic and repetitive *ooo-look* call. Locally common resident throughout region but more widespread in winter.

FERAL PIGEON/ROCK DOVE *Columba livia* Length 33cm

Feral pigeon is descendent of wild rock dove and is now widespread and common, mainly in urban areas. Rock dove is locally common along rocky coasts and rugged, interior terrain including gorges and cliffs. True rock dove is recognised by its blue-grey plumage, two broad, black wingbars, white rump and black-tipped grey tail. Some feral pigeons show ancestral-type plumage but most exhibit wide range of additional or alternative colours and features. Found throughout the region. Feral pigeons are often tame while rock doves are shy and unapproachable.

COLLARED DOVE *Streptopelia decaocto* Length 32cm

Recognised by its rather dainty proportions and sandy-brown plumage with pinkish flush to head and underparts. Shows dark half-collar on nape. Black wingtips and white outer tail feather most noticeable in flight. In display, glides on bowed wings. Repetitive song comprises *oo-oo-oo* phrases. Feeds on seeds and shoots. Resident, usually associated with human habitation, often in villages but also on farms; often seen in pairs. Range expanded dramatically NW across Europe in 20th century. Commonest in E Mediterranean and essentially absent from Iberia.

TURTLE DOVE *Streptopelia turtur* Length 27cm

Has proportions of collared dove but is smaller. Body plumage mostly blue-grey and pinkish with chestnut-brown on mantle; dark feather centres give a scaly appearance to back. Long, mainly black tail appears wedge-shaped in flight due to white corners. At close range, black and white barring on neck can be seen. Presence often indicated by purring song. Favours orchards and agricultural land with scrub. Common passage migrant and widespread nester, present May–August.

CUCKOO *Cuculus canorus* Length 33cm

Male's familiar *cuck-oo* call heard more often than bird itself is seen during first six weeks after arrival in late April; female utters bubbling call. Secretive but sometimes perches on fence posts. In low-level flight, recalls sparrowhawk. Male and most females have grey head and upperparts, and barred white underparts. Juvenile and some females have brown, barred plumage, juvenile with pale nape. Nest parasite of songbirds. Widespread, April–August.

GREAT SPOTTED CUCKOO *Clamator glandarius* Length 38–40cm

Larger than cuckoo, with crest and broader wings and tail. Adult has dark grey crest; upperparts otherwise dark brown with distinct white tips to feathers on back, wings and tail. Underparts white with buffish flush to throat. Juvenile lacks adult's crest, and plumage has browner hue; feather tips pale yellow and has chestnut primaries. Favours open woodland. Nest parasite of crows. Present May–August, mainly Iberia, S France, N Italy and Turkey.

BARN OWL *Tyto alba*   Length 34cm
Beautiful and distinctive owl, usually seen at dusk or after dark, caught in car headlights;
flight leisurely and slow on rounded wings. Perched birds from W of region shows orange-
buff upperparts, speckled with tiny black and white dots; facial disc heart-shaped, underparts and underwing coverts white. Birds from E of region are similar but have orange-buff
underparts and underwing coverts. Favours open agricultural land and grassland with
woodland and scrub. Often nests in buildings. Widespread resident in W and central
Mediterranean but scarce in E.

EAGLE OWL *Bubo bubo*   Length 60–75cm
An immense bird and Europe's largest owl. Body is broad and dumpy with mainly brown
plumage marked with black streaks and spots on underparts and streaked and marbled on
upperparts. Head has prominent ear tufts and large, orange eyes. Chin and throat have
pale feathering and legs and feet are feathered too. Flight is buzzard-like on broad, rounded wings. Despite size, generally difficult to locate since spends daytime roosting on shaded cliff ledges. Deep, booming call heard at dusk. Widespread but generally scarce resident of cliffs and gorges.

TAWNY OWL *Strix aluco*   Length 38cm
Plumage colour rather variable but usually a rich chestnut-brown. At close range, streaked
underparts look greyish and upperparts are well-marked with dark streaks; eyes black.
Caught in car headlights, can look deceptively pale. Roosts unobtrusively during day
among branches and foliage of trees; sometimes discovered and mobbed by small songbirds. Utters sharp *kew-ick* call but best known for male's familiar hooting calls. Usually
associated with broad-leaved woodland. Widespread and rather common in suitable habitats throughout region.

SCOPS OWL *Otus scops*   Length 19–20cm
Small, rather slender owl with proportionately long wings and conspicuous ear tufts.
Adult seen in two colour forms, either grey-brown or rufous. Close view reveals delicate
pattern of bars and streaks on plumage; shows striking black and white lines on scapulars.
Eyes yellow but often closed in roosting birds. Favours woodlands, olive groves and the
outskirts of villages. Utters monotonous sonar-blip call throughout night; occasionally
gives short bursts of call in daytime too. Widespread summer visitor April–September;
occasionally overwinters.

LITTLE OWL *Athene noctua*   Length 22cm
Generally the commonest owl in the region. Also the easiest one to see since it is partly
diurnal. Size and rounded appearance normally allow identification. At close range, large
white spots can be seen on most parts of grey-brown plumage and the staring yellow eyes
glare back at observer. Perches on fenceposts and dead branches, often bobbing head and
body. Favours agricultural land and often nests and roosts in buildings. Calls include cat-
like *kiu*. Widespread throughout.

NIGHTJAR *Caprimulgus europaeus*   Length 27cm
Nocturnal habits and cryptic markings make this a difficult bird to see in daytime. Brown,
grey and black plumage resembles wood bark. Sits motionless on ground, even when
approached closely. At dusk, takes to the wing and hawks insects. Looks long-tailed and
narrow-winged in flight; male has white on wings and tail. Male utters churring song for
hours on end at night. Favours open conifer woodland, maquis and heaths. Widespread
summer visitor, May–August.

RED-NECKED NIGHTJAR *Caprimulgus ruficollis*   Length 30–32cm
Similar to nightjar but larger and with proportionately longer wings and tail. Adult has
mainly rufous brown plumage, conspicuously marked with pale spots and pale line on
scapulars. Close view reveals buffish-orange throat and collar, with white 'moustache' and
chin. In flight, both sexes show white on wings and outer tail feathers. Favours open stone
pine woodlands and sand dunes. Summer visitor, present April–August. Range restricted
to warm, dry regions of Iberia.

KINGFISHER   *Alcedo atthis*   Length 16–17cm
Dazzlingly attractive bird but colours often appear muted when bird is seen sitting in shade of vegetation. Has orange-red underparts and mainly blue upperparts; electric-blue back seen to best effect when bird is observed in low-level flight. Invariably seen near water and uses overhanging branches to watch for fish. When feeding opportunity arises, plumages headlong into water, catching prey in bill; fish is swallowed whole, head first, and sometimes stunned by beating head on branch. Nests in holes excavated in bank. Widespread resident breeding species, from Iberia to N Greece; favours rivers and lakes. Widespread in E Mediterranean outside breeding season. Often forced to move to new habitats such as reservoirs and coasts, if favoured sites dry up.

WHITE-BREASTED KINGFISHER   *Halcyon smyrnensis*   Length 26–29cm
Stunningly attractive, medium-sized kingfisher. Adult has chestnut head, neck and belly and dazzling white throat and upper breast. Back, tail and wings are iridescent blue but with darker wing coverts and black tips to primary feathers. Has disproportionately large, bright red bill and red legs. Juvenile is similar to adult but with duller colours. Favours wetlands with open water and usually breeds in riverbanks. Usually perches on over-hangs, often in shade. However, will also feed over adjacent areas of dry land, employing similar wait-and-see tactics to catch mole-crickets and other insects. Utters rattling and whistling calls when excited. Resident in small numbers in E Mediterranean, particularly along S coast of Turkey; occasionally wanders in winter.

PIED KINGFISHER   *Ceryle rudis*   Length 25–26cm
Medium-sized kingfisher with extremely distinctive plumage. Adult male has striking black and white upperparts. Underparts essentially white but has two distinct black breast bands. Adult female is similar to male but has one, not two, breast bands. Juvenile is sim-ilar to adult female but breast band is grey not black. Legs and large bill are black in all birds. Often perches beside open water when trying to fish but will also hover when suit-able branches or posts are not available. Often associated with freshwater lakes and rivers but also occurs on sheltered coasts. Scarce resident in E Mediterranean, particularly S coast of Turkey; occasionally wanders in winter.

✓ **BEE-EATER**   *Merops apiaster*   Length 27–29cm
The quintessential Mediterranean bird whose bubbling *pruuupp* calls are such a feature of the months of May to August. Has amazingly colourful plumage. Adult has a chestnut crown and nape, grading to yellow on the back and rump; uppertail is green with two pro-jecting central feathers and underparts are blue except for black-bordered yellow throat. In flight, wings show chestnut and blue on upper surface. Close views of perched birds reveal dark mask through eye and white forecrown. Juvenile is similar to adult but colours are duller and lacks tail projections. Often seen flying in flocks, circling and gliding in pursuit of insects. Usually returns to perch with prey and removes stings from bees and wasps by knocking them against perch. Colonial nester in sand banks. Hunts over agricul-tural land, marshes and rivers. Widespread and common summer visitor.

ROLLER   *Coracias garrulus*   Length 30–32cm
A colourful bird of crow-like proportions and size. Adult has blue head, neck and under-parts, palest on forehead, and shows dark patch through eye. The back is chestnut and the rump and tail are bluish-purple. In flight, wings look striking with dark blue flight feath-ers contrasting with pale blue coverts and darker shoulder. The legs and feet are dark. Juvenile is similar to adult but with duller plumage. Favours dry, open country with scat-tered trees. Often perches on wires or dead branches and scans the ground below for lizards and large insects; these are caught and dispatched with robust, hook-tipped bill. Widespread passage migrant and locally common breeding species, mainly in Iberian Peninsula, Greece and Turkey. Present in the region May–August.

HOOPOE   *Upupa epops*   Length 26–28cm

An elegant and distinctive bird when seen well but plumage, and habit of creeping along ground, can make it surprisingly well camouflaged. When feeding on ground, adult appears mainly pale pinkish brown except for black and white barring on wings. However, in flight, is transformed by broad wings into striking black and white bird; the effect is emphasised by slow, butterfly-like flight pattern. White rump is striking as bird flies away from observer. Feeds by probing ground for invertebrates with long, down-curved bill. Erectile crest of barred pink feathers is raised in excitement. Favours open agricultural land and areas of short grass. Nests in tree holes and in holes in stone walls. Utters diagnostic *hoo-poo-poo* call. Widespread and common summer visitor to most of the region, present March–September. Year-round resident in S Iberian Peninsula.

WRYNECK   *Jynx torquilla*   Length 16–17cm

An extraordinary member of the woodpecker family. Its intricately marked plumage looks remarkably like tree bark and affords the bird superb camouflage. Adult has marbled and streaked grey, black and brown upperparts. Shows dark eyestripe, which continues as a line on side of neck and across scapulars. Underparts whitish with dark streaks and bars, and yellow-buff wash on throat and upper breast. Generally shy and unobtrusive. Feeds mainly on the ground, especially on ants. Nests in tree holes. Generally silent but, on breeding grounds, utters raptor-like piping calls. Favours open woodlands and orchards. Local summer visitor to central Mediterranean, present May–September; absent or scarce as a breeding species in Iberia and E of region. Widespread passage migrant.

MIDDLE SPOTTED WOODPECKER   *Dendrocopus medius*   Length 20–22cm

Distinctly smaller than great spotted woodpecker and with proportionately smaller bill. Adult has red crown, which is brightest and most extensive in male birds. Upperparts mainly black but shows bold white patch on scapulars and white barring across flight feathers. Face is mainly white; unlike great spotted, black moustache does not connect with black stripe on nape. Breast and flanks have black streaks; underparts show buffish wash to belly grading to pink on vent. Favours open orchards and broad-leaved woodlands. Excavates holes in decaying trees for nesting. Generally silent but occasionally utters subdued jay-like calls. Widespread but distinctly local resident in E Mediterranean, particularly Greece and Turkey; present on some of the wooded Greek Islands.

LESSER SPOTTED WOODPECKER   *Dendrocopus minor*   Length 14–15cm

A small and unobtrusive woodpecker, which is much the same size as a nuthatch. Has barred, black and white upperparts creating ladder-backed appearance; underparts whitish. Has black and white markings on head; male has red crown. Not especially shy but difficult to locate, especially during summer months when feeding among canopy of leaves in treetops. Not very vocal but utters raptor-like call for a few weeks in spring at start of breeding season. Nests in holes excavated in branches. Favours open broad-leaved woodlands and orchards. Widespread but local resident from S Spain to Turkey.

GREAT SPOTTED WOODPECKER   *Dendrocopus major*   Length 23cm

The largest black-and-white woodpecker likely to be seen in the region. Upperparts mainly black with white patches on wings; has black moustache that connects with black nape and black bar on shoulder, the effect being to enclose the white cheeks. Underparts whitish except for red on vent and undertail. Adult male only has small red patch on nape but this is not always easy to see; juvenile has red cap. In typical undulating flight, birds show rounded, black and white chequered wings with conspicuous white shoulder patches. In spring, male drums loudly on tree trunk to advertise territory; also utters sharp *tchick* alarm call. Excavates hole in trunk for nesting and also uses bill to probe for insect larvae in timber. Favours broad-leaved woodlands and parks. Widespread and locally common resident from Iberian Peninsula to N Greece.

SKYLARK   *Alauda arvensis*   Length 18cm
Superficially similar to meadow pipit but has a stout bill and a short crest that can be raised. Plumage rather nondescript with streaked, sandy-brown upperparts and paler underparts. Shows a pale supercilium and buffish cheeks. Wings show pale wingbars at rest and white trailing edge in flight. Tail has white margins, most easily seen in flight. During breeding season, delivers incessant trilling and fluty song, often in flight; resident birds sing throughout year and migrating flocks utter contact calls that contain elements of song. Widespread in grassy areas throughout, although absent from hot, dry regions. Numbers increase outside breeding season and mainly a winter visitor to E Mediterranean.

WOODLARK   *Lullula arborea*   Length 15cm
Small, short-tailed lark, with wonderful, yodelling song often delivered in flight. Adult has sandy-brown streaked plumage with dark-bordered chestnut ear coverts and white supercilia that meet on nape. Has streaked cap and short crest giving square-ended appearance to head. At rest, wing shows black and white bar at bend of leading edge. Juvenile similar to adult but less well marked. Associated with warm, dry lowlands with short vegetation and scattered clumps of trees; also in open pine woodland. Widespread resident and winter visitor.

CRESTED LARK   *Galerida cristata*   Length 17cm
The region's most familiar lark, partly on account of its predilection for feeding alongside roads and tracks. Similar in size to skylark but body is more bulky and has longer bill and characteristic spiky crest. Adult plumage mainly sandy brown with dark streaking on crown, back, chest and flanks. Face marked with pale supercilium, eyering and throat and dark moustachial stripe. Tail has buff outer feathers and underwing coverts are orange-buff. Favours dry habitats with sparse vegetation. Sings fluty song, which contains elements of mimicry. Widespread resident but absent from most islands in W of region.

THEKLA LARK   *Galerida theklae*   Length 17cm
Superficially very similar to crested lark but less barrel-chested in appearance and has shorter, but thicker, bill; crest is more complete and less spiky than that of crested lark. Adult has grey-brown upperparts with contrasting pale underparts. Has dark streaks on crown and back; streaks on breast and flanks thickened to form spots. Shows similar facial markings to crested lark. Underwings are pale buff. Favours stony, garrigue habitats and sand dunes near coasts. Resident restricted mainly to Iberian Peninsula; also occurs on Balearic Islands (where crested lark is absent) and locally in S France.

SHORT-TOED LARK   *Calandrella brachydactyla*   Length 13–14cm
Small and rather compact lark with rather stubby, finch-like bill. Has sandy-brown upperparts that show faint streaking. Face is marked with rufous-brown crown, bold and pale supercilium, brown cheeks and white throat. Underparts are mainly white with faint streaking forming indistinct band across chest and dark patches on sides of breast. Closed wing is well marked with row of dark-centred feathers with pale margins. Tail has pale margins. Widespread summer visitor, present April–September, and particularly common in Iberia, Greece and Turkey. Favours open steppe terrain and dried margins of lakes and saltpans; often found on ploughed fields on migration.

CALANDRA LARK   *Melanocorypha calandra*   Length 18–19cm
Large, distinctive lark with proportionately short tail and large bill. Has sandy brown upperparts with dark streaks on crown, nape and back. Face shows pale supercilium, eyering and throat. Underparts mainly white but with black patches on sides of breast with small spots extending onto flanks. Tail has white outer feathers. In flight, shows dark trailing margin to wing and black underwing; latter feature easiest to see when bird is singing in flight. Widespread, especially in Iberia, Greece and Turkey. Flock-forming and nomadic in winter.

ALPINE SWIFT *Apus melba*   Length 20–22cm

By far the largest swift in the region and also the easiest to identify thanks to its distinctive plumage. Invariably seen in flight when bulky body and crescent-shaped wings are apparent. In good light, adult looks sandy-brown above. Seen from below, note the white throat separated from the white belly by a dark collar; underparts otherwise appear dark. Nests on cliffs and buildings such as church towers. Otherwise seen in parties on cliffs and mountains. Summer visitor.

PALLID SWIFT *Apus pallida*   Length 16–17cm

Similar to swift but distinguishable with care. In good light, plumage looks sandy brown, not black; has pale forehead and throat. Wing feathers can look translucent when seen against the light. In silhouette, and compared to swift, has proportionately bulkier body, broader wings and shorter, more rounded tail forks. A summer visitor to the region, present April–September. Occurs S Iberia, Corsica, Sardinia, S Italy and Greece. Favours villages and coasts.

✓**SWIFT** *Apus apus*   Length 16–17cm

The commonest swift in the region. Recognised in flight by its anchor-shaped outline and all-black plumage except for paler throat and forehead. Tail is more deeply forked than that of pallid swift but this feature often not apparent since forks are sometimes held closed. Extremely vocal, and parties of swifts are frequently heard screaming as they chase one another through narrows streets or over rooftops. Favours towns and villages. Summer visitor throughout.

?**SAND MARTIN** *Riparia riparia*   Length 12cm

Small hirundine, often seen in groups. In flight, upperparts are sandy brown. Seen from below, shows white belly separated from white throat by brown chest band; white on throat extends up side of neck as half collar. Tail is short and slightly forked. Nests in colonies in sand banks. Common passage migrant. Nests in Iberia, Italy and E Mediterranean and present March–September.

✓**CRAG MARTIN** *Ptyonoprogne rupestris*   Length 14cm

Similar to sand martin but bulkier and with broader wings; lacks that species' dark chest band. Upperparts uniformly dusky brown; underparts grey-buff with dark chin. In flight, shows diagnostic pair of pale patches near tip of tail. Widespread resident throughout region. During summer months, usually found in mountains and gorges. In winter, moves to lower elevations, often on coasts.

✓**RED-RUMPED SWALLOW** *Hirundo daurica*   Length 16–17cm

Similar to swallow but has bulkier body and tail streamers that curve inwards. Adult has blue-black upperparts except for buffish-orange nape and pale rump. Underparts, including underwing, pale; shows streaks on breast. Juvenile much duller than adult and with short tail streamers. Summer visitor, mainly to Iberia, Greece and Turkey. Cup-shaped mud nest built in abandoned buildings and under bridges.

✓**SWALLOW** *Hirundo rustica*   Length 19cm

The commonest hirundine. Recognised by pointed wings and tail with long streamers; these are shorter in juvenile and female than male. Upperparts blue-black and underparts white except for brick-red throat and forecrown and blue-black chest band. Sits on wires. Utters *vit* call in flight; male has twittering song. Nests in buildings. Widespread summer visitor; overwinters in S Iberia.

✓**HOUSE MARTIN** *Delichon urbica*   Length 12–13cm

Easily identified in flight by white underparts and blue-black upperparts showing conspicuous white rump. Could possibly be confused with poor view of red-rumped swallow but appreciably smaller and lacking that species' tail streamers and orange-buff nape. Nests in colonies on buildings, constructing almost spherical mud nests under eaves and overhangs. Widespread summer visitor throughout the region, present March–September. Often feeds over water.

BIRDS

Tree Pipit ✓

MEADOW PIPIT *Anthus campestris*   Length 14–15cm
A medium-sized pipit with rather nondescript plumage comprising streaked brown upperparts and pale underparts, the latter with buffish wash to breast and steaks on throat, breast and flanks. Shows two pale wingbars and a pale supercilium. The legs are pinkish-flesh. White outer tail feathers usually observed in flight when bird utters *pseet-pseet-pseet* call. Favours open areas with short grass. A widespread and common winter visitor to most of the region, present October–March. Usually seen in flocks. Prior to departure in spring, sometimes heard delivering trilling, descending song in flight.

RED-THROATED PIPIT *Anthus cervinus*   Length 15cm
An extremely distinctive pipit in most plumages. In spring, adult has striking brick red face and neck; intensity of colour does vary, however, and birds with buffish faces are not uncommon. Underparts otherwise pale buff, streaked heavily on chest and flanks. Upperparts dark brown, heavily streaked with black and white. Autumn birds appear essentially black and white with heavy streaking on breast. Legs of all birds are buffish-yellow. Passage migrant in spring and autumn. Commonest in E Mediterranean and sometimes seen in sizeable flocks, in the company of meadow pipits. Favours areas of short grassland.

TAWNY PIPIT *Anthus campestris*   Length 16.5cm
A pale, wagtail-like pipit. Adult has essentially sandy-brown upperparts, which are much less marked than on other pipits and usually appear uniformly coloured. Wings show wingbars formed by pale-fringed, dark-centred covert feathers. Face is pale with long, pale supercilium. Underparts mostly unmarked and grade from pale buff on neck and breast to white on belly. Tail is proportionately long and brown with pale edges to outer feathers. Legs long and flesh-coloured. Utters house sparrow-like *chirrupp* call; repetitive song comprises bursts of short phrases. Favour dry sandy habitats with scattered grass clumps. Widespread summer visitor.

WHITE WAGTAIL *Motacilla alba*   Length 18cm
Familiar, long-bodied black and white bird, often seeing running on ground. Pumps tail up and down and utters distinctive *chissick* call. Adult summer male has black cap, nape, throat and upper breast. Face and underparts white with back is grey. Tail has white outer feathers. Winter male has black confined to upper breast only; plumage otherwise similar to summer male but more grubby. Summer female similar to summer male but contrast less intense; winter female and juvenile similar but lose black cap and plumage appears grubby. Widespread resident; numbers boosted in winter by migrants. Favours open, grassy areas.

GREY WAGTAIL *Motacilla cinerea*   Length 18cm
A long-bodied, waterside bird with blue-grey upperparts and lemon-yellow underparts. Male has black throat in summer; this feature absent in female and winter male. Invariably associated with water, mostly fast-flowing streams and rivers. Perches on boulders, pumping tail up and down. Utters *chsee-tsit* call in bounding flight. Widespread resident across most of region but distinctly local thanks to habitat preferences. Mostly a winter visitor to E Mediterranean.

YELLOW WAGTAIL *Motacilla flava*   Length 16–17cm
Widespread summer visitor, forming distinct geographical races, males of which are separable with care on head markings. All adult males have greenish-yellow mantles, darker wings with two pale wingbars and dark tail with white outer feathers; underparts bright yellow. Blue-headed wagtail *M.f.flava* (B) has blue-grey cap, white supercilium, dark cheeks, white chin and yellow throat; Spanish *M.f.iberiae* (D) is similar but cap greyer and throat white. Grey-headed *M.f.thunbergi* has grey head, dark cheeks and yellow throat; ashy-headed *M.f.cinereocapilla* has dark grey cap, black cheeks, white throat and no supercilium; black-headed *M.f.feldegg* (C) has wholly black cap and cheeks and yellow throat. Adult male yellow *M.f.flavissima (A)*, and females of all races, have yellow heads. Favours marshes.

98

WREN *Troglodytes troglodytes*   Length 9–10cm
A tiny bird, recognised by dumpy proportions, brown plumage and habit of cocking its tail upright. Close inspection reveals plumage to be rufous brown on upperparts and barred buffish-brown on underparts. Closed wing shows barring on primary feathers and heads has prominent white supercilium. Creeps through low vegetation in search of insects and can look rather mouse-like. Song loud and warbling, ending in trill; has rattling alarm call. Widespread resident.

DUNNOCK *Prunella modularis*   Length 14–15cm
Unobtrusive bird, adult of which has chestnut-brown back, blue-grey underparts, streaked flanks and needle-like bill; juvenile similar but more uniformly brown and streaked. Feeds quietly, often on ground, searching for insects and seeds. Call a thin *tseer*. Widespread winter visitor, present from October–March. Breeds locally inland, where elevation of mountains creates cooler climate.

ALPINE ACCENTOR *Prunella collaris*   Length 18cm
Rather dumpy bird, adult of which has blue-grey head, breast and belly. Upperparts dark brown and rump rufous; underparts pale with chestnut streaks on flanks and black and white undertail coverts. Closed wing marked with white dots and shows white chin speckled with black dots. Juvenile similar to adult but colours more subdued. Local winter visitor to the region, favouring rocky headlands and rugged, stony hilltops.

ROBIN *Erithacus rubecula*   Length 14cm
A dumpy, familiar bird. Adult has reddish-orange face and breast with whitish belly and grey-brown flanks; upperparts brown, grading to grey on side of neck. Juvenile has streaked brown upperparts and underparts with crescent-shaped markings. Utters sharp *tic* alarm call. Male sings variation of melancholy song at most times of year. Favours broad-leaved woodland and scrub. Widespread resident throughout, although absent as a breeding species from hot, arid coasts.

NIGHTINGALE *Luscinia megarhynchos*   Length 16–17cm
Present mid-April–August. Heard far more easily than bird itself is seen. Has a powerful, musical song, delivered both by day and at night and audible over long range. Has rich brown upperparts and chestnut-red lower back and tail; underparts pale grey-buff. Favours woodland with dense scrub layer. Widespread and common. Thrush nightingale *L.luscinia* is similar but olive-brown upperparts contrast with rufous-brown tail; has speckled breast; passage migrant through E of region.

BLUETHROAT *Luscinia svecica*   Length 14cm
Unobtrusive, robin-sized bird. Adult has brown upperparts, pale belly and pale supercili- iu. Tail is dark brown with reddish-orange bases to outer feathers. Breeding male has shiny blue throat with either white or red central spot; throat is bordered below by black, white and chestnut bands. In winter, male has pale throat. Female similar to winter male but with black moustache and necklace. Mainly a winter visitor, commonest in Iberia. Favours marshes and scrub.

REDSTART *Phoenicurus phoenicurus*   Length 14cm
Male has black and grey on head and back, and red breast; shows white supercilium. Female has grey-brown upperparts and orange wash to pale underparts; both sexes have red tail, pumped up and down. Favours open broad-leaved woodland. Widespread passage migrant; local breeding species, present April–September.

BLACK REDSTART *Phoenicurus ochruros*   Length 14cm
Striking red tail seen in all plumages. Breeding male (A) has otherwise blackish plumage with white panel on wings and orange vent and undertail coverts. Winter male and female (B) at all times have rather uniform grey-brown plumage. Legs and bill black in all birds. Favours rocky mountains and the outskirts of villages. Widespread resident in W Mediterranean but mainly a winter visitor to E.

STONECHAT   *Saxicola torquata*   Length 12–13cm
Small, dumpy chat with relatively short tail. In breeding season, male is handsome with
black head, white on side on neck, dark back, reddish orange breast and pale underparts.
Female and winter male have duller plumage. Often perches openly, flicking tail and
announcing presence with harsh *tchak* call, like two pebbles being knocked together.
Scratchy, whitethroat-like is song sometimes delivered in flight but also from song perch.
Widespread resident favouring heaths, scrub, maquis and sand dunes.

WHINCHAT   *Saxicola rubetra*   Length 12–13cm
Superficially similar to stonechat but male has brown, streaked upperparts and conspicuous pale stripe above eye; underparts pale but with orange-buff flush on throat and upper
breast. Female has similar stripe but plumage generally much more subdued in colour
than that of male. Favours rank grassland and scrubby slopes. Perches on low wires and
bushes. Has *tik* call and chattering song. Local breeding species, present from
April–September, but also a widespread passage migrant, seen in especially good numbers in spring.

NORTHERN WHEATEAR   *Oenanthe oenanthe*   Length 14–15cm
Male (B) has blue-grey crown and back, black mask and wings, and pale underparts with
orange-buff wash on breast. Female and juvenile (A) have mainly sandy-brown plumage.
Both sexes show white rump in flight. Perches low and nests in burrows. Utters *chak*
alarm call like two pebbles being knocked together and has scratchy song. Widespread
summer visitor, present March–September. Favours open grassland, heaths and cliffs.
Common and widespread passage migrant, seen mainly on coasts. Often the first migrant
to arrive and the last to leave the region.

ISABELLINE WHEATEAR   *Oenanthe isabellina*   Length 16.5cm
Superficially similar to female northern wheatear but larger and with grubby sandy-
brown plumage; shows less contrast between upperparts and underparts than other
wheatears. Flight feathers have pale fringes and shows white rump in flight. Generally
adopts rather upright stance on ground and appears to have relatively long legs. Favours
dry, sandy terrain and steppe habitat. Summer visitor, present April–September. Range
restricted to E Mediterranean, mainly NE Greece and Turkey.

BLACK-EARED WHEATEAR   *Oenanthe hispanica*   Length 14.5cm
Adult male is seen in two races, western pale-throated and eastern black-throated, both of
which have black wings and pale back and underparts. Pale-throated form (A) has pale
head except for black mask. Dark-throated form has black face and throat and pale crown.
Both have white rump and tail marked with inverted black 'T'. Females (B) of both races
are similar to their respective males but with subdued plumages. Widespread summer visitor, present April–September; favours dry, stony ground. Utters scratchy, repetitive song
and grating call.

CYPRUS PIED WHEATEAR   *Oenanthe cypriaca* N. Cyprus: Mch'06   Length 14cm
Adult male has dusky-centred white crown and nape, white underparts and otherwise
black plumage with white rump. Female has similar plumage pattern to male but pale elements are suffused with buffish-orange. Summer visitor to Cyprus, present
March–September. Favours stony ground. Similar pied wheatear *O.pleschanka* is a scarce
passage migrant in E Mediterranean; male looks strikingly black and white.

RUFOUS BUSHCHAT   *Cercotrichas galactotes*   Length 15cm
Resembles a cross between a large warbler and a nightingale apart from broad, graduated
tail. Adult from Iberian Peninsula has rufous-brown upperparts, brightest and most rufous
on rump and tail; tip of tail is marked with black and white. Face shows long, pale super-
cillium and dark eyestripe. E European birds have grey-brown, not rufous, plumage.
Favours scrub and maquis, often along dried river courses. Summer visitor to S Iberia,
Greece and Turkey.

ROCK THRUSH *Monticola saxatilis* Length 18.5cm
Distinctive thrush-like bird with the stance of a wheatear. Summer male has blue head, neck and upper back, brown wings and orange-red underparts and tail; white lower back seen best in flight. Adult female and juvenile have scaly brown upperparts, brown wings with pale feather margins and orange-buff, scaly underparts; tail is red. Winter male similar to female but head greyer. Favours dry rocky slopes. Widespread but local summer visitor.

BLUE ROCK THRUSH *Monticola solitarius* Length 20cm
In poor light, resembles an all-dark, outsized wheatear. Adult male has essentially blue plumage, brightest on head and underparts and darkest on wings and tail. Female and juvenile grey-brown, recalling female blackbird; both show spotted throat and scaly underparts. Male sings loud, melodious song from rocky vantage point; alarm call a sharp *tak-tak*. A widespread resident throughout the region, and found on most islands. Favours rocky coasts, gorges and mountains.

RING OUZEL *Turdus torquatus* Length 24cm
Superficially similar to blackbird but black male has striking white crescent on breast; at close range, pale margins to feathers can be seen along with pale patch on wing. Female has brown plumage, the feathers with conspicuous pale margins giving scaly appearance; pale crescent on breast is less striking than on male. Seen mainly as a winter visitor to the region, commonest in S Iberia, S France, N Greece and S Turkey. Favours rough, stony slopes, including vineyards.

✓ **BLACKBIRD** *Turdus merula* Length 25cm
Familiar open country and woodland bird. Male easily identified by thrush-like appearance and all-black plumage; yellow eyering and bill are usually conspicuous. Female and juvenile have brown plumages. Utters harsh *tchak* call in alarm, often at dusk or if predator located. Male is an excellent songster. Feeds on worms, insects, fruits and berries. Widespread resident throughout the region but numbers swollen in winter by influx of birds from N Europe.

FIELDFARE *Turdus pilaris* Length 25–26cm
A large thrush, often seen in large, flighty flocks that utter chattering calls. Recognised by grey head, chestnut back and pale, spotted underparts with yellow wash on breast; pale grey rump and white underwings noticeable in flight. A winter visitor throughout the region. Numbers build up as the winter progresses and are largest when conditions are harsh further north. Favours open country.

REDWING *Turdus iliacus* Length 21cm
Small, well-marked thrush with grey-brown upperparts, prominent white stripe above eye, neatly spotted pale underparts and orange-red flush on flanks and underwings. Widespread winter visitor across the region. Flocks are nomadic and numbers vary from year to year according to the weather. Often associates with fieldfares. Favours open country and woodland. Utters high-pitched *tseerp* call.

SONG THRUSH *Turdus philomelos* Length 23cm
Easily told from mistle thrush by small size, more dainty appearance and orange-red underwing. Upperparts are warm brown with hint of orange-buff wingbar; underparts pale but well marked with dark spots and with a buff wash to breast. Song loud and musical, phrases repeated two or three times. Flight call a thin *tik*. Widespread winter visitor and local breeding species. Favours open woodland.

✓ **MISTLE THRUSH** *Turdus viscivorus* Length 27cm
Larger than song thrush with white underwings. Upperparts grey-brown with faint white wingbar. Pale underparts show large, dark spots; in flight, note white tips to outer tail feathers. Juvenile has white, teardrop-shaped spots on back and scaly underparts. Has loud, rattling alarm call; song contains brief phrases and long pauses. Widespread resident and winter visitor. Favours open woodland.

FAN-TAILED WARBLER   *Cisticola juncidis*   Length 10cm
Has sandy-buff upperparts with dark streaks on crown, mantle and wings. Belly pale; underparts otherwise buffish-brown. Face shows pale supercilium. Tail fan-shaped and brown, with black and white margin. Favours marshes, arable fields and grassland. Widespread resident but local in E Mediterranean.

CETTI'S WARBLER   *Cettia cetti*   Length 13.5cm
Unobtrusive but has loud, explosive *chee-chippi-chippi-chippi* song. Has dark brown upperparts and pale greyish-buff underparts; tail rounded. Widespread and common resident across the region. Favours marshes and anywhere with bushy cover.

SEDGE WARBLER   *Acrocephalus schoenobaenus*   Length 13cm
Has streaked plumage with sandy-brown upperparts and paler buff underparts; head shows distinctive dark eyestripe and pale supercilium. Widespread passage migrant; often pauses beside marshes and well-vegetated ditches on migration through region. Scratchy song often heard in spring. Alarm call a sharp *chek*.

MOUSTACHED WARBLER   *Acrocephalus melanopogon*   Length 14cm
Similar to sedge warbler but has very dark cap, long pale supercilium and dark eyestripe grading to grey cheeks. Back is streaked and brown and underparts whitish with sandy-brown flanks. Song scratchy but musical, often with piping, wader-like notes. Widespread but local due to association with large reedbeds.

REED WARBLER   *Acrocephalus scirpaceus*   Length 12–13cm
Has nondescript sandy-brown upperparts, pale underparts and dark legs. Recognised by song, which contains grating and chattering elements and some mimicry; often delivered from reed stem. Local breeding species; common passage migrant.

GREAT REED WARBLER   *Acrocephalus arundinaceus*   Length 19–20cm
Similar to reed warbler but appreciably larger and with longer, stouter bill. Has sandy-brown upperparts, darkest on crown and most rufous on rump. Underparts pale buff with rufous wash on flanks; face shows pale supercilium. Widespread summer visitor and passage migrant. Favours dense reedbeds and marshy river margins.

MARSH WARBLER   *Acrocephalus palustris*   Length 12–13cm
Similar to reed warbler but has paler throat, yellowish-buff underparts and pinkish legs. Best told by song, which is mimetic, and includes other European songsters and species from African wintering grounds. Scarce passage migrant.

MELODIOUS WARBLER   *Hippolais polyglotta*   Length 13cm
Recalls outsized willow warbler with large bill. Upperparts greenish-brown and underparts yellow. Autumn juveniles often bright yellow. Summer visitor to W of region. Similar icterine warlber *H.icterina* is brighter; seen on migration in E.

OLIVACEOUS WARBLER   *Hippolais pallida*   Length 13cm
Has pale olive-brown upperparts and creamy-white underparts with buffish wash to flanks. Head has indistinct pale supercilium and flat crown. Bill dark and rather long. Locally common summer visitor to S Iberia, Greece and Turkey. Song a scratchy warble. Olive-tree warbler *H.olivetorum* is similar but larger; occurs Greece and Turkey.

DARTFORD WARBLER   *Sylvia undata*   Length 12–13cm
Perched birds show compact body and long tail cocked up at an angle. Male has blue-grey upperparts, reddish underparts and white belly; female similar but duller. Male sings scratchy song. Resident of maquis and heaths in W of region.

MARMORA'S WARBLER   *Sylvia sarda*   Length 12cm
Has proportions of Dartford warbler. Male has dull blue-grey plumage, darkest on wings and tail; legs, eye and eyering reddish-orange. Female similar but duller. Resident W Mediterranean islands, mainly Balearics, Corsica and Sardinia.

SUBALPINE WARBLER *Sylvia cantillans*   Length 12cm
Adult male has blue-grey upperparts except for brownish wings. Breast and throat reddish and shows white moustache stripe; belly white. Adult female and juvenile similar to adult male but plumage subdued; pale moustache often visible. Favours maquis and woodland clearings. Widespread summer visitor, Iberia to W Turkey.

SPECTACLED WARBLER *Sylvia conspicillata*   Length 12.5cm
Adult male has dark grey head, white throat and white eyering; upperparts otherwise sandy brown except for chestnut patch on wings. Underparts pinkish grey. Female and juvenile similar to male but with subdued plumage. Favours low maquis, garrigue and areas of glasswort. Skulking. Local summer visitor.

LESSER WHITETHROAT *Sylvia curruca*   Length 13–14cm
Has blue-grey crown, dark mask and grey-brown back and wings; throat and underparts are white. Male usually has brighter plumage than female, sometimes with pink flush to breast. Summer visitor to E Mediterranean and widespread passage migrant elsewhere. Utters *chek* alarm call and male sings rattling song.

WHITETHROAT *Sylvia communis*   Length 14cm
Male often perches high, revealing white throat, blue-grey crown, rufous back and wings, and pale underparts with buffish tone on breast. Female drabber. Scratchy song often delivered in dancing song flight. Alarm call a harsh *chek*. Favours scrub, heaths, maquis and farmland with hedgerows. Widespread summer visitor.

GARDEN WARBLER *Sylvia borin*   Length 14cm
A rather nondescript bird with uniform grey-brown upperparts and paler, buffish underparts. Lack of distinguishing plumage features is made up for by attractive song, similar to that of blackcap. Favours wooded areas with dense undergrowth. Widespread passage migrant and local breeding species across region.

BLACKCAP *Sylvia atricapilla*   Length 14cm
Male has grey-brown upperparts, paler underparts and distinctive black cap. Female and juvenile are similar but with chestnut brown cap. Male's song is attractive and musical with chattering and fluty elements. Widespread passage migrant and local summer visitor to E of region; year-round resident in W.

RÜPPELL'S WARBLER *Sylvia ruepelli*   Length 14cm
Adult male has distinctive black head with striking white moustache and bright red eye and eyering; upperparts otherwise grey and underparts greyish. Female and juvenile similar to male but plumage more subdued. All birds have reddish legs. Favours maquis-covered rocky slopes. Summer visitor to Greece and Turkey.

SARDINIAN WARBLER *Sylvia melanocephala*   Length 13.5cm
Adult male has black hood, white throat and red eye and eyering; upperparts otherwise grey and underparts greyish-white. Female and juvenile similar to male but plumage duller. All birds have reddish legs. Favours scrub patches and open woodland. Widespread resident in W and central Mediterranean; local in E.

ORPHEAN WARBLER *Sylvia hortensis*   Length 15cm
Adult male has dark hood, pale throat and striking white eyes; upperparts otherwise grey brown and underparts whitish with pink flush to breast. Female and juvenile similar to male but plumage duller and browner. Favours open woodland, olive groves and scrub-covered slopes. Widespread but local summer visitor.

CYPRUS WARBLER *Sylvia melanothorax*   N.Cyprus: Mch'06   Length 13.5cm
Adult male has black hood, yellowish eye and red eyering, and white moustache; underparts are grey with black bars and upperparts are grey. Female and juvenile similar to male but plumage duller and browner. All birds have reddish legs. Favours maquis scrub. Summer visitor, entirely restricted to Cyprus.

108

BONELLI'S WARBLER *Phylloscopus bonelli* Length 11.5cm
Highly active warbler. Adult from W of region has pale grey head, mainly grey-green upperparts and whitish underparts; shows yellow rump and yellow patch on wings. Juvenile and adult from E of region similar but plumage duller, showing less contrast. Male sings trilling song; calls include *chi-irp* in eastern birds and *hu-eet* in western birds. Favours cork oak, chestnut or pine woodland, usually around 1000m above sea level. Widespread summer visitor, present April–August.

CHIFFCHAFF *Phylloscopus collybita* Length 11cm
Adult birds from most of region have dull olive-brown upperparts and pale yellow underparts with buff wash on flanks. Eastern birds generally greyer than western birds and Iberian forms appear yellow-buff. Juveniles often appear rather yellow. All birds have black legs. Song usually a variation on *chiff-chaff* theme; calls include *hu-eet*. Favours woodland and scrub. Widespread passage migrant. Winter visitor to S of region and generally resident further N and inland.

WILLOW WARBLER *Phylloscopus trochilus* Length 11cm
Very similar to chiffchaff but has olive-yellow upperparts and pale, yellowish white underparts; juvenile has brighter, more yellow plumage. Flesh-coloured legs seen in all birds and distinguish silent individuals from chiffchaff. Song a tinkling, descending phrase, sometimes heard on migration. Call a soft *hoo-eet*. Widespread passage migrant. Similar wood warbler *P.sibilatrix* is also seen on migration; has olive-green upperparts, yellow throat and white underparts.

GOLDCREST *Regulus regulus* Length 9cm
Tiny bird with needle-like bill and proportionately large eye and head. Upperparts greenish with two pale wingbars; underparts yellowish buff. Adult male has black-bordered orange crown, that of female being yellow; juvenile lacks adult's crown markings. Widespread winter visitor to much of W and central Mediterranean although absent from S Iberia. Resident around Turkish coast in pine woodland. Song a repeated, high-pitched trill; call thin and high-pitched.

FIRECREST *Regulus ignicapillus* Length 9cm
Similar to goldcrest but more brightly coloured. Adult male has black-bordered orange-yellow crown stripe, white supercilium and black eyestripe; crown of female is yellow. Upperparts mainly olive-green with bronze patch on side of neck; underparts white. All birds have two pale wingbars. Widespread resident and winter visitor. Favours mature mixed woodland, often with large, mature conifers.

PIED FLYCATCHER *Ficedula hypoleuca* Length 13cm
Male (A) has black upperparts, white underparts and white band on otherwise black wing. Female (B) has black elements of male's plumage replaced by brown. Catches insects in flight. Widespread passage migrant, easiest to see in spring.

COLLARED FLYCATCHER *Ficedula albicollis* Length 13cm
Male similar to male pied but has more extensive white on forehead and striking white collar; shows pale rump and more white on wings. Female essentially inseparable from female pied in the field. Passage migrant, commonest in E. Similar male semi-collared *F.semitorquata* has white half collar; rare summer visitor to Greece and Turkey.

RED-BREASTED FLYCATCHER *Ficedula parva* Length 11.5cm
All adults have greyish head and brown upperparts apart with white patches at base of tail. Throat and upper breast reddish in male breeding plumage; buffish in female and immature. Frequently flicks tail. Passage migrant, mainly in E Mediterranean.

SPOTTED FLYCATCHER *Muscicapa striata* Length 14cm
Adult has grey-brown upperparts, streaked on crown; underparts pale, heavily streaked on breast; juvenile similar but with spotted breast. Adopts upright stance and makes insect-catching sorties from perch. Common summer visitor.

PENDULINE TIT   *Remiz pendulinus*   Length 11cm
Adult has stubby bill, grey head, black mask, and chestnut back; flight feathers and tail black and underparts whitish with buffish wash on flanks. Juvenile has subdued plumage and no face mask. Widespread but local resident of large reedbeds.

CRESTED TIT   *Parus cristatus*   Length 11–12cm
Has conspicuous black and white crest and black lines on otherwise white face; back brown and underparts pale. Presence indicated by trilling call. Resident in Iberia, S France and N Greece. Favours pine, cork oak and beech woodland.

BLUE TIT   *Parus caeruleus*   Length 11–12cm
Has blue, green and yellow in plumage with striking black and white markings on face; juvenile similar to adult but lacks blue in plumage. Utters chattering *tserr err err err* call and whistling song. Widespread woodland resident.

GREAT TIT   *Parus major*   Length 14cm
Has bold black and white markings on head and black bib forming line, running down chest, broader in male than female. Underparts otherwise yellow and upperparts mainly greenish. Juvenile has sombre plumage with no white on head. Typical song, a loud *teecha teecha teecha*. Widespread woodland resident throughout the Mediterranean region.

COAL TIT   *Parus ater*   Length 11–12cm
Warbler-like tit with black and white markings on head and conspicuous white patch on nape. Back and wings slate-grey with two white wingbars; underparts pinkish buff. Cyprus birds are darker overall. Song higher pitched than that of great tit. Widespread resident of pine forests; more coastal in winter.

MARSH TIT   *Parus palustris*   Length 12cm
Has black cap and bill, white cheeks and throat, brown upperparts and buffish underparts. Call a loud *pitchoo*. Resident of broad-leaved woodland in central and E Mediterranean, usually inland. Similar sombre tit *P.lugubris* is larger; occurs in orchards in Greece and Turkey.

LONG-TAILED TIT   *Aegithalos caudatus*   Length 14cm
Shows pinkish wash to underparts and pinkish buff on back. Has tiny, stubby bill, long tail and rounded body. Seen in flocks outside breeding season. Calls include a wren-like trill. Widespread resident of scrub and woods.

KRÜPER'S NUTHATCH   *Sitta krueperi*   Length 12cm
Has blue-grey upperparts and pale greyish white underparts. Shows black eyestripe, white supercilium and chestnut patch on breast; black on forecrown more extensive in male than female. Favours pine forests in Turkey and Lesvos. Endemic Corsican nuthatch *S.whiteheadi* is similar; lacks chestnut on breast.

NUTHATCH   *Sitta europaea*   Length 14cm
Dumpy bird with chisel-like bill. Often descends tree trunk head-downwards. Has blue-grey upperparts, black eyestripe, white cheeks and orange-buff underparts. Utters falcon-like call. Widespread resident of broad-leaved and mixed woodlands.

ROCK NUTHATCH   *Sitta neumayer*   Length 15cm
Larger and paler than nuthatch with proportionately longer bill. Upperparts pale grey and underparts white with buff wash to belly. Favours warm, rocky terrain and builds large mud nest in crevice. Widespread resident in Greece and Turkey.

SHORT-TOED TREECREEPER   *Certhia brachydactyla*   Length 12–13cm
Has streaked brown upperparts and white underparts, washed buff on flanks; bill long and downcurved and shows pale supercilium behind eye. Creeps unobtrusively up tree trunks. Widespread resident of pine and mixed woodland.

RED-BACKED SHRIKE *Lanius collurio*   Length 17cm
Male (A) has reddish back, pale underparts flushed with pink, and blue-grey cap with dark mask; tail black with white on sides at base. Female (B) similar but colours and markings less distinct; shows crescent markings on underparts. Juvenile brown and scaly due to crescent markings on plumage. Favours scrub. Often perches on wires. Catches insects and sometimes impales them. Summer visitor, S France to Turkey. Widespread passage migrant, especially common in E Mediterranean in spring.

ISABELLINE SHRIKE *Lanius isabellinus*   Length 17cm
Formerly considered to be a race of red-backed shrike. Male has pale grey-brown upperparts, black mask and reddish tail; female similar but plumage colours, other than tail, more subdued. Juvenile similar to juvenile red-backed but greyer above and with red tail. Scarce passage migrant through E Mediterranean.

GREAT GREY SHRIKE *Lanius excubitor*   Length 24cm
Recalls a small bird of prey and, at a distance, looks very white. At close range, birds from most of range show grey cap and back, black mask and wings, and white underparts. Birds from Iberia are similar but show a pink wash to underparts. Favours open country with bushes; often perches on wires. Catches lizards and insects. Resident in Iberia; winter visitor to rest of region.

LESSER GREY SHRIKE *Lanius minor*   Length 20cm
Male has grey crown and back, broad black eyestripe that continues across forehead, and black wings; underparts whitish but flushed with pink on breast and flanks, and tail black with white outer feathers. Favours open country and farmland with scattered clumps of bushes; often perches on wires. Summer visitor and passage migrant, mainly to E of region, from N Italy to Turkey.

WOODCHAT SHRIKE *Lanius senator*   Length 18cm
Distinctive and well-marked shrike. Male has chestnut crown and nape with upperparts otherwise black except for white markings on wings and shoulder and white rump; underparts white. Female similar but colours duller. Juvenile grey-brown and scaly-looking. Favours open country and farmland with scattered scrub. Often perches on wire fences. Summer visitor throughout the Mediterranean.

MASKED SHRIKE *Lanius nubicus*   Length 18cm
Elegant, slim-bodied shrike. Male has mainly black upperparts with white on wings and shoulder and white forehead and supercilium; underparts white with pinkish orange wash to flanks. Female similar but colours and pattern less distinct. Juvenile is grey-brown and scaly-looking. Favours olive groves, orchards and open pine woodland. Locally common summer visitor to N Greece and Turkey.

STARLING *Sturnus vulgaris*   Length 22cm
Adult's dark plumage has green sheen in summer; in winter, acquires numerous white spots. Bill is yellow in summer but dark in winter. Juvenile is buff-brown, acquiring adult-like plumage in first autumn. Varied song includes clicks and whistles; also imitates other birds and man-made sounds. Widespread resident, except in Iberia; winter visitor throughout region, including Iberia.

SPOTLESS STARLING *Sturnus unicolor*   Length 22cm
Summer male has purple sheen to dark plumage; throat feathers long. Has pale tips to feathers on head, back and underparts in winter. Bill yellow in summer, black in winter. Juvenile similar to juvenile starling but darker. Resident Iberia, Corsica, Sardinia and Sicily. Starling's winter range extends to these areas.

GOLDEN ORIOLE *Oriolus oriolus*   Length 24cm
Male has bright yellow and black plumage, and red bill; female duller and with streaked underparts. Often surprisingly difficult to see in dappled foliage. Male utters fluty *wee-lo-weeow* song. Widespread summer visitor to woods and copses.

JAY *Garrulus glandarius* — Length 34cm
Colourful bird, but wary nature means that colours are seldom seen well. Has pinkish buff body plumage except for white undertail and rump, latter most conspicuous as bird flies away; this feature emphasised by black tail. Wings have black and white pattern and chequerboard patch of blue, black and white. Utters loud, raucous *kraah* call. Widespread resident throughout the region. Favours broad-leaved woodland; also in pine forests. Buries acorns where oaks present.

MAGPIE *Pica pica* — Length 46cm
Familiar and unmistakable black and white bird. In good light, greenish blue sheen can be seen on rounded wings and long tail. Often seen in small groups outside breeding season, frequently uttering loud, rattling alarm calls. An opportunistic feeder, taking insects, fruit, animal road kills and young birds and eggs. Associated with lowland open country with scattered trees. Widespread and common resident throughout most of region.

AZURE-WINGED MAGPIE *Cyanopica cyana* — Length 35cm
A distinctive and elegant crow. Adult has black cap, brown back and rump and buffish white underparts; wings and tail are azure-blue. Juvenile is similar but has duller plumage. Utters a whistling call. Gregarious at all times; in breeding season, nests in loose colonies with all members of flock helping nesting birds. Favours woodland, including cork oak forests, olive groves, and pine plantations. Resident restricted to S and C Iberian Peninsula.

CHOUGH *Pyrrhocorax pyrrhocorax* — Length 40cm
A jackdaw-sized bird with glossy, all-dark plumage and bright red legs and long, down-curved bill; juvenile has shorter, duller bill than adult. Outside breeding season, forms flocks. Recognised in flight by broad, 'fingered' wingtips and frequently uttered *chyah* call. Probes ground for insects. Favours inland cliffs and rocky coasts. Widespread resident in Iberian Peninsula but rather local in S France, Apennines, Sicily, mainland Greece, Crete and S Turkey.

JACKDAW *Corvus monedula* N. Cyprus : Mch '06 — Length 33cm
The most familiar small crow. Has mainly smoky-grey plumage; at close range, pale eye and grey nape are obvious. Aerobatic in flight, frequently uttering sharp *chack* calls. Walks with characteristic swagger. Favours sea cliffs and farmland. Nests in tree holes, rock crevices and in buildings. Opportunistic feeder with omnivorous diet. Widespread resident across the Mediterranean.

RAVEN *Corvus corax* — Length 64cm
Largest European member of the crow family with all-dark plumage. Has massive bill and shaggy, ruffed throat; plumage has an oily sheen in good light. Often seen in flight when recognised by long, thick neck and wedge-shaped tail. Very aerobatic, tumbling and rolling in mid-air. Utters loud, deep *cronk* call. Widespread resident, mainly on rocky coasts, inland cliffs and rugged terrain.

CARRION/HOODED CROW *Corvus corone* N. Cyprus : Mch '06 Length 47cm
Two races occur in region. All-dark carrion crow *C.c.corone* (A) occurs throughout Iberian Peninsula and S France. Hooded crow *C.c.cornix* (B) occurs from N Italy, Corsica and Sardinia eastwards and has black head, wings and tail but otherwise grey plumage. Usually associated with farmland and open country but also visits outskirts of villages to scavenge. Widespread and common.

ROOK *Corvus frugilegus* — Length 46cm
Large member of the crow family with glossy black plumage. Adult has bare, white facial patch at base of long bill; this feature is absent in immature birds. Winter visitor to the region and invariably seen in flocks. Locally common in former Yugoslavia, N Greece and Turkey; local in N Spain. Favours farmland, particularly ploughed fields and short grassland.

TREE SPARROW *Passer montanus*   Length 14cm

Sexes similar and easily distinguished from house sparrow by chestnut cap and nape, and black patch on otherwise white cheeks; plumage otherwise streaked brown on back with pale underparts. Juvenile lacks black cheek patch. Utters house sparrow-like chirps but also sharp *tik tik* in flight. Often associated with outskirts of villages and untidy arable farms, taking advantage of frequent grain spills. Nests in tree holes or, occasionally in white stork's nests. Widespread but rather local resident across much of the region but a winter visitor only to S Iberia, S Greece and coastal Turkey.

 ✔ **HOUSE SPARROW** *Passer domesticus*   Length 14–15cm

Male (A) has grey crown, cheeks and rump, chestnut-brown nape, back and wings, pale underparts and black throat. Female (B) is rather nondescript with streaked buff and grey-brown plumage. Small groups of birds often encountered sitting on roofs, uttering familiar sparrow chirps. Frequently dust-bathes. Usually nests in roof spaces or holes in walls but occasionally builds large and untidy nest in bush. Can become remarkably tame when not disturbed. Widespread resident, mainly associated with human habitation, but absent from Sardinia.

 SPANISH SPARROW *Passer hispaniolensis*   Length 15cm

Distinctive and attractively marked sparrow. Male has white cheeks framed by chestnut crown, nape and sides of neck, and black throat and bib. Upperparts otherwise boldly streaked with chestnut, black and white; shows two pale wingbars. Underparts otherwise white but heavily patterned with black arrow-head markings. Bill black in breeding season but paler at other times. Female has plumage almost indistinguishable from that of female house sparrow. Gregarious at all times and breeds colonially; nests constructed in trees, buildings and nests of white storks. Winter visitor to S Spain but resident further N in Iberia; resident in Sardinia but summer visitor only to N Greece and Turkey.

 ROCK SPARROW *Petronia petronia*   Length 14cm

A rather dumpy-looking sparrow with nondescript plumage. Adults of both sexes superficially resemble female house sparrow. Upperparts, including wings and rumps, are grey-brown and streaked with buff and black. Underparts are mostly white but with buff-brown streaks on breast, flanks and undertail feathers. Head is marked with pale crown stripe, dark stripe on side of crown, pale supercilium and dark eyestripe. Throat is pale except for brown stripe; in spring, male shows diagnostic yellow spot in centre of throat. Favours arid rocky terrain. Locally common resident from Iberia to Turkey.

 ✔ **CHAFFINCH** *Fringilla coelebs*   Length 15cm

Colourful male has reddish pink face and underparts, blue crown and chestnut back; female is more uniformly buffish brown but, like male, has prominent white shoulder patch and white wingbar. Song comprises a descending trill with characteristic final flourish. Call a distinct *pink pink*. Feeds mainly on insects during summer months but seeds taken in winter when birds gather in sizeable flocks. Varied choice of habitat includes broad-leaved and conifer woodland, farmland and gardens. Widespread and common resident throughout but numbers increase in winter due to influx of birds from further N in Europe.

BRAMBLING *Fringilla montifringilla*   Length 14–15cm

In winter plumages (those most commonly seen in region) superficially similar to chaffinch but always shows orange-buff on shoulder, breast and flanks; white rump seen in flight. Female and immature birds have buffish grey face with characteristic dark, parallel lines down nape. Male has dark brown head, which in breeding plumage (sometimes seen in late winter), becomes black. Calls include a harsh *eerp*. Favours open woodland and usually seen in flocks, sometimes with chaffinches; especially fond of fallen beech mast. Widespread winter visitor but absent from S Iberia, S Italy and most islands in region.

HAWFINCH   *Coccothraustes coccothraustes*   Length 18cm
Distinctive, even in silhouette, because of relatively large size (for a finch) and proportionately massive, conical bill. Has pinkish buff, orange-buff and chestnut elements to plumage; colours of male are brighter than those of female. Large white wingbar obvious in undulating flight. Commonest call a sharp, robin-like *tik*. Favours broad-leaved woodland and feeds on hard-cased seeds, notably hornbeam. Local resident, mainly Greece; widespread winter visitor.

SERIN   *Serinus serinus*   Length 11.5cm
A tiny, well-marked finch. Male has bright yellow head, breast and rump. Plumage otherwise streaked greenish-brown; shows two pale wingbars, forked tail and stubby bill. Female and juvenile are similar but colours more subdued. Male sings jingling song and calls include a distinctive *tirililit*, similar in pitch to call of pied wagtail. Favours orchards, open forests and mature gardens. Forms flocks outside breeding season. Widespread resident throughout the region.

SISKIN   *Carduelis spinus*   Length 12cm
Male in breeding plumage (sometimes seen in late winter) has striking yellow and green plumage with black bib and forehead. Female and winter male have more subdued colours but always show two yellow wingbars and yellow rump in flight. Calls include a twittering *tsweee*. Forms flocks outside breeding season. Favours wooded areas, often beside water, and feeds mainly on seeds. Widespread winter visitor throughout region although numbers vary from year to year.

GREENFINCH   *Carduelis chloris*   Length 14–15cm
In full breeding plumage, male is very bright yellow-green but for most of year colours are duller; female has grey-green plumage and juvenile is streaked. All birds show yellow wing patches and have yellow rumps and side to tail. Bill pinkish and conical, used for feeding on seeds. Outside breeding season, forms flocks. Utters a wheezy *weeeish* call. Favours wooded terrain with plenty of open ground for feeding. Widespread resident throughout the Mediterranean.

GOLDFINCH   *Carduelis carduelis*   Length 12cm
The only bird in the region with combination of yellow wingbars and white rump. Adult has red and white on face, black cap extending down sides of neck, buffish back, and white underparts with buff flanks. Juvenile has brown, streaked plumage but yellow wingbars as adult. Favours meadows and fallow arable fields with plenty of seed-bearing plants. Widespread resident but numbers boosted in winter by birds from northern Europe.

BULLFINCH   *Pyrrhula pyrrhula*   Length 14–16cm
Male has rosy-pink face and breast, black cap and blue-grey back. Female similar but with duller colours. Both sexes have characteristic white rump, seen as bird flies away. Favours woodland scrub and hedgerows. Utters soft, piping call. Local resident, mainly S France and N Greece but more widespread in winter.

LINNET   *Carduelis cannabina*   Length 13–14cm
Male has grey head and chestnut back. In breeding season, acquires rosy-pink patch on forecrown and on breast; these features are absent in winter months when male is similar to streaked, grey-brown female. Male often perches prominently to deliver twittering, warbling song. Forms flocks outside breeding season. Favours scrub, maquis and arable fields. Widespread resident throughout region.

CROSSBILL   *Loxia curvirostra*   Length 16–17cm
Has evolved crossed-tipped mandibles to extract seeds from conifer cones; seldom seen away from mature specimens of these trees. Male has mainly red plumage, that of female being yellowish green. Feeds high in trees but often visits pools to drink. Flights call a sharp *kip kip*. Presence of feeding birds often indicated by sound of falling cones. Locally common resident of extensive conifer forests.

CORN BUNTING *Miliaria calandra*   Length 18cm
A large but rather nondescript bunting with streaked brown plumage and large but stubby bill. Best identified by its distinctive, jingling song sometimes likened to sound of jangling keys; often delivered from fencepost or overhead wire. Also characteristically flutters wings and dangles legs in flight. Widespread resident throughout the Mediterranean region, favouring farmland with fences and hedges.

YELLOWHAMMER *Emberiza citrinella*   Length 16–17cm
Male is particularly striking with mainly bright yellow head and underparts, and chestnut back and wings; female has more subdued colours and juvenile is sandy-brown and streaked. In spring, male sings a much repeated, chirping song. Feeds on insects and seeds, often on ground. Forms flocks outside breeding season, sometimes mixing with finches and other buntings. Widespread winter visitor from N Spain to Turkey but absent from most islands. Favours open farmland. Cinereous bunting *E. cineracea* has grey-brown plumage and yellowish head. Summer visitor to Lesvos and S Turkey only.

CIRL BUNTING *Emberiza cirlus*   Length 16–17cm
Superficially yellowhammer-like but male easily told by black throat and eyestripe, and olive-grey nape and breast-band. Female has paler yellow throat than female yellowhammer but best separated by olive-grey, not chestnut, rump, or by association with male. In spring, male delivers tuneless, rattling song, similar to that of lesser whitethroat; in breeding season, favours maquis and open woodland. Outside breeding season, forms small flocks which feed on arable land. Widespread resident from Iberia to W Turkey.

ORTOLAN BUNTING *Emberiza hortulana*   Length 16cm
Male has grey-green head and breast with pale yellow throat, moustache and eyering. Upperparts reddish-brown and streaked while underparts are reddish-orange. Female similar to male but colours subdued; shows streaking on breast. Juvenile pale brown and streaked but with pale throat and moustache. All birds have pink bill. Flight call a sharp chip; male delivers *see-see-see* song. Favours agricultural land and rocky slopes, usually inland. Local summer visitor.

ROCK BUNTING *Emberiza cia*   Length 16cm
Male has blue-grey head and breast, the face boldly marked with black stripes. Upperparts streaked brown and underparts reddish-orange. Female similar to male but colours subdued. Juvenile has brown, streaked plumage. Male sings rapid warbling song. Local resident, mainly Iberia, Greece and Turkey, of warm, rocky slope usually inland. More widespread and at lower elevations in winter.

CRETZSCHMAR'S BUNTING *Emberiza caesia*   Length 16cm
Superficially similar to ortolan but male has blue-grey head with orange-red moustache and throat; eyering buff. Upperparts streaked reddish-brown and underparts orange-red. Female similar to male but colours subdued. All birds have reddish bill and legs. Summer visitor to E of region, mainly Greece, Turkey and Cyprus; occurs on most islands. Favours dry, rocky slopes.

BLACK-HEADED BUNTING *Emberiza melanocephala*   Length 17cm
Large, robust bunting. Male has black head, bright yellow underparts and chestnut back; wings and tail are black. Female has sandy-brown and grey plumage and easiest to tell by association with male. Favours arable farmland; male perches on wires. Short, rasping song. Summer visitor, May–August, to E of region, mainly Greece, Turkey and Cyprus.

REED BUNTING *Emberiza schoeniclus*   Length 15cm
In breeding plumage, male has black head except for white moustache stripes; underparts pale and upperparts chestnut-brown. In winter, black elements of male's plumage less distinct. Female has brown streaked plumage and dark moustache stripes at all times. In flight, all birds show white outer tail feathers. Widespread winter visitor, favouring farmland and marshes.

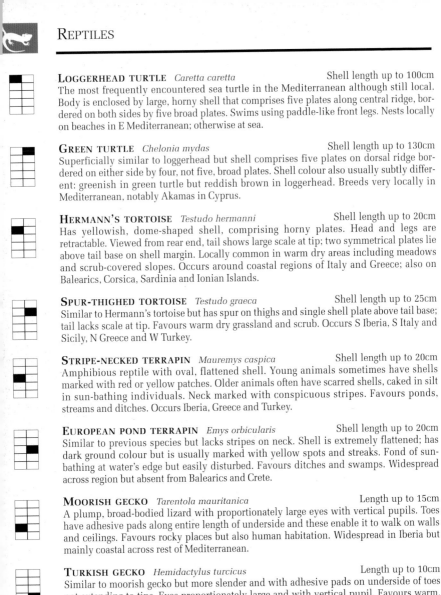

LOGGERHEAD TURTLE *Caretta caretta*   Shell length up to 100cm
The most frequently encountered sea turtle in the Mediterranean although still local.
Body is enclosed by large, horny shell that comprises five plates along central ridge, bordered on both sides by five broad plates. Swims using paddle-like front legs. Nests locally
on beaches in E Mediterranean; otherwise at sea.

GREEN TURTLE *Chelonia mydas*   Shell length up to 130cm
Superficially similar to loggerhead but shell comprises five plates on dorsal ridge bordered on either side by four, not five, broad plates. Shell colour also usually subtly different: greenish in green turtle but reddish brown in loggerhead. Breeds very locally in
Mediterranean, notably Akamas in Cyprus.

HERMANN'S TORTOISE *Testudo hermanni*   Shell length up to 20cm
Has yellowish, dome-shaped shell, comprising horny plates. Head and legs are
retractable. Viewed from rear end, tail shows large scale at tip; two symmetrical plates lie
above tail base on shell margin. Locally common in warm dry areas including meadows
and scrub-covered slopes. Occurs around coastal regions of Italy and Greece; also on
Balearics, Corsica, Sardinia and Ionian Islands.

SPUR-THIGHED TORTOISE *Testudo graeca*   Shell length up to 25cm
Similar to Hermann's tortoise but has spur on thighs and single shell plate above tail base;
tail lacks scale at tip. Favours warm dry grassland and scrub. Occurs S Iberia, S Italy and
Sicily, N Greece and W Turkey.

STRIPE-NECKED TERRAPIN *Mauremys caspica*   Shell length up to 20cm
Amphibious reptile with oval, flattened shell. Young animals sometimes have shells
marked with red or yellow patches. Older animals often have scarred shells, caked in silt
in sun-bathing individuals. Neck marked with conspicuous stripes. Favours ponds,
streams and ditches. Occurs Iberia, Greece and Turkey.

EUROPEAN POND TERRAPIN *Emys orbicularis*   Shell length up to 20cm
Similar to previous species but lacks stripes on neck. Shell is extremely flattened; has
dark ground colour but is usually marked with yellow spots and streaks. Fond of sun-bathing at water's edge but easily disturbed. Favours ditches and swamps. Widespread
across region but absent from Balearics and Crete.

MOORISH GECKO *Tarentola mauritanica*   Length up to 15cm
A plump, broad-bodied lizard with proportionately large eyes with vertical pupils. Toes
have adhesive pads along entire length of underside and these enable it to walk on walls
and ceilings. Favours rocky places but also human habitation. Widespread in Iberia but
mainly coastal across rest of Mediterranean.

TURKISH GECKO *Hemidactylus turcicus*   Length up to 10cm
Similar to moorish gecko but more slender and with adhesive pads on underside of toes
not extending to tips. Eyes proportionately large and with vertical pupil. Favours warm,
sunny areas, among stones and agave plants or in houses. Mostly nocturnal. Widespread
in coastal areas across whole of Mediterranean.

KOTSCHY'S GECKO *Cyrtodactylus kotschyi*   Length up to 10cm
A rather slender gecko with slender-looking toes and narrow tail. Toes lack adhesive pads
and looked kinked. Essentially nocturnal but sometimes discovered during daytime resting under stones or bark. Restricted to E Mediterranean from N Greece, Greek Islands and
Turkey to Cyprus.

CHAMELEON *Chamaeleo chamaeleon*   Length up to 30cm
Unmistakable reptile with large head and proportionately large, bulging eyes; feet and
prehensile tail used for grasping stems and branches. Moves extremely slowly but catches
insects with lightning speed using extensible tongue. Found in bushes and scrub. Local in
S Iberia, Crete and Cyprus; introduced elsewhere.

IBERIAN ROCK LIZARD *Lacerta monticola* Length up to 20cm
A slender, delicate-looking lizard, most individuals having characteristic green or green-ish yellow underside. Adult has variably blotched upperside, that of male often being suf-fused with green. Young male often has blue-green tail. Restricted to W France and Iberia but confined to rocky slopes in mountains.

SAND LIZARD *Lacerta agilis* Length up to 20cm
Most individuals show pale and dark stripes along length of body, latter usually broken up into blotches. Male in breeding season has green body; at other times, colours more sub-dued and often similar to sandy brown female. Favours heaths and grassland. Occurs locally SW France, former Yugoslavia and N Greece.

EYED LIZARD *Lacerta lepida* Length up to 45cm
A large, robust lizard. Young animals are olive green and marked all over with dark-mar-gined pale eyespots. Adult is mainly green with blue spots along flanks. Head is propor-tionately large, more so in male than female. Favours maquis scrub, open woodland and olive groves with stone walls. Occurs Iberia and S France.

COMMON WALL LIZARD *Podarcis muralis* Length up to 20cm
A slender lizard with a rather narrow, pointed head. Colour and pattern variable but usu-ally has black and white barring on tail. Female usually has uniform brown body but male often shows dark blotches on flanks and back. Throat usually pale and belly orange. Favours rocky slopes. Widespread from N Spain to Greece.

BALKAN WALL LIZARD *Podarcis taurica* Length up to 20cm
A robust lizard with a proportionately large, pointed head. Ground colour of upperparts mostly green. Some males are otherwise unmarked but most show variable pattern of black blotches on flanks and pale stripes along body. Most females show pale stripes along body. Favours short grassland. Common in Greece.

LARGE PSAMMODROMUS *Psammodromus algirus* Length up to 20cm
Distinctive lizard with proportionately long tail and large, flat and keeled scales on back and flanks. Body colour brown with two pale stripes along flanks; male often has blue spot on shoulder. Underparts whitish. Favours maquis, open woodland and scrub. Widespread in Iberia and local in SW France.

SLOW WORM *Anguis fragilis* Length up to 40cm
Legless, superficially snake-like lizard. Adults are usually orange-bronze; female usually darker than male; male sometimes has blue spots on back. Young animals yellow-gold with dark dorsal stripe and flanks. Favours scrub, grassland and heaths. Widespread but from absent S Iberia, Balearics, Corsica and Sardinia.

THREE-TOED SKINK *Chalcides chalcides* Length up to 40cm
Snake-like lizard with minute limbs. Body colour olive-bronze, often with dark stripes along length of body. Extremely fast and agile, moving by means of wriggling from side to side. Retreats into cover at first sign of danger. Favours damp grassland. Occurs Iberia, S France, Italy, Sardinia and Sicily.

OCELLATED SKINK *Chalcides ocellatus* Length up to 30cm
Robust and distinctive skink with plump, cylindrical body and thick, tapering tail. Body colour sandy brown but usually well-marked with black and white spots. Favours scrub and dunes and burrows well. Wary and fast-moving when disturbed. Locally common in Sardinia, Sicily, Greece and Crete.

AGAMA *Agama agama* Length up to 30cm
A robust and distinctive lizard. Body is rather flattened and has conspicuously spiny scales, most noticeable on neck, flanks and legs. Colour mostly brown; can change exact shade quickly. Favours dry, rocky places and fond of sunbathing. Locally common N Greece, Corfu, Lesvos, Mykonos, Naxos and SW Turkey.

WESTERN WHIP SNAKE   *Coluber viridiflavus*   Length up to 150cm
A large and distinctive snake. The front third of most individuals is well-marked with
black and yellow blotches; black and yellow stripes along body length are seen towards
tail end. Mostly black individuals do occur. Favours maquis, open woodland and rocky
slopes. Occurs N Spain, S France, Italy, Corsica and Sardinia.

LARGE WHIP SNAKE   *Columber jugularis*   Length up to 200cm
A long snake with smooth scales and proportionately slender body; eye has round pupil.
Body colour usually reddish brown or olive-brown, palest on underside. Fast-moving,
diurnal species that hunts mainly lizards. Favours rocky slopes, maquis and vineyards.
Main range N Greece but also occurs on many Aegean Islands.

LEOPARD SNAKE   *Elaphe situla*   Length up to 100cm
A beautifully patterned snake. Ground colour of body is usually silvery grey but well-
marked with dark-bordered red spots or stripes. Favours warm, rocky slopes, field margins with stone walls. Hunts mainly small mammals as an adult. Occurs Greece including
some Aegean Islands, former Yugoslavia and S Italy.

LADDER SNAKE   *Elaphe scalaris*   Length up to 150cm
A large snake with a proportionately large head. Adults are usually uniformly yellow-
brown or olive with two indistinct dark stripes along back. Young individuals are olive-
yellow and boldly marked with black ladder markings on back. Favours vineyards, open
woodland and maquis. Occurs Iberia and S France.

GRASS SNAKE   *Natrix natrix*   Length up to 125cm
Has olive-green ground colour, variably marked with dark spots and stripes; shows characteristic black-bordered yellow collar. Favours damp habitats and swims well.
Widespread but absent Balearics and Crete. Viperine snake *N.maura* is similar but has
dark zigzag along back. Occurs Iberia, S France and Balearics.

SMOOTH SNAKE   *Coronella austriaca*   Length up to 70cm
Slender snake small, pointed head. Eye has round pupil. Body grey-brown; marked with
dark spots. Head shows dark stripe from neck to nostril, passing through eye. Favours
maquis and heaths. Widespread; absent S Iberia and many islands.

SOUTHERN SMOOTH SNAKE   *Coronella girondica*   Length up to 60cm
Similar to smooth snake but head has more rounded profile and shows dark stripe from
neck to eye, not continuing to nostril. Favours open woods, heaths and rocky slopes.
Occurs Iberia, S France, Italy and Sicily.

MONTPELIER SNAKE   *Malpolon monspessulanus*   Length up to 200cm
A large, back-fanged snake with angular head; ridged eyebrows create menacing expres-
sion. Body colour of adult usually uniformly grey-brown; young animals are often spotted.
Favours warm, dry habitats. Occurs Iberia, S France and S Balkans.

ASP VIPER   *Vipera aspis*   Length up to 60cm
Venomous, well marked snake with slightly upturned snout; eye has vertical pupil. Body
colour grey-brown but marked with dark zigzag along back. Favours warm, rocky slopes
and mountains. Occurs N Iberia, S France, Italy and Sicily.

NOSE-HORNED VIPER   *Vipera ammodytes*   Length up to 60cm
Similar to asp, with distinct zigzag markings, but has pronounced 'horn' on nose. Hisses
loudly when disturbed and extremely venomous. Favours sunny, rocky slopes. Occurs
mainly Greece and Turkey but also N Italy and some Greek Islands.

WORM SNAKE   *Typhlops vermicularis*   Length up to 30cm
An extraordinary snake that looks extremely worm-like. Body lacks distinct head and tail
ends. Body usually shiny brown and eyes reduced to small, dark spots. Favours warm, dry
lowlands; sometimes found by turning stones. E of region only.

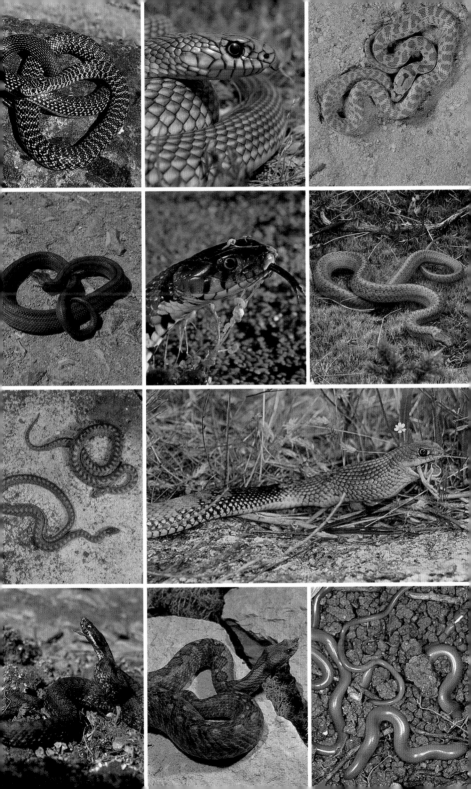

FIRE SALAMANDER *Salamandra salamandra*   Length up to 25cm
A large and distinctive salamander. Ground colour is black but body is boldly marked
with yellow or orange spots and blotches. Favours forested areas and seldom found far
from water; usually occurs in upland, inland regions. Essentially nocturnal but occasionally discovered in daytime after heavy rainfall or by turning stones. Widespread across the
region but absent from warm, dry coastal districts and most islands.

SHARP-RIBBED SALAMANDER *Pleurodeles waltl*   Length up to 30cm
A large, robust salamander with proportionately large, flat head. Has diagnostic row of
warts along flanks through which ribs project in some animals. Tail long and flattened.
Body colour olive-brown with dark spots; belly usually orange or yellow. Often associated
with seasonally drying habitats such as ponds and ditches; aestivates beneath stones during summer months. Restricted to central and S Iberian Peninsula but there locally common.

MARBLED NEWT *Triturus marmoratus*   Length up to 15cm
A boldly marked newt whose upperparts are variably marbled with green and black at all
times. In breeding season, male develops dorsal crest that is barred black. Adult female
and young animals have orange dorsal stripe. Belly greyish in all animals. Returns to
water to breed but otherwise often found in dry habitats including open woodland,
maquis and heaths. Range is restricted to Iberian Peninsula and S France.

GREAT CRESTED NEWT *Triturus cristatus*   Length up to 15cm
A large, mainly dark newt with distinctly warty skin. Body colour usually brownish with
black spots but belly usually bright orange or yellow with dark spots. In breeding season,
male develops ragged dorsal crest and pale lateral band on tail. Usually associated with
permanent ponds and lakes and sometimes found in water throughout year. Otherwise
hides beneath stones during daytime and dry weather. Occurs from SE France eastwards;
absent Iberia and most islands.

SMOOTH NEWT *Triturus vulgaris*   Length up to 10cm
A comparatively small newt with smooth skin. Body colour mostly dark olive-brown,
variably marked with dark spots; belly orange and throat white, both marked with dark
spots. In breeding season, male develops ragged dorsal crest and more intense dark spots.
Breeds in ponds and ditches but otherwise found in surrounding woodland and scrub.
Occurs from N Italy eastwards.

MIDWIFE TOAD *Alytes obstetricans*   Length up to 5cm
A small, compact toad with a proportionately large head; eyes large with vertical pupils.
Body colour olive-brown or dull green with paler belly. During late spring and early sum-
mer, male carries strings of eggs, wound around hind legs to form a cluster. Favours scrub,
open woodland and rocky habitats. Call recalls that of Scops owl. Widespread in Iberian
Peninsula and S France.

WESTERN SPADEFOOT *Pelobates cultipes*   Length up to 10cm
A plump toad with proportionately large head and eyes; has a vertical pupil. Body is vari-
ably marbled with olive-green and yellow-buff. Hind foot has prominent 'spade', used for
digging burrows. Breeds in pools but otherwise found in sandy areas. Occurs Iberia and
SW France. Replaced in SE France and N Italy by common spadefoot *P.fuscus* and in N
Greece and Turkey by eastern spadefoot *P.syriacus*.

GREEN TOAD *Bufo viridis*   Length up to 10cm
Distinct, plump toad with body variably marbled with green and buff; eye has horizontal
pupil. Breeds in shallow pools, usually on sandy soil. Often encountered on farmland on
outskirts of villages. Male's song is trilling and insect-like. Mainly nocturnal. Occurs from
Italy eastwards; also found on Balearics, Corsica and Sardinia.

COMMON TOAD *Bufo bufo* Length up to 15cm
A large, squat toad; females generally larger than males. Body colour usually uniformly olive-brown or sandy brown on upperside; reddish individuals do occur. Underside usually greyish. Skin is covered in distinct warts. Eye is orange-bronze with horizontal pupil. Breeds in shallow pools but at other times of year often found in rather dry habitats including open woodland and heaths. Widespread throughout the region but absent from many islands including Balearics.

NATTERJACK *Bufo calmita* Length up to 9cm
Attractive toad with proportionately short limbs and rather flattened body. Upper body usually uniformly olive-brown or sandy with conspicuous warts and diagnostic yellow dorsal stripe; underside greyish. Walks rather than hops from danger. Eye golden coloured with horizontal pupil. Favours shallow, often brackish or seasonally drying pools for breeding. Otherwise often found in rather dry habitats; burrows well in loose soil. Occurs Iberia and SW France.

PAINTED FROG *Discoglossus pictus* Length up to 7cm
A well-marked and distinctive frog. Body colour mainly olive-brown but marked with distinct darker brown blotches and spots on upper body; underside pale. Some individuals show broad, pale dorsal stripe. Distinguished from frogs of genus *Rana* by having rounded, not horizontal, pupil. Favours shallow pools and stream margins, even where water is brackish. Restricted mainly to S and W Iberian Peninsula, Sicily and Malta.

COMMON TREE FROG *Hyla arborea* Length up to 5cm
An attractive little frog with mainly bright green body and distinct brown stripe along entire length of flanks; throat whitish. Disc-like suckers on tips of fingers and toes enable animal to climb through vegetation with ease. Mainly nocturnal but sometimes discovered sitting in full sun on foliage. Male has inflatable vocal sac under chin. Favours marshes, reedbeds and riverside vegetation. Widespread but absent from S Iberia, SW France and Balearics.

STRIPELESS TREE FROG *Hyla meridionalis* Length up to 5cm
Superficially similar to common tree frog with bright green body and proportionately long limbs. However, lacks that species' dark flank stripe although mask-like dark stripe usually present though eyes. Throat usually greenish. Favours marshes, reedbeds and streamside vegetation. Restricted mainly to S Iberian Peninsula, S France and Balearic Islands.

MARSH FROG *Rana ridibunda* Length up to 15cm
A large and robust frog with a rather pointed snout. Body colour usually olive-green and well-marked with dark spots. Vocal sacs grey and backs of thighs are body colour, marbled with black and white. Favours all sorts of watery habitats and often abundant where conditions are ideal. Sings noisily during breeding season. Occurs Iberia, S France, Balearics, Greece and Turkey.

POOL FROG *Rana lessonae* Length up to 9cm
Similar to marsh frog with ground colour of body varying from green to olive-brown and variably patterned with dark blotches and spots; some individuals have pale dorsal stripe. Distinguishing features include white vocal sacs and yellow marbling seen on back of thighs. Favours all sorts of water bodies but sometimes found on land. Occurs mainly S France, Italy and Sicily.

EDIBLE FROG *Rana esculenta* Length up to 12cm
Similar to pool frog but with proportionately longer hind limbs; the two species are separable only with care and experience. Body colour ranges from green to olive-brown with dark blotches and spots. Some individuals show a pale dorsal stripe; vocal sac white. Favours ponds and lakes. Occurs mainly S France, Italy, Corsica and Sicily.

SCARCE SWALLOWTAIL *Iphiclides podalirius*   Wingspan 80mm
Has long tail streamers on hindwing. Upperwing is pale yellow with dark transverse bands; hindwing has red and blue eyespot and blue crescents. Underwing has upperwing pattern but subdued colours. Widespread; absent from many islands.

SWALLOWTAIL *Papilio machaon*   Wingspan 80–90mm
Upperwings are yellow with network of black veins; margins have black-bordered blue spots and yellow crescents. Hindwing shows red eyespot and tail streamers. Underwing has pattern of upperwing but subdued colours. Widespread and common.

SOUTHERN FESTOON *Zerynthia polyxena*   Wingspan 50–60mm
Upperwings have yellow ground colour and black markings, with red spots on hindwing in particular; underwings similar but yellow is less intense with more red on forewing. Flies spring and autumn. Widespread from S France eastwards.

EASTERN FESTOON *Zerynthia cerisyi*   Wingspan 55–65mm
Similar to southern festoon with yellow ground colour to upperwings but less extensive black markings; shows blue and red spots on hindwing. Underwings pale yellow. Occurs from former Yugoslavia and N Greece eastwards. Flies April–May.

LARGE WHITE *Pieris brassicae*   Wingspan 60mm
Male has pale upperwing except for dark tip on forewing and dark mark on leading edge of hindwing. Female similar but shows two dark spots on upper forewing. Underwings have two dark spots on forewings and yellowish hindwings. Widespread.

SMALL WHITE *Artogeia rapae*   Wingspan 50mm
Off-white upperwings show greyish tip and single spot on male forewing and two spots and dark tip in female. Underside of forewing has yellow tip and dark spot; that of hindwing is yellowish. Widespread and common. Occurs spring to autumn.

GREEN-VEINED WHITE *Artogeia napi*   Wingspan 50mm
Upperwing is white with veins marked by grey scaling; forewing has dark tip, female with two dark spots and male with one. Underwings yellowish with veins marked with greenish-grey scales. Widespread and common. Occurs spring to autumn.

ORANGE-TIP *Anthocharis cardamines*   Wingspan 35mm
Male has orange tip to upper and lower surface of forewing; hindwing is white on upper surface and marbled greenish-yellow below. Female similar to male but orange colour replaced by dark grey. Widespread except S Iberia and Balearics.

MOROCCO ORANGE-TIP *Anthocharis belia*   Wingspan 35mm
Male is similar to male orange tip but ground colour of upperwings is pale yellow not white; underside of hindwing marbled green. Female has white ground colour to upperwings and paler orange tip than male. Occurs S Iberia, S France and N Italy.

DAPPLED WHITE *Euchloe ausonia*   Wingspan 35mm
Ground colour of upperwings is white; forewing has dark grey spot and tip while hindwing has faint grey marbling. Underwings marbled yellow-green on hindwing; forewing is tipped yellow and has dark spot. Widespread. Flies in spring.

GREEN-STRIPED WHITE *Euchloe belemia*   Wingspan 35mm
Upperwings mainly white but forewing has dark central spot and dark, speckled tip; hindwing has grey bands. Underside of forewing similar to upperside; underside of hindwing has green bands. Occurs S Iberia. Flies March–May.

BATH WHITE *Pontia daplidice*   Wingspan 50mm
Upperwings white with faint grey marbling and dark spots. Hindwings marbled yellow-green on underside; that of forewing is white with greenish tip and two dark spots. Widespread and common. Flies spring to autumn. A powerful migrant.

CLOUDED YELLOW *Colias crocea*   Wingspan 50mm
Both sexes have orange upperwings with chocolate-brown border; forewing has dark central spot. Female has yellow spots on brown border. Underwings of both sexes are yellow with black and red markings. Widespread, flying April–October.

PALE CLOUDED YELLOW *Colias hyale*   Wingspan 50mm
Similar to clouded yellow but upperwings lemon yellow; female paler than male. Both sexes have dark central forewing spot and dark border with pale spots. Underwing pale yellow. Occurs mainly S France and flies May–October.

BRIMSTONE *Gonepteryx rhamni*   Wingspan 60mm
Shape distinctive, forewings with prominent hooked tip. Male is bright yellow while female is very pale green. Underwings bear a few reddish marks. Widespread, favouring scrub and open woodland. Hibernates from autumn to spring.

CLEOPATRA *Gonepteryx cleopatra*   Wingspan 60mm
Similar wing shape to brimstone but male has bright yellow wings, forewings with central orange flush; female has very pale yellow wings. Favours meadows and flower-rich scrub. Widespread throughout the region, mainly seen in spring.

WOOD WHITE *Leptidea sinapis*   Wingspan 40mm
A delicate butterfly with distinctly rounded wings. Upperwings white, the forewings tipped grey, more distinct in male than female. Underwings of both sexes variably marked with grey-green scaling. Widespread, spring and autumn.

BLACK-VEINED WHITE *Aporia crategi*   Wingspan 60mm
Unmistakable with rounded, almost translucent wings boldly marked with black veins. Favours open woods and nearby scrub and meadows. Often drinks at pools. Widespread but absent from many islands. Flies July–August.

TWO-TAILED PASHA *Charaxes jasius*   Wingspan 70–80mm
Has strongly angled forewings and hindwings with prominent streamers. Upperwings rich brown with creamy-yellow margins. Underwings marbled maroon, purple, orange and white. Widespread. Flies spring and autumn. Larva feeds on strawberry tree.

COMMA *Polygonia c-album*   Wingspan 45mm
Has ragged-edged wings. Upperwings orange with dark spots; underwings grey-brown with 'comma' marking on hindwing. Widespread, flying April–September. Similar southern comma *P.egea* has less distinct 'comma' mark; mainly Italy eastwards.

SOUTHERN WHITE ADMIRAL *Limenitis reducta*   Wingspan 50mm
Has rounded wing outline, upperwings blackish with broad, white markings forming a band; underwings reddish-orange with broad white spots forming continuous patch on hindwing. Favours woodland rides. Widespread from N Spain eastwards.

SMALL TORTOISESHELL *Aglais urticae*   Wingspan 42mm
Attractive butterfly with jagged wing margins. Upperwings orange with black and yellow patches; dark border has blue spots. Underwings grey-brown and buff. Favours flower-rich sites. Widespread, flying March–October.

PAINTED LADY *Vanessa cardui*   Wingspan 60mm
Arguably the region's most familiar butterfly. Upperwings pinkish-orange with dark and white markings; underwings marbled brown, buff and white. Widespread in meadows, coasts and scrub. Flies April–October. Highly migratory.

RED ADMIRAL *Vanessa atalanta*   Wingspan 60mm
Upperwings jet black and beautifully marked with red transverse band on forewings and red margin on hindwings; forewings tipped with white spots. Underwings marbled black, brown, blue and white. Widespread; flies mainly spring and autumn.

BUTTERFLIES

LARGE TORTOISESHELL *Nymphalis polychloros*   Wingspan 80mm
Upperwings are orange-brown with yellow and black patches and dark border.
Underwings are grey-brown. Favours open woodland and scrub. Adults emerge early
summer and hibernate to the following spring. Widespread; absent many islands.

PEACOCK *Inachis io*   Wingspan 60mm
Attractive species. Upperwings maroon with large eyespot on each wing; those on
forewings are yellow, blue and maroon and those on hindwing are blue and buff.
Underwings grey-brown. Summer adults hibernate until spring. Widespread.

CAMBERWELL BEAUTY *Nymphalis antiopa*   Wingspan 80mm
Distinctive species. Upperwings maroon, bordered with spots and showing cream margin;
underwings grey-brown with pale margin. Favours wooded areas. Summer adults hibernate until spring. Widespread; absent S Iberia and many islands.

HIGH BROWN FRITILLARY *Fabriciana adippe*   Wings 60mm
Upperwings orange-brown with black spots. Shows green scales and silver spots on
underside of hindwing; underside of forewing orange with dark spots. Favours grassland.
Flies July–August. Widespread; absent from islands in W of region.

SILVER-WASHED FRITILLARY *Argynnis paphia*   Wingspan 60mm
Has angled forewings and rounded hindwings. Upperwings orange-brown with dark spots
and lines. Underwings greenish-buff with silver sheen on hindwing. Favours open woodland. Flies mid-summer. Widespread but absent S Iberia and Balearics.

DARK GREEN FRITILLARY *Mesoacidalia aglaja*   Wingspan 60mm
Fast flier with rounded wings. Upperwings orange-buff with dark spots and stripes.
Underside greenish with silver spots on hindwings; forewings orange-buff with silver and
dark spots. Favours grassland. Widespread; absent from many islands.

CARDINAL *Pandoriana pandora*   Wingspan 70mm
Similar to silver-washed but larger. Upperwings orange-buff with dark spots and lines and
greenish scales. Underside green and pink with dark spots on forewing; female has silver
stripes on hindwing. Flies mid-summer. Widespread.

QUEEN OF SPAIN FRITILLARY *Issoria lathonia*   Wingspan 40–45mm
Wings have rather angular outline. Upperwings orange with dark spots. Underside
orange-buff with dark spots on forewing and large silvery spots on hindwing. Has several
broods and so seen April–October. Widespread in grassy places.

HEATH FRITILLARY *Mellicta athalia*   Wingspan 45–50mm
Delicate fritillary with rounded wings. Upperwings orange with network of dark markings. Underwings orange, buff and creamy white; dark spots absent. Favours open woodland. Flies May–August. Widespread; absent S Iberia and many islands.

KNAPWEED FRITILLARY *Melitaea phoebe*   Wingspan 50mm
Upperwings orange-buff with variable dark markings; best feature is large orange crescent
on forewing. Underwings pale with network of black lines and orange spots. Widespread
in flowery places; absent many islands. Flies May–August.

SPOTTED FRITILLARY *Melitaea didyma*   Wingspan 40–50mm
Attractive species with orange upperwings marked with a relatively small number of dark
spots. Underside shows orange forewings with dark spots and underwings with orange
and buff bands. Flies June–August. Widespread in grassy places.

GLANVILLE FRITILLARY *Melitaea cinxia*   Wingspan 40mm
Upperwings orange-buff with network of black markings. Underside pale with dark-mar-
gined orange bands and black spots (five on submarginal band). Favours grassy slopes.
Seen in spring and autumn. Widespread; absent S Iberia and many islands.

138

PROVENCAL FRITILLARY *Mellicta dieone*   Wingspan 40mm
Upperwings orange-brown with network of black markings. Underwings patterned with buff, orange and black. Favours flowery meadows, often on mountain slopes. Flies late spring. Occurs S France and E and S Iberian Peninsula.

PEARL-BORDERED FRITILLARY *Clossiana euphrosyne*   Wingspan 43mm
Upperwings orange-brown with black spots and lines. Underside buffish-orange; forewings have dark spots and hindwings have seven silver spots on margins plus pale patches in centre. Flies spring and autumn. Occurs N Sprain to Greece.

VIOLET FRITILLARY *Clossiana dia*   Wingspan 35mm
Upperwings orange-brown with black spots and other markings. Underside of forewings orange-buff with dark spots; that of hindwing marbled with violet-brown and white. Flies May–August; favours open woods. Occurs N Spain to N Greece.

MARSH FRITILLARY *Euphydryas aurinia*   Wingspan 40–50mm
Upperwings show pattern of orange, yellow and dark brown. Underwings orange-buff, marked with orange and cream patches. Favours both wet and dry grassland. Flies May–July. Widespread from Iberia to N Greece; absent most islands and Italy.

DUKE OF BURGUNDY *Hamearis lucina*   Wingspan 30mm
Resembles tiny fritillary but unrelated to that family. Upperwings dark brown with orange spots. Underwings orange-buff with black and white spots and patches. Favours open woodland and grassland. Flies May–June. Occurs N Iberia to N Greece.

MARBLED WHITE *Melanargia galathea*   Wingspan 50mm
Upperwings marbled with black and white; pattern on underwings similar but black replaced by grey and white by cream. Favours grassland. Flies June–September. Widespread but absent from Balearics, Corsica, Sardinia and Crete.

SPANISH MARBLED WHITE *Melanargia ines*   Wingspan 50mm
Similar to marbled white but black markings less extensive and ground colour is creamy white; underwing pattern similar to that on upperwing but colours less intense. Favours meadows, often on mountain slopes. Widespread in Iberia.

ROCK GRAYLING *Hipparchia alcyone*   Wingspan 60mm
Upperwings dark brown with cream band; small spot on each wing, forewing with large eyespot. Underside marbled grey, brown and white; forewing has cream band with eyespot. Favours uplands. Local in Iberia, S France, Italy and N Greece.

GRAYLING *Hipparchia semele*   Wingspan 50mm
Upperwings brown with eyespots in yellow-buff band. Underside marbled grey, brown and white on hindwing; forewing has yellow-buff patch and two eyespots. Favours stony places. Flies June–August. Widespread but absent from some islands.

TREE GRAYLING *Hipparchia statilinus*   Wingspan 50mm
Upperwings dark brown with faint pale band and dark eyespots. Underside marbled pinkish grey, brown and white with two large eyespots on forewing. Favours open woods on rocky ground. Flies July–September. Widespread; absent from some islands.

THE HERMIT *Chazara briseis*   Wingspan 50–60mm
Upperwings dark brown with two eyespots on each wing; forewing shows pale band. Underside marbled buff, brown and grey with two eyespots on forewing. Favours dry stony terrain. Flies June–July. Occurs E Iberia to N Greece; absent from most islands.

STRIPED GRAYLING *Pseudotergumia fidia*   Wingspan 60mm
Upperwings dark brown with variable white markings; two eyespots on forewing. Underside grey-brown with white patches and jagged band; two eyespots seen on forewing. Favours rocky, grassy slopes. Flies July–August. Iberia and S France.

GIANT BANDED GRAYLING *Britesia circe*   Wingspan 60–70mm
Impressive butterfly whose black upperwings show a white band on both wings. Underside marbled grey, brown, black and white; eyespot on forewing. Favours open woodland. Flies June–August. Widespread from Iberia to N Greece.

RINGLET *Aphantopus hyperantus*   Wingspan 45–50mm
Upperwings dark brown in female, black in male; two dark spots on hindwing, also sometimes on forewing. Underside of both sexes dark brown with white-ringed eyespots. Favours grassy places. Flies June–July. Mainly N Iberia and S France.

THE DRYAD *Minois dryas*   Wingspan 50–60mm
Upperwings brown with two blue-centred black eyespots on forewing and one on hindwing. Underside has similar pattern to upperside but ground colour less rich. Favours grassland. Flies June–August. Occurs N Iberia, S France and N Italy.

MEADOW BROWN *Maniola jurtina*   Wingspan 50mm
Upperwings brown; forewing has eyespot contained within orange patch, larger in female than male. Underside of hindwing is brown with paler band; that of forewing orange and buff with eyespot. Favours grassland. Widespread June–August.

GATEKEEPER *Pyronia tithonus*   Wingspan 40mm
Upperwings orange with dark brown border and single, twin-pupilled eyespot on forewing. Underside of hindwing grey and brown with orange band; forewing pattern similar to upperside. Favours scrub and grassland. Widespread July–August.

SPANISH GATEKEEPER *Pyronia bathseba*   Wingspan 35–50mm
Upperwings orange-buff with brown border with twin-pupilled eyespot on forewing and four smaller eyespots on hindwing. Underwing pattern similar to upperwing but has broad cream band on hindwing. Flies April–June. Iberia and S France.

SMALL HEATH *Coenonympha pamphilus*   Wingspan 30mm
Upperwings orange-brown with brown margin and dark spot on forewing. Underside of forewing orange with grey-brown margin and dark spot; that of hindwing marbled grey-brown and white. Favours grassland. Flies May–August. Widespread.

CORSICAN HEATH *Coenonympha corinna*   Wingspan 30mm
Upperwings orange-brown with dark border and eyespot on forewing. Underside of forewing orange with an eyespot; hindwing reddish-grey with pale streak and small spots. Favours grassy slopes. Flies June–August. Corsica and Sardinia.

DUSKY HEATH *Coenonympha dorus*   Wingspan 35mm
Upperwings orange-brown with dusky scaling; eyespot on forewing, smaller spots on hindwing. Underside of forewing orange with eyespot; hindwing dusky with pale stripe and several eyespots. Favours grassy slopes. Iberia, S France and N Italy.

WALL BROWN *Lasiommata megera*   Wingspan 45mm
Upperwings orange-buff with network of brown lines; single eyespot on forewing, several smaller ones on hindwing; Underside of forewing similar to upperwing; hindwing marbled grey and brown. Favours rocky places. Widespread May–August.

LARGE WALL BROWN *Lasiommata maera*   Wingspan 45–50mm
Upperwings orange-buff in female, grey-brown in male, with network of dark lines; large, twin eyespot on forewing, smaller ones on hindwing. Underside of forewing similar to upperwing; hindwing marbled grey-brown. Widespread June–August.

SPECKLED WOOD *Pararge aegeria*   Wingspan 45mm
Upperwings dark brown with pale patches, these being pale cream in north of range and orange-buff in south. Underside of forewing similar to upperwing; hindwing marbled brown. Favours open grassy woods. Flies April–October. Widespread.

BUTTERFLIES

ILEX HAIRSTREAK *Nordmannia ilicis* Wingspan 35mm
Upperwings brown with orange patch on forewings and orange spot on rear margin of hindwing. Underside grey-brown with broken white line; orange submarginal spots on hindwing. Favours oak woods. Flies June–July. Occurs from N Iberia eastwards.

FALSE ILEX HAIRSTREAK *Nordmannia esculi* Wingspan 35mm
Upperwings dark brown; females have two orange spots on rear margin of hindwing, males have one. Underside grey-brown with broken white line; reddish submarginal spots on hindwing. Favours oak scrub. Flies June–July. Iberia and S France.

BLUE-SPOT HAIRSTREAK *Strymondia spini* Wingspan 35mm
Male upperwings dark brown with two orange spots on hindwing; female has brown wings with broad orange bands. Underside greyish with white streak and blue spot on hindwing. Favours scrub. Flies June–July. Widespread; absent most islands.

WHITE-LETTER HAIRSTREAK *Strymondia w-album* Wingspan 35mm
Upperwings dark brown. Underside brown with fused row of orange submarginal spots on hindwing; white streak on both wings, forming letter 'w' on hindwing. Favours woods and scrub with elms. Flies in July. Occurs from N Iberia eastwards.

BLACK HAIRSTREAK *Strymondia pruni* Wingspan 35mm
Upperwings brown with submarginal orange spots on both wings. Underside brown with jagged white streak and orange band fringed with black dots. Favours blackthorn scrub. Flies July. Occurs S France eastwards; absent from S of region.

GREEN HAIRSTREAK *Callophrys rubi* Wingspan 25mm
Upperwings brown. Underside green with slight iridescence and broken white streak. Favours open woodland, heaths and maquis. Flies April–June. Widespread throughout the Mediterranean, including most islands.

BROWN HAIRSTREAK *Thecla betulae* Wingspan 45mm
Upperwings brown with orange patch at base of tail streamer; female has orange patch on forewing. Underside orange with black and white lines. Favours scrub and open woodland. Flies July–August. Occurs mainly NE Iberia, S France and N Italy.

PURPLE HAIRSTREAK *Quercusia quercus* Wingspan 35–40mm
Male upperwings iridescent purple; those of female brown with purple patch on forewing. Underside greyish-lilac with white streaks; has orange spot at base of tail streamer. Favours oak woodland. Flies July–August. Widespread.

SCARCE COPPER *Heodes virgaureae* Wingspan 30–40mm
Male upperwings orange with dark margin; those of female orange brown with dark spots. Underside orange-buff with dark spots; has white spots on hindwing. Favours grassy slopes. Flies July–August. Local from N Iberia eastwards.

PURPLE-EDGED COPPER *Palaeochrysophanus hippothoe* Wingspan 35–40mm
Male upperwings orange with dark margin; purple streaks on border of hindwing. Female upper forewing orange with dark spots; hindwing brown with orange margin. Underside grey-brown with dark spots. Favours meadows. Flies June–July. Local.

SMALL COPPER *Lycaena phlaeas* Wingspan 30–40mm
Upperwing ground colour brown; forewing has broad orange patch with dark spots while hindwing has orange margin. Underside pattern similar to upperside but colours less intense. Favours grassland. Flies April–October. Widespread.

PURPLE-SHOT COPPER *Heodes alciphron* Wingspan 40mm
Upperwings dull orange with dark spots; male wings have purplish hue. Underside grey-brown with dark spots; has orange submarginal spots on hindwing. Favours flowery meadows. Flies June–July. Widespread but absent from most islands.

SOOTY COPPER *Heodes tityrus*   Wingspan 30–35mm
Upperwings brown with patches of orange on forewings and submarginal orange band on both wings. Underside grey-brown with dark spots and border of orange spots. Favours flowering meadows. Flies spring and autumn. Occurs N Iberia eastwards.

GREEN-UNDERSIDE BLUE *Glaucopsyche alexis*   Wingspan 35mm
Male upperwings violet with dark margin; those of female similar but dark margin more extensive. Underside brown with black spots and green scaling at wing bases. Favours grassy slopes. Flies April–May. Occurs from N Iberia eastwards.

LONG-TAILED BLUE *Lampides boeticus*   Wingspan 35mm
Male upperwings bluish-lilac with dark margin to forewing and dark spot at base of tail streamer; female similar to male but browner. Underside brown with concentric buff bands; has eyespots near base of tail streamer on hindwing. Favours grassland. Flies May–October. Widespread.

LANG'S SHORT-TAILED BLUE *Syntarucus pirithous*   Wingspan 25mm
Male upperings lilac-blue with faint dark barring; female similar but barring more apparent. Underside marbled grey-buff and white; two eyespots at base of tail streamer. Favours grassy slopes. Flies March–October. Widespread.

PROVENCAL SHORT-TAILED BLUE *Everes alcetas*   Wingspan 30–35mm
Male upperwings violet-blue with dark margin; those of female are dark brown. Underside pale grey with black spots. Favours flowery meadows. Flies April–September. Local S France, N Italy, N Greece and Corsica.

SHORT-TAILED BLUE *Everes argiades*   Wingspan 30mm
Male upperwings violet-blue with dark margin; those of female are dark brown. Underside pale grey with small dark spots and orange spots near margin of hindwing. Favours flowery meadows. Flies May–August. Occurs from N Iberia eastwards.

SILVER-STUDDED BLUE *Plebejus argus*   Wingspan 25–30mm
Male upperwings violet-blue with dark margin and white border; those of female are brown with submarginal orange spots. Underside grey-brown with black spots and orange submarginal band. Favours grassy heaths. Flies May–August. Widespread.

MAZARINE BLUE *Cyaniris semiargus*   Wingspan 30mm
Male upperwings violet-blue; those of female dark brown. Underside brown with small, white-ringed black spots and blue scaling at wing bases. Favours flowery meadows. Flies June–July. Widespread throughout region.

COMMON BLUE *Polyommatus icarus*   Wingspan 32mm
Male upperwings blue; those of female brown with variable amounts of blue and orange submarginal spots. Underside grey-brown with white-ringed black spots and orange submarginal spots. Favours meadows. Flies May–October. Widespread.

ADONIS BLUE *Lysandra bellargus*   Wingspan 32mm
Male upperwings iridescent blue, the white margin interrupted by black lines; those of female brown with varying amounts of blue. Underside grey-brown with white-ringed black spots and orange submarginal spots. Favours chalk grassland. Flies spring and autumn. Widespread but absent from most islands.

CHALKHILL BLUE *Lysandra coridon*   Wingspan 40mm
Male upperwings pale blue with dark margin; those of female are brown with orange submarginal spots on hindwing. Underside grey-brown with white-ringed black spots and orange submarginal spots on hindwing. Favours chalk grassland. Larval foodplants include vetches. Flies July–August. Widespread but absent from S Iberia, S Italy, S Greece and most islands.

BUTTERFLIES

SMALL BLUE *Cupido minimus* Wingspan 25mm
Upperwings sooty brown; male has violet-blue scaling wing bases. Underside blue-grey with blue scaling at wing bases and small black spots. Favours chalk grassland. Flies June–July. Widespread; absent S Iberia and most islands.

BROWN ARGUS *Aricia agestis* Wingspan 25mm
Upperwings chocolate brown with row of orange submarginal crescents. Underside grey-brown with black spots and submarginal orange spots. Favours flowery slopes. Flies May–August. Widespread from N Iberia eastwards; absent from Balearics.

RED-UNDERWING SKIPPER *Spialia sertorius* Wingspan 20–25mm
Upperwings dark brown with variable white markings. Underside grey-brown on forewing and reddish brown on hindwing, both with extensive white marks. Favours grassy slopes. Flies May–August. Widespread but absent from Balearics and Crete.

GRIZZLED SKIPPER *Pyrgus malvae* Wingspan 20mm
Upperwings dark brown with numerous white spots. Underside is grey-brown on forewing and orange-brown on hindwing, both with white marks. Favours meadows and grassy woodland rides. Flies April–August. Widespread; absent from many islands.

DINGY SKIPPER *Erynnis tages* Wingspan 25mm
Rather moth-like with marbled grey-brown upperwings. Underside reddish brown with indistinct pale spots. Favours meadows and grassy scrub. Flies May–August. Widespread but absent from most islands in region.

MALLOW SKIPPER *Carcharodus alceae* Wingspan 30mm
Upperwings attractively marbled pinkish-buff, brown and white. Underside grey-brown with white spots and flecks. Favours grassy slopes where mallows (larval foodplants) are common. Flies April–August. Widespread throughout.

MARBLED SKIPPER *Carcharodus lavatherae* Wingspan 30–35mm
Upperwings marbled buffish white and pale olive-brown. Underside pale greenish-buff with white marks. Favours grassy slopes. Flies May–August. Widespread from S France eastwards; absent from most islands and very local in Iberia.

LARGE SKIPPER *Ochlodes venatus* Wingspan 25mm
Upperwings orange-brown with darker brown margins. Underside buffish orange with faint yellow markings. Favours grassy meadows. Flies June–July. Widespread but absent from S Iberia, Balearics, Corsica and Sardinia.

SILVER-SPOTTED SKIPPER *Hesperia comma* Wingspan 25mm
Upperwings dark brown with yellow-buff spots. Underside greenish buff with silvery white spots, most extensive on hindwings. Favours calcareous grassland. Flies July–August. Widespread but absent from many islands, S Italy and S Greece.

SMALL SKIPPER *Thymelicus sylvestris* Wingspan 25mm
Upperwings orange-brown with darker brown margin. Underside orange-brown on forewing and grey-brown on hindwing. Tips of antennae orange-brown. Favours grassland. Flies May–August. Widespread but absent from many islands.

ESSEX SKIPPER *Thymelicus lineola* Wingspan 25mm
Similar to small skipper but tips of antennae black. Upperwings orange-brown with dark margin. Underside orange-brown on forewing and buffish brown on hindwing. Favours grassland. Flies May–August. Widespread; absent from Balearics and Crete.

LULWORTH SKIPPER *Thymelicus acteon* Wingspan 25mm
Upperwings olive-brown, forewings with crescent of yellowish spots. Underside orange-buff with indistinct pale markings on forewings. Favours grassy slopes. Flies May to July. Widespread but absent from Balearics, Corsica and Sardinia.

Syntomis phegea   Wingspan 40mm
A distinctive day-flying moth; forewings appreciably larger than hindwings. Wings violet-blue (a greenish iridescence is visible in some lights) with large white spots. Body greenish blue with two yellow bands. Favours flowery meadows and slopes. Flies June–August. Flight sluggish. Widespread but local.

5-SPOT BURNET *Zygaena trifolii*   Wingspan 35mm
A colourful day-flying moth and one of several superficially similar species. Forewings dark with greenish metallic sheen and five red spots. Hindwings red with a dark border. Yellow and black larvae feed on trefoils. Favours flowery meadows. Flies May–June. Widespread and locally common.

LAPPET MOTH *Gastropacha quercifolia*   Wingspan 60–70mm
Shape and manner in which wings are held afford this species superb camouflage when resting among dead or fallen leaves. Upperwings reddish-brown with scalloped margins and scalloped dark concentric lines. Favours woodland and scrub. Flies June–July. Widespread and locally common but easily overlooked.

GIANT PEACOCK MOTH *Saturnia pyri*   Wingspan 120–150mm
An impressive insect and Europe's largest moth. Upperwings beautifully patterned with grey and brown; both pairs of wings each have a single large eyespot and a pale cream border. Body and bases of wings hairy. Larva green with arrays of spines on each segment. Favours scrub and maquis. Flies April–June. Common.

EMPEROR MOTH *Saturnia pavonia*   Wingspan 60–70mm
An attractive day-flying moth. Female has forewings marbled brown, grey and red and hindwings orange and brown. Smaller male has forewings patterned grey and white with orange hindwings. Pale margins and conspicuous eyespots seen on all wings of both sexes. Larva green with tufts of black hairs on each segment. Favours heaths and maquis. Flies April–May. Widespread.

EYED HAWKMOTH *Smerinthus ocellatus*   Wingspan 80mm
A large and attractive moth. Forewings, which normally conceal hindwings, are marbled brown, grey and buff. Hindwings, which are revealed when insect is threatened, are reddish pink with a large, black-bordered blue eyespot. Larva is green with oblique stripes on each segment and a tail horn. Adult flies May–June. Favours woodland, gardens and scrub. Widespread and common.

DEATH'S-HEAD HAWKMOTH *Acherontia atropos*   Wingspan 110mm
One of Europe's most impressive moths with a striking yellow-buff skull and crossbones marking on the thorax. Forewings are blackish but marbled with brown, white and buff. Hindwings are yellow with bands of black. Abdomen is banded black and yellow. Adult can hiss loudly when disturbed. Larva large and yellow with blue oblique stripes on each segment and shrivelled-looking tail horn; feeds on potato leaves. Adult flies May–October. Widespread and common.

CONVOLVULUS HAWKMOTH *Agrius convolvuli*   Wingspan 110mm
A large and impressive moth, sometimes seen visiting garden flowers (especially tobacco plant) at dusk, collecting nectar using its long proboscis. Forewings beautifully patterned with grey and brown to resemble tree bark. Hindwings grey-buff. Abdomen banded with pink, white and black. Found in all sorts of open habitats. Flies May–October. Widespread and common.

PRIVET HAWKMOTH *Sphinx ligustri*   Wingspan 100mm
A large and attractive moth. Forewings subtly patterned with brown, buff and black. Hindwings marked with dark and buff bands and with pink flush at base. Abdomen shows pale dorsal band along length and sides marked with pink and black bands. Larva bright green with oblique purple stripes on each segment and black shiny tail horn. Favours gardens, maquis and woodland. Flies June–July. Common.

OLEANDER HAWKMOTH *Daphnis nerii* Wingspan 95mm
Attractively marked moth with proportionately narrow wings and long body. Wings patterned with various shades of green, along with lilac, pink and brown. Favours scrub and river courses where larval foodplant, oleander, grows. Flies June–September. Sometimes seen in gardens at dusk visiting nectar-bearing flowers. Widespread and fairly common throughout the region. Larva is green with a pale lateral stripe and blue anterior spot on side.

BEDSTRAW HAWKMOTH *Hyles gallii* Wingspan 75mm
A boldly marked moth with pointed wings and a rather plump body. Forewings olive-brown with pale central stripe and grey margin. Hindwings have a pale stripe that is flushed pink at base. Favours well-vegetated habitats where species of bedstraws, the larval foodplants, flourish. Flies May–July. Widespread and generally common throughout the region. Larva is olive with black-ringed white spots on the sides of each segment.

SPURGE HAWKMOTH *Hyles euphorbiae* Wingspan 80mm
A well-marked moth, superficially similar to bedstraw hawkmoth. Forewings olive-brown with broad pale stripe along length and pale pink margin. Hindwings show a black-bordered pink band. Favours wide variety of habitats, wherever spurges, the larval foodplants, grow; larva itself is strikingly patterned yellow, red and black. Flies May–July. Widespread throughout region.

STRIPED HAWKMOTH *Hyles lineata livornica* Wingspan 80mm
A beautiful moth whose olive-brown forewings are strikingly patterned with pale stripes; hindwings have brown-bordered pink band. Thorax marked with two longitudinal pale stripes. Favours scrub, maquis and gardens and often seen visiting flowers at dusk in hot weather. Flies May–August. Widespread and generally common throughout the region. Larva is black above and creamy below.

SILVER-STRIPED HAWKMOTH *Hippotion celerio* Wingspan 75mm
A narrow-wing, narrow-bodied moth. Forewings buffish brown with dark streaks and a silvery-white stripe along length. Hindwings are pink towards the base and marked with dark streaks. Favours all sorts of open, flower-rich habitats including gardens. Often seen on the wing at dusk and occasionally in daytime too. Flies May–September. Widespread throughout the region. Larva is green with anterior false eye spot.

ELEPHANT HAWKMOTH *Dielephila elpenor* Wingspan 64mm
A beautifully marked moth with rather narrow wings. Forewings marked with pink and olive-buff. Hindwings bright pink with black base. Body olive-yellow with pink longitudinal stripes. Favours scrub, river margins and meadows. Flies May–August. Widespread and locally common throughout the region. Strange, snake-like larva has eyespots near head end.

HUMMINGBIRD HAWKMOTH *Macroglossum stellatarum* Wingspan 45mm
A familiar day-flying moth, often seen visiting garden flowers, using long proboscis to extract nectar. Forewings dark brown and hindwings mainly orange but with dark base and margin. Favours all sorts of open, grassy habitats. Flies June–August. Widespread and generally common throughout. Larva is pale green with pale longitudinal stripes along the sides.

WILLOWHERB HAWKMOTH *Prosperinus prosperina* Wingspan 50mm
An attractive moth with proportionately short wings. Forewings mainly pale green with broad dark green transverse band containing dark spot; margin ragged-edged and dark green. Hindwings yellow and brown. Favours open, flower-rich terrain and sometimes seen flying in daytime. Flies June–August. Widespread. Larva is brown and lacks tail horn that characterises the larvae of most other hawkmoth species.

DRINKER MOTH *Philodoria potatoria*   Length at rest 35–40mm
Wings yellow-buff with oblique brown line across forewing and two pale spots; wings held in tent-like manner over body at rest. Larva large, brown and hairy; feeds on grasses. Favours damp meadows. Flies July. Widespread but local.

LACKEY *Malacosoma neustria*   Length at rest 17mm
Wings are buffish-brown, forewings with two transverse dark brown lines; body and wing bases hairy. Larvae live gregariously and construct silken tents. Favours scrub. Flies July–August. Widespread but absent from hot dry areas.

PUSS MOTH *Cerura vinula*   Length at rest 35mm
Wings are greyish-white with dark lines along and between the veins. Body and wing bases are hairy. Larva is large and plump with a squat head and two whip-like 'tails'. Favours scrub and open woodland. Flies May–June. Widespread.

BUFF-TIP *Phalera bucephala*   Length at rest 30mm
Forewings mainly silvery-grey with dark lines that add to appearance of tree bark; forewing tipped with buffish-yellow patch, the effect resembling a broken twig. Favours woodland. Flies June–July. Widespread and locally common.

PALE PROMINENT *Pterostoma palpina*   Length at rest 30mm
Forewings conceal hindwings at rest; marbled grey and buff pattern and jagged margins create impression of tree bark. Favours scrub and open woodland. Flies May–June. Widespread but absent from hot dry regions.

PINE PROCESSIONARY MOTH *Thaumetopoea pityocampa*   Length at rest 17mm
Best known for large silken tents constructed in pine trees by gregarious larvae and their processional marching habits. Adult has grey-buff wings with dark brown lines. Favours pine forests. Flies May–July. Widespread and common.

BLACK ARCHES *Lymantria monacha*   Length at rest 22mm
Forewings white and beautifully patterned with black lines; hindwings (hidden at rest) grey-buff. Body banded pinkish-red and black. Favours wooded habitats. Flies July–September. Widespread and locally common.

GARDEN TIGER MOTH *Arctia caja*   Wingspan 60–70mm
At rest, creamy-white and chocolate-brown forewings conceal striking hindwings that are orange with dark spots; these are revealed when moth is alarmed. Flies July–August. Larva brown and extremely hairy. Widespread.

JERSEY TIGER MOTH *Euplagia quadripunctaria*   Wingspan 55mm
Best known in region for mass appearance at misnamed 'Valley of the Butterflies' on Rhodes where dry summer months are spent in this damp, wooded valley. Forewings dark brown with two pale transverse stripes; hindwings orange-red with dark spots. Flies July–August. Widespread.

RUBY TIGER MOTH *Phragmatobia fuliginosa*   Length at rest 22mm
Forewings dark ruby red and hindwings a variable shade of reddish-blue. Favours open woodland and scrub. Flies July. Widespread but absent from hot dry areas.

HEART AND DART *Agrotis exclamationis*   Length at rest 20mm
Forewings grey-brown with two dark markings, one streak-like, the other rounded and heart-shaped; grey hindwings concealed at rest. Favours all types of well-vegetated habitats. Flies June–July. Widespread.

FLAME SHOULDER *Ochropleura plecta*   Length at rest 18mm
At rest, forewings conceal pale hindwings and are reddish brown with a pale streak along the leading edge, behind which are black and white marks. Favours all types of well-vegetated habitats. Flies May–July. Widespread.

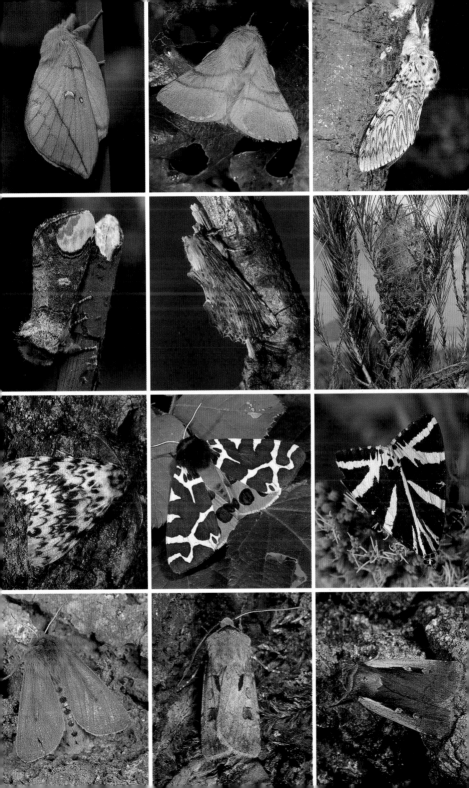

LARGE YELLOW UNDERWING *Noctua pronuba* Length at rest 25mm
Forewing colour variable, from marbled buffish brown to more uniform dark brown. Underwings orange-yellow with narrow black submarginal band. Found in all types of well-vegetated habitats. Flies June–October. Widespread and common.

BROAD-BORDERED YELLOW UNDERWING *Noctua fimbriata* Length at rest 25mm
Upperwing colour variable, from buffish brown to dark chestnut; darker specimens are usually beautifully marbled. Underwings orange-yellow with broad submarginal black band. Favours scrub and open woodland. Flies June–September. Widespread.

BROOM MOTH *Ceramica psi* Length at rest 22mm
Forewing ground colour variable, from chestnut to dark brown; always shows characteristic pale spot on hind edge of forewings. Favours all types of well-vegetated habitats. Flies May–June. Widespread but rather local.

CLOUDED DRAB *Orthosia incerta* Length at rest 15mm
Forewing colour variable but usually suffused with buffish purple and showing two pale-margined spots. Favours woodland, scrub and mature gardens. Flies February–April. Widespread and common.

HEBREW CHARACTER *Orthosia gothica* Length at rest 20mm
Upperwings marbled brown and grey with distinctive black mark that has semi-circular section removed as if by a hole punch. Favours woods, gardens and meadows. Flies February–April. Widespread and common.

EARLY GREY *Xylocampa areola* Length at rest 18mm
Forewings usually pale pinkish-grey but sometimes darker; subtly patterned with black markings. Favours open woodland and scrub. Flies February–April. Widespread but absent from hot dry areas.

GREEN-BRINDLED CRESCENT *Allophyes oxyacanthae* Length at rest 20mm
Forewings variable but usually beautifully marbled with green and brown; show curved white mark on trailing edge. Favours open woodland, scrub and gardens. Flies October–November. Widespread but absent from hot dry areas.

CRIMSON SPECKLED *Utetheisa pulchella* Length at rest 20mm
Forewings white but speckled with red and black dots. Hindwings white with black margin. Favours open flowery terrain including abandoned arable fields and meadows. Flies April–October. Widespread and common.

KNOTGRASS *Acronicta rumicis* Length at rest 20mm
Forewings grey marbled with black lines; show black-centred white spots and white submarginal line. Hindwings grey. Favours open well-vegetated terrain such as meadows. Flies June–August. Widespread.

GREY DAGGER *Acronicta psi* Length at rest 23mm
Forewing soft grey but with distinct black dagger markings. Favours wooded terrain, including orchards and mature gardens. Flies June–August. Widespread and locally common but absent from hot dry areas.

BIRD'S-WING *Dypterygia scabriuscula* Length at rest 20mm
Forewings mainly blackish-brown but with distinct pale patches near tip of trailing margin; also show pale buff patch on thorax. Overall effect produces good camouflage on tree bark. Favours woodland. Flies May–August. Widespread.

LIGHT ARCHES *Apamea lithoxylaea* Length at rest 25mm
Forewings usually pale straw-brown, suffused orange-buff towards the margin and with variable faint dark streaking. Favours all types of well-vegetated habitats. Flies June–July. Widespread but absent from hot dry areas.

SCARCE SILVER LINES *Bena prasinana*   Length at rest 17mm
Forewings leaf-shaped and green with two silvery white diagonal lines; underwings white in male and yellowish in female. Favours broad-leaved woodland. Flies June–July. Widespread throughout the region but rather local.

BURNISHED BRASS *Diachrisia chrysitis*   Length at rest 21mm
A stunning moth when in good condition. Forewings patterned with metallic golden scaling. Shows tufts of hairs when viewed in profile. Favours well-vegetated areas including meadows. Flies spring and autumn. Widespread.

THE HERALD *Sciolopteryx libatrix*   Length at rest 20mm
Wings often held flattened, giving moth triangular outline. Forewings have ragged margins; ground colour brown with patches of orange-red. Favours all sorts of well-vegetated habitats. Flies spring and autumn. Widespread.

THE SPECTACLE *Abrostola triplasia*   Length at rest 18mm
When viewed from head-on, shows distinctive 'spectacle' markings. Forewings grey with darker central band; shows pale tuft of hairs on thorax. Favours open woodland, scrub and meadows. Flies May–July. Widespread but local.

SILVER Y *Plusia gamma*   Length at rest 21mm
Forewings marbled grey with patches of brown and with distinct silvery white 'Y' marking. Shows tufts of hairs along back when viewed in profile. Often flies during the day in hot weather. Favours all types of vegetated habitats. Flies April–October. A strong migrant. Widespread and very common.

BEAUTIFUL GOLDEN Y *Autographa pulchrina*   Length at rest 21mm
Superficially similar to silver Y but forewings are marbled brown not grey and 'Y' marking is broken not complete. Favours open woodland, scrub and grassland. Flies May–July. Widespread and commmon.

PINE BEAUTY *Panolis flammea*   Length at rest 18mm
Forewings beautifully marked with orange, brown and grey; pale spot usually seen near leading edge. Favours pine forests. Widespread and locally common.

ANGLE-SHADES *Phlagophora meticulosa*   Length at rest 27mm
Forewings have ragged margin; leading edge is rolled in at rest. Forewing colour is variable but often olive-green or pale brown with pink and brown triangular mark. Favours all well-vegetated habitats. Flies March–November. Widespread.

LEOPARD MOTH *Zeuzera pyrina*   Length at rest 35mm
Forewings sparingly covered with white scales; these are often lost and wings can look almost transparent except for black spots. Body covered in white scales. Favours broad-leaved woodland. Flies June–August. Widespread but local.

PEBBLE HOOKTIP *Drepana falcataria*   Length at rest 28mm
An attractive species whose forewings have hooked tips. Wing colour buffish brown, the forewings with a dark spot and transverse lines. Favours woods and heaths. Flies May–June. Widespread.

LARGE EMERALD *Geometra papilionaria*   Wingspan 42mm
A beautiful moth but colours are brightest when newly emerged. Rounded wings are emerald green with transverse pale wavy lines. Favours heaths and broad-leaved woodland. Flies July–August. Widespread but local.

MAGPIE MOTH *Abraxas grossulariata*   Wingspan 38mm
Easily recognised by patterns of black spots and yellow bands on otherwise white wings. Often rests rather conspicuously on leaves during daytime. Favours woods, scrub and gardens. Flies July–August. Widespread.

MOTHS

EARLY THORN *Selenia dentaria*   Wingspan 45mm
Wings have jagged, irregular margins. Ground colour of wings varies from buffish-brown
to chocolate brown; forewings show three transverse dark lines and dark tip. Favours
scrub, woodland and gardens. Flies spring and autumn. Widespread.

LILAC BEAUTY *Apeira syringaria*   Wingspan 40mm
Resemblance to dead leaf enhanced by creased leading edge to forewing. Wings lilac-buff,
marbled with white and orange and with brown transverse line. Favours broad-leaved
woodland. Flies June–September. Widespread but local.

ORANGE MOTH *Angerona prunaria*   Wingspan 40mm
Attractive moth, male of which has orange-brown wings, those of female being yellowish.
Forewings of both sexes marked with numerous short, transverse lines. Favours woods
and heaths. Flies June–July. Widespread but local.

THE FOUR-SPOTTED *Tyta luctuosa*   Wingspan 23mm
Well marked moth with one white patch on each of the wings, which are otherwise brown.
Flies during daylight in sunshine but also after dark. Favours field and open woods. Flies
May–August. Widespread in W of region.

Dicestra sodae   Wingspan 35mm
Wings have pale brown ground colour with delicate darker markings and dark
kidney-shaped spot on forewings. Mainly coastal; larval foodplants include
prickly saltwort and various goosefoots. Flies May–June. Widespread.

SMALL RANUNCULUS *Mamestra dysodea*   Wingspan 30mm
Attractively marked moth with forewings patterned with grey and brown to give lichen-
like effect. Favours open country; larval foodplants include cultivars and wild species of
lettuce. Flies May–July. Widespread.

L-ALBUM WAINSCOT *Mythimna L-album*   Wingspan 35mm
Distinctive moth with straw-brown forewings marked with dark streaks and white 'L'
shaped mark. Favours open country; larva feeds on grasses. Flies May–July and readily
comes to light. Widespread.

THE ALCHYMIST *Catephia alchymista*   Wingspan 40mm
Often difficult to locate because dark wings afford resting moth good camouflage. When
disturbed, however, reveals striking white patch on hindwing. Favours open woodland.
Flies May–July. Widespread.

THE PALE SHOULDER *Acontia lucida*   Wingspan 30mm
Attractive moth with areas of white on head, thorax and base of forewings and on leading
edge of forewings. Flies during sunny spells and also after dark. Favours open habitats.
Flies May–August. Widespread.

PEACH BLOSSOM *Thyatira batis*   Wingspan 35mm
Attractive moth with forewings that are marked with pinkish spots and blotches. Favours
open woodlands and hedgerows; larva feeds on bramble leaves. Flies May–July and comes
to light. Widespread.

MUSLIN MOTH *Diaphora mendica*   Wingspan 40mm
Male has reddish buff wings, female white; both sexes have black spots on wings. Night-
flying male comes to light; female often diurnal. Favours open grassy areas and larval
foodplants include plantains. Flies May–June. Widespread.

DARK ARCHES *Apamea monoglypha*   Wingspan 50mm
Forewing colour variable but usually dark brown with jagged white lines and dark streaks.
Favours open grassy habitat; larva feeds on grasses. Flies May–September in several
broods. Widespread.

OTHER INSECTS

TREE CRICKET *Oecanthus pellucens*   Body length 20mm
Delicate, almost translucent insect. Wings held flat over body. Antennae very long and thin. Difficult to locate during daytime. At night, detected by soft, trilling call. Favours foliage of shrubs. Seen June–October. Widespread in E.

WOOD CRICKET *Nemobius sylvestris*   Body length 7mm
Tiny dark brown cricket with tiny forewings and no hindwings. Head shiny and dark and antennae long. Occurs among leaf litter in broad-leaved woods, especially beech. Seen as different stages in life cycle throughout year. Local.

FIELD CRICKET *Gryllus campestris*   Body length 24mm
An impressive cricket. Jet black in young instars but adults short yellow on wings and orange on hind legs. Head proportionately large and bulbous. Lives in burrows in short grassland. Male sings at entrance in spring. Widespread.

SCALY CRICKET *Mogoplistes squamiger*   Body length 10mm
Intriguing wingless cricket. Body rather flattened and partly covered in tiny scales. Favours stable shingle shorelines. Easily overlooked since it hides under boulders during daytime; discovered by turning stones. Widespread.

MOLE CRICKET *Gryllotalpa gryllotalpa*   Body length 40mm
Extraordinary insect, suited to burrowing lifestyle by front legs enlarged for digging. Body covered with velvety fur. Hindwings fully formed and can fly. Also swims well. Lives in damp grassland. Found all year. Widespread.

EPHIPPIGER *Ephippiger ephippiger*   Body length 35mm
Recognised by saddle-like plate that covers thorax. Colour variable but usually green or brown. Female has long, curved ovipositor. Male sings chirping *ti-zi* song. Occurs July–November. Favours scrub and vineyards. Widespread.

GREAT GREEN BUSH-CRICKET *Tettigonia viridissima*   Body length 46mm
Has proportionately long wings. Body colour mainly green although often shows brown dorsal stripe and brown on legs. Female has long straight ovipositor. Male's song loud and reeling. Favours scrub. Widespread June–October.

OAK BUSH-CRICKET *Meconema thalassinium*   Body length 15mm
Lacewing-like bush-cricket with slender green body; female has narrow, slightly upcurved ovipositor. Legs long and spindly. Mainly active at night and attracted to lighted windows. Favours broad-leaved woodland. Widespread July–October.

LONG-WINGED CONEHEAD *Conocephalus discolor*   Body length 17–19mm
Has slender body; bright green except for brown stripe on dorsal surface of head and pronotum; brown wings extend to tip of abdomen. Female has long, straight and brown ovipositor. Favours grasses and rushes. Widespread June–September.

GREY BUSH-CRICKET *Platycleis denticulata*   Body length 24mm
Body marbled grey-brown and tawny on back and flanks; underside of abdomen yellow. Female has upcurved ovipositor. Favours areas of short grassland. Widespread in W of region, July–October.

ROESEL'S BUSH-CRICKET *Metrioptera roeselii*   Body length 15–18mm
Body colour varies from green to brown but always shows pale margin to entire side flap of pronotum. Forewings reach halfway along abdomen. Favours damp meadows. Seen July–September. Widespread; absent from hot, dry southern parts.

Pycnogaster inermis   Body length 40mm
A robust, almost cylindrical bush-cricket. Pronotum flap neatly folded like sides of a box; 'V' shape cut into hind margin. Body colour green, marbled with brown. Favours scrub and maquis. Seen May–August. Confined to Iberian Peninsula.

ITALIAN GRASSHOPPER *Calliptamus italicus*   Body length 25–35mm
A plump, squat-bodied grasshopper; head flattened when viewed in profile and has pegs between front legs. Body colour marbled brown; some individuals show pale stripe running along sides of pronotum and wings. Inner surface of hind legs is flushed red. Male sings by rubbing jaws. Female larger than male. Favours grassland and arable fields. Seen July–November. Locally very common.

MIGRATORY LOCUST *Locusta migratoria*   Body length 50mm
A large and impressive grasshopper. Most females are marbled green and brown while most males are marbled buff and brown. Occurs in two phases: commoner solitary phase has swollen appearance to pronotum while gregarious phase pronotum more flattened and like other grasshoppers. Flies well and at speed. Favours scrub and grassland. Seen mainly June–November. Widespread in S of region.

EGYPTIAN GRASSHOPPER *Anacridium aegyptium* April 06 N. Cyprus Body length 30–50mm
Superficially locust-like. Adult has more uniformly grey-brown body colour and a pronotum that is distinctly ridged, like plates of armour; nymph is usually green. Head is rather bulbous and eyes are striped. Female larger than male. Flies well and at speed. Favours scrub, maquis and orchards. Can be found throughout year. Widespread in S of region.

RUFOUS GRASSHOPPER *Gomphocerippus rufus*   Body length 15–20mm
Recognised by rufous-brown body colour and antennae that are clubbed at the tip, the base of the tip being black and the tip conspicuously white. Male smaller than female but with more strongly clubbed antennae tips. Mature specimens of both sexes show red tip to abdomen. Favours calcareous grassland and warm, sunny sites. Seen July–November. Widespread but local.

COMMON FIELD GRASSHOPPER *Chorthippus brunneus*   Body length 18–24mm
A well-marked grasshopper. Body ground colour varies from green to shades of brown but always mottled and marbled with black and white. Pronotum shows strongly indented and sharply angled white line, bordered with black; black does not extend to hind margin of pronotum. Favours areas of short grassland with areas of bare soil. Seen June–October. Widespread and common.

HEATH GRASSHOPPER *Chorthippus vagans*   Body length 15–18mm
Similar to common field grasshopper but usually mottled grey; black wedge markings on pronotum reach hind margin. Usually dives for cover when disturbed instead of hopping away. Favours heaths and maquis. Local. Seen June–October.

MEADOW GRASSHOPPER *Chorthippus parallelus*   Body length 17–23mm
Both sexes have rather short forewings, which do not reach tip of abdomen, those of female being proportionately very short; hindwings absent. Body colour varies from pure green to pure brown and mixtures of the two; pink and almost black forms also occur. Favours grassland. Widespread, June–October.

NOSED GRASSHOPPER *Acrida hungarica*   Body length 45mm
Rather stick insect-like but hops well. Body slender and head elongated and forward pointed; legs spindly. Favours damp grassland. Widespread May–October.

BLUE-WINGED GRASSHOPPER *Oedipoda caerulescens*   Body length 15–25mm
Body colour marbled grey-brown, providing good camouflage on ground. When disturbed, flies well and shows conspicuous hindwings: bright blue with a black and white margin. Favours dry stony places and dunes. Widespread May–October.

RED-WINGED GRASSHOPPER *Oedipoda germanica*   Body length 15–25mm
Similar to blue-winged grasshopper but eye flashes on hindwings are bright red. Marbled grey-brown body colour affords excellent camouflage when resting on ground. Favours dry, stony places. Seen June to October. Locally common.

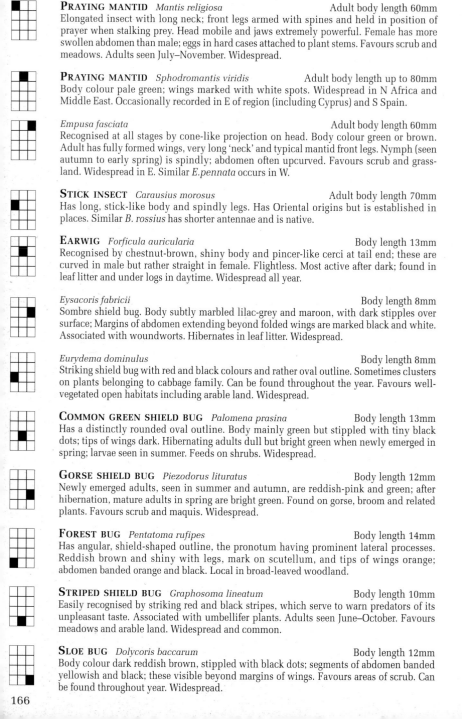

PRAYING MANTID *Mantis religiosa*   Adult body length 60mm
Elongated insect with long neck; front legs armed with spines and held in position of
prayer when stalking prey. Head mobile and jaws extremely powerful. Female has more
swollen abdomen than male; eggs in hard cases attached to plant stems. Favours scrub and
meadows. Adults seen July–November. Widespread.

PRAYING MANTID *Sphodromantis viridis*   Adult body length up to 80mm
Body colour pale green; wings marked with white spots. Widespread in N Africa and
Middle East. Occasionally recorded in E of region (including Cyprus) and S Spain.

Empusa fasciata   Adult body length 60mm
Recognised at all stages by cone-like projection on head. Body colour green or brown.
Adult has fully formed wings, very long 'neck' and typical mantid front legs. Nymph (seen
autumn to early spring) is spindly; abdomen often upcurved. Favours scrub and grassland. Widespread in E. Similar *E.pennata* occurs in W.

STICK INSECT *Carausius morosus*   Adult body length 70mm
Has long, stick-like body and spindly legs. Has Oriental origins but is established in
places. Similar *B. rossius* has shorter antennae and is native.

EARWIG *Forficula auricularia*   Body length 13mm
Recognised by chestnut-brown, shiny body and pincer-like cerci at tail end; these are
curved in male but rather straight in female. Flightless. Most active after dark; found in
leaf litter and under logs in daytime. Widespread all year.

Eysacoris fabricii   Body length 8mm
Sombre shield bug. Body subtly marbled lilac-grey and maroon, with dark stipples over
surface; Margins of abdomen extending beyond folded wings are marked black and white.
Associated with woundworts. Hibernates in leaf litter. Widespread.

Eurydema dominulus   Body length 8mm
Striking shield bug with red and black colours and rather oval outline. Sometimes clusters
on plants belonging to cabbage family. Can be found throughout the year. Favours well-
vegetated open habitats including arable land. Widespread.

COMMON GREEN SHIELD BUG *Palomena prasina*   Body length 13mm
Has a distinctly rounded oval outline. Body mainly green but stippled with tiny black
dots; tips of wings dark. Hibernating adults dull but bright green when newly emerged in
spring; larvae seen in summer. Feeds on shrubs. Widespread.

GORSE SHIELD BUG *Piezodorus lituratus*   Body length 12mm
Newly emerged adults, seen in summer and autumn, are reddish-pink and green; after
hibernation, mature adults in spring are bright green. Found on gorse, broom and related
plants. Favours scrub and maquis. Widespread.

FOREST BUG *Pentatoma rufipes*   Body length 14mm
Has angular, shield-shaped outline, the pronotum having prominent lateral processes.
Reddish brown and shiny with legs, mark on scutellum, and tips of wings orange;
abdomen banded orange and black. Local in broad-leaved woodland.

STRIPED SHIELD BUG *Graphosoma lineatum*   Body length 10mm
Easily recognised by striking red and black stripes, which serve to warn predators of its
unpleasant taste. Associated with umbellifer plants. Adults seen June–October. Favours
meadows and arable land. Widespread and common.

SLOE BUG *Dolycoris baccarum*   Body length 12mm
Body colour dark reddish brown, stippled with black dots; segments of abdomen banded
yellowish and black; these visible beyond margins of wings. Favours areas of scrub. Can
be found throughout year. Widespread.

Rhopalus subrufus   Body length 9mm
A rather delicate-looking bug. Body reddish, stippled with black, and with black on eyes
and abdomen. Favours open woodlands and meadows with scrub; often associated with
St John's-worts and thyme-related plants. Widespread.

FIRE BUG *Pyrrhocoris apterus*   Body length 10mm
Body mainly bright red with black head and legs, and black spots on thorax and abdomen.
Often congregates at food sources such as tree sap and seed clusters. Will also attack
defenceless insects. Widespread. Easiest to find May–August.

ASSASSIN BUG *Rhinocoris iracundus*   Body length 14mm
Body mainly orange-red but with black leg joints and dark hairs on head and thorax;
abdomen banded orange and red. Uses long, piercing rostrum to feed on body juices of
prey which comprise mainly soft-bodied insects. Often lurks on flowers. Seen
May–August. Widespread.

Lygaeus saxatilis   Body length 11mm
Another striking bug. Body mainly black but with bright red patches on head, thorax and
wings, and red bands on abdomen. Found on a wide variety of plants in warm, sunny
areas. Widespread.

CICADA *Tibicen plebejus*   Length 35mm
A large insect with a squat dark body and large, transparent wings. Nymph lives underground; empty skins sometimes found where adult has emerged. Male produces loud,
shrill song. Found in open pine forests, June–August. Mainly in S.

CICADA *Cicada orni*   Length 30mm
Body colour usually grey-green and wings long and translucent, with dark spots near the
margin. Newly emerged adults sometimes found near empty nymphal skins. Favours
open pine forests. Adults occur June–August. Song audible only to those with good hearing. Widespread in S.

CICADA *Cicadetta argentata*   Length up to 25mm
Body colour dark brown with reddish brown markings on thorax and between abdominal
segments; wing veins reddish brown. Newly emerged adults found resting on low vegetation. Favours open scrub. Adults seen June–August. Widespread. Similar *C. montana* has
mainly all-dark body, lacking reddish brown markings.

COMMON FROGHOPPER *Philaenus spumarius*   Length 6mm
Adult is oval in outline; colour variable but usually marbled brown. Jumps well. Nymph
is green and, like adult, feeds on plant sap; creates froth mass in which it lives. Common
and widespread, June–August. One of several similar species.

Cercopis vulnerata   Length 9mm
Distinctive, shiny red and black froghopper. Found resting on low vegetation and jumps
well to escape danger. Common and widespread in hedgerows, open woods and meadows; seen from May–August. Absent from especially hot, dry areas. Adult feeds on plant
sap; nymph found on roots.

Elymana sulphurella   Length 5mm
A delicate little leafhopper with greenish body and dark eyes; wings green but becoming
pale towards the tips. Favours dry grassy places. Widespread from June–October. One of
several similar species.

TERMITE *Reticulitermes lucifugus*   Length 2mm
Tiny soft-bodied insect that lives in large colonies in dead wood and stumps. Workers are
all pale with rounded heads; soldiers have dark brown elongated heads with protruding
jaws. Widespread but mainly coastal. Similar *Kalotermes flavicollis* has pronotum rectangular not rounded on rear edge.

ANT-LION *Myrmeleon formicarius*   Body length 30mm
Superficially damselfly-like insect with a long narrow body that is dark brown; has transparent wings and these are held in tent-like manner over body when at rest. Antennae are clubbed. Flight is weak and fluttery. Mostly active after dark and sometimes attracted to outside lights. Carnivorous larva is found in sandy soil and lives at bottom of conical pit into which ants and other insects fall. Adults are seen May–August; sometimes disturbed from vegetation during daytime. Widespread and common in warm, dry areas.

ANT-LION *Palpares libelluloides*   Body length 45mm
A large and impressive day-flying insect that bears a passing resemblance to a damselfly or dragonfly. Antennae are clubbed and eyes are dark and proportionately large. Thorax and abdomen are yellow-brown with a dark dorsal stripe. Wings are transparent but marked with brown blotches and spots. Larva lives among plant debris at soil surface and is a voracious predator of other invertebrates. Favours maquis, sand dunes and open grassland. Adult is seen May–September. Widespread and locally common.

THREAD LACEWING *Nemoptera bipennis*   Body length 12mm
An extremely elegant insect with a span across the forewings of 40mm. The hindwings form tail streamers, each 40mm long. Body is slender and marked with pale lime green and black. Eyes are dark and antennae are long and slender. Translucent forewings are blotched with pale lime green and black. Hindwing tail streamers are pale with three distinct dark bands. Favours stony slopes and open woodland. Flies April–August. Widespread in E Mediterranean. Similar species occur throughout the region.

Libelluloides coccajus   Wingspan 60mm
A distinctive insect, sometimes called a 'butterly-lion'. Head and eyes proportionately large and dark and body broad and black; antennae long and clubbed-tipped. Forewings mainly transparent but veins marked in black and showing black area at base of wing flanked by yellow patches. Hindwings have black base, broad central yellow band and transparent tip marked with black veins. Active in daytime and fast-flying, hawking for insects on the wing. Favours dry stony and wooded slopes and open woodland. Flies April–July. Widespread in warm dry areas, especially in S and W of region.

Libelluloides macaronius   Wingspan 60mm
Similar to *L.coccajus* but hindwings in particular narrower. Head large and marked with yellow and black; thorax yellow and black and abdomen bulbous and black; antennae long and clubbed-tipped. Forewings transparent but with yellow veins and dark stripe along length. Hindwings with black patch at base and black crescent mark near tip; otherwise transparent with yellow veins. Favours grassy slopes. Flies June–August. Widespread in E of region.

LACEWING *Chrysopa carnea*   Length 15mm
Familiar insect with green body, beady iridescent eyes and transparent, well-veined wings; these are held in tent-like manner over body when at rest. Antennae long and slender. Often hibernates indoors and body turns from green to pink. Larva is voracious predator of aphids and other small insects; camouflages itself by creating home from empty skins of prey items. Favours woodland and scrub. Widespread but absent from hot dry areas.

Osmylus fulvicephalus   Length 25mm
A relative of lacewings and a large and impressive insect. Has a dark body, reddish head, beady black eyes and long, slender antennae. Wings proportionately large and held in tent-like manner at rest; wings are mainly transparent with brownish hue and marked with dark spots. Favours open woodland, usually near water. Flies April–August. Widespread but absent from hot dry areas.

CLUB-TAILED DRAGONFLY *Gomphus vulgatissimus*   Length 50mm
Male has tip of abdomen swollen and both sexes show eyes spaced wide apart. Body of both sexes mainly black but with conspicuous yellow markings in immature specimens, these becoming lime-green when mature. Favours flowing water, including rivers with silt-covered beds; nymphs live part-buried in silt. Adults fly April–June. Widespread from S France and Italy eastwards but absent from Iberian Peninsula and most islands.

Gomphus pulchellus   Length 55mm
An attractive dragonfly with widely-spaced eyes. Thorax marked with lime-green and black while abdomen has yellow and black stripes along length; tip of abdomen is not swollen in male. Mostly associated with ponds, lakes and ditches and nymphs live in stagnant waters. Adult flies April–July. Usually wary of disturbance and quickly retreats from danger. Confined to Iberian Peninsula and S France but there locally common.

Onychogomphus uncatus   Length 55m
A striking dragonfly with widely-spaced blue eyes and a swollen-tipped abdomen in the male. Body colour mainly yellow but conspicuously marked with black bands on abdomen and black stripes on thorax. Favours fast-flowing streams and rivers with clear water. Adult flies June–September. Occurs Iberian Peninsula, S France and N Italy; locally common,

EMPEROR DRAGONFLY *Anax imperator*   Length 78mm
A large and impressive dragonfly. Male has sky blue abdomen, that of female being greenish blue; both sexes show dark dorsal line along length of abdomen. Extremely active and wary. Associated with lakes, pond and canals and characteristically hunts over open water, away from the margins. Nymph is large, predatory and has rounded outline to head. Adult flies May–August. Widespread throughout the region, including many islands.

HAIRY DRAGONFLY *Brachytron pratense*   Length 55mm
A compact and distinctive dragonfly, recognised by the coating of hairs that covers the thorax and abdomen of females in particular. Has relatively large eyes that meet for a short distance on the dorsal surface. Body of male mainly blue and black, that of female yellow, yellow-green and black. Favours canals, ditches and pools and nymph lives among plant stems. Adult flies March–July. Widespread, but absent from S Iberia, S Italy and most islands.

SOUTHERN HAWKER *Aeshna cyanea*   Length 70mm
A large, active species. Shows broad green stripes on thorax and abdomen with markings of similar colouration on abdomen, except for last three segments in male where markings are blue. Favours ponds, lakes and canals. Sometimes seen hunting away from water, especially during first few weeks after emergence. Flies June–October. Widespread from Iberia to Italy.

MIGRANT HAWKER *Aeshna mixta*   Length 60mm
A medium-sized dragonfly with eyes that meet for a considerable distance. Body of male is dark brown with blue markings while that of female is dark brown with yellow markings. Associated with ditches and pools with stagnant, sometimes brackish water. Adults often seen well away from water and are strongly migratory. Adult flies June–October. Widespread and common.

BROWN HAWKER *Aeshna grandis*   Length 74mm
Recognised, even in flight, by brown body and bronze wings. At rest, blue spots on second and third segments of male's abdomen can be seen. Found on well-vegetated ponds, lakes and canals. Patrols hunting territory around margins, which is defended against intruding dragonflies. Flies June–October. Occurs mainly N Spain, S France and N Italy.

BLACK-LINED SKIMMER *Orthetrum cancellatum*   Length 50mm
Mature male has blue eyes and black-tipped blue abdomen with orange-yellow spots on
sides. Female and immature male are yellow-brown with black lines on abdomen. Wings
of both sexes are clear, even at base. Skims low over water and uses regular perches over
bare ground beside water. Favours marshes, lakes and ditches, sometimes even where
water is brackish. Nymph lives part-buried in silt and debris. Adult flies June–August.
Widespread throughout the region and found on most islands.

KEELED SKIMMER *Orthetrum coerulescens*   Length 42mm
A rather small dragonfly. Mature male has powdery blue abdomen, the prunescence sometimes lost in places by wear. Female and immature male are yellow-brown with black
lines on abdomen. Wings of both sexes are clear at the base. Favours stagnant stream margins, marshy pools, ponds and lakes; nymph lives part-buried in silt. Skims low over
water and males defend territories against other males. Immatures in particular are often
seen far from water. Adult flies May–September. Widespread throughout the region.

FOUR-SPOT CHASER *Libellula quadrimaculata*   Length 45mm
A medium-sized, distinctive dragonfly. Adult abdomen is slightly flattened in both sexes
and is brown with orange patches on sides of each segment; tip of abdomen is tipped
black. Forewing has orange base and two black spots on leading edge, one in middle and
one near tip. Hindwing has orange and black patches at base and two black spots similarly placed to those on forewing. Favours marshes, ditches and pools and nymph lives part-
buried in silt. Adults hunt around water margins. Flies April–September. Widespread but
absent from some islands.

BROAD-BODIED CHASER *Libellula depressa*   Length 43mm
Has broad, flattened abdomen with wings that are dark brown at base. Abdomen of mature
male is sky blue with small yellow spots on sides of segments; in female and immature
male, abdomen is brown with conspicuous yellow spots on side. Favours ponds, canals
and marshes and nymphs live part-buried in silt. Adults patrol water margins and use regular perches from which aerial forays are made. Immatures in particular are often seen
well away from water. Adult flies May–September. Widespread throughout the
Mediterranean region.

COMMON DARTER *Sympetrum striolatum*   Length 36mm
Mature male has blood-red abdomen but in immature male and female this is orange
brown. Head and eyes of all individuals are reddish brown. Patrols water margins but
immatures in particular are often seen well away from water. Favours marshes, pools,
ditches and ponds. Nymph lives among pondweeds. Adult flies June–November.
Widespread and often very common. Red-veined darter *S.fonscolombii* is similar but has
yellowish base to wings; similar range and habitat preferences.

RUDDY DARTER *Sympetrum sanguineum*   Length 35mm
A small, delicate-looking dragonfly. Male has distinctive constriction towards front of
abdomen giving 'waisted' appearance. Mature male has blood-red abdomen but in immature male and female this is orange-brown. Frequently perches on waterside vegetation
with wings depressed slightly. Males defend territories against other males. Favours
marshes, pools and ponds, sometimes in rather stagnant water. Nymph is found among
pondweeds. Adult flies June–October. Widespread throughout the Mediterranean region.

Crocothemis erythraea   Length 42mm
Mature male has bright red body, including the head and eyes. Immature male and female
have yellowish-brown body although head and eyes are usually reddish. All individuals
show a yellow-orange patch at base of hindwings; most intense in mature male. Favours
stagnant pools and ditches, even where water is brackish. Flies May–November.
Widespread and common throughout the region.

LARGE RED DAMSELFLY *Pyrrhosoma nymphula*   Length 35mm
A distinctive, bright red damselfly; abdomen marked with black, more extensive on female than male. Associated with a wide range of freshwater habitats including ponds, lakes, canals and marshes. Flight rather weak and frequently settles on waterside vegetation. Flies April–September. Widespread; absent from many islands.

BLUE-TAILED DAMSELFLY *Ishnura elegans*   Length 32mm
Both sexes are easily identified by the mainly dark body with segment eight of the abdomen sky blue. Favours a wide variety of freshwater habitats including lakes, canals and marshes; nymphs will tolerate brackish or stagnant water. Flies March–September. Occurs from N Spain eastwards; absent from many islands.

COMMON BLUE DAMSELFLY *Enallagma cyathigerum*   Length 32mm
Male has blue abdomen with black markings; that on segment two usually mushroom-like, resembling dot attached to stalk. Green and black female is similar to females of other small damselflies; identified with certainty by ventral spin on abdomen segment eight. Flies May–October. Widespread; absent from most islands.

BANDED DEMOISELLE *Calopteryx splendens*   Length 45mm
Male has blue body with metallic sheen; smoky wings show a conspicuous blue 'thumbprint' mark. Female has green body with metallic sheen and greenish brown wings. Favours clean streams; sometimes also in ponds. Flies May–September. Widespread but absent from most of Iberia, S Italy and most islands.

BEAUTIFUL DEMOISELLE *Calopteryx virgo*   Length 45mm
Similar to banded demoiselle but wings of male more uniformly dark bluish brown with metallic sheen; those of female are duller than female banded demoiselle. Body of male is bluish, that of female being green; metallic sheen seen in both sexes. Favours fast-flowing water. Flies May–August. Widespread throughout.

EMERALD DAMSELFLY *Lestes sponsa*   Length 35mm
Slender damselfly with small wings. Body dark green with bronze metallic sheen; powdery blue dusting seen on ventral side of thorax and at base and tip of abdomen in mature individuals. Favours stagnant pools and marshes, usually in foothills. Flies June–November. Widespread; absent from Italy and most islands.

SCARCE EMERALD DAMSELFLY *Lestes dryas*   Length 35mm
Similar to emerald damselfly but dark marking on wings (pterostigma) is shorter and brown, not black. Body is dark green with metallic sheen; powdery blue dusting seen in mature individuals. Favours marshes, forest pools and ponds, usually in foothills. Flies June–November. Widespread; absent from most islands.

WHITE-LEGGED DAMSELFLY *Platycnemis pennipes*   Length 40mm
Has greenish body when immature but mature individuals of both sexes are mainly white to pale blue; each abdominal segment is marked with narrow black line. Middle and hind legs have enlarged white segments. Favours lakes and large ponds. Flies May–September. Absent from most of Iberia but widespread elsewhere.

SOUTHERN DAMSELFLY *Coenagrion mercuriale*   Length 35mm
A delicate little damselfly. Body mainly sky blue with black markings; that on segment two of abdomen resembles symbol of Mercury: trident shape with swollen patch on stalk and straight line at base. Favours gently flowing streams in marshy areas. Flies April–August. Widespread from Iberia to former Yugoslavia.

AZURE DAMSELFLY *Coenagrion puella*   Length 33mm
Male is sky blue with black bands along length of abdomen and black 'U' markings on segment two of abdomen; female is mostly black but with tip of abdomen blue. Favours marshes, canals and ponds and nymph lives in still water. Adult flies April–September. Widespread throughout the region.

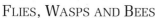

Volucella zonaria   Body length 21mm
A large and impressive wasp-mimicing hoverfly. The abdomen is marked with orange and black stripes and the front of the head is orange-yellow; the wings have a yellowish sheen. Favours wooded areas and scrub. Flies April–July. Widespread.

HORSE FLY   *Tabanus bromius*   Body length 14mm
A robust, biting fly. Abdominal segments show yellowish brown and black markings. Flies July–August and commonly found around cattle and other livestock; can inflict a painful bite. Carnivorous larva lives in damp soil. Widespread.

COMMON HOUSE-FLY   *Musca domestica*   Body length 8mm
Extremely common and widespread visitor to houses. Has red eyes and mostly dark body except for orange patches on abdomen. Close inspection reveals sharp bend in fourth long vein of wing. Attracted to rubbish where eggs are laid. Widespread.

FLESH-FLY   *Sarcophaga carnaria*   Body length 15mm
Adult has greyish body but shows chequered markings on abdomen; eyes red and feet proportionately large. Attracted to carrion and carcasses on which female gives birth to live young. Seldom ventures indoors. Common and widespread.

GERMAN WASP   *Vespa germanica*   Length 18mm
Has typical yellow and black wasp colours and markings; seen head on, face has three black dots. Grey, papery nest is built underground or sometimes in loft space. Collects large numbers of insects to feed its larvae. Widespread.

HORNET   *Vespa crabro*   Length 30mm
An impressive insect; the largest yellow-striped wasp in the region. Recognised by its size and by its tawny brown and dull yellow colours. Favours wooded areas; usually nests in dead trees. Colony active May–September. Widespread but local.

HONEY BEE   *Apis mellifera*   Length 12mm
Widely kept in hives for honey. In wooded areas, wild colonies nest in tree holes. Network of wax cells form comb in which honey is stored and young are raised. Adults often seen collecting pollen from flowers. Widespread.

CARPENTER BEE   *Xylocopa violacea*   Body length 22mm
A large and impressive bee. Recognised by its almost black body and wings that have violet sheen; eyes dark red. Nests is dead wood. Most active April–September. Favours open flower-rich terrain. Widespread and common.

SAND DIGGER WASP   *Ammophila sabulosa*   Body length 20mm
Favours sandy areas, including coastal sand dunes. Often seen dragging immobilised caterpillar larger than itself back to burrow in which eggs are laid; burrow entrance is then plugged with soil. Flies April–August. Widespread.

PAPER WASP   *Polistes gallicus*   Body length 10mm
Resembles a true wasp in miniature but has as proportionately smaller, hairless abdomen. Nest comprises exposed umbrella-shaped arrangement of cells, often suspended from a ceiling. Most active April–September. Widespread.

THREAD-WAISTED WASP   *Sceliphron spirifex*   Body length 25mm
Recognised by the long narrow 'waist' that forms the front half of the abdomen. Body mainly black but shows conspicuous yellow bands on legs. Nest constructed of mud and stocked with spiders. Favours dry sunny areas. Widespread.

HAIRY SAND WASP   *Podalonia viatica*   Body length 20mm
Recognised by extremely narrow 'waist; the rear half of the abdomen is swollen and egg-shaped. Body hairy and mainly black although front half of swollen part of abdomen is reddish. Nests in sandy soil and catches caterpillars. Widespread.

Scolia flavifrons Body length up to 30mm
Impressive and rather intimidating wasp relative. Body mostly black but with tow yellow bands on upper surface of abdomen, each band sometimes almost divided into two by central dark line. Favours bare sunny ground. Flies May–July. Widespread.

BUMBLEBEE *Bombus terrestris* Length 24mm
Female appears from hibernation in early spring and visits flowers on sunny days. Builds nest in burrow. Body blackish and furry with buffish yellow band at front of thorax and on abdomen; tip of abdomen buff. Widespread. Many similar species.

WOOD ANT *Formica rufa* Body length 10mm
One of numerous ant species found in region. Forms large colonies, these easily recognised as sizeable mounds of dry plant material. Reddish brown workers seen collecting caterpillars. Favours upland woodland clearings. Widespread.

Hoplia caerulea Length 10mm
An attractive chafer beetle. Male's body is covered with metallic blue scales; these are greyish in female. Favours lush vegetation in damp habitats. Adults seen June–August. Widespread and locally common.

ROSE CHAFER *Cetonia aurata* Length 18mm
An impressive beetle whose body is green with a striking metallic sheen. Active in sunny weather and often found visiting flowers on which it feeds. Adult seen April–October. Widespread and common. Several similar species also occur.

GREEN TIGER BEETLE *Cicindela campestris* Length 14mm
An active, ground-dwelling beetle of sandy places including heaths and dunes. Upperparts usually green with pale spots on wing cases; legs and thorax margins are shiny bronze. Adults seen April–July. Widespread and locally common.

Trichodes apiarius Length 14mm
A brightly coloured beetle; parts of body are extremely hairy. Wing cases marked with red and blue-black bands; body otherwise blackish. Often found on flowers, particularly umbellifers. Adults seen May–July. Widespread.

Strangalia quadrifasciata Length 20mm
Has a rather narrow body and proportionately very long antennae. Body mainly dark but wing cases marked with four yellow bands. Often found feeding on flower heads. Seen May–August. Favours wooded areas. Widespread.

OIL BEETLE *Meloe proscarabeus* Length 26mm
Produces pungent oil when alarmed. Has shiny, bluish body with small wing cases that do not cover swollen-looking abdomen. Favours flower-rich grassy areas. Adults are seen April–June. Widespread. Several similar species also occur.

7-SPOT LADYBIRD *Coccinella 7-punctata* Length 6mm
Distinctive little beetle with oval, domed body outline. Wing cases reddish-orange and, at rest, these show seven black spots; anterior spot embraces both wing cases. Adults and larvae feed on aphids. Adults seen March–October.

SCARAB BEETLE *Scarabeus sacer* Body length up to 30mm
All-black beetle recognised by broad thorax, spiky anterior end to body and habit of pushing balls of dung with its hind legs; these are eventually buried. Common on bare, often sandy ground in S. Several similar species occur across region.

Oxythyrea funesta   Length 12mm
Distinctive beetle with mainly dark body, upper surface marked with irregular white spots; metallic sheen to body sometimes visible. Usually found feeding in flowers; April–July. Widespread and often common.

GARDEN CHAFER *Phyllopertha horticola*   Length 12mm
Has dark green head and thorax and reddish brown abdomen. Adults often seen feeding in flowers and particularly active in sunny weather, May–July. Larvae feed on plant roots. Widespread and common. Several similar species in region.

WOODLOUSE *Porcellio sp*   Length up to 20mm
Terrestrial crustacean recognised by protective armoured plates. Has 7 pairs of walking legs. Commonly found under stones during daytime. Emerges after dark to forage on decaying vegetation when humidity is high. Several species in region.

TENBRIONID BEETLE   Length 25mm
A rounded-bodied beetle, commonly seen walking across coastal sands with purposeful but awkward gait. E of region only. One of a group of beetles associated with this habitat and with representatives across the Mediterranean.

GREAT SILVER BEETLE *Hydrophilus piceus*   Length 40mm
Large and impressive water beetle with streamlined outline. Appears silvery when seen underwater. Sometimes discovered after dark in late spring near water but on land, even on wet road surfaces. Widespread. Larva feeds on water snails.

GROUND BEETLE *Calosoma sycophanta*   Length up to 30mm
Large and intimidating ground beetle with metallic sheen to green, ribbed elytra. Active predator of shrub-dwelling moth larvae and usually encountered walking among scrub branches in search of prey. Widespread and locally common.

CENTIPEDE *Scolopendra cingulata*   Length up to 9cm
A formidable-looking centipede. Body long, flattened and orange-brown, comprising numerous segments, each with one pair of legs. Head possesses large fangs. Favours stony maquis and garrigue. Hides under stones during daytime. Widespread.

LONG-LEGGED CENTIPEDE *Scutigera coleoptrata*   Length up to 3cm
A distinctive centipede with a long, narrow body; each segment bears one pair of extremely long legs, the last pair being particularly long. Body colour grey-brown. Favours stony, sometimes cultivated ground. Hides under stones in daytime.

SCORPION *Buthus occidentalis*   Length up to 3cm
Has squat body comprising armoured cephalothorax, bearing mandibles and dorsal eye-spots, and segmented abdomen; last five segments narrow, curved over body and armed with sting. Broad pincers on front legs. Hides under stones in daytime.

SCORPION *Euscorpius sp*   Length up to 3.5cm
Cephalothorax and main part of abdomen are dark grey-brown; front legs, including long, narrow pincers, and last five segments of abdomen, including sting, are orange-brown. Hides under stones during daytime. Widespread in E of region.

FRESHWATER CRAB   Carapace width up to 5cm, but usually smaller
Carapace and legs are brown, marbled with buff; leg joints often reddish. Stalked eyes are black-tipped. Favours shady freshwater streams that do not dry up in summer. Usually hides under stones and overhangs in daytime. Local in E.

YELLOW-AND-BLACK FLAT-BACKED MILLIPEDE   Length up to 60mm
Has distinctive warning colours and two pairs of walking legs per segment. Most active after dark but often seen on cool days or mornings and evenings in spring. Favours open, stony ground. Widespread in E of region.

Argiope bruennichi   Female body length 20mm
Female abdomen is yellow and white with striking black lines. Carapace is silvery and legs are brown but marked with dark bands. Male is small and easily overlooked. Web has vertical thickened strands. Seen June–October. Widespread.

Micrommata virescens   Body length 10–15mm
Female has bright green and yellow abdomen; body otherwise dull green. Smaller male has red and yellow abdomen and otherwise dull green body. Favours lush vegetation in damp habitats. Seen April–July. Widespread but local.

Micrommata ligurina   Body length 10–15mm
Attractively marked spider with mainly green body; tubular-shaped abdomen is marked with white-bordered dark median stripe. Favours low, tangled vegetation, often in damp places. Widespread in W of region.

GARDEN SPIDER *Araneus diadematus*   Body length up to 12mm
Female larger than male. Ground colour of body and legs grey-brown or reddish. Abdomen has row of white dots down centre and transverse white streaks forming a cross. Favours well-vegetated habitats. Adults seen June–October. Widespread.

Araneus ceropegius   Body length up to 10mm
Female larger than male. Abdomen marbled with yellow, black and white; shows white stripe along length of abdomen with marbled yellow central line. Favours rank vegetation. Adults seen June–September. Widespread.

Thomisus onustus   Body length up to 10mm
Female much larger than male with colour uniform but variable: white, yellow or pink forms are all common. Abdomen has swollen, angular appearance. Invariably found on flowers. Favours heaths and maquis. Seen June–August. Widespread.

Misumena vatia   Body length up to 10mm
Colour of female is variable but usually white, creamy yellow or pale green; invariably found on flower that matches colour and catches insects that visit. Male is smaller and darker. Favours heaths and maquis. Common, May–August.

LADYBIRD SPIDER *Eresus niger*   Body length 10–15mm
Female is all dark with squat, flattened body. Smaller male has bright red abdomen with four black spots; legs marked with white rings. Female is mainly subterranean. Male wanders above ground in spring. Widespread in W of region.

Philaeus chrysops   Body length 8–11mm
Small but active jumping spider. Male has bright red abdomen with dark median band; colours of female's abdomen are more subdued. Favours open, stony ground. Seen mainly in spring and early summer. Widespread.

SHEEP TICK *Ixodes ricinus*   Body length up to 8mm
A familiar arachnid. Spider-like larvae are sometimes found crawling among vegetation or over clothing; attach themselves to mammals, including humans, and become bloated with blood. Widespread in open country.

Araneus alsine   Body length up to 10mm
Female has proportionately large, button-shaped abdomen that is pinkish orange and generally unmarked; male is similar but smaller and narrower-bodied. Favours shady vegetation. Widespread.

Eusparassus dufourii   Body length up to 15mm
Active, ground-dwelling spider. Entire body covered in dense coating of hairs, variously coloured to give marbled grey-brown, white and black appearance; shows marked with dark bands. Favours sandy ground with short vegetation. W of region.

SOWERBY'S SLUG *Milax sowerbyi*   Length up to 60mm
Body colour rather variable, from pale brown speckled with black to all dark; shows distinctive orange line along keel and orange rim to breathing pore. Burrows underground during daytime. Favours cultivated land. Widespread.

YELLOW SLUG *Limax flavus*   Length up to 100mm
A large, yellowish slug; body marbled and mottled with olive brown. Tentacles blue and mantle has thumbprint pattern of concentric rings. Favours gardens and cultivated land. Remains hidden during daytime. Widespread and common.

ROUND-MOUTHED SNAIL *Pomatias elegans*   Shell length up to 15mm
Shell bluntly conical and strongly ridged; mouth is rounded and can be sealed by circular plate that fits tightly when animal retracts inside shell. Favours open woods and rocky slopes on calcareous soils. Widespread but local.

STRIPED SNAIL *Cernuella virgata*   Shell diameter up to 20mm
Viewed from above, shell is neatly and tightly coiled with alternating spiral bands of brown and off-white; viewed from the side, shell is globular. Favours calcareous soils on dunes and grassland. Widespread but local.

Trochoidea elegans   Shell diameter up to 10mm
Distinctive shell is greyish white almost perfectly conical, the whorls being rather flattened; the mouth is rather flattened. Favours dry grassland and rather bare scree slopes. Widespread and locally common.

POINTED SNAIL *Cochlicella acuta*   Shell length up to 21mm
Has a rather narrow shell, rounded at the mouth end but narrowing and pointed towards the tip; shell colour variable but usually off-white with irregular brown markings. Favours calcareous grassland and dunes, often near sea. Widespread.

Theba pisana   Shell diameter up to 22mm
Viewed from above, shell is rounded in outline; seen from the side, appears rounded but smoothly flattened top and bottom. Shell colour variable but often pale brown with dark brown spiral stripes; larger of these sometimes contain pale spots. Favours dunes and dry grassland. Aestivates on plant stems. Widespread.

Eobania vermiculata   Shell diameter up to 30mm
Shell rounded from above but flattened when seen from side; mouth rather flattened. Favours cultivated land and grassland. Widespread and common.

GARDEN SNAIL *Helix aspersa*   Shell diameter up to 40mm
Shell rounded with large round mouth. Shell colour brown, marbled with grey and black; palest towards centre. Shell shows rough growth ridges. Body colour grey-brown. Favours cultivated areas and gardens. Widespread.

BROWN-LIPPED SNAIL *Cepaea nemoralis*   Shell diameter up to 21mm
Shell glossy but colour extremely variable and often striped; shell lip almost always dark brown. Favours open woods, scrub-covered slopes and grassland. Widespread in W of region.

GREAT POND SNAIL *Lymnaea stagnalis*   Shell length 45mm
A large water snail with a brown, conical shell. Sometimes moves along underside of surface film of water. Sausage-shaped gelatinous egg masses sometimes found on water plants. Favours pond, lakes and canals. Widespread and often common.

RAMSHORN *Planorbis sp*   Shell diameter up to 35mm
Several species of ramshorns occur in the region, varying in size but all with tightly spiralled, flattened shells. Young animals usually have smooth shells, those of older snails being ridged. Favours rather stagnant waters. Widespread.

COASTAL AND MARINE PLANTS AND ANIMALS

CORALLINE SEAWEED *Corallina officinalis*   Length up to 75mm
A hardened, chalky seaweed. Branches regularly and evenly to produce feathery, fern-like outline. Colour pinkish-red. Stem appears segmented and base is attached to rocks with chalky encrustation. Widespread on lower shore.

ENCRUSTING SEAWEED *Lithophyllum incrustans*   Forms extensive patches
Grows as chalky encrustation on rocks, these being irregular in outline, thickness and texture. Colour pinkish-red but often has powdery, chalky coating. Widespread and common in clear water from mid- to lower-shore.

LICHEN *Caloplaca marina*   Up to 7cm across
Forms a rounded encrustation which is bright orange-yellow in colour; surface of lichen is usually granular. Grows on rocks near the coast, always above the high water mark. Widespread and common.

LICHEN *Lichina pygmaea*   Up to 4cm across
A tufted, branching lichen that forms low, matted clumps that are blackish when dry and extremely dense. Grows on rocks at or below the high tide mark, often beside barnacles. Widespread and common.

BREADCRUMB SPONGE *Halichondria panicea*   Thickness up to 2cm
An encrusting animal that often forms large patches on rocky overhangs from the middle shore downwards. Colour rather variable but often bright orange. Spongy surface is pitted with openings through which seawater passes. Widespread.

BATH SPONGE *Spongia officinalis*   Up to 25cm across
Forms globular mass attached to rocks in coastal waters; usually easy to see when snorkelling. Surface pitted with pores. Colour variable but often green or brown when alive. Regrettably, frequently collected and killed for sale as bath sponge.

HYDROID *Corymorpha nutans*   Length up to 20mm
A curious relative of jellyfish that lives attached to rocks and compacted sand, sometimes in fairly shallow water. Body almost transparent; comprises thick stem and bulbous head that carries slender tentacles. Widespread and locally common.

HYDROID *Aglaophenia tubulifera*   Length up to 75mm
A curious marine invertebrate that resembles a stylised feather growing on a long stalk; forms large colonies attached rocks and empty shells in shallow to deep water. Egg-like reproductive bodies born on short stalks. Widespread.

PORTUGUESE MAN-O'-WAR *Physalis physalis*   Float length up to 30cm
Colonial jellyfish-like animal, recognised by large grey-blue float under which are suspended trailing tentacles (each an individual organism) of varying length and function. Pelagic but sometimes blown inshore. Has dangerous stinging cells.

JELLYFISH *Cotolorhiza tuberculata*   Up to 20cm across
Body comprises orange-buff domed 'umbrella' below which is suspended a stalk from which dense clusters of tentacles arise; some of these are swollen- and purple-tipped. Pelagic but sometimes carried into inshore waters. Widespread and common.

JEWEL ANEMONE *Corynactes viridis*   Height up to 2cm
More closely related to corals than true sea anemones. Forms colonies attached to rock on lower shore. Body colour usually pale buffish white but sometimes pale green; tentacles tipped with iridescent pinkish purple. Widespread.

PLUMOSE ANEMONE *Metridium senile*   Height up to 7cm
Body comprises smooth stalk tipped with dense array of slender tentacles; base is firmly attached to rocks. Colour variable but often creamy white or buff; pink and brown forms also occur. Widespread in W Mediterranean.

BEADLET ANEMONE *Actinia equina* Height up 5cm
Attaches itself to rocks in shallow water with sucker-like base. Colour variable but commonly seen as either red or green forms. Tentacles form ring around oral opening. Tentacles extended when immersed but, when exposed to air or disturbed, they are retracted and anemone becomes jelly-like blob. Widespread and common.

Anthopleura ballii Height up to 6cm
Elongate sea anemone with furrowed and warty, orange-pink column. Has around 50 pinkish-grey tentacles arranged around oral opening. Found in shallow water where rock overhangs provide shade. Widespread.

DAISY ANEMONE *Cereus pedunculatus* Height up to 12cm
Base is broader than the height of column. Body colour variable but usually dark olive-grey or yellowish; shows pale streaks and spots. Oral opening and tentacles have intricate markings. Attaches to rocks; also boulders buried in sand.

RAGWORM *Nereis diversicolor* Length up to 10cm
Predatory annelid worm of sandy substrates in shallow water. Has toothed jaws proboscis at the head end with tufts of hair-like chaetae on each of the 100 or so segments. Distinct blood vessel runs length of body. Burrows freely.

LUGWORM *Arenicola marina* Length up to 18cm
A burrowing annelid worm of muddy and sandy substrates in shallow waters. Holes and casts mark entrances to its U-shaped burrow. Segments in anterior half of body are swollen, posterior ones less so. Important food for many wading birds.

PEACOCK WORM *Sabella pavonina* Height up to 20cm
Intriguing marine annelid worm that lives in tube constructed of sand and mud particles glued together by mucus; these stand proud of substrate in which they are embedded. When immersed, radiating gills appear for feeding and breathing.

COMMON ORMER *Haliotis lamellosa* Length up to 7cm
Shell rather flattened and almost semicircular in outline with large respiratory holes; opening on underside very large. Upper surface is ridged and brown while underside has mother-of-pearl coating. Widespread and common.

SLIT-LIMPET *Emarginula elongata* Length up to 2cm
Viewed from above, shell has oval outline, radiating ridges and distinct slit down leading edge. Seen from the side, curved outline resembles the crest of a wave. Shell colour usually white to pale yellow. Widespread on rocky shores.

KEYHOLE LIMPET *Diodora italica* Length up to 4cm
Viewed from above, shell is oval in outline with ridges and furrows radiating from an off-centre keyhole-like opening. Shell colour varies from greyish white to grey-brown. Favours rocky shores. Widespread.

MEDITERRANEAN LIMPET *Patella lusitanica* Length up to 4cm
Conical shell is often almost symmetrical. Upper surface ridged and colour variable but usually greenish grey or brown. Under surface usually shows alternating light and dark radiating bands. Widespread on rocky shores.

LARGE TOPSHELL *Gibbula magus* Height up to 2cm
Shell conical and comprising about eight whorls. Shell colour grey-green but marked with reddish blotches in undamaged specimens. Found among stones and seaweeds in shallow waters. Widespread.

Gibbula varia Height up to 2cm
Shell conical, comprising six or so whorls. Shell colour variable but usually grey-brown with dark radial stripes. Favours rocks, often in deep water.

PAINTED TOPSHELL *Calliostoma zizyphinum*　　　　　Height up 25mm
Spiral shell forms an almost perfectly smooth-sided cone and comprises nine or so whorls. Whorls are marked with spiral ridges and colour is grey-brown with reddish patches. Mouth large and rounded. Found on rocky and shingle shores.

PHEASANT SHELL *Tricolia pullus*　　　　　Height up to 8mm
Spiral shell has an oval outline and comprises four whorls, the lowermost one being the largest. In life, large oval mouth to shell can be closed by an operculum. Shell colour reddish-brown; paler in worn specimens. Rocky shores.

SMALL PERIWINKLE *Littorina neritoides*　　　　　Height up to 5mm
A tiny shell with a large body whorl and mouth, and pointed spire. Shell colour dark grey-brown but sometimes has chalky encrustation. Found in rocky crevices in splash zone on rocky shores, often as aggregations. Widespread and common.

TOWER SHELL *Turritella communis*　　　　　Height up to 50mm
Distinctive spiral shell, which is long, narrow and pointed. Whorls are spirally ridged and shell colour is usually reddish-brown or off-white. Favours coasts with a sandy or muddy substrate. Widespread, particularly in E.

NEEDLE SHELL *Bittium reticulatum*　　　　　Height up to 15mm
Long, narrow shell that is sharply pointed. Surface of whorls is textured with spiral and lateral ridges and grooves. Whorls themselves have a concave outline. Favours shallow waters on rocky shores. Widespread, particularly in E.

COMMON CERITH *Cerithium vulgatum*　　　　　Height up to 60mm
Attractive and ornamented shell. Whorls spirally arranged to create pointed appearance; whorls show a spiral median furrow flanked by rib-like processes. Shell colour usually marbled brown and white. Favours muddy, stony shores.

ROCK CERITH *Cerithium rupestre*　　　　　Height up to 25mm
A pointed conical shell. Similar to common cerith but with more rounded outline; whorls lack that species' distinctly indented, spiral median furrow but are armed with rib-like processes. Favours rocky shores. Widespread.

COMMON WENDLETRAP *Clathrus clathrus*　　　　　Height up to 40mm
An elegant narrowly pointed shell. Whorls have a concave outline and have transverse ridges that give a sculptured appearance. Shell colour usually whitish, marbled with brown. Mouth is rounded. Favours sandy shores with rock.

PURPLE SEA-SNAIL *Ianthina janthina*　　　　　Height up to 15mm
Easily recognised by the shell's intense purple colour. Shell rather rounded and surprisingly fragile. In life, animal surrounds itself by a float of bubbles trapped in mucus. Pelagic, drifting at surface of sea. Sometimes washed inshore.

Cymbium olla　　　　　Length up to 110mm
Large and exotic-looking shell with a low spire and an extremely wide opening. Outer surface of shell is glossy orange-brown; inner surface of opening is paler. Locally common in southern Portugal only.

BONNET LIMPET *Capulus ungaricus*　　　　　Length up to 25mm
Shell is superficially cap-like, narrowing to a peaked curved-tipped apex. Outer surface of shell is ridged and sutured, and often coated with algae. In life, often attaches itself to other, larger shells. Widespread.

CHINAMAN'S HAT *Calyptraea chinensis*　　　　　Width up to 12mm
A flattened but almost perfectly conical shell comprising shallow, indistinct spiral whorls; these are more apparent when shell is viewed from below. Shell colour usually grey-brown. Found mainly on shingle beaches. Widespread.

SLIPPER LIMPET *Crepidula fornicata*   Length up to 30mm
Shell is oval in outline and domed in profile. Outer surface is grey-brown and ridged; inner surface has broad opening giving shell shoe-like appearance. In life, found in clusters: males on top mature to become females on bottom.

PELICAN'S-FOOT SHELL *Aporrhais pes-pelicani*   Height up to 40mm
A distinctive shell with spiral whorls forming a pointed apex; body whorl has four broad, flattened and pointed extensions bearing passing resemblance to a webbed bird's foot. Favours mud and gravel shores. Widespread.

NECKLACE SHELL *Natica alderi*   Height up to 15mm
A globular shell with a large body whorl and rounded opening; inner rim of opening has distorted appearance. Outer surface of shell is grey-brown, marbled with reddish streaks. Burrows in sandy substrates. Widespread.

EUROPEAN COWRIE *Trivia monacha*   Length up to 15mm
Bead- or bean-like shell that has a slit-like aperture along the length of the under surface; the rest of the shell is ribbed and extremely shiny. In life, mantle of animal covers most of shell. Favours rocky shores. Common.

KNOBBED HELMET SHELL *Cassidaria rugosa*   Height up to 130mm
A large shell, rounded or oval in outline. Shell comprises six or so whorls, the body whorl being the largest; all are marked with spiral ridges. Opening looks ear-shaped thanks to reflexed lips. Founds on gravel substrates in shallow water.

GIANT TUN SHELL *Dolium galea*   Height up to 150mm
A large and rather rounded shell, the body whorl representing the bulk of shell volume; whorls are marked with shallow, spiral ridges. Opening is rounded but with reflexed inner lip. Shell colour grey-brown. Lives in deep water.

STING WINKLE *Ocenebra ericacea*   Height up to 50mm
Shell is oval in outline but extremely sculptured and with distinct spiral ridges around the five whorls. Feeds by drilling holes in shells of oysters and related molluscs and then sucking out body tissue. Widespread in calm, shallow water.

MUREX *Murex brandaris*   Height up to 80mm
Distinctive shell. Main body of shell is rounded with a short, spiral apex, but whorls are armoured with spiral rows of long spines and long siphon channel extends from opening. A source of a purple dye favoured in the past.

MUREX *Murex trunculus*   Length up to 70mm
Overall outline of shell is oval but whorls are heavily ridged and ribbed; opening is oval with short siphon canal. Together with *M. brandaris*, often found discarded beside fishermen's lobster pots. A predator of smaller molluscs.

Pyrene scripta   Height up to 20mm
A smoothly elongate-oval shell comprising six or so whorls. Outer surface of shell is off-white but marbled with reddish-brown. Outer lip of oval opening is toothed. Found on rocky coasts. Widespread.

NETTED DOG WHELK *Nassarius reticulatus*   Length up to 30mm
Shell is oval in outline with a pointed apex; surface of the 7 whorls is neatly sculptured with ridges and ribs to give netted appearance. Opening is ear-shaped due to reflexed inner lip; outer lip is toothed. Under stones on muddy shores.

THICK-LIPPED DOG WHELK *Nassarius incrassatus*   Length up to 15mm
Shell is oval in outline, similar in appearance to *N. reticulatus*. Surface of the seven whorls is marked with ridges and ribs. Oval opening has pronounced thick outer lip; inner lip reflexed. Found under stones on muddy and rocky shores.

MOTTLED TRITON *Pisania maculosa*   Height up to 25mm
Smoothly oval shell comprising five whorls, the body whorl being the largest. Mouth is oval and outer lip is toothed. Shell ground colour is greenish-grey, marbled with reddish brown. Found on rocky shores. Widespread.

MEDITERRANEAN CONE SHELL *Conus mediterraneus*   Height up to 50mm
Unique and distinctive shell comprising shortly conical spire and elongate conical body whorl. Opening is slit-like. Shell colour yellowish-white, marbled with reddish brown. Found on silt and muddy shores. Widespread.

TUSK SHELL *Dentalium vulgare*   Length up to 50mm
A distinctive shell that is curved, white and tapering; resembles a miniature elephant's tusk. In life, found buried in sand in shallow water but often washed up in good numbers. Widespread.

NOAH'S ARK SHELL *Arca noae*   Length up to 80mm
Unusual bivalve mollusc. When two valves are held together, bears a fanciful resemblance to the hull of a boat. Outer surface ribbed and brown; inner surface white. Lives attached to rocks by means of byssus threads. Widespread.

Gastrana fragilis   Length up to 45mm
Bivalve mollusc with equal valves, each being oval in outline. Outer surface of shell is greenish-brown and marked with concentric growth ridges; inner surface is smooth and whitish. Burrows in soft substrates. Widespread.

PANDORA SHELL *Pandora albida*   Length up to 35mm
Bivalve mollusc, each valve being curved pear-shaped in outline; upper valve is flat while lower valve is depressed and trough-like. In life, found resting on soft substrates such as sand and silt. Widespread.

Spisula subtruncata   Length up to 30mm
Robust little bivalve mollusc, each valve being roughly triangular in outline with the outer margin curved. Outer surface with concentric ridges and bands of reddish brown and white; inner surface whitish. Burrows in soft substrates.

STRIPED VENUS *Venus striatula*   Length up to 40mm
Each valve is rather triangular in outline, the outer margin being curved. Outer surface is scored with concentric growth ridges and radiating bands of reddish brown and yellow-buff; inner surface white. Lives buried in sand. Widespread.

BEARDED HORSE MUSSEL *Modiolus barbatus*   Length up to 60mm
Has typical mussel-like outline and equal valves, each being fan- or wedge-shaped. Outer surface of shell is bluish brown and covered in bristly hairs; inner surface is smooth and whitish. Lives attached to rocks with byssus threads.

COMMON MUSSEL *Mytilus edulis*   Length up to 100mm
Familiar bivalve mollusc, which is wedge-shaped in outline. Outer surface is bluish black with concentric growth ridges; inner surface is smooth and bluish white. Lives attached to rocks in shallow water. Widespread and common.

QUEEN SCALLOP *Chlamys opercularis*   Length up to 80mm
Bivalve with typical scallop-shaped shell: outline is rounded with unequal basal projections; lower valve is flatter than upper one. Outer surface has 20 or so radiating ribs; colour variable but often pinkish or brown. Sandy shores.

VARIEGATED SCALLOP *Chlamys varia*   Length up to 60mm
A rather delicate-looking scallop. Shell outline is rather elongate-rounded with pronounced basal projection on one side only. Shell is marked with 28 or so radiating ribs; colour variable but often purplish brown. Widespread.

FAN MUSSEL *Pinna nobilis* Length up to 40cm
Large and distinctive, fan-shaped bivalve; the two valves are similar. Outer surface is brown and scaly; inner surface is smooth. In life, it is found upright and part-buried in sand or silt, attached by byssus threads to buried rock.

GAPING FILE SHELL *Lima hians* Length up to 25mm
Superficially scallop-shaped but outline curved, elongate and asymmetrical. Shell valves do not meet along concave edge and leave gaping slit. Outer surface of shell shows radiating scaly ridges. Attached to rocks with byssus threads.

THORNY OYSTER *Spondylus gaederopus* Length up to 100mm
Large bivalve with rather asymmetrical scallop-shaped shell. Upper valve flatter than lower one; both are covered with sharp spines. Outer surface reddish-brown; inner surface smooth and white. Attached to rocks with byssus threads.

SADDLE OYSTER *Anomia ephippium* Length up to 50mm
Bivalve with oyster-like appearance. Upper valve is thick, convex and marked with irregular concentric growth ridges on outer surface; lower valve is flat and thin with an indented opening. Attached to rocks and other shells with byssus threads.

EUROPEAN OYSTER *Ostrea edulis* Length up to 100mm
Bivalve with rounded, irregular outline. Outer surface of shell comprises overlapping, irregular plates with jagged margins; inner surface has mother-of-pearl coating. Upper valve flat; lower valve concave. On silt in shallow water.

PORTUGUESE OYSTER *Crassostrea angulata* Length up to 100mm
Bivalve with irregular elongate-oval outline; upper valve flat while lower valve is concave. Outer surface is greenish brown and with sculptured growth ridges. Attached to rocks and stones in shallow water. S Iberia only.

Topes aureus Length up to 30mm
Bivalve with irregular oval outline. Outer surface of shell is pinkish brown and beautifully patterned with dark brown zigzag markings; inner surface is pale and smooth, showing faint zigzag patterning. Burrows in soft substrates.

DOG COCKLE *Glycymeris glycymeris* Length up to 80mm
Attractive and robust bivalve with a rounded outline; the valves are equal. Outer surface is yellowish brown, marked with concentric growth rings and irregular dark lines; inner surface white and smooth. Burrows in soft substrates.

BANDED WEDGE SHELL *Donax vittatus* Length up to 30mm
Rather delicate bivalve, oval in outline but rather triangular towards hinge site. Outer surface whitish purple with radiating rays of yellow brown; inner surface bluish white. Burrows in sand. Widespread.

PEPPERY FURROW SHELL *Scrobicularia plana* Length up to 60mm
Bivalve with rounded-oval outline; the valves are equal. Outer surface is buffish brown and marked with concentric growth ridges; furrows between ridges often appear dark. Inner surface white and smooth. Burrows in soft substrates. Common.

THIN TELLIN *Tellina tenuis* Length up to 20mm
Delicate little bivalve with flattened, equal valves. Outer and inner surfaces variable in colour but often pink or orange; marked with concentric bands of light and dark. Burrows in sand. Widespread and common.

Tellina planata Length up to 40mm
Distinctly oval bivalve with flattened valves. Outer surface is marked with concentric growth ridges; colour variable but usually pinkish or yellowish but with olive-brown coating around margin. Inner surface white. Burrows in sand.

Actaeon tornatilis — Length up to 20mm
Shell is fragile and oval, comprising seven or so whorls, the body whorl being the largest. Shell colour pinkish brown but whorls marked with spiral pale band; opening slit-like. Living animal partly envelops shell. Sandy shores.

RAZORSHELL *Pharus legumen* — Length up to 120mm
Elongate bivalve with equal valves. Outline of shell is straight with sides gently rounded. Outer surface of shell is yellow-brown, often with worn paler patches; shell marked with concentric growth ridges. In life, burrows in sand.

CURVED RAZORSHELL *Ensis ensis* — Length up to 120mm
Elongate bivalve with equal valves. Outline of shell is distinctly curved. Shell colour mottled white and yellow-brown; shell marked with concentric growth rings. In life, burrows in sand in shallow water. Widespread.

POD RAZORSHELL *Ensis siliqua* — Length up to 200mm
Elongate bivalve with equal valves. Outline of shell is straight with roughly parallel sides along entire length. Shell colour mottled white and yellow-brown; shell marked with concentric growth ridges. Burrows in sand. Widespread.

Solenocurtus strigillatus — Length up to 80mm
Bivalve with equal valves; shell outline is oblong with rounded corners. Shell colour pale greyish-pink with paler radiating rays; concentric growth rings are conspicuous. Burrows in soft substrates in shallow water. Widespread.

SEA SLUG *Greilada elegans* — Length up to 40mm
Attractive, brightly coloured mollusc. Body is bright orange with intense blue-violet spots. Has branched gills midway along dorsal surface. Often found in shallow water with bryozoans on which it feeds. Widespread.

SEA SLUG *Polycera quadrilineata* — Length up to 30mm
Elegant mollusc. Body is mainly white but with prominent orange spots and streaks; tentacles on head, and those flanking the dorsal gills, are also orange-tipped. Found in shallow water. Widespread.

SEA SLUG *Berthella plumula* — Length up to 50mm
Delicate-looking mollusc with oval body that is yellow and slightly translucent. Body tissue surrounds fingernail-like white shell. Has two pairs of tentacles at head and gill on right side of body. Favours shallow water. Feeds on sea-squirts.

SEA HARE *Aplysia punctata* — Length up to 200mm
An intriguing slug-like mollusc with an elongate olive-brown body. Head end has two pairs of stout tentacles; has flaps of skin along dorsal side of body. Often seen moving in shallow water; exudes purple dye if disturbed. Widespread.

COMMON OCTOPUS *Octopus vulgaris* — Length up to 1m
Unmistakable mollusc with rounded body and large, conspicuous eyes. Has two rows of suckers on its long, flexible tentacles. Body colour can be varied at will by animal to reflect mood or serve as camouflage. Found on rocky shores. Widespread.

GOOSE BARNACLE *Lepas anatifera* — Length up to 40mm
Body of animal is protected by five translucent plates that are bluish white. Typically found in large groups attached to driftwood by 15cm long retractable stalk. Normally pelagic but often washed-up on exposed beaches after gales.

STAR BARNACLE *Chthalamus stellatus* — Shell width up to 10mm
Forms encrusting communities on rocks on exposed shores. Body of animal is protected by volcano-like shell comprising six calcareous plates. Central oval opening is sealed by four plates when exposed to air. Widespread.

SQUAT LOBSTER *Galathea strigosa*   Length up to 12cm
Distinctive crustacean with abdomen folded under carapace. Body is red but marked with blue lateral bands. Walking legs are proportionately long and spiny, the first pair being longest and having pincers. Found under stones on rocky shores.

COMMON LOBSTER *Homarus gammarus*   Length up to 40cm
In life, body is blue and only turns red when boiled. Defends itself with massive pincers. Has a scavenging diet. Large specimens found among rocks in deep water but smaller individuals are sometimes discovered in rock pools. Widespread.

BROAD-CLAWED PORCELAIN CRAB *Porcellana platycheles*   Carapace width 13mm
An extremely flattened crab with a rounded carapace and very broad pincers. Upper surface sandy brown and rather hairy; hairs trap silt. Underside white and porcelain-like. Found under stones where silt and debris collect. Widespread.

SPINY SPIDER CRAB *Maia squinado*   Carapace length up to 18cm
Carapace is oval-triangular in outline and covered in large spines; two prominent ones found between eyes. Walking legs long and spindly, the first pair bearing pincers. Found on rocky shores, from shallow water downwards. Widespread.

MASKED CRAB *Corystes cassivelaunus*   Carapace length 4cm
Distinctive crab with carapace much longer than it is broad. Pincer-bearing front pair of walking legs is extremely long. Sometimes found washed up dead on shore; in life burrows in sand, using long antennae to allow seawater to reach gills.

SWIMMING CRAB *Macropipus depurator*   Carapace length up to 4cm
Carapace rounded but leading edge is armed with sharp spines, three of which are seen between eyes. Last joint of fifth pair of walking legs is flattened to form a paddle. Body colour reddish brown. Found on sandy shores. Widespread.

EDIBLE CRAB *Cancer pagurus*   Carapace width up to 15cm
Recognised by 'piecrust' appearance to the margin of the carapace and its pinkish orange colour; the tips of the broad pincers are black. Small specimens often found among rocks in shallow water; larger individuals favour deep water. Common.

MARBLED CRAB *Pachygrapsus marmoratus*   Carapace width up to 3cm
Carapace typically rather square in outline and marbled with green, blue and brown. First pair of legs bear pincers. Associated with rocky shores and often found in shady crevices in vicinity of pools in splash zone. Widespread.

MEDITERRANEAN SHORE CRAB *Carcinus mediterraneus*   Carapace width up to 4cm
Body colour usually greenish or olive-brown; shows three blunt teeth between the eyes. Found among rocks and seaweed in shallow water. Scavenging diet. Common and widespread throughout the region.

HERMIT CRAB *Eupagurus bernhardus*   Body length up to 9cm
Body size difficult to determine since animal lives inside empty mollusc shell; shell exchanged for larger one as animal grows. Body colour reddish brown. Right pincer larger than left; used to block shell entrance when crab retreats inside.

COMMON PRAWN *Palaemon serratus*   Length up to 5cm
Often trapped in pools but difficult to spot until it moves because of transparent body; close inspection reveals array of purplish brown dots and lines. Has long antennae and toothed rostrum between eyes. Swims backwards.

CUSHION-STAR *Asterina gibbosa*   Diameter up to 5cm
Has five radiating arms projecting from otherwise pentagonal body outline. Upper surface is rough and usually blotched pinkish yellow and grey-brown; underside yellowish grey with numerous tube-feet. Found under rocks in shallow water.

RED STARFISH *Echinaster sepositus*   Diameter up to 20cm
An impressive and distinctive starfish. The body is small but the five radiating legs are long and narrow; these are rather rounded in cross-section. Upper surface of body is bright red and rather sculptured; underside has rows of suckered tube-feet. Found mainly on rocks; sometimes in shallow water but mainly at medium depths. Widespread and fairly common.

SPINY STARFISH *Marthasterias glacialis*   Diamter up to 30cm
Has rather slender arms, which are usually olive-brown in colour and bear larger and conspicuous pink spines; the radiating arms are often upturned at the tip. The underside is much paler. Sometimes occurs in comparatively deep water but can also be found in pools in relatively shallow areas. Favours rocky substrates. Widespread and fairly common.

BRITTLESTAR *Ophiocomina nigra*   Disc diameter up to 2.5cm
A delicate little invertebrate. Body comprises a central, flattened disc and five radiating and narrow arms; the surfaces of both the disc and the arms are rather spiny. Colour usually brownish but disc generally darker than legs. Legs often partly broken off and regenerating. Found by searching under rocks and among seaweeds on rocky shores. Widespread.

ROCK URCHIN *Paracentrotus lividus*   Diameter up to 5cm
A delicate little sea-urchin. Living animal is variable in colour but often green or reddish brown; body covered in spines, each of which is up to 3cm long. Dead animal loses spines to reveal rounded, flattened test which is chalky green with radiating rows of pores. Found on rocks with encrusting seaweeds, sometimes in shallow water but often deeper. Widespread.

HEART URCHIN *Echinocardium cordatum*   Length up to 8cm
A distinctive sea-urchin. Most familiar as the smooth, pale brown and potato-like test of the dead animal which is washed up on the tideline. In life, it is covered by a dense mat of fine spines, most of which are directed backwards. Burrows in sand and sometimes found near surface in shallow water. Widespread and common in suitable habitats.

PURPLE SEA-URCHIN *Sphaerechinus granularis*   Diameter up 12cm
An attractive sea-urchin. In life, almost spherical test is purple and covered in rather short, white-tipped purple spines. Dead animal loses spines and test becomes chalky pinkish purple; oral opening on underside of test is large and has ten radiating slits. Favours rocks with encrusting algae and sometimes found in shallow water. Widespread.

SEA-CUCUMBER *Stichopus regalis*   Length up to 30cm
Bizarre sausage- or cucumber-shaped animal with a slightly lumpy outline. Skin on upper surface is rough and leathery and body colour is usually yellow, mottled with white and brown. Underside is slightly flattened and has three rows of tube-feet used for movement Sometimes found in shallow water on sandy substrates but often in deeper water. Widespread and common.

RED SEA-SQUIRT *Halocynthia papillosa*   Height up to 5cm
An intriguing chordate animal; affinities with vertebrate animals only apparent in tiny, pelagic larva. Adult has flagon-shaped body which is reddish orange and attached to rocks and stones in shallow water. Conspicuous exhalent and inhalent pores allow the passage of seawater through body. Widespread.

STAR ASCIDIAN *Botryllus schlosseri*   Star diameter up to 5mm
Encrusting, colonial animal. Forms tough mats on shaded surfaces of rocks in shallow water. Individuals are arranged in star-like fashion around a common opening. Colour variable; usually seen as white stars on purplish background.

CONGER EEL *Conger conger*   Length up to 2m
Extremely muscular, snake-like fish whose skin lacks scales and is variable in colour. Favours rocky coasts, often in deep water but sometimes in shallow enough seas to be found when snorkelling. Hides in rock crevices. Widespread.

POLLACK *Pollachius pollachius*   Length up to 1m
Has cod-like appearance and lateral line that curves gently over pectoral fin. Body colour silvery grey, mottled with brown. Often seen in shallow water around jetties and rocky outcrops, sometimes in shoals. Widespread.

GREATER PIPEFISH *Syngnathus acus*   Length up to 50cm
Bizarre little fish with worm-like body and elongate, snout-like mouth. One of several similar species and best told by large size when adult and tapering, curved snout which is longer than the rest of the head. Among seaweeds and rocks.

THICK-LIPPED GREY MULLET *Chelon labrosus*   Length up to 50cm
Body has silvery grey appearance. Head is angular and mouth relatively small; lip of upper jaw is very thick. First dorsal fin has spiny rays. A common fish of estuaries and shallow, sheltered coasts. Widespread. Several similar species.

BARRACUDA *Sphyraena sphyraena*   Length up to 1m
An elongated, well-marked predatory fish. Head is long and tapering with powerful jaws and prominent teeth. Body is rounded with well-spaced fins. Often seen in shoals, patrolling over sandy substrates. Widespread and locally common.

BASS *Dicentrarchus labrax*   Length up to 15cm
A powerful, deep-bodied fish with spiky dorsal fins. When small, often found in shoals near mouths of estuaries and in sheltered coastal water. Larger specimens solitary off shingle or rocky shores. Body colour olive-grey with silver sheen.

BALLAN WRASSE *Labrus bergylta*   Length up to 40cm
Deep-bodied fish with proportionately large head. Body colour variable but often green or brown, marbled with reddish-brown; scales relatively large. Found among rocks and seaweeds in shallow water. Widespread and common.

CORKWING WRASSE *Crenilabrus melops*   Length up to 15cm
A beautiful fish. Variable colours and patterns but usually mainly blue, marbled with deep pink bands and lines. Favours clean, rocky coasts and usually easy to see in calm water daring among seaweeds in rock gullies. Widespread.

LESSER WEEVER *Echiichthys vipera*   Length up to 20cm
Usually lives part-buried in soft substrates with only upward-pointing mouth and eyes on top of head visible. Head is proportionately large and body tapering. Has venomous spine on gill cover. Often found in shallow water. Widespread.

SAND GOBY *Pomatoschistus minutus*   Length up to 8cm
Delicate-looking fish with a proportionately large head and narrow, tapering body. Usually lives part-buried in sand, hence eyes are on top of head. Body colour sandy brown with darker mottling on back and stripes on flanks.

GREY GURNARD *Eutrigla gurnardus*   Length up to 30cm
A distinctive fish with a tapering body and pectoral fins partly divided into three feeler-like rays, used in sensory detection. Usually found near rocky outcrops on muddy or sandy seabeds; sometimes near jetty piers. Widespread.

RED SCORPIONFISH *Scorpaena scrofa*   Length up to 50cm
A squat fish. The proportionately large head has spine-tipped flaps, spines on the gill covers being venomous. Dorsal fin also spiny and poisonous. Body colour reddish, marbled with brown. On sand, usually away from shore.

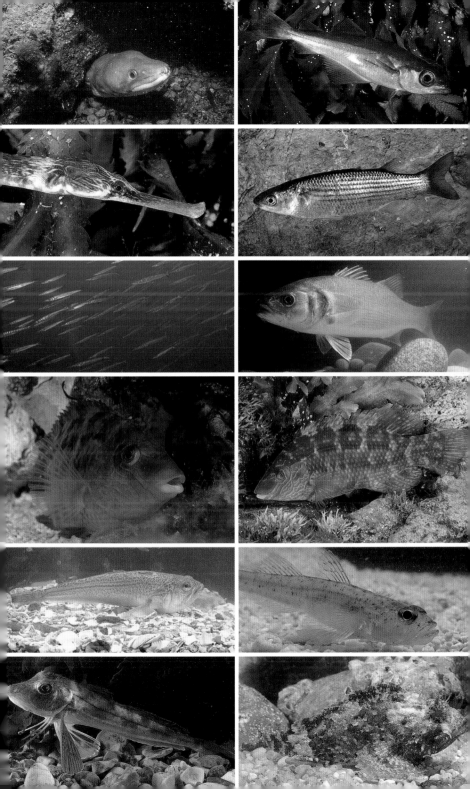

CORNISH SUCKER *Lepadogaster lepadogaster* Length up to 6cm
A strange-looking fish with a flattened, tadpole-like appearance and rather pointed snout. Body colour usually reddish and blotched. Has two bluish, eye-like markings on back of head behind true eyes. Clings to rocks on rocky coasts.

SOLE *Solea solea* Length up to 25cm
Flattened fish with oval outline and very short tail whose fin is not separated from dorsal and anal fins by any distinct tail stock. Lies with right-hand side uppermost and both eyes appear on that side. Widespread on silt in shallow water.

FLOUNDER *Platichthys flesus* Length up to 17cm
Flatfish with rounded-oval outline and long dorsal and anal fins separated from tail fin by distinct tail stock; dorsal fin starts near eye. Right-hand side lies uppermost; both eyes appear on that side. Shallow brackish and marine waters.

MORAY EEL *Muraena helena* Length up to 1.2m
Superficially snake-like fish. Body is elongated, muscular and blotched brown and yellow. Head is pointed and mouth is armed with sharp teeth. Dorsal fin starts behind head and runs entire length of body, fusing with tail fin; pectoral and pelvic fins absent. Lives in rock crevices. Widespread and locally common.

JOHN DORY *Zeus faber* Length up to 50cm
Distinctive and unmistakable fish. Seen from the side, body is almost circular and head and eyes are proportionately very large. Shows dark spot on side of body and dorsal fin that bears extremely long curved spines. Occasionally seen in shallow coastal waters. Widespread and locally common.

RED MULLET *Mullus surmeletus* Length up to 35cm
Has reddish upper body and paler flanks and belly. Head has steep profile, large eyes set on upper surface; mouth has two long barbels. Favours rocky and sandy substrates. Widespread and common. Similar M.barbatus has even steeper forehead.

COMMON DRAGONET *Callionymus lyra* Length up to 25cm
Slender tapered fish with scale-less body and upwards-pointing eyes. First dorsal fin has 4 spines, the first two of which are extremely long; second dorsal fin has spines of equal length. Body colour mottled brown but breeding male is marked with blue and yellow.

TUNA *Thunnus thynnus* Length up to 3m
Large and impressive fish with streamlined, muscular body and proportionately large head. Body is bluish above and silvery white below. Tail is narrow and curved and tail stock is keeled above and below. Favours open water and often found in large schools. Widespread but severely over-fished in many areas.

SEAHORSE *Hippocampus ramulosus* Length up to 15cm
Charming little fish, easily recognised by appearance alone. Head has a snout and a 'mane' which continues down back. Swims in upright posture using dorsal fin. Uses tail to grasp marine plants. Favours shallow waters, particularly among eel-grass. Widespread and common. Similar *H.hippocampus* occurs in similar habitats; distinguished by proportionately shorter snout and lack of 'mane'.

BLUE SHARK *Prionace glauca* Length up to 3m
A long and comparatively slender-bodied shark with a pointed snout, long curved pectoral fins. Dorsal fin is triangular and comparatively small and tail fin has relatively long upper lobe. Sometimes gathers in groups where feeding is good. Widespread and common. Similar mako shark *Isurus oxyrinchus* also occurs in region; upper lobe of tail stock only slightly longer than lower one. Great white shark *Carcharadon carcharias* is much larger and has a proportionately larger, blunter head; occurs locally in the Mediterranean.

ALEPPO PINE   *Pinus halepensis*   Height up to 20m
Mature tree has stout bole, often rather distorted trunk with reddish bark, and irregular crown. Needles are slender, paired and up to 15cm long. Cones are reddish, oval and about 10cm long. Widespread and often planted on dunes.

CALABRIAN PINE   *Pinus brutia*   Height up to 20m
Similar to aleppo pine with stout bole and often distorted trunk. Paired needles are up to 15cm long but thicker (1–2mm) than those of aleppo pine. Grows on coastal foothills in E of region, including Crete, Turkey and Cyprus.

STONE PINE OR UMBRELLA PINE   *Pinus pinea*   Height up to 30m
Has broad, flattened crown. Foliage dense and trunk tall and straight. Reddish grey bark of mature trees peels to reveal orange patches. Needles paired, twisted and up to 20cm long. Cones brown, ovoid and 15cm long. Widespread on sandy soils.

AUSTRIAN PINE   *Pinus nigra nigra*   Height up to 35m
Mature tree has tall, straight trunk and conical crown; bark grey-brown and rough. Paired needles 15cm long with toothed margins. Cones round and 8cm long. Widely planted. Similar Corsican pine *C.n.maritima* native to Corsica and Italy.

TROODOS PINE   *Pinus nigra pallasiana*   Height up to 25m
Mature tree has a straight thick trunk and a dense oval crown. Bark is grey-brown and rough, and needles are stiff, curved, 10cm long and borne in tufts. Cones ovoid and 7–8cm long. Endemic to mountains on Cyprus notably the Troodos range.

MARITIME PINE   *Pinus pinaster*   Height up to 32m
Mature tree has tall, rather slender trunk, often kinked low down; yellowish brown bark cracks into rectangular plates. Crown open and irregular in shape. Needles paired and 20cm long. Widespread on sandy soils, often near coasts.

MONTEREY PINE   *Pinus radiata*   Height up to 45m
Mature tree has domed or flattened crown and spreading lower branches that sometimes droop. Needles in groups of three, each 15cm long. Cones ovoid. Native to SW USA but widely planted in W of region, often as a wind-break.

GRECIAN FIR   *Abies cephalonica*   Height up to 35m
Mature tree has a narrow, conical shape. Prickly green needles are 3cm long and arise from all around the twigs. Cones are upright, elongate-oval and brown; length 15cm. Forms dense forests in mountains of Greece.

ATLAS CEDAR   *Cedrus atlantica*   Height up to 40m
Mature tree is domed and broadly conical in outline. Bark is grey and deeply fissured. Needles are borne in clusters on shoots; needle length up to 3cm. Cones are upright, 5cm long and ovoid. Native to N Africa but widely planted elsewhere.

CYPRUS CEDAR   *Cedrus brevifolia*   Height up to 20m
A flat-topped, open-crowned tree. Has large ascending branches leading to smaller horizontal lateral branches. Needles dark green, 2cm long and in clusters. Female cones oval, 6cm long and reddish. Native to Troodos Mountains on Cyprus.

NORFOLK ISLAND PINE   *Araucaria heterophylla*   Height up to 15m
Distinctive tree with palm frond-like side branches comprising upward-pointing shoots arising from a lateral branch. Stem tall and slender. Native to Norfolk Island near New Zealand but widely planted for its ornamental value.

MONTEREY CYPRESS   *Cupressus macrocarpa*   Height up to 35m
Spreading and often straggly-looking; domed crown. Leaves small and scale-like. Bark reddish. Male cones rounded, 5cm across and yellow; female cones rounded, 4cm across, green but maturing purple. Native to SW USA but widely planted.

COMMON JUNIPER *Juniperus communis*   Height up to 5m
Sometimes seen as a small tree but more usually as a compact shrub. Evergreen and aromatic. 2cm long needle-like leaves borne in whorls of three on three-angled twigs. Male cones small and yellow. Female cones 2cm across; green, ripening blue then black. Widespread on limestone and in mountains.

PRICKLY JUNIPER *Juniperus oxycedrus*   Height up to 12m
Evergreen shrub or small tree. Sharply pointed needle-like leaves in whorls of three; two pale bands on upper surface (one on common juniper). Female cones are rounded and ripen to red berries. Favours dry stony areas. Widespread.

SYRIAN JUNIPER *Juniperus drupacea*   Height up to 18m
Evergreen, tall and columnar when mature. Needles in whorls of three. Female cones rounded and 2cm across; green, ripening to brown. From N Greece eastwards.

PHOENICEAN JUNIPER *Juniperus phoenicea*   Height up to 8m
Straggly evergreen shrub or small tree. Young leaves are 1.5cm long, narrow and pointed and borne in whorls of three; mature leaves are scale-like and 1mm long. Female cones are 1.5cm across and rounded; green, ripening red. Coastal.

JOINT-PINE *Ephedra fragilis*   Height up to 1m
A low, much-branched shrub comprising narrow grey-green branches that snap off easily at the nodes. Leaves tiny and scale-like. Mature seeds borne in berry-like fruits. Often found growing on coastal cliffs and riverbanks. Widespread.

SWEET CHESTNUT *Castanea sativa*   Height up to 35m
Familiar deciduous tree with spreading branches. Bark silver in small specimens but brown and spirally fissured when mature. Leaves glossy, dark green and lanceolate, with toothed margins. Shiny brown nuts borne in spiky green cases.

WALNUT *Juglans regia*   Height up to 30m
Spreading tree with domed crown. Bark of mature tree fissured and grey. Compound leaves comprise 7–9 oval leaflets. Seeds (edible walnuts) are borne in green fruits. Native but widely planted and cultivated throughout the region.

KERMES OAK *Quercus coccifera*   Height up to 5m
Dense evergreen shrub or small tree. Leaves are glossy and holly-like, the margins with conspicuous teeth. Acorns are 1.5cm long and borne in spiny cups. Widespread on stony ground and a typical member of the maquis community.

HOLM OAK *Quercus ilex*   Height up to 30m
Domed evergreen tree, often branching from low down. Leaves are glossy and oval, the margins sometimes slightly toothed. Acorns are 2cm long and borne in scaly cups. Native but widely planted, especially in coastal districts.

CORK OAK *Quercus suber*   Height up to 20m
Domed evergreen tree, often branching from low down. Bark is corky and fissured in mature trees; often stripped, revealing red trunk. Leaves are oval and glossy. Acorns are 2cm long and borne in scaly cups. Native but also widely planted.

VALONIA OAK *Quercus macrolepis*   Height up to 15m
Domed, semi-evergreen tree with finely fissured bark. Leaves are oval, the margins with up to seven conspicuous teeth. Acorns are up to 2cm long and borne in scaly cups. Occurs from the Balkans eastwards. Locally common.

CYPRUS GOLDEN OAK *Quercus alnifolia*   Height up to 8m
Shrubby, much-branched evergreen tree. Leaves are leathery with toothed margins; upper surface glossy green, under surface with golden downy hairs. Acorns are 3cm long and borne in small scaly cups. Native to the mountains of Cyprus.

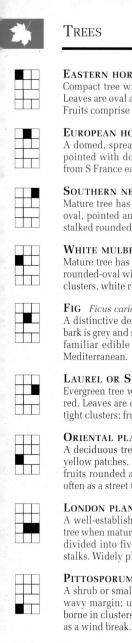

EASTERN HORNBEAM *Carpinus orientalis* Height up to 10m
Compact tree with dense ascending branches, a rounded crown and grey fissured bark. Leaves are oval and pointed with a double-toothed margin. Male catkins are yellow-green. Fruits comprise clusters of winged nuts. SE of region.

EUROPEAN HOP-HORNBEAM *Ostrya carpinifolia* Height up to 18m
A domed, spreading tree with many level branches when mature. Leaves are oval and pointed with double-toothed margins. The hop-like fruits are borne in clusters. Native from S France eastwards, mainly in hilly country.

SOUTHERN NETTLE TREE *Celtis australis* Height up to 12m
Mature tree has an open, spreading crown and a straight trunk with silver bark. Leaves oval, pointed and toothed, similar to those of stinging nettle. Flowers in May. Fruits are stalked rounded and solitary, red, ripening to black. Widespread.

WHITE MULBERRY *Morus alba* Height up to 15m
Mature tree has a domed crown and a thick bole to the trunk. Leaves are 18cm long and rounded-oval with a heart-shaped base. Flowers are spike-like. Fruits are drupes, borne in clusters, white ripening purple. Widely planted in region.

FIG *Ficus carica* Height up to 5m
A distinctive deciduous tree with an open crown and spreading, often curved, branches; bark is grey and smooth. Leaves are deeply lobed and up to 20cm long. Fruits ripen to form familiar edible fig. Possibly native in E of region but widely cultivated throughout Mediterranean.

LAUREL OR SWEET BAY *Laurus nobilis* Height up to 15m
Evergreen tree with ascending branches and a pointed crown. Bark is grey and twigs are red. Leaves are oval, dark green, leathery and aromatic. Flowers are yellow and borne in tight clusters; fruits are black berries. Widespread.

ORIENTAL PLANE TREE *Platanus orientalis* Height up to 30m
A deciduous tree with spreading branches. Bark is smooth and brown, flaking to reveal yellow patches. Leaves are 17cm long and deeply divided into pointed lobes. Flowers and fruits rounded and borne on drooping stalks. Native to E of region but widely planted, often as a street tree.

LONDON PLANE *Platanus x hispanica* Height up to 40m
A well-established hybrid between American and oriental planes. A tall and spreading tree when mature. Bark is brown, peeling to reveal pale patches. Leaves are 22cm long and divided into five palmate lobes. Flowers and fruits are rounded and borne on hanging stalks. Widely planted as a street and shade tree.

PITTOSPORUM *Pittosporum undulatum* Height up to 10m
A shrub or small tree with dense branches and foliage. Leaves are oval-lanceolate with a wavy margin; usually dark green, glossy on upper surface. Short, scented flowers are borne in clusters; the fruits are rounded. Native to New Zealand but widely planted, often as a wind break.

FIRE THORN *Pyracantha coccinea* Height up to 1.5m
Dense evergreen shrub; stems armed with thorns. Leaves oval, leathery and dark green. Five-petalled white flowers are borne in flat clusters. Fruits are bright red and berry-like; appear during winter months. Native in E; widely planted.

QUINCE *Cydonia oblonga* Height up to 7m
A dense, much-branched tree with a flat crown. Leaves are oval and 10cm long, with entire margins; they are smooth above but felted below. Pink, five-petalled flowers appear April–May and are 5cm across. The 3cm long pear-shaped fruits ripen to golden-yellow. Native to Asia but widely cultivated.

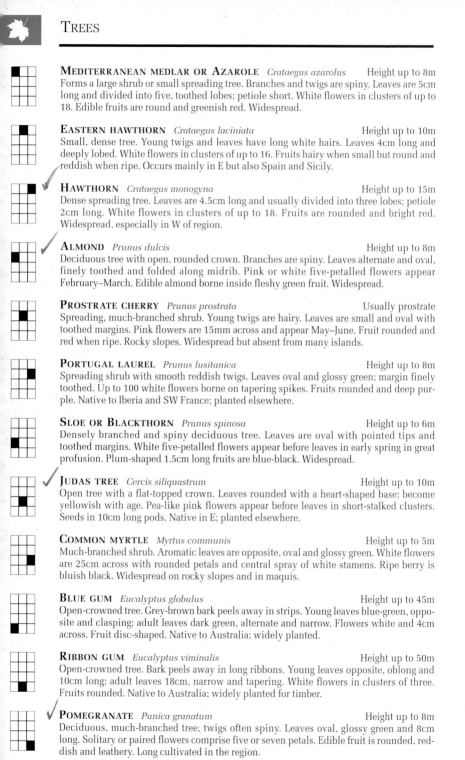

MEDITERRANEAN MEDLAR OR AZAROLE *Crataegus azarolus* Height up to 8m
Forms a large shrub or small spreading tree. Branches and twigs are spiny. Leaves are 5cm long and divided into five, toothed lobes; petiole short. White flowers in clusters of up to 18. Edible fruits are round and greenish red. Widespread.

EASTERN HAWTHORN *Crataegus laciniata* Height up to 10m
Small, dense tree. Young twigs and leaves have long white hairs. Leaves 4cm long and deeply lobed. White flowers in clusters of up to 16. Fruits hairy when small but round and reddish when ripe. Occurs mainly in E but also Spain and Sicily.

HAWTHORN *Crataegus monogyna* Height up to 15m
Dense spreading tree. Leaves are 4.5cm long and usually divided into three lobes; petiole 2cm long. White flowers in clusters of up to 18. Fruits are rounded and bright red. Widespread, especially in W of region.

ALMOND *Prunus dulcis* Height up to 8m
Deciduous tree with open, rounded crown. Branches are spiny. Leaves alternate and oval, finely toothed and folded along midrib. Pink or white five-petalled flowers appear February–March. Edible almond borne inside fleshy green fruit. Widespread.

PROSTRATE CHERRY *Prunus prostrata* Usually prostrate
Spreading, much-branched shrub. Young twigs are hairy. Leaves are small and oval with toothed margins. Pink flowers are 15mm across and appear May–June. Fruit rounded and red when ripe. Rocky slopes. Widespread but absent from many islands.

PORTUGAL LAUREL *Prunus lusitanica* Height up to 8m
Spreading shrub with smooth reddish twigs. Leaves oval and glossy green; margin finely toothed. Up to 100 white flowers borne on tapering spikes. Fruits rounded and deep purple. Native to Iberia and SW France; planted elsewhere.

SLOE OR BLACKTHORN *Prunus spinosa* Height up to 6m
Densely branched and spiny deciduous tree. Leaves are oval with pointed tips and toothed margins. White five-petalled flowers appear before leaves in early spring in great profusion. Plum-shaped 1.5cm long fruits are blue-black. Widespread.

JUDAS TREE *Cercis siliquastrum* Height up to 10m
Open tree with a flat-topped crown. Leaves rounded with a heart-shaped base; become yellowish with age. Pea-like pink flowers appear before leaves in short-stalked clusters. Seeds in 10cm long pods. Native to E; planted elsewhere.

COMMON MYRTLE *Myrtus communis* Height up to 5m
Much-branched shrub. Aromatic leaves are opposite, oval and glossy green. White flowers are 25cm across with rounded petals and central spray of white stamens. Ripe berry is bluish black. Widespread on rocky slopes and in maquis.

BLUE GUM *Eucalyptus globulus* Height up to 45m
Open-crowned tree. Grey-brown bark peels away in strips. Young leaves blue-green, opposite and clasping; adult leaves dark green, alternate and narrow. Flowers white and 4cm across. Fruit disc-shaped. Native to Australia; widely planted.

RIBBON GUM *Eucalyptus viminalis* Height up to 50m
Open-crowned tree. Bark peels away in long ribbons. Young leaves opposite, oblong and 10cm long; adult leaves 18cm, narrow and tapering. White flowers in clusters of three. Fruits rounded. Native to Australia; widely planted for timber.

POMEGRANATE *Punica granatum* Height up to 8m
Deciduous, much-branched tree; twigs often spiny. Leaves oval, glossy green and 8cm long. Solitary or paired flowers comprise five or seven petals. Edible fruit is rounded, reddish and leathery. Long cultivated in the region.

CAROB OR LOCUST TREE   *Ceratonia siliqua*   Height up to 10m
Much-branched evergreen with dense foliage. Pinnate leaves comprise 2–5 pairs of ovate, leathery leaflets, with notched tip and wavy margin. Flowers greenish and lacking petals. Flattened seeds in 20cm long pods. Widespread on stony ground.

CORNELIAN CHERRY   *Cornus mas*   Height up to 8m
Straggly deciduous tree with downy-tipped twigs. Leaves are ovate with a rounded base and pointed tip. Clusters of yellow flowers are borne on short stalks before leaves appear. Fruit is a bright red berry. Favours scrub, mainly in E of region.

DOGWOOD   *Cornus sanguinea*   Height up to 4m
Usually seen as a much-branched shrub. Winter twigs are dark red. Leaves are ovate with a pointed tip and 3–4 pairs of distinct veins. Creamy flowers in clusters. Clusters of black berries in autumn. Widespread on calcareous soils.

SILVER WATTLE OR MIMOSA   *Acacia dealbata*   Height up to 30m
Elegant tree with greenish-grey bark; twigs and leaves covered in silvery hairs. Leaves fern-like, divided into narrow leaflets. Yellow flowers borne in clusters of round heads. Seedpods long and flat. Introduced from Australia for ornament.

SYDNEY GOLDEN WATTLE   *Acacia longifolia*   Height up to 10m
Small tree with a dense crown. Leaves bright green, ovate-rounded and with distinct veins. Yellow flowers borne in 5cm long spikes. Seedpods long and straight, constricted between seeds. Native of Australia; widely planted.

SWAMP WATTLE   *Acacia retinodes*   Height up to 10m
Small tree with upward-spreading branches. Leaves are long and narrow. Yellow flowers are borne in clusters of rounded heads, each 5mm or so across. Pod is straight, constricted between seeds. Native of Australia; widely planted.

BLACKWOOD   *Acacia melanoxylon*   Height up to 40m
Imposing tree with a long trunk and grooved bark. Leaves are bright green, long narrow, and often curved. Creamy white flowers borne in clusters of rounded heads. Pods are long, flattened and twisted. Native of Australia; widely planted.

ALBIZIA OR PINK SIRIS   *Albizia julibrissin*   Height up to 12m
Small tree with spreading branches. Leaves fern-like and pinnately divided. Flowers pink and plume-like. Pods 15cm long and brown. Native of Asia; widely planted. Plume Albizia *A.lophantha* from Australia is similar but flowers yellow.

FALSE ACACIA OR ROBINIA   *Robinia pseudacacia*   Height up to 30m
Upright deciduous tree with an open crown; suckers freely. Pinnate leaves comprise 3–10 pairs of oval leaflets. White pea-like flowers borne in 20cm long pendulous clumps. Pods are 10cm long and smooth. Native of USA; widely planted.

CLAMMY LOCUST   *Robinia viscosa*   Height up to 15m
Small spreading tree. Pinnate leaves comprise 3–10 pairs of oval-elongate leaves; these turn bright orange in autumn. Twigs and leaf stalks are sticky. Pink pea-like flowers are borne in pendulous clumps. Native of USA but widely planted.

CHINESE WISTERIA   *Wisteria sinensis*   Length up to 15m
Vigorous climber, woody at the base. Pinnate leaves comprise usually 9–1 oval leaflets. Lilac, pea-like flowers borne in pendulous clumps, April–May. Pod is oblong and downy.

PAGODA TREE   *Sophora japonica*   Height up to 22m
Open-crowned deciduous tree with twisted branches. Pinnate leaves comprise 3–8 pairs of oval leaflets, hairy on under surface. Pale pink pea-like flowers in terminal clusters in autumn. Pods green and narrow. Introduced; widely planted.

HONEY LOCUST *Gleditsia triacanthos*   Height up to 45m
Has domed crown and spines on branches and trunk. Leaves pinnate (18 pairs of oval leaflets) or bipinnate (14 pairs of leaflets). Clusters of greenish flowers appear in June. Pods brown, flattened and 40cm long. Alien but widely planted.

FLAMBOYANT TREE *Delonix regia*   Height up to 15m
Deciduous, spreading tree. Bipinnate leaves comprise numerous narrow leaflets. Scarlet flowers, 8cm across, appear June–August and comprise five spoon-shaped petals. Pod up to 50cm long. Native of Madagascar but widely planted.

LEMON *Citrus limon*   Height up to 10m
Small, domed tree. Branches and twigs spiny. Alternate leaves are oval and glossy with a toothed margin. White, highly scented flowers appear early spring in leaf axils. Fruit the familiar, edible lemon. Widely cultivated throughout the region.

SWEET ORANGE *Citrus sinensis*   Height up to 10m
Small, rounded tree. Alternate leaves are oval and waxy. White, fragrant flowers appear mostly in May, borne in leaf axils. Fruit is familiar, edible orange; ripens in winter. Widely cultivated throughout the Mediterranean.

SEVILLE ORANGE *Citrus aurantium*   Height up to 10m
Small, rounded tree. Leaves are alternate, oval and waxy. White flowers are highly scented and appear mostly in May, borne in leaf axils. Fruit is the familiar large, bitter Seville orange; used for making marmalade. Widespread.

GRAPEFRUIT *Citrus paradisi*   Height up to 12m
Medium-sized, rounded and much-branched tree. Leaves are oval, 15cm long and have winged petioles. White flowers appear in spring, borne in leaf axils. Fruit is familiar edible grapefruit; ripens in winter. Widely cultivated.

TANGERINE *Citrus deliciosa*   Height up to 8m
Small, spreading and domed tree with spiny branches. Leaves narrow-oval. Small white flowers appear in spring, borne in leaf axils. Fruit is familiar edible tangerine; usually only 7cm or so in diameter. Widely cultivated.

TREE OF HEAVEN *Ailanthus altissima*   Height up to 20m
Has a high, spreading crown; suckers freely at base. Pinnate leaves comprise up to 25 oval, pointed and shiny leaflets. Greenish, strong-smelling flowers appear June–July, borne on spikes. Seeds reddish and winged. Widely planted shade tree.

PERSIAN LILAC OR INDIAN BEAD TREE *Melia azedarach*   Height up to 15m
Distinctive, open-crowned tree. Bipinnate leaves comprise numerous small, oval and toothed leaflets. Scented flowers comprise five or six narrow lilac petals and appear June. Fruits bead-like and pinkish yellow. Widely planted.

MONTPELIER MAPLE *Acer monspessulanum*   Height up to 15m
Small, domed tree. Bark grey and fissured and twigs reddish. Leaves are up to 17cm long and comprise three to five lobes. Yellow flowers appear in spring, borne in upright clusters. Fruits are winged. Native to Balkan uplands.

BRAZILIAN PEPPER TREE *Schinus terebrinthifolia*   Height up to 12m
Much-branched evergreen tree; also known as christmasberry. Pinnate leaves comprise up to 13 pairs of narrow leaflets that smell of pepper when crushed. Flowers are white, tiny and borne in clusters. Fruits are bright red. Native of S America; planted for ornament.

BOX *Buxus sempervirens*   Height up to 5m
Dense evergreen shrub. Young twigs downy. Ovate dark green leaves glossy on upper surface, paler below. Flowers small and green. Fruit green ripening brown. Local. Balearic box *B.balearica* is similar but leaves larger. Balearics and S Spain.

TURPENTINE TREE *Pistacia terebrinthus*　　　　　　　Height up to 10m
Straggly small tree. Twigs and foliage resinous. Pinnate leaves with up to 9 leaflets; leaf axis round. Greenish purple, petal-less flowers in clusters March–April. Fruits ovoid, red ripening brown. Widespread; scrub on calcareous soils.

MASTIC TREE OR LENTISC *Pistacia lentiscus* *N. Cyprus :* *in flower, March 2006*　Height up to 8m
Straggly evergreen shrub. Leaves and fruit aromatic. Pinnate leaves comprise 3–6 pairs of oval leaflets; leaf axis winged. Clusters of purplish petal-less flowers appear April. Fruits rounded-ovoid, red ripening black. Widespread; rocky areas.

PISTACHIO *Pistacia vera*　　　　　　　　　　Height up to 6m
Straggly deciduous shrub. Leaves either simple ovate or pinnate with up to 3 leaflets; leaf axis winged. Small green flowers, borne in spikes, appear in spring. Fruits have reddish skin; hard-cased edible nut inside. Widely planted.

FOXGLOVE TREE *Paulownia tomentosa*　　　　　　Height up to 15m
Deciduous tree with open, upright crown. Leaves broadly ovate with heart-shaped base and pointed tip. Spikes of pinkish-lilac, five-lobed, trumpet-shaped flowers appear before leaves in spring. Fruit is ovoid and green. Widely planted.

INDIAN BEAN TREE *Catalpa bignonioides*　　　　　Height up to 20m
Deciduous spreading tree. Long-stalked leaves are ovate with heart-shaped base and pointed tip; turn yellow in autumn. Bell-shaped flowers are 5cm long, white with purple and yellow marks. Fruit is bean-like and long. Widely planted alien.

STORAX *Styrax officinalis*　　　　　　　　　Height up to 7m
Spreading, deciduous shrub, covered in minute stellate hairs. Leaves ovate and 7cm long. White, pendulous flowers, borne in terminal clusters, appear April–May. Fruit berry-like, grey and hairy. Native from Italy eastwards; planted elsewhere.

MANNA ASH OR FLOWERING ASH *Fraxinus ornus*　　Height up to 24m
Deciduous tree with flattish crown. Bark and twigs grey. Pinnate leaves 30cm long with up to 9 ovate downy leaflets. Clusters of creamy, fragrant and four-petalled flowers appear with leaves in spring. Fruits have narrow wings. Widespread.

PHILLYREA *Phillyrea latifolia*　　　　　　　Height up to 15m
Dense evergreen with domed crown. Leaves ovate with dark green upper surface and pale vein; under surface pale. Clusters of small greenish flowers appear in leaf axils May–July. Fruit a blackish, rounded berry. Native but widely planted.

OLIVE *Olea europaea*　　　　　　　　　　Height up to 15m
Evergreen with gnarled, twisted trunk in old trees. Leaves narrow lanceolate, grey-green and 8cm long. Spikes of creamy four-petalled flowers appear July–September. Fruit is familiar olive; takes a year to ripen fully. Widely planted.

STRAWBERRY TREE *Arbutus unedo*　　　　　　Height up to 9m
Spreading evergreen with reddish bark. Leaves glossy, narrow lanceolate and 10cm long. Clusters of pendulous white flowers, each 9mm long, appear in winter. Fruits reddish orange and berry-like. Maquis, scrub and open woods, mainly in W.

EASTERN STRAWBERRY TREE *Arbutus andrachne*　Height up to 12m
Evergreen with reddish, peeling bark. Glossy ovate leaves are 10cm long; broader than those of A.unedo. Upright clusters of whitish flowers appear in spring. Fruit orange and berry-like. Native to E of region, from Aegean eastwards.

BANANA *Musa cavendishii*　　　　　　　　Height up to 3m
Herbaceous, tropical-looking plant. Leaves up to 2m long and 50cm across with conspicuous midrib; often split at margins. Long, pendulous spikes of flowers eventually form green berries from which bananas ripen. Widely cultivated.

CANARY ISLAND DATE PALM *Phoenix canariensis*   Height up to 20m
Mature plant comprises a tall, scarred and ridged trunk and a dense crown. Leaves are 5m or more long with up to 200 pairs of narrow leaflets. Creamy yellow flowers are borne in 2m long clusters. Fruits are 2cm long and inedible. Native to Canary Islands but widely planted in Mediterranean region.

DATE PALM *Phoenix dactylifera*   Height up to 35m
Similar to *P.canariensis* but mature plant is taller, more slender and with fewer leaves in crown. Leaves are 4m long with numerous pairs of narrow leaflets. Creamy flowers are borne in long clusters. Fruits are familiar, edible dates. Probably of Middle Eastern and North African origins but widely planted.

CHILEAN WINE PALM *Jubaea chilensis*   Height up to 30m
Mature plant has tall, 2m thick, scarred trunk. Crown has mostly erect leaves. Leaves are 4m long with split-tipped leaflets in two rows. Upright clusters of purple flowers are 1.5m long. Fruits yellow and fleshy. Native of Chile but widely planted in the region and a common ornamental plant.

CHUSAN PALM *Trachycarpus fortunei*   Height up to 14m
Mature plant has shaggy, layered appearance due to old leaf bases that persist and cover trunk; living leaves overlap one another. Leaves are 1m long and deeply divided. Yellow flowers are borne in spikes. Fruits are purplish and clustered. A native of China but widely planted for its ornamental value.

PETTICOAT PALM *Washingtonia filifera*   Height up to 15m
Trunk of mature tree is mostly hidden by fringe of hanging dead leaves. Living leaves are 2m long and deeply divided; white fibres link the divisions. White flowers are borne in 5m long clusters. Black ovoid fruit borne in hanging clusters. Native of USA but widely planted.

DWARF FAN PALM *Chamaerops humilis*   Height up to 3m
Grazing normally limits plant to a compact shrub; protected plants develop tall trunk. Palmate leaves are 1m across and deeply divided. Flowers borne on 30cm long spikes. Fruits rounded and yellow. Widespread native; mainly near coasts.

PELLITORY-OF-THE-WALL *Parietaria judaica*   Height up to 7cm
Spreading, downy perennial found on walls and rocky ground. Oval, long-stalked leaves borne on much-branched red stems. Clusters of flowers appear March–October, at leaf bases. Widespread, often in slightly damp situations.

HOP *Humulus lupulus*   Height up to 6m
Twining, square-stemmed climber of hedgerows and scrub. Leaves are divided into 3–5 coarse-toothed lobes. Male flowers in open clusters; female flowers are green cone-like hops that ripen brown and are harvested for beer brewing. Widespread.

BIRTHWORT *Aristolochia rotunda*   Height up to 15cm
Distinctive, rather upright perennial. Oval leaves have a heart-shaped base and clasp the stem. Mouth of tubular yellow-brown flowers is shaded by overlapping lip; flowers appear April–June. Favours stony slopes and open woods. Widespread.

CRETAN BIRTHWORT *Aristolochia cretica*   Height up to 20cm
Spreading, hairy perennial. Leaves heart- or kidney-shaped and short-stalked. Flowers tubular and curved; opening splayed and darker than outer walls of the tube; flowers March–April. Rocky, scrub-covered slopes. Crete and Karpathos.

Aristolochia longa
Hairy perennial. Leaves triangular with a heart-shaped base and a short stalk. Flowers greenish brown overtopped with a reddish-tinged lip. Favours stony ground, in open woods and scrub. Widespread.

COMMON NETTLE *Urtica dioica*   Height up to 1m
Has stinging hairs. Oval leaves toothed with pointed tips; in opposite pairs. Flowers March–July in pendulous catkins; male and female on separate plants. Widespread. Roman nettle *U.pilulifera* similar; female flowers in rounded heads.

MEMBRANOUS NETTLE *Urtica dubia*   Height up to 75cm
Upright stinging plant. Leaves oval with a heart-shaped base. Flowers February–May in pendulous catkins; male and female on same plant. Favours disturbed ground and often on wasteground or outskirts of villages. Widespread across region.

CANNABIS *Cannabis sativa*   Height up to 2m
Tall, aromatic plant. Source of hemp and cannabis drug. Leaves comprise 3–9 narrow lanceolate leaflets. Flowers borne in successions of rounded heads along side shoots; male and female on separate plants. Occasional on wasteground.

CYTINUS *Cytinus hypocistis*   Height up to 6cm
Bizarre-looking plant. Stems covered with overlapping, pinkish yellow scales. Clusters of 4-lobed yellow flowers appear March–June, each 10mm long. Favours maquis and garrigue, parasitic on white-flowered Cistus species. Widespread.

Cytinus ruber   Height up to 6cm
Similar to *C.hypocistis* but overlapping stem scales are red, not yellowish. Clusters of pale pink 4-lobed flowers appear March–June, each 10mm long. Favours maquis and garrigue, parasitic on pink-flowered *Cistus* species. Widespread.

CYNOMORIUM *Cynomorium coccineum*   Height up to 20cm
Above ground, appears as very short stem, covered with overlapping scales, supporting deep purple, club-shaped spike of densely packed tiny flowers; April–May. Parasitic on plants of salt-laden, sandy and rocky ground. Widespread.

SEA KNOTGRASS *Polygonum maritimum*   Spreading and usually prostrate
Blue-green, narrow-lanceolate leaves are leathery with inrolled margins; appear alternately along stems which are covered in papery sheaths. Clusters of 5-petalled flowers appear March–August. Coastal sand and shingle. Widespread.

Rumex bucephalphorus   Height up to 15cm
Upright perennial with narrow-oval leaves. Greenish flowers appear in spiked clusters April–August. Whole plant often turns red. Favours dry, sandy places, often on stabilised sand dunes. Widespread.

SEA BEET *Beta vulgaris*   Height up to 40cm
Sprawling perennial. Fleshy leaves are glossy green and oval with a heart-shaped base. Spikes of small, greenish purple flowers appear February–May. Favours coastal habitats including rocky cliffs and stabilised shingle. Widespread.

GLASSWORT *Salicornia europaea*   Height up to 30cm
Yellowish-green, fleshy annual; fancifully resembles a miniature cactus. Usually much-branched and looks segmented. Tiny flowers appear August–September at stem junctions. Typical saltmarsh plant. Tolerates seawater immersion. Widespread.

SHRUBBY GLASSWORT *Arthrocnemum fruiticosum*   Height up to 1m
Tangled, straggling perennial. Bases of stems are reddish and woody. Young shoots fleshy, bluish green and much-branched. Tiny flowers appear August–October at stem junctions. Found mainly on saltmarshes. Widespread but local in E.

SEA-PURSLANE *Halimione portulacoides*   Height up to 1m
Spreading perennial, all parts of which are mealy. Grey-green leaves are oval at the base of the plant but are narrower further up stem. Yellow flower spikes appear July–October. Grows mainly on saltmarshes. Widespread and common.

SMALL RED GOOSEFOOT *Chenopodium botryrodes* Usually prostrate
Fleshy plant with red stems. Leaves triangular with irregular margins; red on under surface when mature. Small reddish flowers appear in terminal clusters June–August. Favours salt-laden soils, especially saltmarshes. W of region.

FAT HEN *Chenopodium album* Height up to 1m
Upright annual with green leaves that look matt due to mealy coating; leaf shape varies from oval to diamond-shaped. Spikes of whitish flowers appear June–October. Widespread on disturbed arable land and wasteground.

ANNUAL SEABLITE *Suaeda maritima* Height up to 50cm
Much-branched annual that forms small clumps, which vary from yellowish green to reddish. Leaves are rather swollen and cylindrical. Tiny greenish flowers appear August–September. Favours saltmarshes and mudflats. Widespread.

SHRUBBY SEABLITE *Suaeda vera* Height up to 1m
Much-branched perennial shrub that varies in colour from yellowish green to reddish. Leaves are swollen and cylindrical; densely crowded on stems. Tiny flowers appear August–September. Favours coastal rocks and shingle. Widespread.

SPEAR-LEAVED ORACHE *Atriplex hastata* Height up to 50cm
Much-branched upright annual. Leaves are grey-green, triangular with pointed, spreading bases; mealy when young. Reddish yellow clusters of flowers appear in leafy spikes July–October. Favours sandy soils and often coastal. Widespread.

GRASS-LEAVED ORACHE *Atriplex littoralis* Height up to 50cm
Much-branched upright annual. Stems are reddish and leaves are green and narrow; mealy when young. Green flowers are borne in rounded clusters along leafless shoots. Mainly coastal, often on stabilised sandy shores. Mainly in W of region.

PRICKLY SALTWORT *Salsola kali* Height up to 50cm
Spiky-looking, prickly annual, typical of sandy beaches. Leaves are swollen, flattened-cylindrical and spiny-tipped. Tiny solitary flowers appear July–October in leaf bases. Mainly coastal and widespread throughout Mediterranean.

PIGWEED *Amaranthus retroflexus* Height up to 1m
Upright robust annual with hairy upper stem. Short-stalked leaves are oval or diamond-shaped; hairy on under surface. Dense clusters of small, whitish green flowers are borne in branched spikes, June–October. Widespread alien.

✓ **BOUGAINVILLEA** *Bougainvillea spectabilis* Height up to 10m
Familiar spiny climber. Dark green leaves are mainly opposite along stems. Small, pale flowers are surrounded by large purple, petal-like bract; appear February–October. Widely planted around houses and parks, and sometimes along roadsides.

HOTTENTOT FIG *Carpobrotus edulis* Height up to 50cm
Spreading, carpet-forming perennial. Lower stems woody and leaves fleshy, narrow tapering and pointed, and 3-angled. Flowers yellow and 8cm across; appear mainly April–July. Fruit fleshy and fig-like. Widespread alien, mainly coastal.

RED HOTTENTOT FIG *Carpobrotus acinaciformis* Height up to 50cm
Spreading, carpet-forming perennial. Stems woody at base and leaves fleshy, narrow and 3-angled; broadest in middle. Flowers reddish purple and 10cm across; appear April–July. Widespread alien, mainly coastal.

CORAL-NECKLACE *Illecebrum verticillatum* Prostrate
Charming, trailing annual of damp, sandy ground beside drying-up ponds; usually at inland and upland sites. Plant comprises reddish stems, which bear opposite, bright green leaves and clusters of white flowers, mainly May–August. Local.

ICE PLANT *Mesembryanthemum crystallinum* Prostrate
Mat-forming annual covered with crystalline hairs. Leaves oval and mostly unstalked. Flowers pale yellow and 25–30mm across; appear May–August. Favours bare coastal ground, often on saltmarshes. Widespread as far W as Greece.

Mesembryanthemum nodiflorum Prostrate
Mat-forming plant covered with small woolly-crystalline hairs. Leaves narrow and fleshy. Flowers whitish and 25–30mm across; appear April–August. Found near the coast among rocks and on sandy soils. Widespread.

BALEARIC SANDWORT *Arenaria balearica* Mainly prostrate
Mat-forming perennial comprising masses of stems bearing small oval leaves. Flowers white and 6–7mm across with petals not notched; borne on slender upright stems April–July. Grows among rocks on Balearics, Corsica, Sardinia and Sicily.

CRETAN MOUSE-EAR *Cerastium scaposum* Mainly prostrate
Creeping mat-forming plant with stems often reddish and leaves oval and hairy. Flowers white and 10mm across, with notched petals; borne on upright stems March–June. Favours rocky places on limestone. Crete only.

SNOW-IN-SUMMER *Cerastium tomentosum* Height up to 6cm but mainly prostrate
Mat-forming perennial covered in greyish woolly hairs. Leaves narrow with inrolled margins. Flowers white and 20–30mm across with notched petals; appear April–June. Favours rocky ground. Native to Italy but naturalised elsewhere.

STICKY MOUSE-EAR *Cerastium glomeratum* Height up to 40cm
Stickily-hairy annual. Leaves are pointed-oval and borne in opposite pairs. The white, 5-petalled flowers are 10–15mm across and are carried in clustered heads; appear April–October. Widespread on bare ground throughout the region.

COMMON CHICKWEED *Stellaria media* Height up to 30cm
Common annual of disturbed ground, including gardens, flower beds and arable land. Often prostrate and spreading. Leaves oval, fresh green and in opposite pairs; upper leaves unstalked. White flowers area 5–10mm across; seen all year. Widespread.

PARONYCHIA *Paronychia argentea* Prostrate
Mat-forming plant with reddish stems and narrow tapering leaves in opposite pairs. Tiny flowers are borne in rounded clusters comprising mainly silvery bracts; appear January–July. Favours bare ground such as sand dunes. Widespread.

GREATER SEA-SPURREY *Spergularia media* Height up to 30cm
Straggly, trailing perennial, often found growing through other vegetation. Stems reddish and leaves narrow and borne in tufts at stem nodes. Flowers pinkish-purple, 5-petalled and 10mm across; March–June. Salt-laden soils. Widespread.

CORNCOCKLE *Agrostemma githago* Height up to 70cm
Upright plant with narrow, grass-like leaves. Flowers comprise five reddish-pink petals and long, narrow radiating sepals; appear May–August. Formerly much more widespread in wheat fields than today; now rather scarce due to herbicides.

✓ **CARTHUSIAN PINK** *Dianthus carthusianorum* Height up to 60cm
Upright perennial with narrow leaves. Flowers comprise five pinkish red petals with jagged margins; borne in clusters above greenish brown bracts April–July. Favours dry, grassy places. Local, mainly in upland areas.

MONTPELIER PINK *Dianthus monspesselanus* Height up to 50cm
Upright, clump-forming perennial with narrow leaves. Fragrant flowers comprise five pink petals with ragged margins; appear March–May. Favours rocky places, usually in upland areas. Local, mainly Italy and France.

Silene colorata   Height up to 30cm
Upright annual with downy, oval leaves; stalked at base. Flowers usually pink but some-times white, with five deeply notched petals and club-shaped calyx; appear February–May. Abandoned arable land and sandy soil. Widespread and common.

SMALL-FLOWERED CATCHFLY *Silene gallica*   Height up to 20cm
Upright, branched and stickily-hairy annual with narrow-oval leaves. Flowers 7–10mm across and white, pink or white with a red centre; appear March–May. Favours arable land and sandy soil. Widespread throughout the region.

ITALIAN CATCHFLY *Silene italica*   Height up to 50cm
Upright perennial; upper parts sticky. Leaves grey-green, hairy and elliptical. Flowers comprise five white petals, each divided into two lobes; inrolled during day but unfurl in evening. Flowers April–July. Stony arable land. Widespread.

BLADDER CAMPION *Silene vulgaris*   Height up to 50cm
Upright perennial with oval, slightly fleshy leaves. Flowers 30–35mm across with five white petals, each deeply notched; appear March–July. Calyx tube inflated. Favours arable ground and stony soil. Widespread and common.

WHITE CAMPION *Silene alba*   Height up to 70cm
Upright stickily-hairy perennial. Leaves oval and stalked. Flowers 20–30mm across, white and 5-petalled, each deeply notched; appear March–June. Favours disturbed arable land. Widespread.

SAND CATCHFLY *Silene conica*   Height up to 20cm
Upright, stickily-hairy annual with lanceolate leaves. Flowers pinkish and 5mm across, with five slightly notched petals; appear March–June. Favours sandy ground near the sea, often on stabilised sand dunes. Widespread.

KOHLRAUSCHIA *Kohlrauschia velutina*   Height up to 20cm
Slender, upright annual or biennial with narrow, pointed leaves. Flowers 8mm across with five petals, each lobed and with central red veins; one flower opens at a time, in suc-cession February–May. Stony ground and garrigue. Widespread.

LEONTICE *Leontice leontopetalum*   Height up to 50cm
Branched perennial with grey-green leaves variably divided into oval lobes. Flowers yel-low, up to 15mm across with 6–8 petals; borne in heads, February–April. Fruit inflated. Favours disturbed arable land. E of region only.

STINKING HELLEBORE *Helleborus foetidus*   Height up 70cm
Robust strong-smelling perennial. Leaves divided into 7–10 toothed lobes; lower ones persist over winter. Green, purple-rimmed and bell-shaped flowers, 15–20mm across, appear January–May. Woods on Balearics, Corsica, Sardinia and Sicily.

Helleborus cyclophyllus   Height up to 70cm
Robust perennial with leaves divided into 5–9 toothed leaflets that are hairy below; leaves do not persist over winter. Leaves yellow and cup-shaped, 40–50mm across; appear February–May. Wooded slopes in mainland Balkans only.

Helleborus lividus   Height up to 60cm
Robust, hairless perennial. Leaves divided into three toothed or untoothed leaflets; veined and marbled with red. Flowers pinkish-yellow, cup-shaped and 40–50mm across; appear November–April. Wooded slopes in Balearics.

FRAGRANT CLEMATIS *Clematis flammula*   Height up to 5m
Woody, deciduous climber. Leaves bipinnate with oblong to oval leaflets. Flowers white, 4-petalled, 20–30mm across and fragrant; appear May–August. Favours stony ground, often in scrub or maquis. Widespread throughout but local.

Anemone blanda   Height up to 30cm
Upright hairy perennial with leaves divided into broad, toothed lobes. Flowers 25–40mm across with 11–15 petals; usually white, pink, blue or purple. Flowers appear March–May. Stony ground, mainly uplands, from Greece eastwards.

CROWN ANEMONE *Anemone coronaria*   Height up to 30cm
Upright, hairy perennial with leaves deeply dissected into narrow toothed lobes. Flowers 40–70mm across with 5–8 petals; usually red, pink, blue or purple. Flowers appear January–April. Stony, often agricultural ground. Widespread.

PEACOCK ANEMONE *Anemone pavonia*   Height up to 30cm
Upright, hairy perennial. Basal leaves divided into broad, oval and toothed lobes; stem leaves narrow and tapering. Flowers 30–60mm across with 7–12 petals; usually red, pink or purple, often pale-centred; appear February–April. Stony ground, commonest in E.

EARLY YELLOW PHEASANT'S-EYE *Adonis vernalis*   Height up to 40cm
Upright annual with feathery leaves divided into narrow lobes. Flowers bright yellow and 50–80mm across with 10–20 petals; appear February–May. Stony, disturbed ground and arable fields. Widespread from S France eastwards.

PHEASANT'S-EYE *Adonis annua*   Height up to 30cm
Upright branched annual with feathery, finely divided leaves. Flowers bright red and 10–25mm across with 5–8 petals and spreading green petals; appear February–June. Stony disturbed soils and arable fields. Widespread across region.

YELLOW PHEASANT'S-EYE *Adonis microcarpa*   Height up to 40cm
Branched, upright annual with feathery, finely divided leaves. Flowers bright yellow and 15–30mm across with 5–8 petals; appear February–May. Stony disturbed ground including vineyards and arable fields. Widespread but local.

LOVE-IN-A-MIST *Nigella damascena*   Height up to 20cm
Hairless annual with feathery, finely divided leaves. Elegant blue flowers 20–30mm across, comprise five petal-like structures and numerous stamens; appear April–July. Fruit inflated. Widespread on stony ground. Several similar species.

HAIRY BUTTERCUP *Ranunculus sardous*   Height up to 40cm
Hairy annual with lower leaves divided into three lobes; middle lobe unstalked. Upper leaves unlobed. Pale yellow flower, 15–25mm across, appear April–August; sepals reflexed. Grassy fields and arable land. Widespread but local in E.

BULBOUS BUTTERCUP *Ranunculus bulbosus*   Height up to 40cm
Hairy annual with leaves divided into three lobes, each of which is stalked. Flowers bright yellow and 20–30mm across; appear April–August. Sepals reflexed. Favours dry grassland and arable fields. Widespread.

CORN BUTTERCUP *Ranunculus arvensis*   Height up to 40cm
Upright, often hairless annual with leaves divided into narrow lobes. Pale yellow flowers are 10–12mm across; appear March–June. Favours disturbed ground and arable fields. Widespread across region.

Ranunculus muricatus   Height up to 20cm
Hairless, much-branched annual with kidney-shaped basal leaves and narrow, 3–5 lobed upper leaves. Flowers bright yellow and 12–15mm across; appear February–May. Fruit round-headed and spiny. Damp and cultivated ground. Widespread.

JERSEY BUTTERCUP *Ranunculus paludosus*   Height up to 40cm
Hairy perennial with basal leaves divided into broad lobes; upper leaves comprise three narrow lobes. Flowers bright yellow and 20–30mm across; appear February–May. Sepals not reflexed. Widespread in seasonally flooding ground.

CELERY-LEAVED BUTTERCUP *Ranunculus sceleratus*　　　Height up to 50cm
Fresh green, hairless annual. Lower leaves are celery-like and divided into three lobes.
Flowers yellow and 5–10mm across; borne in clusters and appearing May–September.
Favours marshes and wet grazing meadows. Widespread.

LESSER CELANDINE *Ranunculus ficaria*　　　Height up to 25cm
Clump- or mat-forming perennial. Leaves heart-shaped, glossy and dark green. Flowers
yellow or yellowish-white with 8–12 petals and 3 sepals; 20–50mm across and appear
February–May, opening only in sunshine. Widespread in scrub and woods.

TURBAN BUTTERCUP *Ranunculus asiaticus*　　　Height up to 25cm
Annual with rounded 3-lobed basal leaves and smaller, narrow stem leaves. Flowers 5-
petalled and 30–70mm across; colour variable but often red, white, yellow or pink with
black stamens. Flowers appear March–May. Stony ground in E of region.

Paeonia broteroi　　　Height up to 1m
Perennial with basal leaves divided into 17 or more leaflets; dark green above but blue-
green below. Typical peony flowers are reddish purple and 8–10cm across; appear
May–June. Stony ground with scrub in Iberian Peninsula.

CLUSIUS' PEONY *Paeonia clusii*　　　Height up to 1m
Perennial with leaves divided into 30 or more, narrow leaflets. Flowers usually white but
sometimes pink; 7–12cm across and appearing March–May. Favours stony slopes among
scrub. Endemic to Crete and Karpathos.

Paeonia cambessedesii　　　Height up to 70cm
Perennial with leaves divided into oval leaflets that are veined purple on upper surface
and flushed reddish below. Flowers pinkish purple and 6–10cm across; appear March to
May. Stony slopes among scrub. Endemic to Balearics.

Paeonia arietina　　　Height up to 1m
Perennial with leaves divided into 12–15 broadly oval leaflets that are hairy below.
Flowers reddish purple and 8–14cm across; appear May–June. Stony ground from N Italy
eastwards. Several similar peony species occur in region.

CAPER *Capparis spinosa*　　　Height up to 2m
Straggling, spiny shrub with rounded-oval leaves. Flowers are 50–70mm across and comprise 4 white petals; stamens numerous and purple. Flowers May–July. Fruit is green and
berry-like. Flower bud is the edible caper. Widespread on stony ground.

OPIUM POPPY *Papaver somniferum*　　　Height up to 1m
Annual with leaves that are oval with lobed margins; upper leaves clasp the stem. Flowers
are 40–90mm across; colour variable but often purple with a dark centre, or white.
Flowers appear April–July. Widespread throughout.

✓ **COMMON POPPY** *Papaver rhoeas*　　　Height up to 60cm
Hairy annual with much-branched leaves. Flowers are 40–60mm across and scarlet, some-
times dark centred; anthers bluish. Flowers March–June. Seed capsule rounded.
Disturbed and cultivated ground. Widespread; abundance reduced by herbicides.

LONG-HEADED POPPY *Papaver dubium*　　　Height up to 60cm
Hairy annual with leaves divided into narrow lobes. Flowers red and 40–60mm across
with violet anthers; appear March–June. Seed capsule oblong and smooth. Cultivated and
disturbed ground. Widespread across region.

PRICKLY POPPY *Papaver argemone*　　　Height up to 50cm
Hairy annual with deeply divided leaves. Flowers are red, sometimes with a dark centre,
and 35–45mm across; appear March–June. Seed capsule elongate and bristly. Cultivated
ground, often near the sea. Widespread as far E as Greece.

ROUGH POPPY *Papaver hybridum*   Height up to 50cm
Hairy annual with leaves deeply divided. Flowers deep red with a dark centre and
20–40mm across; appear February–June. Seed capsule rounded, ribbed and bristly.
Favours cultivated and disturbed ground. Widespread across region.

SMALL POPPY *Papaver minus*   Height up to 20cm
Short, hairy annual with finely divided leaves. Flowers red, sometimes black-centred, and
10–20mm across, not opening widely; appear April–May. Favours cultivated and disturbed ground. Widespread in E of region.

MEDITERRANEAN POPPY *Papaver apulum*   Height up to 1m
Impressive hairy annual with deeply divided leaves. Flowers bright red with a dark centre
and 40–50mm across; appear March–June. Seed capsule rounded and bristly. Cultivated
and disturbed ground. Widespread from S Italy to Balkans.

YELLOW HORNED-POPPY *Glaucium flavum*   Height up to 50cm
Blue-grey, clump-forming perennial of shingle beaches. Leaves pinnately divided, clasping upper ones having shallow toothed lobes. Flowers yellow and 60–90mm across;
appear June–September. Widespread and common in suitable coastal sites.

RED HORNED-POPPY *Glaucium corniculatum*   Height up to 30cm
Bristly annual or biennial with pinnately lobed leaves, the upper ones clasping the stem.
Flowers red or orange and 30–50mm across; appear April–June. Favours disturbed and
cultivated ground near the sea. Widespread across region.

COMMON FUMITORY *Fumaria officinalis*   Height up to 20cm
Scrambling or spreading annual with much-divided leaves, the lobes all in one plane.
Crimson-tipped pink flowers are 6–7mm long, spurred and two-lipped; borne in spike-
like heads April–October. Favours arable fields. Widespread.

RAMPING-FUMITORY *Fumaria capreolata*   Height up to 40cm
Scrambling annual with much-divided grey-green leaves, the lobes appearing rounded.
Purple-tipped white flowers and 10–14mm long, spurred and two-lipped; borne in spike-
like heads March–June. Stony, often cultivated land. Widespread.

WOAD *Isatis tinctoria*   Height up to 1m
Upright biennial. In first year, appears as basal rosette of leaves. In second year, stem
appears bearing clasping, arrow-shaped leaves. Flowers yellow and 3–4mm across; borne
in dense clusters April–July. Stony ground, mainly in W.

CUT-LEAVED DAME'S VIOLET *Hesperis laciniatus*   Height up to 1m
Hairy biennial or perennial. Leaves oval with wavy and lobed margins. Flowers 4-
petalled, usually purple and 15–25mm across; borne in tall, open heads April–July. Pod
slender and up to 150mm long. Stony ground, Iberia eastwards to Greece.

SAND STOCK *Malcolmia littorea*   Height up to 25cm
Downy, greyish perennial with elliptical, deeply-toothed leaves. Flowers 4-petalled, purple and 15–20mm across; borne in open, terminal heads March–June. Favours sand, shingle and rock near the coast. Widespread in W Mediterranean.

Malcolmia flexuosa   Height up to 20cm
Hairy annual with oblong leaves that often have toothed margins. Flowers 4-petalled, purple or pink and 10–15mm across; borne terminal clusters February–May. Pod narrow, up
to 50mm long and wavy. Coastal stony ground, mainly in E.

WALLFLOWER *Cheiranthus cheiri*   Height up to 70cm
Upright perennial with narrow oval or lanceolate leaves. Fragrant flowers are yellow or
orange and 20–25mm across; borne in terminal heads March–May. Pod long, slender and
flattened. Favours cliffs and walls and widely naturalised.

CYPRUS ROCKCRESS *Arabis cypria*   Height up to 10cm
Hairy annual with basal rosette of oval, toothed leaves; stem leaves smaller and arrow-or heart-shaped. Flowers 4-petalled, purple and 5–8mm across; appear March–May. Rock crevices, often several plants together. Endemic to Cyprus mountains.

SEA STOCK *Matthiola sinuata*   Height up to 30cm
Grey-green, hairy biennial or perennial. Leaves oblong and deeply toothed; lobes rounded. Flowers 4-petalled, pinkish-purple and 20–25mm across; appear February–May. Pod long and sticky. Coastal sandy ground. Widespread, commonest in W.

HOARY STOCK *Matthiola incana*   Height up to 30cm
Grey-green, hairy biennial or perennial. Leaves oblong and untoothed. Flowers 4-petalled, pinkish-purple 25–30mm across; appear February–May. Pod long and hairy. Sandy and stony ground near coasts. Widespread as far E as Turkey.

THREE-HORNED STOCK *Matthiola tricuspidata*   Height up to 40cm
Grey-green, woolly annual. Leaves oblong with rounded, shallow lobes. Flowers 4-petalled, purple and 20–30mm across; appear February–May. Pod is long and split into 3 at tip. Coastal sandy ground. Widespread across region.

CRETAN ALYSSOIDES *Alyssoides cretica*   Height up to 30cm
Grey-green, hairy perennial. Leaves oblong, deeply-lobed. Flowers 8–14mm across and yellow; appear March–June. Pods round and hairy. Endemic to rocks on Crete and Karpathos. Similar alyssoides *A.sinuata* occurs rocks on Adriatic coasts.

GOLDEN ALYSSUM *Alyssum saxatile*   Height up to 30cm
Grey-green perennial. Leaves, oblong-elliptical, sometimes with shallow-lobed margins. Flowers yellow and 4–8mm across; borne in terminal clusters March–June. Pod round and flattened. Rocky places from Italy to Turkey.

SWEET ALISON *Lobularia maritima*   Height up to 15cm
Grey, much-branched and often hairy annual. Leaves narrow and untoothed. Flowers scented, white and 3–4mm across; borne in dense heads February–June. Pod flattened and oval. Stony and sandy ground. Widespread; also planted in gardens.

BURNT CANDYTUFT *Aethionema saxatile*   Height up to 15cm
Branched, upright perennial. Oval leaves often overlap one another along stem. Flowers pinkish and 3–5mm across; appear in terminal heads March–May. Favours stony and rocky ground. Widespread but local from E Iberia to N Greece.

Biscutella fruitescens   Height up to 30cm
Hairy annual. Leaves oblong with rounded lobes; form basal rosette and appear up stem. Flowers yellow, 3–5mm across, in dense clusters February–May. Rocky places, SW Spain and Balearics. Similar biscutella *B.didyma* occurs elsewhere in region.

EVERGREEN CANDYTUFT *Iberis sempervirens*   Height up to 30cm
Branched, evergreen perennial with narrow, rounded-tipped leaves. Flowers white; borne in flat-topped clusters April–June. Pods oval, flattened and notched-tipped. Rocky ground in mountains. Widespread but local E Spain to N Greece.

WILD CABBAGE *Brassica oleracea*   Height up to 1.25m
Tough perennial found on coastal cliffs, mainly on calcareous soils. Lower leaves grey-green, large and fleshy; often ravaged by larvae of large white butterfly. Flowers yellow, 10–20mm across; appear April–July. Occurs Iberia to S Italy.

Brassica fruiticulosa   Height up to 40cm
Clump-forming, hairy perennial. Leaves spoon-shaped or oblong, margins with rounded lobes. Flowers yellow and 8–12mm across; appear in small clusters, often drooping, April–July. Rocky ground, Iberia to N Greece; absent from most islands.

WHITE MUSTARD *Sinapis alba*   Height up to 80cm
Upright, hairy annual with stalked and pinnately-lobed leaves. Flowers yellow and
15–20mm across; borne in terminal clusters February–July. Pod long and beaked; constricted between seeds. Common and widespread on disturbed ground.

ERUCA *Eruca sativa*   Height up to 1m
Bristly annual with stalked, pinnately-lobed leaves; terminal leaflet largest. Flowers white
with purple veins, 20–30mm across, in terminal heads February–June. Pods beaked and
flattened. Disturbed ground. Sometimes grown as a salad crop. Widespread.

SEA ROCKET *Cakile maritima*   Height up to 25cm
Spreading, grey-green and fleshy annual with pinnately-lobed leaves. Flowers pinkish
purple and 7–12mm across; borne in clusters February–July. Pods oval to diamond-
shaped. Favours stabilised sandy beaches. Widespread across region.

✓ **SEA RADISH** *Raphanus maritimus* ssp *maritimus*   Height up to 60cm
Robust, roughly hairy annual. Lower leaves pinnately divided but upper ones narrow and
entire. Flowers yellow and 15–25mm across; appear April–September. Favours stabilised
coastal shingle and sand. Widespread in W of region only.

WHITE MIGNONETTE *Reseda alba*   Height up to 70cm
Upright perennial with pinnately divided leaves comprising 10 or more lobes. Flowers
white and 6-petalled; borne in spikes, January–May. Favours disturbed and cultivated
ground, mainly on calcareous soils. Widespread across region.

WILD MIGNONETTE *Reseda lutea*   Height up to 70cm
Biennial or perennial of disturbed calcareous ground. Leaves pinnately divided compris-
ing 3–5 lobes. Flowers yellow-green and 6-petalled; borne in tall spikes
March–September. Widespread across region.

WELD *Reseda luteola*   Height up to 1.2m
Upright biennial of disturbed sandy or calcareous ground. Has basal rosette of narrow
leaves in first year only. Tall flower spike appears in second year with narrow stem leaves.
Yellowish 4-petalled flowers appear April–July. Widespread.

BITING STONECROP OR WALLPEPPER *Sedum acre*   Height up to 10cm
Mat-forming perennial with crowded, fleshy leaves that are pressed close to stem; taste
hot. Flowers bright yellow, 5-petalled and 10–12mm across; appear May–July. Sandy and
stony ground, and walls. Widespread; absent from much of E and many islands.

✓ **WHITE STONECROP** *Sedum album*   Height up to 5cm
Mat-forming, tufted perennial with fleshy, egg-shaped leaves that are pressed close to
stem and often tinged red. Flowers white, 5-petalled and 6–9mm across; appear May–July.
Stony ground and old walls. Widespread.

ANNUAL STONECROP *Sedum annuum*   Height up to 5cm
Mat-forming annual with fleshy, egg-shaped but flattened leaves that are pressed close to
stem and often reddish. Flowers yellow, five-petalled and 5–7mm across; appear
April–June. Stony ground. Widespread but mainly in mountains.

✓ **NAVELWORT** *Umbilicus rupestris*   Height of flower spike up to 15cm
Distinctive perennial. Leaves rounded and fleshy, with a depressed centre above the leaf
stalk. Spikes of whitish flowers appear March–June. Found on cliffs, banks and old walls,
often in shaded sites. Widespread.

BURNET ROSE *Rosa pimpinellifolia*   Height up to 50cm
Clump-forming deciduous shrub. Stems armed with straight thorns and stiff bristles.
Leaves comprise 7–11 oval leaflets. Creamy white flowers, 30–50mm across, appear
May–July. Sandy and calcareous soils. Local, S France to N Greece.

THORNY BURNET *Sarcopoterium spinosum*   Height up 60cm
Spiny, much-branched perennial. Often forms a low, rounded shrub. Leaves small, pinnately divided with 9–15 leaflets. Flowers rounded, 20mm across and green; February–April. Fruits rounded and red. Garrigue and stony ground. Mainly in E.

PARSLEY-PIERT *Aphanes arvensis*   Creeping
Easily overlooked downy annual. Leaves fan-shaped and deeply divided into three lobes; superficially parsley-like. Flowers tiny and green, appearing April–June. Favours dry, bare ground. Widespread and often common.

THORNY BROOM *Calycotome infesta*   Height up to 3m
Spiny, much-branched shrub; young shoots downy. Leaves trifoliate with oval leaflets; smooth above, hairy below. Flowers solitary, yellow and 12–18mm long; January–May. Pods 25–30mm long and hairless. Maquis and garrigue. W of region.

HAIRY THORNY BROOM *Calycotome villosa*   Height up to 3m
Spiny, much-branched shrub. Leaves trifoliate with oval leaflets; smooth above, hairy below. Flowers solitary or in clusters, yellow and 12–18mm long; appear January–May. Pods 25–30mm long and hairy. Maquis and garrigue. Widespread.

BROOM *Cytisus scoparius*   Height up to 2m
Much-branched deciduous shrub with ridged, 5-angled green twigs. Leaves usually trifoliate with oval leaflets. Flowers yellow and 20mm long; appear April–June. Pods 30–40mm long, hairy on margins, ripening black. Sandy soils. Widespread.

TELINE *Teline linifolia*   Height up to 1.5m
Spreading, spineless shrub. Leaves trifoliate with narrow-oval, downy leaflets, pale below. Flowers yellow, 15–18mm long; borne in leafy clusters, April–May. Stony ground in scrub and open woods. Iberia, Balearics and S France.

DYER'S GREENWEED *Genista tinctoria*   Height up to 1m
Spineless shrub. Leaves narrow-oval and sometimes downy. Flowers yellow and 8–15mm long; borne in clusters, April–June. Pods hairless and oblong. Favours grassy places. Widespread but absent from many islands.

COMMON GORSE *Ulex europaeus*   Height up to 2m
Spiny, evergreen shrub. Leaves trifoliate when young. Spines are straight, 15–25mm long and grooved. Flowers yellow, 16–20mm long and smell of coconut; appear March–September. Sandy or rocky ground. Native to W of region; planted elsewhere.

Lygos monosperma   Height up to 3m
Spineless, much-branched shrub. Leaves silvery and narrow; soon shed. Flowers white, 10–12mm long; appear in dense sprays, February–April. Pods oval and rough. Favours coastal sandy soil. Occurs S Iberia only.

SPANISH BROOM *Spartium junceum*   Height up to 3m
Spineless shrub comprising numerous radiating, blue-green, reed-like stems. Leaves narrow and soon shed. Flowers yellow and 20–25mm long; appear May–August. Favours maquis, open woodland and roadsides. Widespread; commonest in W and C.

NARROW-LEAVED LUPIN *Lupinus angustifolius*   Height up to 80cm
Upright, hairy annual. Leaves narrow and downy below. Flowers deep blue, pea-like and 11–13mm long; borne in spiked heads March–May. Pods hairy, ripening black. Garrigue and stony, disturbed ground. Widespread across region.

MEDITERRANEAN LUPIN *Lupinus varius*   Height up to 50cm
Upright, downy-hairy annual. Leaves elongate-oval and hairy below. Flowers deep blue with white or purple central patch, and 15–17mm long; borne in spiked heads March–June. Pods hairy, ripening brown. Sandy soils. From Iberia to Greece.

GOAT'S-RUE *Galega officinalis* Height up to 1.5m
Shrubby perennial. Leaves pinnately divided with 4–8 pairs of elongate-oval leaflets. Flowers pinkish-lilac and 10–15mm long; in spikes June–August. Pods constricted between seeds. Scrub and grassland. Widespread, Iberia to Turkey.

TRAGACANTH *Astragalus massiliensis* Height up to 25cm
Spiny, much-branched perennial. Spine-tipped leaves comprise 6–12 pairs of elongate-oval leaflets that are hairy below. Flowers white and 14–17mm long; borne in heads April–June. Stony and rocky ground. W Mediterranean only.

Astragalus balearicus Height up to 25cm
A so-called 'hedgehog plant' on account of its domed and extremely spiny habit. Leaves comprise 3–5 pairs of oval, hairy leaflets. Flowers white and 10–12mm long; in heads of 4–5 flowers, April–June. Stony ground. Endemic to Balearics.

PITCH TREFOIL *Psoralea bituminosa* Height up to 80cm
Hairy perennial that smells of bitumen. Leaves comprise 3 narrow-oval leaflets. Flowers bluish-lilac and 15–20mm long; borne in heads, April–July. Pods curved-tipped. Favours stony, often disturbed ground. Widespread.

COMMON VETCH *Vicia sativa* Height up to 75cm
Scrambling, hairy annual. Leaves comprise 3–8 pairs of oval leaflets and end in branched tendrils. Flowers pinkish purple and 15–20mm long; in groups of one or two, January–April. Ripe pods are black. Widespread, often grown for fodder.

BUSH VETCH *Vicia sepium* Height up to 1m
Scrambling, hairy perennial. Leaves comprise 5–9 pairs of leaflets ending in branched tendrils. Flowers pale lilac and 12–15mm long; in groups of 2–6, March–August. Stony slopes, grassland and garrigue. Widespread, commonest in W.

YELLOW VETCH *Vicia lutea* Height up to 50cm
Scrambling, hairy annual. Leaves with 4–10 pairs of narrow leaflets. Flowers pale yellow, sometimes flushed pink, and 25–35mm long; in groups of 1–3, April–August. Pods yellow and hairy. Arable fields and grassland. Widespread, mainly in W.

FODDER VETCH *Vicia villosa* Height up to 1m
Attractive, scrambling and hairy annual. Leaves comprise 4–12 pairs of narrow oval leaflets and end in branched tendrils. Flowers 10–20mm long and usually purple; in heads of 10–30, March–June. Widespread, often grown for fodder.

FALSE SAINFOIN *Vicia onobrychioides* Height up to 1m
Hairy perennial with leaves comprising 4–11 pairs of narrow oval leaflets. Flowers violet with a pale keel and 17–24mm long; in heads of 4–12 flowers, April–June. Favours disturbed, often stony ground. Widespread, Iberia to Turkey.

HAIRY TARE *Vicia hirsuta* Height up to 60cm
Slender, scrambling annual with leaves comprising 4–10 pairs of narrow leaflets and ending in branched tendrils. Flowers pale lilac and 2–4mm long; in heads of 1–8 flowers, May–July. Pods 2-seeded. Grassy and cultivated ground. Widespread.

HAIRY YELLOW VETCHLING *Vicia hybrida* Height up to 60cm
Hairy annual with leaves comprising 3–8 pairs of oblong leaflets. Flowers pale yellow or purplish, 20–30mm long and solitary; appear March–June. Favours cultivated ground and grassy field margins, often on sandy soil. Widespread.

BROAD-LEAVED EVERLASTING-PEA *Lathyrus latifolius* Height up to 2m
Sprawling perennial. Stems winged, sometimes hairy. Leaves with 1 pair of narrow oval leaflets and a branched tendril. Flowers 20–30mm long, usually pink or purple; in groups of 5–10 flowers, June–August. Grassy places, Iberia to Greece.

GRASS VETCHLING *Lathyrus nissolia*   Height up to 1m
Slender, climbing annual. Leaves narrow and grass-like, without tendrils. Flowers crimson, solitary or paired, and 10–18mm long; appear February–June. Favours grassy places; easily missed when not in flower. Widespread; absent from many islands.

YELLOW VETCHLING *Lathyrus aphaca*   Height up to 80cm
Scrambling, grey-green annual. Angled stems carry pairs of leaf-like stipules; leaves reduced to tendrils. Solitary yellow flowers are borne on long stalks; appear February–May. Grassy places and fallow cultivated ground. Widespread.

WILD PEA *Pisum sativum*   Height up to 1.5m
Scrambling or climbing annual. Leaves comprise 1–3 pairs of oval leaflets, ending in branched tendrils. Flowers blue, purple or white and 15–35mm long; in groups of 1–3, April–July. Pods brown. Garrigue and stony ground. Widely cultivated.

LARGE YELLOW REST-HARROW *Ononis natrix*   Height up to 60cm
Shrubby perennial with a woody base. Leaves sticky and comprise 3 oval leaflets with toothed margins. Flowers yellow and 10–20mm long, with darker veins on standard petal; in leafy heads, April–July. Sandy and stony ground. Widespread.

WHITE MELILOT *Melilotus albus*   Height up to 1m
Hairless annual or biennial with leaves comprising 3 oblong leaflets. Flowers white and 4–5mm long; borne in tall spikes, May–August. Favours disturbed and cultivated ground, including olive groves. Widespread.

RIBBED MELILOT *Melilotus officinalis*   Height up to 2m
Upright, hairless biennial with leaves comprising 3 oblong leaflets. Flowers yellow and 4–7mm long; borne in tall spikes, May–July. Ripe pods brown. Favours cultivated or disturbed ground. Local, Iberia to Turkey; absent from most islands.

TREE MEDICK *Medicago arborea*   Height up to 4m
Much-branched, silvery grey shrub. Leaves comprise 3 broadly oval leaflets. Flowers are yellow and 12–15mm long; borne in groups of 4–8, April–June. Pods flat and spirally coiled. Favours rocky slopes and roadsides. Widespread.

LARGE DISK MEDICK *Medicago orbicularis*   Height up to 15cm
Sprawling annual with leaves comprising 3 diamond- or wedge-shaped leaflets. Flowers are yellow and 2–5mm long; borne in groups of 1–5, February–June. Pods 15mm across, flat and spirally coiled. Cultivated and disturbed soil. Widespread.

LUCERNE *Medicago sativa*   Height up to 75cm
Downy perennial with leaves comprising 3 narrow, toothed leaflets which broaden towards the tip. Flowers purple and 12–15mm long; in heads of 5–40 flowers, March–June. Pods spirally coiled. Grown as a fodder crop; widely naturalised.

SEA MEDICK *Medicago marina*   Prostrate
Creeping, downy and silvery grey perennial. Leaves comprise 3 oval leaflets which broaden towards the tip. Flowers yellow and 6–8mm long; borne in clusters of 5–12 flowers, February–June. Pods spirally coiled. Widespread on coastal sands.

COMMON BIRD'S-FOOT TREFOIL *Lotus corniculatus*   Usually creeping
Trailing perennial. Leaves comprise 5 leaflets but appear trifoliate since lower pair is sited at stalk base. Flowers yellow or orange and 10–16mm long; in heads of 2–7, April–July. Pods arranged like a bird's foot. Grassy places. Widespread.

SOUTHERN BIRD'S-FOOT TREFOIL *Lotus creticus*   Prostrate
Silvery grey, hairy perennial. Leaves comprise 5 oblong leaflets. Flowers yellow with dark tip to keel, 12–18mm long; in heads of 2–6 flowers, March–May. Pods borne in splayed clusters. Coastal habitats. Widespread; absent from most islands.

GREATER BIRD'S-FOOT TREFOIL *Lotus uliginosus*   Height up to 50cm
Straggling perennial with hollow stems. Leaves grey-green and downy; comprise five leaflets but appear trifoliate. Flowers yellow and 10–18mm long; borne in heads of 5–12, May–July. Damp grassland and marshes. Widespread.

ORANGE BIRD'S-FOOT *Ornithopus pinnatus*   Prostrate
Creeping, hairy annual. Leaves comprise 3–7 pairs of narrow oval leaflets, ending in a terminal leaflet, not a tendril. Flowers orange-yellow, 6–8mm long; borne in heads of 1–5, February–May. Widespread, particularly in W of region.

NARROW-LEAVED CRIMSON CLOVER *Trifolium angustifolium*   Height up to 50cm
Branching, hairy annual with stiff stems. Leaves comprise 3 narrow lanceolate leaflets. Flowers pink and 10–12mm long; borne in elongate-ovoid heads, April–July. Favours dry soils including garrigue. Widespread.

WHITE CLOVER *Trifolium repens*   Height up to 40cm
Creeping perennial whose stems root at the nodes. Leaves comprise 3 oval leaflets, often bearing white marks. Flowers creamy white, browning with age, and 7–10mm long; borne in rounded heads, April–July. Widespread in grassland.

SHIELD CLOVER *Trifolium clypeatum*   Height up to 30cm
Hairy annual. Leaves comprise 3 wedge- or diamond-shaped leaflets. Flowers white, becoming pink and 20–25mm long; in stalked heads, February–April. Sepals expand and flatten in fruit. Damp grassy places, often in maquis. E of region only.

ALSIKE CLOVER *Trifolium hybridum*   Height up to 30cm
Sprawling, hairless perennial. Leaves comprise 3 broadly oval, green and unmarked leaflets. Flowers usually purple or white, ageing pink then brown; 7–10mm long and borne in rounded heads, April–July. Local, avoiding hot dry areas.

STRAWBERRY CLOVER *Trifolium fragiferum*   Height up to 20cm
Sprawling, often creeping perennial; stems often root at nodes. Leaves comprise 3 oval leaflets. Flowers pink and 6–7mm long; borne in rounded heads, May–October, which expand in fruit becoming strawberry-like. Widespread in grassy places.

Trifolium speciosum   Height up to 25cm
Hairless annual with leaves comprising 3 oval leaflets, the terminal one on a short stalk. Flowers violet and 8–10mm long; borne in rounded heads, April–June, which expand and persist in fruit. Stony ground. Occurs from Sicily eastwards.

HOP TREFOIL *Trifolium campestre* Mch'06 : N. Cyprus   Height up to 25cm
Hairy annual with leaves comprising oval or oblong leaflets. Flowers yellow and 4–5mm long; borne in rounded heads, February–June, these becoming brown and hop-like when in fruit. Widespread on cultivated and stony ground.

WOOLLY TREFOIL *Trifolium tomentosum*   Height up to 25cm
Sprawling, hairless annual with leaves comprising 3 oval leaflets. Flowers pink and 3–4mm long; borne in heads, March–June, these expanding and become rounded and woolly. Grassy places and field margins. Widespread.

CRIMSON CLOVER *Trifolium incarnatum*   Height up to 35cm
Branching, upright and hairy annual. Leaves comprise 3 rounded or heart-shaped leaflets. Flowers crimson and 10–12mm long; in elongate cone-shaped heads, April–July. Widespread in grassy places, but absent most islands. Grown for fodder.

LONG-HEADED CLOVER *Trifolium incarnatum* ssp *molinerii*   Height up to 30cm
Branching, upright and hairy annual. Similar to *T. incarnatum* but flowers yellowish white or pinkish white; individual flowers 10–12mm long, borne in cone-shaped heads, April–June. Grassy places, often near the sea. Mainly W of region.

PURPLE CLOVER *Trifolium purpureum*   Height up to 50cm
Upright, hairy annual with leaves comprising 3 narrow leaflets. Flowers reddish-purple
and 16–25mm long; borne in cone-shaped heads, March–July. Native of disturbed, stony
ground, S France, Sicily and Balkans; cultivated elsewhere.

STAR CLOVER *Trifolium stellatum* ✓ Mch '06 · N Cyprus   Height up to 20cm
Upright, hairy annual. Leaves comprise 3 oval to heart-shaped leaflets. Flowers pink and
8–12mm long; borne in rounded heads, March–July. Star-shaped calyx lobes conspicuous
after flowering. Widespread in grassy places.

EASTERN STAR CLOVER *Trifolium dasyurum*   Height up to 30cm
Upright, hairy annual. Similar to *T.stellatum* but leaves narrow-oval. Flowers pinkish-pur-
ple and 10–14mm long; borne in egg-shaped heads, which are often paired, March–July.
Widespread from Greece eastwards, including Cyprus.

SEA CLOVER *Trifolium squamosum*   Height up to 10cm
Sprawling, hairy annual with leaves comprising 3 oval leaflets. Flowers pale pink and
5–7mm long; in heads, March–May. Narrow calyx lobes persist after flowering; heads then
resemble miniature teasels. Widespread. Damp coastal ground.

DRAGON'S TEETH *Tetragonolobus maritimus*   Height up to 30cm
Spreading perennial with leaves comprising 3 oval leaflets. Flowers yellow, 25–30mm long
and solitary; borne on stalks just above leaf-like bracts. Pods 30–60mm long, green ripening
brown. Grassy places. Widespread; absent from hot dry areas.

MEDITERRANEAN KIDNEY VETCH *Anthyllis vulneraria*   Height up to 30cm
Tufted silky-hairy perennial. Leaves comprise pairs of narrow leaflets; lower leaves with
single leaflet. Flowers reddish-purple and 12–15mm long; in kidney-shaped heads,
March–July. Dry grassy places. Widespread; absent Iberia and Italy.

BLADDER VETCH *Anthyllis tetraphylla*   Height up to 20cm
Spreading, hairy annual. Leaves comprise 5 leaflets; terminal one largest. Flowers pale yel-
low and 8–12mm long; in clusters of 1–7, February–June. Pod inflated and bladder-like.
Cultivated ground and garrigue. Widespread.

CROWN VETCH *Coronilla varia*   Height up to 50cm
Scrambling, much-branched perennial. Leaves comprise 7–12 pairs of narrow oval leaflets.
Flowers usually pink or whitish and 10–15mm long; in heads of 10–20. Pods beaded and
20–40mm long. Grassy places. Widespread; absent from most islands.

MEDITERRANEAN SCORPION-VETCH *Coronilla securidaca*   Height up to 35cm
Sprawling, hairless annual. Leaves comprise 4–7 pairs of oblong leaflets. Flowers yellow
and 4–8mm long; borne in heads on long stalks, March–May. Pods straight with a curved,
pointed tip. Grassy places and field margins, S France eastwards.

MEDITERRANEAN HORSESHOE-VETCH *Hippocrepis unisiliquosa* Height up to 30cm
Much-branched annual with leaves comprising 3–7 pairs of oval leaflets. Flowers yellowish, usually solitary and 4–7mm long; appear March–June. Pods 20–40mm long, comprising horseshoe-shaped segments. Cultivated ground and garrigue. Widespread.

ITALIAN SAINFOIN *Hedysarum coronarium*   Height up to 1m
Upright, hairy perennial. Leaves comprise 3–5 rounded-oval leaflets that are hairy below.
Flowers reddish purple and 12–15mm long; borne in cone-shaped heads, April–June.
Native in W, on cultivated ground and garrigue. Cultivated elsewhere.

SPINY SAINFOIN *Hedysarum spinosissimum*   Height up to 30cm
Sprawling, hairy annual. Leaves comprise 4–8 pairs of oblong leaflets. Flowers pale pink
and 8–11mm long; in clusters of 2–10 flowers, February–May. Pods beaded with hooked
spines. Stony ground and garrigue. Common, but distribution patchy.

CYPRIOT SAINFOIN *Onobrychis venosa* Height up to 30cm
Branched, hairy perennial. Leaves comprise 3–4 pairs of oval leaflets, green with purple-brown veins. Flowers creamy yellow, veined purple and 9–10mm long; borne in conical spikes, February to May. Endemic to Cyprus, favouring garrigue.

CRETAN EBONY *Ebenus creticus* Height up to 50cm
Grey-green, hairy shrub. Leaves comprise 3–5 narrow, silky-hairy leaflets. Flowers pink with crimson veins and 10–15mm long; borne in conical spikes, April–June. Stony slopes and cliffs. Endemic to Crete.

BARBADOS PRIDE *Caesalpina pulcherrima* Height up to 5m
Evergreen, prickly shrub. Leaves comprise numerous opposite pairs of oblong-oval leaflets. Flowers large and showy, orange-yellow with long red stamens; appear July–August. Alien species, grown for its ornamental value.

BERMUDA BUTTERCUP *Oxalis pes-caprae* Height up to 25cm
Bulbous, mat-forming perennial. Leaves superficially clover-like, comprising 3 heart-shaped leaflets on a long stalk. Flowers yellow and 30mm across with 5 petals; appear November–May. Cultivated and disturbed ground. Widely naturalised.

PINK OXALIS *Oxalis articulata* Height up to 30cm
Hairy perennial. Clover-like leaves comprise 3 heart-shaped leaflets, borne on long stalks. Flowers pink, 5-petalled and up to 25mm across; appear May–October. Disturbed and cultivated ground. Grown in gardens and sometimes naturalised.

TUBEROUS CRANE'S-BILL *Geranium tuberosum* Height up to 50cm
Hairy, branching perennial. Stems reddish and leaves green and finely pinnately divided. Flowers pinkish-purple with dark veins. 15–25mm across; borne in clusters, February–April. Stony slopes and cultivated soils. Widespread in E.

DOVE'S-FOOT CRANE'S-BILL *Geranium molle* Height up to 20cm
Spreading, very hairy annual. Leaves hairy and rounded but margins cut into 5–7 lobes, each one itself having a 3-lobed margin. Flowers pink, 5–10mm across with notched petals; in pairs, March–May. Stony ground and field margins. Widespread.

ROUND-LEAVED CRANE'S-BILL *Geranium rotundifolium* Height up to 30cm
Upright, hairy annual. Leaves rounded but margins cut into 5–7 lobes, each one itself having a 3-lobed margin. Flowers pink and 10–12mm across with unnotched petals; in small clusters, March–May. Field margins and stony ground. Widespread.

CUT-LEAVED CRANE'S-BILL *Geranium dissectum* Height up to 45cm
Sprawling, hairy annual. Leaves are deeply dissected into very narrow lobes. Flowers pinkish and 8–10mm across with petals sometimes notched; appear February–May. Favours field margins and damp grassland. Widespread.

SMALL-LEAVED CRANE'S-BILL *Geranium pusillum* Height up to 30cm
Sprawling, branching and hairy annual. Leaves rounded but deeply divided into 5 lobes, each one of which is itself 3-lobed. Flowers pale lilac and 4–6mm across; appear February–May. Stony ground, grassy field margins and garrigue. Widespread.

LONG-STALKED CRANE'S-BILL *Geranium columbinum* Height up to 40cm
Hairy annual. Leaves divided into 5 lobes each one of which is itself deeply divided. Flowers pink and 12–20mm across; borne on long stalks, up to 25mm long, March–May. Rough ground, usually on calcareous soils. Widespread.

SHINING CRANE'S-BILL *Geranium lucidum* Height up to 30cm
Almost hairless annual. Shiny leaves are green, sometimes tinged red, and divided into 5–7 rounded lobes. Flowers pink and 10–14mm across; appear March–May. Favours shaded rocky slopes and banks, mostly on limestone. Widespread.

HERB-ROBERT *Geranium robertianum*   Height up to 40cm
Aromatic, hairy annual; stems and leaves sometimes flushed reddish. Leaves hairy and
deeply cut into 3–5 lobes. Flowers pink with orange pollen and 14–18mm across; appear
March–September. Shady banks, woods and cliffs. Widespread.

LITTLE ROBIN *Geranium purpureum*   Height up to 20cm
Similar to *G.robertianum* but smaller and less aromatic. Leaves divided into 5 lobes, each
of which is deeply divided. Flowers pink, 7–14mm across with yellow pollen; appear
March–September. Walls, stony ground and shingle. Widespread.

COMMON STORK'S-BILL *Erodium cicutarium*   Height up to 25cm
Stickily-hairy annual. Leaves finely pinnately divided and feathery. Flowers pink and
10–18mm across, petals easily lost; borne in clusters, February–June. Favours bare, grassy
places, garrigue and sand dunes. Widespread.

SYRIAN BEAN CAPER *Zygophyllum fabago*   Height up to 1m
Upright, hairless perennial. Leaves comprise two oval and fleshy leaflets with projecting
leaf stalks. Flowers whitish, 9–11mm across, borne on stalks arising from leaf axils,
May–August. Native in E Mediterranean, naturalised in W.

FAGONIA *Fagonia cretica*   Height up to 40cm
Much-branched perennial. Leaves comprise 3 lanceolate, spine-tipped leaflets. Flowers
purple and 9–10mm across; appear February–June. Favours stony ground and garrigue,
mostly on calcareous soils. Widespread but local; commonest in E.

YELLOW FLAX *Linum flavum*   Height up to 50cm
Upright, hairless perennial. Leaves lanceolate with 3–5 conspicuous veins. Bell-shaped
flowers are 25–30mm across and comprise 5 yellow petals; borne in clusters, April–July.
Rocky ground and garrigue. Italy and former Yugoslavia.

PERENNIAL FLAX *Linum perenne*   Height up to 50cm
Upright, hairless perennial. Leaves narrow and grass-like with 1–3 veins. Flowers dark
blue and 25–30mm across with petals 3–4 times longer than sepals; appear January–June.
Grassy places and field margins. Locally common, Iberia to Greece.

Linum tenuifolium   Height up to 30cm
Upright, hairless perennial with some non-flowering shoots. Leaves narrow, with flat margins. Flowers pinkish and 15–25mm across; appear April–July. Grassy places on rocky
slopes. Widespread across much of Mediterranean.

UPRIGHT YELLOW FLAX *Linum strictum*   Height up to 35cm
Upright, mostly hairless annual. Leaves narrow and rough, with inrolled margins. Flowers
yellow and 10–15mm across; borne in spikes, March–May. Favours rocky slopes and
sandy soil. Widespread across the region.

PURPLE SPURGE *Euphorbia peplis*   Prostrate
Creeping hairless annual with grey-green foliage and reddish purple stems. Leaves oppo-
site and oblong-oval. Flowers green and brown; appear May–July. Fruit capsule purple.
Shingle and sandy beaches. Widespread.

TREE SPURGE *Euphorbia dendroides*   Height up to 2m
Branched, upright perennial shrub. Leaves lanceolate with rounded tips; present in
autumn and winter only. Flowers with yellowish bracts; borne in umbels, April–June.
Rocky slopes near the seas. Widespread.

SUN SPURGE *Euphorbia helioscopia*   Height up to 50cm
Upright, little-branched annual. Leaves spoon-shaped, broadest near the tip. Flowers with
yellow bracts, lacking petals and sepals; borne in umbels, January–July. Favours disturbed
ground and cultivated soils. Widespread.

GREEK SPINY SPURGE *Euphorbia acanthothamnos*   Height up to 40cm
A 'hedgehog' plant, forming dense, spiny mounds; spines appear at tips of branches, which fork regularly. Leaves oval and bright green. Flowers with yellow bracts; appear March–May. Stony slopes and garrigue in E Mediterranean.

BROAD-LEAVED GLAUCOUS SPURGE *Euphorbia myrsinites*   Height up to 30cm
Radially spreading, often prostrate perennial with oval, blue-green and fleshy leaves. Flowers with rounded yellow bracts; appear March–June. Favours rocky slopes and garrigue habitat on Balearics and Corsica eastwards.

✓ **NARROW-LEAVED GLAUCOUS SPURGE** *Euphorbia rigida*   Height up to 40cm
Radially spreading, upright perennial with fleshy leaves, blue-green often flushed with purple. Flowers with rounded yellow bracts; appear March–May. Favours rocky slopes and garrigue. Widespread from Italy eastwards.

CAPER SPURGE *Euphorbia lathyris*   Height up to 120cm
Upright perennial with reddish stems and blue-green opposite and oval to heart-shaped leaves. Flowers green, appearing April–July. Fruits poisonous and comprise rounded capsules resembling edible capers. Stony ground, S France to Greece.

PETTY SPURGE *Euphorbia peplus*   Height up to 30cm
Upright, hairless annual. Branched stems carry oval, blunt-tipped and stalked leaves. These are topped by umbels of greenish flowers, comprising oval bracts; appear March–September. Cultivated and disturbed ground. Widespread.

SEA SPURGE *Euphorbia paralias*   Height up to 60cm
Upright, blue-green perennial with stout stems that bear whorl-like arrays of close-packed, grey-green and fleshy leaves. Flowers comprise yellowish bracts; appear February–September. Coastal stabilised sand dunes. Widespread.

✓ **CYPRESS SPURGE** *Euphorbia cyparissias*   Height up to 40cm
Upright, clump-forming perennial. Stems carry arrays of close-packed, needle-like leaves and growing tips resemble conifer shoots. Flowers with yellowish bracts; appear March–June. Rocky and stony ground. Iberia to Turkey; absent from most islands.

LARGE MEDITERRANEAN SPURGE *Euphorbia characias*   Height up to 150cm
Impressive clump-forming perennial. Stout stems carry grey-green, oval leaves. Flowers with green bracts and dark red glands; borne in large umbels, February–June. Rocky slopes, maquis and garrigue. Iberia eastwards to former Yugoslavia.

✓ **POINSETTIA** *Euphorbia pulcherrima*   Height up to 3m
Large evergreen shrub. Leaves oval, with a pointed tip. Flowers comprise small green glands surrounded by large oval, pointed-tipped red bracts; appear November–May. Widely planted in parks and gardens, and on roadsides.

ANNUAL MERCURY *Mercurialis annua*   Height up to 40cm
Upright, mostly hairless annual. Leaves, narrow-oval, opposite and toothed. Flowers yellowish; borne on stalked spikes, male and female on separate plants, October–April. Cultivated and disturbed ground. Widespread.

✓ **CASTOR OIL PLANT** *Ricinus communis*   Height up to 5m
Large, often red-tinged shrub. Leaves palmate, with 5–9 toothed lobes. Flowers in long spikes: females with red stigmas are terminal, with whitish males below; appear February–October. Fruit ovoid and spiny. Cultivated ground. Widespread.

CNEORUM *Cneorum tricoccon*   Height up to 1m
Evergreen hairless shrub. Leaves narrow and rounded-tipped. Flowers 6–8mm across, yellow with 3–4 petals; appear March–June. Fruits comprise 3 rounded lobes, red ripening black. Rocky slopes and maquis. Iberia to Italy; absent from most islands.

RUE *Ruta graveolens*   Height up to 40cm
Evergreen, clump-forming shrub. Leaves aromatic, blue-green and pinnately divided, lower ones most noticeably so. Flowers yellow and 4- or 5-petalled; in heads April–July. Dry stony ground. Locally native but widely naturalised.

FRINGED RUE *Ruta chalepensis*   Height up to 60cm
Evergreen, clump-forming shrub. Leaves aromatic, blue-green and pinnately divided, lower ones most noticeably so. Flowers yellow with 4 or 5 petals showing fringed margins; in heads April–July. Stony ground, mainly in E Mediterranean.

COMMON MILKWORT *Polygala vulgaris*   Height up to 30cm
Trailing or upright perennial. Leaves are alternate, narrow and pointed. Flowers 5–8mm long and usually blue, pink or white; borne in loose clusters, April–July. Favours grassy places, often on calcareous soils. Widespread; commonest in W.

NICE MILKWORT *Polygala nicaeensis*   Height up to 30cm
Trailing or upright perennial. Leaves are alternate and narrow with rounded tips. Flowers 8–11mm long and usually pink, blue or white; borne in loose clusters April–July. Favours garrigue and maquis. S France and N Italy only.

DODONAEA *Dodonaea viscosa*   Height up to 3m
Upright evergreen shrub. Leaves elongate-oval and sticky. Flowers green and reddish; borne in pendant clusters, May–July. Fruits are winged and reddish. Alien species, widely planted for hedging and shelter.

KASHMIR BALSAM *Impatiens balfourii*   Height up to 1m
Branched hairless annual. Leaves oval, toothed and pointed-tipped. Flowers pink and white and 30–40mm across; borne in groups of 4–8, June–October. Favours damp, shady ground. A garden escape that is naturalised in places.

CHRIST'S THORN *Paliurus spina-christi*   Height up to 2.5m
Extremely spiny, much-branched shrub with zigzag stems. Leaves oval, 3-veined and toothed. Flowers tiny and yellow; in clusters, April–September. Fruit disc-shaped. Favours maquis, garrigue and scrub. Widespread across region.

GRAPE VINE *Vitis vinifera*   Length up to 20m or more
Scrambling or climbing shrub. Leaves palmately divided into 5–7 lobes; borne alternately along stem with opposite tendrils. Flowers small and green; in clusters, May–June. Fruits are the familiar edible grapes. Widely cultivated.

✓ **COMMON MALLOW** *Malva sylvestris*   Height up to 1.5m
Upright or spreading perennial. Leaves are rounded at base but 5-lobed on stem. Flowers pink with purple veins and 25–30mm across; appear May–September. Fruits comprise hairy nutlets. Cultivated and disturbed ground. Widespread.

✓ **DWARF MALLOW** *Malva neglecta*   Height up to 50cm
Upright, hairy annual. Flower pale pinkish-lilac or whitish and 10–15mm across; appear April–September. Fruits comprise smooth nutlets. Favours cultivated and disturbed ground. Widespread.

MUSK MALLOW *Malva moschata*   Height up to 75cm
Upright, mainly hairless perennial. Leaves rounded and 3-lobed at the base but increasingly dissected up the stem. Flowers pale pink and 30–60mm across; appear May–July. Grassy places and field margins. Widespread; absent from most islands.

ROUGH MARSH-MALLOW *Althaea hirsuta*   Height up to 30cm
Often sprawling hairy annual. Leaves rounded to heart-shaped at the base but increasingly dissected up the stem. Flowers pink and 15–25mm across; appear March–May. Favours dry cultivated and disturbed ground. Widespread.

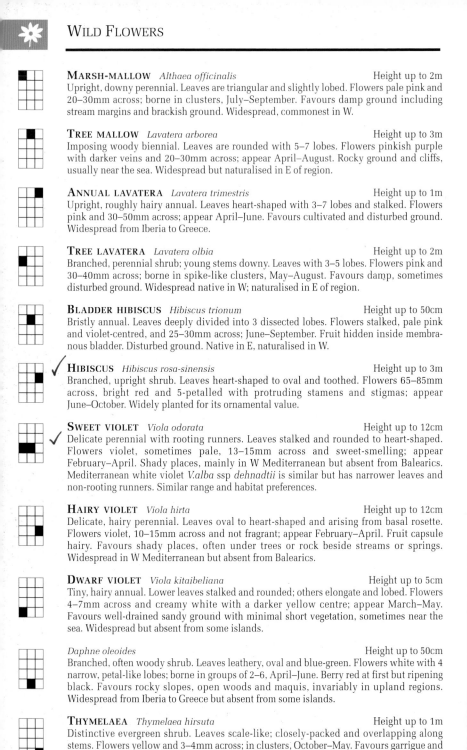

MARSH-MALLOW *Althaea officinalis*   Height up to 2m
Upright, downy perennial. Leaves are triangular and slightly lobed. Flowers pale pink and 20–30mm across; borne in clusters, July–September. Favours damp ground including stream margins and brackish ground. Widespread, commonest in W.

TREE MALLOW *Lavatera arborea*   Height up to 3m
Imposing woody biennial. Leaves are rounded with 5–7 lobes. Flowers pinkish purple with darker veins and 20–30mm across; appear April–August. Rocky ground and cliffs, usually near the sea. Widespread but naturalised in E of region.

ANNUAL LAVATERA *Lavatera trimestris*   Height up to 1m
Upright, roughly hairy annual. Leaves heart-shaped with 3–7 lobes and stalked. Flowers pink and 30–50mm across; appear April–June. Favours cultivated and disturbed ground. Widespread from Iberia to Greece.

TREE LAVATERA *Lavatera olbia*   Height up to 2m
Branched, perennial shrub; young stems downy. Leaves with 3–5 lobes. Flowers pink and 30–40mm across; borne in spike-like clusters, May–August. Favours damp, sometimes disturbed ground. Widespread native in W; naturalised in E of region.

BLADDER HIBISCUS *Hibiscus trionum*   Height up to 50cm
Bristly annual. Leaves deeply divided into 3 dissected lobes. Flowers stalked, pale pink and violet-centred, and 25–30mm across; June–September. Fruit hidden inside membranous bladder. Disturbed ground. Native in E, naturalised in W.

HIBISCUS *Hibiscus rosa-sinensis*   Height up to 3m
Branched, upright shrub. Leaves heart-shaped to oval and toothed. Flowers 65–85mm across, bright red and 5-petalled with protruding stamens and stigmas; appear June–October. Widely planted for its ornamental value.

SWEET VIOLET *Viola odorata*   Height up to 12cm
Delicate perennial with rooting runners. Leaves stalked and rounded to heart-shaped. Flowers violet, sometimes pale, 13–15mm across and sweet-smelling; appear February–April. Shady places, mainly in W Mediterranean but absent from Balearics. Mediterranean white violet *V.alba* ssp *dehnadtii* is similar but has narrower leaves and non-rooting runners. Similar range and habitat preferences.

HAIRY VIOLET *Viola hirta*   Height up to 12cm
Delicate, hairy perennial. Leaves oval to heart-shaped and arising from basal rosette. Flowers violet, 10–15mm across and not fragrant; appear February–April. Fruit capsule hairy. Favours shady places, often under trees or rock beside streams or springs. Widespread in W Mediterranean but absent from Balearics.

DWARF VIOLET *Viola kitaibeliana*   Height up to 5cm
Tiny, hairy annual. Lower leaves stalked and rounded; others elongate and lobed. Flowers 4–7mm across and creamy white with a darker yellow centre; appear March–May. Favours well-drained sandy ground with minimal short vegetation, sometimes near the sea. Widespread but absent from some islands.

Daphne oleoides   Height up to 50cm
Branched, often woody shrub. Leaves leathery, oval and blue-green. Flowers white with 4 narrow, petal-like lobes; borne in groups of 2–6, April–June. Berry red at first but ripening black. Favours rocky slopes, open woods and maquis, invariably in upland regions. Widespread from Iberia to Greece but absent from some islands.

THYMELAEA *Thymelaea hirsuta*   Height up to 1m
Distinctive evergreen shrub. Leaves scale-like; closely-packed and overlapping along stems. Flowers yellow and 3–4mm across; in clusters, October–May. Favours garrigue and dry, stony ground. Widespread across region.

BALEARIC ST JOHN'S-WORT *Hypericum balearicum* Height up to 1m
Upright, branched shrub with stems 4-angled when young. Leaves oval with a wavy margin; surface marked with conspicuous lumps. Flowers yellow, 5-petalled and 15–40mm across; appear July–October. Rocky slopes. Endemic to Balearics.

PERFORATE ST JOHN'S-WORT *Hypericum perforatum* Height up to 80cm
Upright perennial with paired, oval leaves that bear translucent dots borne on 2-lined stems. Flowers yellow, 5-petalled and 18–22mm across; appear May–July. Favours dry grassland, scrub and cultivated ground. Widespread.

GREY-LEAVED CISTUS *Cistus albidus* Height up to 1m
Rounded, evergreen shrub. Leaves elliptical and flat with 3 veins and greyish white downy hairs. Flowers pinkish purple and 40–60mm across; appear April–June. Garrigue and open maquis, often on calcareous soil. W of region but not islands.

NARROW-LEAVED CISTUS *Cistus monspeliensis* Height up to 1m
Dense, evergreen shrub. Unstalked leaves are narrow, sticky above and hairy below with 3 veins. Flowers white and 20–30mm across; appear March–June. Garrigue and other stony habitats. Widespread as far E as Cyprus.

SMALL-FLOWERED CISTUS *Cistus parviflorus* Height up to 1m
Spreading, evergreen shrub. Leaves stalked, 3-veined and hairy. Flowers pink and 20–30mm across; appear January–May. Favours garrigue and stony slopes with calcareous soil. Widespread in E Mediterranean as far W as Italy.

SAGE-LEAVED CISTUS *Cistus salvifolius* Height up to 1m
Spreading, evergreen shrub. Leaves oval, 3-veined and stalked, with a wavy margin; hairy above and below. Flowers white and 30–50mm across; appear February–June. Favours maquis, garrigue and stony slopes. Widespread and common.

GUM CISTUS *Cistus ladanifer* Height up to 2m
Sticky, aromatic shrub. Narrow leaves are dark green and shiny above but paler and hairy below. Flowers white, sometimes with dark red spot at petal bases, and 70–100mm across; appear April–June. Maquis and garrigue. Iberia and S France.

Halimium lasianthum Height up to 80cm
Upright, compact shrub. Leaves narrow-oval, dark green above, paler and hairy below. Flowers yellow, sometimes brown-spotted on petal bases, and 12–30mm across; appear April–June. Favours sandy soils. S Iberia only.

Halimium halimifolium Height up to 1m
Branched shrub. Leaves oval to oblong; downy white when young, grey-green when older. Flowers yellow, often with black spot at petal bases, and 20–30mm across; borne in groups, April–June. Maquis and coastal sandy soil. W Mediterranean.

SPOTTED ROCKROSE *Tuberaria guttata* Height up to 30cm
Annual with basal rosette of hairy, oval leaves from which flowering stem arises. Flowers 10–20mm across, yellow but petals dark-spotted at base; appear February–June. Petals easily dislodged. Maquis, garrigue and open ground. Widespread.

COMMON ROCKROSE *Helianthemum nummularium* Height up to 40cm
Spreading undershrub. Leaves paired, narrow and oblong; hairy below. Flowers 12–20mm across and yellow with 5 crinkly petals; appear April–July. Favours dry grassland and garrigue. Widespread but local or absent in much of the E.

HOARY ROCKROSE *Helianthemum canum* Height up to 30cm
Creeping, hairy undershrub. Leaves paired, narrow-oval and grey-green. Flowers yellow and 8–15mm across; borne in groups, April–July. Favours dry grassland and stony slopes on calcareous soils. Iberia to Turkey but absent from some islands.

WHITE ROCKROSE *Helianthemum appeninum* Height up to 50cm
Low, spreading shrub. Leaves variable, from oval to lanceolate; grey-green and woolly below. Flowers with white petals and yellow centre, 14–20mm across; in groups of 2–10, May–July. Dry grassy slopes on rocky ground. Widespread.

Helianthemum obtusifolius Height up to 40cm
Spreading undershrub. Leaves opposite, paired and narrow; hairy below. Flowers pale yellow and 20–28mm across; in groups of up to 10 flowers, May–July. Grassy slopes and garrigue. Endemic to Cyprus.

THYME-LEAVED FUMANA *Fumana thymifolia* Height up to 20cm
Much-branched undershrub. Leaves narrow and thyme-like; opposite lower down stem, irregularly alternate higher up. Flowers yellow and 10–14mm across; in groups of 4–9, April–June. Dry rocky slopes and garrigue. Widespread; absent much of E.

FUMANA *Fumana procumbens* Stem length up to 30cm but prostrate
Spreading, much-branched undershrub. Leaves narrow-oval and alternate. Flowers yellow and 12–18mm across; appear February–June. Favours maquis and garrigue, usually on calcareous soils. Widespread but absent from or local in much of E.

TAMARISK *Tamarix gallica* Height up to 5m
Upright, hairless shrub or small tree. Leaves blue-green, small and scale-like. Flowers pink or white; borne in long, drooping spikes, April–June. Riverbanks and coastal ground. Native in W of region; planted and naturalised elsewhere.

SEA-HEATH *Frankenia laevis* Prostrate
Creeping, mat-forming perennial. Leaves small, narrow and spiky, sometimes with chalky encrustation. Flowers pinkish purple, 5-petalled and 5–7mm across; appear all along stems, May–September. Salt-laden soils, mostly near sea. Widespread.

THYME-LEAVED SEA-HEATH *Frankenia thymifolia* Height up to 25cm
Much-branched undershrub. Leaves small, narrow and spiky; usually coated in chalky encrustation. Flowers pinkish purple, 5-petalled and 6–8mm across; borne in terminal clusters, April–June. Favours salt-laden soils. Mainly S Spain.

SQUIRTING CUCUMBER *Ecballium elaterium* Mainly prostrate
Spreading bristly perennial. Leaves fleshy, toothed and rounded to heart-shaped. Flowers yellow and 15–20mm long; appear February–September. Fruits green and cucumber-like; ripe seeds violently squirted out. Stony ground. Widespread.

WHITE BRYONY *Bryonia cretica* Height up to 4m
Climbing perennial. Leaves with 5 rounded lobes. Also has coiling tendrils. Flowers whitish with dark veins and 10–18mm across; appear April–September. Berries green, ripening red. Scrubby areas on calcareous soils. Widespread.

PRICKLY PEAR *Opuntia ficus-indica* Height up to 5m
Large, spiny succulent comprising green, flattened branches. Flowers yellow and up to 100mm long; appear March–July. Fruit ovoid and yellowish. Favours rocky ground and field margins. Alien but widely cultivated and planted for hedging.

Lythrum junceum Height up to 50cm
Upright, hairless perennial. Leaves narrow and oblong. Flowers 6-petalled, purple and 6–8mm across; appear March–September. Favours damp ground, pool margins and marshes. Widespread across the Mediterranean.

GRASS-POLY *Lythrum hyssopifolia* Height up to 30cm
Upright, hairless perennial. Leaves narrow and pointed. Flowers 3–5mm across, pink with 4–6 petals; appear March–September. Favours damp ground, especially winter-wet hollows on arable land. Widespread across the Mediterranean.

GREATER WILLOWHERB *Epilobium hirsutum*   Height up to 2m
Imposing perennial with hairy stems bearing unstalked hairy leaves in opposite pairs. Flowers 4-petalled, pinkish-purple and 15–25 mm across; borne in terminal groups, June–October. Favours damp ground and river margins. Widespread.

MARSH WILLOWHERB *Epilobium palustre*   Height up to 50cm
Slender perennial with rounded stems that carry opposite pairs of narrow leaves. Flowers are pink or white and 4–7mm across with a club-shaped stigma; appear June–August. Favours damp ground. Widespread but absent from many islands.

MARSH PENNYWORT *Hydrocotyle vulgaris*   Creeping
An atypical umbellifer, best known for its round, dimpled leaves found among low vegetation. Flowers tiny and pinkish but hidden by leaves; appear April–July. Favours marshy ground. Widespread; commonest in W but absent from many islands.

SEA-HOLLY *Eryngium maritimum*   Height up to 60cm
Distinctive perennial. Leaves grey-green or grey-blue and spiny, resembling those of holly. Blue flowers are borne in globular umbels and appear June–September. Favours coastal shingle and sand. Widespread across Mediterranean.

FIELD ERYNGO *Eryngium campestre*   Height up to 60cm
Branched, upright perennial. Leaves lobed and sharp-toothed; stem leaves unstalked. Flowers greenish white; borne in globular heads, below which are spiny bracts, June–October. Widespread although local or absent in parts of E.

ALEXANDERS *Smyrnium olusatrum*   Height up to 1.25m
Distinctive, strong-smelling biennial with leaves three times divided into dark green shiny lobes. Flowers yellowish and borne in rounded umbels, February–May. Favours damp ground, often along field or road margins and in scrub. Widespread.

Smyrnium rotundifolium   Height up to 1.5m
Impressive, hairless biennial with ridged stems. Lower leaves with rounded lobes but stems leaves rounded and clasping the stems. Flowers yellow and borne in rounded umbels, February–May. Favours upland, rocky wooded slopes. Mainly in E.

SHEPHERD'S NEEDLE *Scandix pecten-veneris*   Height up to 30cm
Upright, hairless annual, best known for its long, needle-like and erect fruits. Leaves finely divided and feathery. Flowers white and borne in open umbels, January–July. Favours cultivated and disturbed ground. Widespread.

ROCK SAMPHIRE *Crithmum maritimum*   Height up to 40cm
Grey-green perennial with leaves divided into narrow, fleshy lobes. Flowers greenish yellow and borne in broad umbels, June–September. A characteristic plant of coastal sand, shingle and rocky habitats. Widespread across Mediterranean.

HEMLOCK WATER-DROPWORT *Oenanthe crocata*   Height up to 1.25m
Distinctive, poisonous perennial. Leaves are 2–4 times pinnately divided and are borne on hollow, ridged stems. Flowers white and borne in domed, open umbels, May–July. Favours damp meadows and ditches. Widespread in W Mediterranean.

TUBULAR WATER-DROPWORT *Oenanthe fistulosa*   Height up to 80cm
Upright, grey-green and hairless perennial. Leaves are pinnately divided into tubular lobes. Flowers white and borne in small, rather dense umbels. Favours damp ground, often near the sea. Widespread but local.

FENNEL *Foeniculum vulgare*   Height up to 2m
Distinctive aromatic and grey-green perennial with feathery leaves comprising thread-like leaflets. Flowers yellow and borne in open umbels, April–September. Favours cultivated and disturbed ground, often near the sea. Widespread.

SHRUBBY HARE'S-EAR *Bupleurum fruiticosum* Height up to 2m
Hairless, evergreen and aromatic shrub. Stems reddish and leaves dark green, oval and leathery. Flowers yellowish and borne in broad umbels, April–August. Favours stony slopes and garrigue. Widespread, Iberia to Greece; absent from many islands.

THOROW-WAX *Bupleurum rotundifolium* Height up to 70cm
Upright annual, blue-green but often tinged purple. Leaves rounded, upper ones encircling the stem. Flowers small and yellow with star-shaped yellow bracts; borne in small umbels, May–July. Disturbed and cultivated ground. Widespread.

SICKLE-LEAVED HARE'S-EAR *Bupleurum falcatum* Height up to 1m
Slender, upright perennial. Lower leaves oval to elliptical, upper ones narrow, curved and sickle-like. Flowers small, yellow and borne in small open umbels, June–August. Stony ground and field margins. Widespread; absent from most islands.

SLENDER HARE'S-EAR *Bupleurum tenuissimum* Height up to 50cm
Slender upright or spreading annual. Leaves narrow and pointed. Flowers small, yellow and borne in open, delicate umbels, April–June. Favours salt-laden soils, hence mostly coastal. Widespread but absent from many islands and much of E.

Bupleurum gracile Height up to 40cm
Slender, branched annual. Leaves narrow and 3–5 veined; lower leaves stalked, upper ones unstalked. Flowers yellowish with pointed, membranous bracts; borne in small open umbels, April–June. Garrigue, often coastal. Greece and Turkey.

WILD CELERY *Apium graveolens* Height up to 1m
Upright biennial, smelling strongly of celery. Leaves 1–2 times pinnately divided. Flowers greenish white and borne in umbels 40–60mm across, May–July. Favours salt-laden ground and hence mainly coastal. Widespread except in E.

FOOL'S WATER-CRESS *Apium nodiflorum* Height up to 20cm
Creeping perennial, rooting at the lower nodes. Shiny leaves comprise oval, toothed leaflets. Flowers white and borne in loose umbels, April–August. Favours ditches, wet hollows and muddy river margins. Widespread.

CREEPING MARSHWORT *Apium repens* Height up to 15cm
Creeping perennial, similar to *A.nodiflorum* but rooting at all nodes. Leaves comprise oval, toothed leaflets. Flowers white and borne in small umbels, April–July. Wet hollows, ditches and stream margins. Iberia, S France and N Italy only.

GIANT FENNEL *Ferula communis* Height up to 3m
Imposing and distinctive perennial. Leaves large and feathery, being divided into long, thread-like lobes. Flowers yellow and borne in large, almost spherical umbels, March–June. Favours garrigue, stony ground and roadsides. Widespread.

HOGWEED *Heracleum sphondylium* Height up to 2m
Robust, upright perennial. Leaves broad, hairy and pinnate; borne on hollow, hairy stems. Flowers off-white with unequal petals; borne in large umbels April–July. Favours grassy slopes, roadsides and field margins. Widespread but local.

TORDYLIUM *Tordylium apulum* Height up to 50cm
Upright, hairy annual. Leaves pinnately divided into oval to triangular lobes; lower ones toothed. Flowers white, outer ones with unequal petals; borne in open umbels, March–June. Cultivated and disturbed ground. Widespread.

KNOTTED HEDGE-PARSLEY *Torilis nodosa* Height up to 50cm
Creeping, grey-green and hairy annual. Leaves finely divided. Flowers pinkish white and borne in small, dense umbels, March–August. Fruit egg-shaped and spiny. Cultivated and disturbed ground. Widespread across Mediterranean.

WILD CARROT *Daucus carota*   Height up to 75cm
Upright, hairy biennial. Feathery leaves are 2–3 times pinnately divided into narrow leaflets. Dense umbels pinkish in bud but white in flower with central flower red; appear April–September. Grassy places, often on coast. Widespread.

PSEUDORLAYA *Pseudorlaya pumila*   Height up to 20cm
Branched and extremely hairy annual. Leaves 2–3 times pinnately divided into rounded-oval leaflets. Flowers pinkish and borne on small, open umbels, February–May. Fruits ovoid and spiny. Coastal sand dunes. Widespread across region.

TREE HEATH *Erica arborea*   Height up to 3m or more
Impressive, evergreen shrub. Leaves dark green and needle-like; borne in whorls of 4. Flowers bell-shaped and white; borne in clusters, May–June. Favours maquis, scrubby habitats and open woodland. Widespread but commonest in W Mediterranean and absent from much of E.

PORTUGUESE HEATH *Erica lusitanica*   Height up to 3m
Tall evergreen shrub. Leaves pale green and needle-like; borne in whorls of 4. Flowers pinkish white; borne in clusters, March–May. Favours open woods and heaths, usually on damp soils. Iberian Peninsula only.

Erica multiflora   Height up to 80cm
Small, upright shrub. Leaves dark green and needle-like; borne in whorls of 4–5. Flowers pink and narrow bell-shaped; borne in clusters, November–March. Favours rocky slopes among scrub and open woods. Widespread, Iberia to former Yugoslavia.

BELL HEATHER *Erica cinerea*   Height up to 50cm
Hairless undershrub. Leaves dark green and needle-like; borne in whorls of 3 up the wiry stems. Flowers reddish purple and bell-shape; borne in groups along stems, June–September. Favours heaths and open ground on well-drained sandy or stony soil. Widespread from Iberia to N Italy only.

YELLOW RHODODENDRON *Rhododendron luteum*   Height up to 4m
Deciduous shrub with spreading and upright stems. Leaves oblong-oval and 10cm long. Flowers yellow and trumpet-shaped, 10–15mm long; borne in crowded, globular heads, April–May. Favours damp streamsides in conifer woodland, usually at moderate altitudes. Local and restricted to E Mediterranean only.

Lysimachia atropurpurea   Height up to 50cm
Upright perennial. Alternate leaves are narrow, finely toothed and with wavy margins. Flowers deep purple and borne in terminal spikes, May–July; after flowering, style becomes spine-like and projecting. Favours disturbed sandy ground. Confined to E Mediterranean only.

SEA-MILKWORT *Glaux maritima*   Prostrate
Fleshy, creeping perennial that roots at many of its nodes. Leaves narrow-oval and opposite. Flowers 3–6mm across, with pinkish sepals and no petals; borne along stems, March–September. Coastal habitats. Iberia and S France only.

BROOKWEED *Samolus valerandi*   Height up to 40cm
Creeping perennial with upright stems. Leaves are oval and borne mainly in a basal rosette but also appear alternately up stem. Flowers white and 2–3mm across; borne on stalks alternately up stem, April–July. Favours damp, usually salt-laden or calcareous ground. Widespread across the region.

CORIS *Coris monspeliensis*   Height up to 30cm
Upright perennial. Leaves narrow, recurved and alternate; 2 rows of black dots either side of midrib. Flowers lilac-purple, 9–12mm across, with 5 notched lobes; April–July. Dry sandy or stony ground, often coastal. W and C Mediterranean only.

SCARLET PIMPERNEL *Anagallis arvensis*　　　　　　　　Prostrate
Hairless annual with opposite pairs of unstalked, oval leaves borne on trailing stems. Flowers 4–7mm across, usually red but sometimes blue or pink; borne on stalks along stems, April–October. Disturbed and cultivated ground. Widespread.

Anagallis foemina　　　　　　　　Prostrate
Hairless annual with opposite pairs of narrow, unstalked leaves borne on trailing stems. Flowers 4–7mm across, blue with hairless petal margins (those of *A. arvensis* are hairy); April–October. Mainly on cultivated ground. Widespread.

CHAFFWEED *Anagallis minima*　　　　　　　　Height up to 3cm
Tiny, easily overlooked annual with small, alternate leaves. Minute flowers are 1–2mm across and whitish with petals shorter than sepals; April–August. Damp ground with short vegetation. Widespread. A challenge to find or recognise.

SHRUBBY PIMPERNEL *Anagallis monelli*　　　　　　　　Height up to 50cm
Upright or sometimes spreading perennial. Leaves narrow-oval and borne in whorls or opposite pairs. Flowers 6–12mm across, usually blue but sometimes red or white; borne on stalks, March–June. Dry sandy soil. Iberia, Sardinia and Sicily.

IVY-LEAVED SOWBREAD *Cyclamen hederifolium*　　　　　　　　Height up to 10cm
Tuberous perennial with heart-shaped, ivy-like leaves variegated whitish and dark green. Flowers pink with forked blotch at base of each lobe; appear September–October. Stony ground including maquis and garrigue. S France to Turkey.

SPRING SOWBREAD *Cyclamen repandum*　　　　　　　　Height up to 10cm
Tuberous perennial. Leaves heart-shaped with irregular margins; variegated dark green and silvery. Flowers reddish pink and unmarked; March–May. Bare ground in open woodland. Mainly S France, N Italy, Corsica and Sardinia.

CRETAN SOWBREAD *Cyclamen creticum*　　　　　　　　Height up to 10cm
Tuberous perennial. Leaves heart-shaped with wavy margins; dark green, marbled with whitish. Flowers unmarked and usually white; appear March–May. Favours stony ground, often in shady and damp sites. Endemic to Crete and Karpathos.

BALEARIC SOWBREAD *Cyclamen balearicum*　　　　　　　　Height up to 8cm
Tuberous perennial. Leaves heart-shaped with wavy margins; dark green with down-rolled margins. Flowers white and unmarked: appear March–May. Stony ground, often on shady slopes in open maquis. Balearic Islands and locally in S France.

Armeria pungens　　　　　　　　Height up to 50cm
Tufted perennial, sometimes reaching proportions of a small shrub. Leaves narrow and up to 10cm long. Flowers usually pink; borne in dense heads 20–30mm across, April–July. Stabilised coastal sand dunes. S Iberia, Corsica and Sardinia only.

COMMON SEA-LAVENDER *Limonium vulgare*　　　　　　　　Height up to 30cm
Hairless perennial with basal rosette of stalked and spoon-shaped leaves. Flowers clustered and pinkish lilac; borne in branched, flat-topped heads as arching sprays, July–October. Saltmarshes and mudflats. Widespread, except in E.

LIMONIASTRUM *Limoniastrum monopetalum*　　　　　　　　Height up to 2m
Large, clump-forming shrub. Leaves grey-green and spoon-shaped. Flowers pinkish lilac or bluish lilac; colour varies from plant to plant; appear June–August. Saltmarshes and seawalls. Occurs mainly Iberia to Italy.

WINGED SEA-LAVENDER *Limonium sinuatum*　　　　　　　　Height up to 50cm
Hairy perennial with winged stems. Stalked leaves comprise 4–7 pairs of rounded lobes. Flowers yellowish white but drying purple, both extremes usually seen together on arched sprays; appear March–September. Mainly coastal. Widespread.

YELLOW-WORT *Blackstonia perfoliata* Height up to 30cm
Upright, grey-green annual. Leaves form basal rosette; also up stem in opposite pairs, fused at base around stem. Flowers yellow and 6–8 petalled, opening in sunlight; April–September. Mainly on calcareous or sandy ground. Widespread.

COMMON CENTAURY *Centaurium erythraea* Height up to 25cm
Upright, branching biennial. Has a basal rosette of oval leaves and opposite pairs of leaves on stems. Clusters of pink, 5-petalled flowers appear May–August. Dry, grassy ground, mostly on calcareous soils. Widespread across the region.

SLENDER CENTAURY *Centaurium tenuiflorum* Height up to 15cm
Upright, branching annual. Leaves oval and borne in opposite pairs up stems; no basal rosette. Flowers pale and 5-petalled; borne in clusters, June–August. Favours damp ground, often coastal. Widespread across the region.

LESSER CENTAURY *Centaurium pulchellum* Height up to 15cm
Slender annual, branching from low down. Leaves oval and borne in opposite pairs up stems; no basal rosette. Flowers pink and 5-petalled; borne in clusters, June–August. Short grassland and bare sandy soil; usually on damp ground. Widespread.

OLEANDER *Nerium oleander* Height up to 4m
Dense, poisonous shrub with slender stems. Leaves narrow and leathery. Flowers 5-lobed, 30–40mm across and usually pink; borne in clusters, May–August. Favours gravely ground, especially riverbanks. Widespread across region.

LADY'S BEDSTRAW *Galium verum* Height up to 30cm
Branched perennial. 4-angled stems carry narrow leaves with rolled margins in whorls of 8–12; leaves blacken when dry. Flowers yellow, 4-lobed and 3mm across; in clusters, April–July. Dry, grassy places. Widespread; absent from some islands.

HEDGE BEDSTRAW *Galium mollugo* Scrambling, up to 1.5m
Hairless perennial with square stems that carry narrow leaves in whorls of 6–8. Flowers white, 4-lobed and 2–3mm across; borne in open clusters, May–August. Favours dry grassy habitats. Widespread in W and C but absent from Balearics.

WILD MADDER *Rubia peregrina* Scrambling, up to 2m
Evergreen perennial with long square stems bearing angled bristles. Leaves oval, leathery and dark green; in whorls of 4–8. Flowers whitish, 5-lobed and 5mm across; in clusters, May–July. Scrub and garrigue on stony ground. Widespread.

GOOSEGRASS *Galium aparine* Height up to 1.5m
Sprawling annual. Backward-pointing prickles secure plant in its scrambling progress through vegetation. Leaves narrow and borne in whorls of 6–8. Flowers tiny and white; appear May–July. Fruits have hooked bristles. Widespread.

FIELD MADDER *Sherardia arvensis* Creeping
Hairy annual. Leaves narrow and oval; borne in whorls of 4–6 along stems. Heads of pinkish flowers, each one 3–5mm across, appear March–July. Favours cultivated arable land and disturbed ground. Widespread across the region.

LAURUSTINUS *Viburnum tinus* Height up to 6m
Hairless evergreen shrub. Leaves oval, leathery and short-stalked. Flowers white but pink in bud; 5–9mm across and borne in umbel-like heads, May–July. Fruit a dark blue berry. Favours scrub-covered slopes. Widespread, mainly in W and C.

COMMON DODDER *Cuscuta epithymum* Climbing
Parasitic, leafless plant. Lacks chlorophyll and gains nutrition from host plants, which include species of heath and clover. Clusters, 7–10mm across, of pink flowers are borne on red, twining stems, May–October. Widespread.

SEA BINDWEED *Calystegia soldanella*   Creeping
Spreading, hairless perennial. Leaves are kidney-shaped and borne on long stalks.
Flowers 40–50mm across and pink with white stripes; appear June–August. Favours
coastal sand and shingle. Widespread in most parts of the region.

HEDGE BINDWEED *Calystegia sepium*   Climbing, up to 2–3m
Perennial, twining around other plants to assist its progress. Leaves arrow-shaped and up
to 12cm long. Flowers white and 30–40mm across with basal bracts that do not overlap;
June–September. Favours hedgerows and scrub. Widespread.

GREAT BINDWEED *Calystegia silvatica*   Climbing, up to 2–3m
Perennial, twining around other plants as it grows. Leaves arrow-shaped and up to 12cm
long. Flowers white and 50–90mm across with basal bracts that overlap; appear
June–September. Favours hedges, scrub and walls. Widespread.

HEAVENLY BLUE *Ipomoea tricolor*   Climbing, up to 4m
Twining annual with stalked and heart-shaped leaves. Flowers funnel-shaped, blue and
60–80mm across; appear July–September. Native to C America but grown in gardens and
occasionally escapes.

MALLOW-LEAVED BINDWEED *Convolvulus althaeoides*   Climbing, up to 1m
Twining, hairy perennial. Leaves grey-green; upper ones deeply divided into 5 lobes,
lower ones heart-shaped with wavy margins. Flowers bell-shaped, reddish pink and
30–50mm across; appear March–July. Stony ground. Widespread.

DWARF CONVOLVULUS *Convolvulus tricolor*   Creeping
Spreading, hairy annual. Leaves oval with a heart-shaped base. Flowers funnel-shaped
and tricoloured: yellow and white in centre, blue around margin; appear March–June.
Disturbed ground, often on sand. Widespread except in E.

FIELD BINDWEED *Convolvulus arvensis*   Creeping or climbing, up to 2–3m
Twining, hairless perennial. Twists around other plants to assist its progress. Leaves long-
stalked, arrow-shaped and 20–50mm long. Flowers 15–30mm across, white and pink
striped; appear April–August. Cultivated ground. Widespread.

PURPLE GROMWELL *Buglossoides purpurocaerulea*   Height up to 40cm
Hairy, rather straggly perennial with long lanceolate leaves. Flowers funnel-shaped,
12–15mm across, changing from reddish purple to blue; borne in heads, March–June.
Favours scrub and shady woodland edge. Iberia to Turkey.

CORN GROMWELL *Buglossoides arvensis*   Height up to 30cm
Upright, hairy annual. Leaves oblong to spatula-shaped. Flowers funnel-shaped, 5-lobed
and usually whitish; in small clusters, February–June. Favours cultivated and disturbed
stony ground. Widespread across the region.

Lithodora hispidula   Height up to 30cm
Much-branched, hairy undershrub with narrow-oval leaves. Flowers funnel-shaped, 5-
lobed and 10mm long; pink, white or blue, appearing February–June. Stony slopes and
garrigue. Local in E, including Crete, Karpathos, Cyprus and Turkey.

ONOSMA *Onosma fruticosa*   Height up to 25cm
Spreading, branched and hairy perennial. Leaves narrow-oval. Flowers orange-yellow,
10–14mm long; in hanging clusters, March–May. Stony ground and garrigue. Cyprus
endemic. Similar *O.frutescens* has larger flowers; Greece and Turkey.

HONEYWORT *Cerinthe major*   Height up to 50cm
Upright hairless annual. Leaves fleshy and oval; heart-shaped base clasps the stem.
Flowers 20–30mm long, maroon at base and yellow-tipped; borne in hanging clusters,
March–June. Stony, often disturbed ground. Widespread.

WILD FLOWERS

VIPER'S-BUGLOSS *Echium vulgare* Height up to 80cm
Roughly hairy biennial. Leaves are narrow and pointed; basal leaves stalked. Flowers funnel-shaped, bright blue and 15–20mm long; in dense spikes, April–July. Dry, often sandy or calcareous soils. Widespread; absent Balearics and Cyprus.

BORAGE *Borago officinalis* Height up to 30cm
Bristly, upright annual. Lower leaves are stalked and in a basal rosette; upper leaves clasp the stem. Flowers 5-petalled, 20–25mm across and lilac-blue with dark anthers; appear March–June. Cultivated and disturbed ground. Widespread.

LARGE BLUE ALKANET *Anchusa azurea* Height up to 1.5m
Bristly, branched and upright perennial. Leaves narrow, lower ones stalked. Flowers blue and 10–20mm long, with 5 rounded lobes; borne in clusters March–June. Cultivated ground and garrigue. Widespread across the region.

UNDULATE ANCHUSA *Anchusa undulata hybrida* Height up to 45cm
Bristly biennial or perennial. Leaves narrow-elliptical with wavy margins; lower ones in basal rosette, upper ones clasping stem. Flowers 5-lobed, purple with white centre; in curled heads, March–June. Garrigue and stony ground. Widespread.

PURPLE VIPER'S-BUGLOSS *Echium plantagineum* Height up to 40cm
Softly hairy biennial. Leaves show prominent side veins; stem leaves clasping and heart-shaped at base. Dry sandy ground. Widespread and common. Several similar species occur in region.

LANTANA *Lantana camara* Height up to 1.5m
Much-branched prickly shrub with a pungent smell. Leaves oval to heart-shaped and toothed. Flowers yellow or orange, changing to pink or red; borne in flat-topped heads, May–October. Widely cultivated and occasionally naturalised.

VERVAIN *Verbena officinalis* Height up to 50cm
Upright hairy perennial with square stems. Lower leaves small and narrow, upper ones larger, oval and deeply divided. Flowers pink and 2–5mm across; borne in long spikes, May–September. Dry grassland and disturbed ground. Widespread.

BUGLE *Ajuga reptans* Height up to 20cm
Perennial with creeping runners that root at intervals. Stems hairy on 2 opposite sides. Leaves oval and stalked. Flowers blue-violet and 15mm long; on upright flowering stems, March–July. Grassy places on calcareous soils. Widespread.

BLUE BUGLE *Ajuga genevensis* Height up to 20cm
Perennial that lacks creeping runners. Stems hairy all round. Leaves oval and lobed, lower ones stalked. Flowers blue and 15–20mm long; borne in upright spikes, March–July. Grassy places on calcareous soils. W and C Mediterranean.

GROUND-PINE *Ajuga chamaepitys* Height up to 20cm
Hairy spreading annual, smelling of pine when crushed. Stem leaves are deeply divided into 3 narrow lobes. Flowers yellow and 7–15mm long; borne at leaf nodes, February–July. Favours open disturbed ground on calcareous soils. Widespread.

EASTERN SKULLCAP *Scutellaria orientalis* Height up to 25cm
Spreading, hairy perennial. Leaves narrow heart-shaped with lobed margins. Flowers yellow and 15–20mm long; borne in terminal heads, April–July. Dry, calcareous soils. E Mediterranean and mountains of S Spain.

SKULLCAP *Scutellaria galericulata* Height up to 40cm
Hairy perennial with square stems. Leaves oval, stalked and toothed. Flowers pale blue and 15mm long; on upright, leafy stems, May–August. Damp ground in marshes and beside rivers. Widespread but local or absent in E and from many islands.

280

WILD FLOWERS

WALL GERMANDER *Teucrium chamaedrys*   Height up to 50cm
Upright hairy perennial. Leaves opposite, oval and toothed. Flowers pinkish purple and 10–16mm long; in leafy spikes, April–September. Dry bare ground and areas of short grass, often on calcareous soils. Widespread.

WATER GERMANDER *Teucrium scordium*   Height up to 40cm
Softly hairy perennial, smelling of garlic when crushed. Leaves oval with heart-shaped base. Flowers purple and 7–10mm long; borne in whorls, June–September. Favours marshes and damp ground. Widespread across the region.

WOOD-SAGE *Teucrium scorodonia*   Height up to 40cm
Downy upright perennial. Leaves heart-shaped and stalked. Flowers yellowish, paired and 8–9mm long; borne in spikes, June–September. Stony slopes, open scrub and hedge banks. Iberia to former Yugoslavia; absent from Balearics and Crete.

WHITE HOREHOUND *Marrubium vulgare*   Height up to 60cm
Branching, downy perennial. Leaves oval and heart-shaped at the base with lobed margins. Flowers white and 12–15mm long; borne in whorls up stem, March–October. Stony and rocky ground, often on calcareous soils. Widespread across the region.

JERUSALEM SAGE *Phlomis fruticosa*   Height up to 1.5m
Branched shrub covered in greyish felt-like hairs. Leaves oval and stalked, grey-green above and whitish below. Flowers yellow and 25–35mm long; borne in whorls, April–June. Favours dry stony ground. Widespread in E Mediterranean.

Phlomis purpurea   Height up to 2m
Hairy evergreen shrub. Leaves oblong, grey-green above and whitish below. Flowers purple and 22–25mm long; borne in whorls, April–June. Favours stony and rocky ground, often among scrub. Confined to S Iberian Peninsula.

Phlomis herba-venti   Height up to 70cm
Upright hairy perennial. Leaves oval with a heart-shaped base, grey-green above and whitish and downy below. Flowers pinkish purple and 15–20mm long; borne in whorls, April–July. Favours dry stony and rocky ground. Iberia to Turkey.

Ballota pseudodictamnus   Height up to 40cm
Upright perennial with yellowish downy hairs. Leaves rounded to oval and heart-shaped at the base. Flowers purple and 14–15mm long; borne in whorls, April–May. Rocky and stony ground. Native to Crete and Aegean Islands; cultivated elsewhere.

SELF-HEAL *Prunella vulgaris*   Height up to 20cm
Creeping, downy perennial. Leaves are oval, paired and stalked. Flowers blue-violet and 13–15mm long; borne in dense clusters on leafy stems, May–August. Favours short grassland, mainly on calcareous soils. Widespread.

LARGE SELF-HEAL *Prunella grandiflora*   Height up to 30cm
Creeping, downy perennial. Leaves are oval, paired and stalked. Flowers blue-violet and 25–30mm long; borne in dense clusters on leafy stems, May–August. Dry grassland on calcareous soils. Iberia to Turkey; absent from most islands.

CATMINT *Nepeta cataria*   Height up to 70cm
Upright branched perennial with grey downy hairs and smelling pleasantly of mint. Leaves oval and heart-shaped at base. Flowers white with purple spots and 8–10mm long; in spikes, May–August. Dry calcareous ground. Iberia to Turkey.

DOWNY WOUNDWORT *Stachys germanica*   Height up to 80cm
Downy perennial. Leaves green, oval, heart-shaped at base. Flowers purplish and 15–20mm long; in whorls, May–July. Widespread on dry ground; absent Cyprus and Crete. *S.cretica* similar but oval leaves grey above. Widespread except Iberia.

LARGE RED DEADNETTLE *Lamium garganicum* Height up to 50cm
Spreading, hairy perennial. Leaves triangular, heart-shaped at the base and with toothed margins. Flowers pinkish purple with dark markings and 25–40mm long; borne in heads, February–July. Rocky and stony ground. Widespread in C and E.

HENBIT DEADNETTLE *Lamium amplexicaule* Height up to 20cm
An often trailing, hairy annual. Leaves heart-shaped, toothed and unstalked. Flowers are purple and 14–20mm long; in open, terminal clusters, December–June. Favours cultivated and disturbed ground. Widespread across the region.

RED DEADNETTLE *Lamium purpureum* Height up to 30cm
Branched, downy annual. Leaves are heart-shaped toothed and stalked. Flowers are pinkish purple and 10–17mm long; borne in whorls on upright stems, January–June. Favours cultivated and disturbed ground. Widespread across the region.

BASIL-THYME *Acinos arvensis* Height up to 20cm
Delicate, spreading and hairy annual. Leaves narrow-oval and toothed. Flowers violet purple with white spots and 7–10mm long; borne in whorls, April–July. Dry grassy habitats, often on calcareous soils. Widespread but distribution patchy.

LESSER CALAMINT *Calamintha nepeta* Height up to 40cm
Slender, grey-green and hairy perennial. Leaves rounded-oval with lobed margins. Flowers pale pinkish lilac with darker spots and 10–15mm long; borne in whorls, June–October. Favours dry grassy places, avoiding hot, dry sites. Widespread.

WILD BASIL *Clinopodium vulgare* Height up to 35cm
Aromatic and hairy perennial. Leaves oval, short-stalked and toothed. Flowers pinkish purple with bristly bracts and 15–20mm long; borne in whorls, May–August. Favours dry grassland, mainly on calcareous soils. Widespread, absent from Balearics.

THYME *Thymus vulgaris* Height up to 25cm
Aromatic and often mat-forming perennial. Leaves narrow-ovate and borne in clusters. Flowers pinkish purple and 5–6mm long; in terminal heads, April–July. Dry grassland and garrigue. S France and Italy; naturalised elsewhere.

Thymus camphoratus Height up to 40cm
Aromatic, woody-based perennial, sometimes forming a compact undershrub. Leaves narrow and borne in clusters. Flowers pinkish purple and 4–6mm long; borne in terminal heads, 12–18mm across, April–July. Stony garrigue. S Portugal only.

Thymus capitatus Height up to 50cm
Aromatic, much-branched undershrub with delicate-looking but wiry stems. Leaves narrow and borne in clusters. Flowers pinkish purple and 7–10mm long; borne in ovoid terminal clusters, May–October. Dry sandy and stony ground. Widespread.

MARJORAM *Origanum vulgare* Height up to 50cm
Aromatic, hairy perennial. Leaves oval and pointed; borne in pairs on reddish stems. Flowers pinkish purple and 4–7mm long; borne in dense terminal clusters, June–October. Dry grassland, mainly on calcareous soils. Widespread.

ROSEMARY *Rosmarinus officinalis* Height up to 2m
Aromatic and usually upright shrub. Leaves narrow and leathery; borne in clusters along stems. Flowers 10–12mm long and usually bluish lilac; borne in clusters along stems, January–May. Maquis, garrigue and scrub. Widespread.

FRENCH LAVENDER *Lavandula stoechas* Height up to 1m
Aromatic, much-branched and grey-green shrub. Leaves narrow, untoothed and borne in clusters. Flowers deep purple and 10–50mm long; borne on terminal heads, March–June. Garrigue, maquis and stony ground. Widespread across the region.

SPEAR MINT *Mentha spicata*   Height up to 75cm
Upright, strongly-scented perennial. Leaves are narrow-ovate, toothed and unstalked. Flowers pale lilac and 3–4mm long; borne in long, upright spikes, July November. Favours damp ground. Widely cultivated and frequently naturalised.

PENNYROYAL *Mentha pulegium*   Height up to 30cm
Sweetly aromatic and often creeping perennial. Leaves oval, short-stalked and slightly toothed. Flowers lilac and 5–6mm long; borne in dense whorls at intervals along stem, June–August. Damp ground and marsh margins. Widespread.

HORSE MINT *Mentha longifolia*   Height up to 1m
Upright, downy grey-green perennial. Leaves oblong and sharply-toothed. Flowers lilac and 3–4mm long; borne in clusters in a terminal spike, June–October. Damp marshy ground and river margins. Widespread but absent from most islands.

WATER MINT *Mentha aquatica*   Height up to 50cm
Strongly mint-scented perennial. Leaves oval and toothed; borne on reddish, hairy stems. Flowers lilac-pink and 4–6mm long; borne in dense terminal heads, 2cm long, June–August. Damp ground, sometimes growing in water. Widespread.

SAGE *Salvia officinalis*   Height up to 60cm
Much-branched aromatic shrub. Leaves oval-elliptical and stalked, green above but whitish below. Flowers bluish purple and 25–35mm long; in whorls, May–July. Stony ground and garrigue. Native to Spain, S France; naturalised elsewhere.

CLARY *Salvia sclarea*   Height up to 1m
Upright, strong-smelling and hairy biennial or perennial. Leaves heart-shaped, toothed and stalked. Flowers pale bluish-lilac and 20–30mm long with purple bracts; borne in whorls, May–July. Stony ground. Widespread, often cultivated.

CHINA TEAPLANT *Lycium chinense*   Height up to 2m
Deciduous shrub. Leaves narrow-elliptical, broadest below the middle. Flowers bell-shaped, 5-lobed and pink; May–September. Widespread, grown as a hedging plant. *L.barbarum* is similar but has leaves broadest at the middle.

HENBANE *Hyoscamus niger*   Height up to 75cm
Branched, stickily-hairy and strong-smelling plant. Leaves oval and pointed. Flowers yellowish and dark-veined, 20–30mm across; in one-sided clusters, April–September. Disturbed ground, often coastal. Widespread; absent from some islands.

YELLOW HENBANE *Hyoscamus aureus*   Height up to 75cm
Branched, stickily-hairy biennial or perennial. Leaves roughly heart-shaped but deeply toothed. Flowers bright yellow with a purple centre, 20–30mm across; borne in clusters, February–June. Rocky and stony ground, Crete.

APPLE OF SODOM *Solanum sodomeum*   Height up to 2.5m
Prickly, much-branched perennial. Leaves spiny and broadly oval but deeply lobed. Flowers purple, 5-lobed and 25–30mm across; in clusters, May–September. Berry is green, ripening brown. Stony ground, often near the sea. Widely naturalised.

BLACK NIGHTSHADE *Solanum nigrum*   Height up to 25cm
Spreading annual with stems often blackish. Leaves oval, lobed and stalked. Flowers white, 5-lobed and 10–15mm across with yellow anthers; in clusters, all year. Berry green, ripening black. Disturbed and cultivated ground. Widespread.

SPRING MANDRAKE *Mandragora officinarum*   Height up to 10cm
Perennial with basal rosette of oval, wavy-margined leaves. Flowers greenish white and 5-lobed; appear February–May. Stony disturbed ground, Italy and former Yugoslavia. *M.autumnalis* is widespread; purple flowers, October–December.

THORNAPPLE *Datura stramonium* — Height up to 1.5m
Upright poisonous annual. Leaves broadly oval but with deeply toothed margins. 5-lobed flowers are white, funnel-shaped and erect, 60–100mm long; appear May–August. Fruit is egg-shaped and spiny. Disturbed ground. Widely naturalised.

SHRUB TOBACCO *Nicotiana glauca* — Height up to 5m
Open, upright shrub. Leaves narrow-oval, blue-green and stalked. Flowers narrow trumpet-shaped, 30–40mm long, 5-lobed and yellow. Fruit egg-shaped. Widely naturalised as a garden escape on stony ground.

GREAT MULLEIN *Verbascum thapsus* — Height up to 2m
Upright, grey-green and woolly biennial. Leaves oval with a winged stalk; appear as basal rosette and up flowering stem. Flowers yellow, 5-lobed and 15–30mm across; borne in tall spikes, May–July. Disturbed and rough ground. Widespread.

Verbascum sinuatum — Height up to 1m
Upright and woolly biennial. Leaves oblong-oval with wavy margins. Flowers yellow, 5-lobed and 15–30mm across; borne in clusters on branched inflorescence, April–July. Stony and sandy ground. Widespread across the region.

LESSER SNAPDRAGON *Misopates orontium* — Height up to 50cm
Branched, rather straggly annual. Leaves narrow, opposite at base, alternate higher up stem. Flowers pinkish red and 10–15mm long; appear March–September. Favours cultivated and disturbed ground. Widespread across the region.

SMALL TOADFLAX *Chaenorhinum minus* — Height up to 35cm
Upright but rather straggly annual. Leaves narrow-oval and short-stalked. Flowers yellow and purple, 5–9mm long; appear April–August. Favours cultivated and disturbed ground. Widespread but commonest in W Mediterranean.

THREE-LEAVED TOADFLAX *Linaria triphylla* — Height up to 40cm
Upright, hairless and grey-green annual. Leaves oval, often borne in whorls of three. Flowers white, orange and purple, 20–30mm long; borne in terminal spikes, February–June. Cultivated and disturbed ground. Widespread, commonest in W.

COMMON TOADFLAX *Linaria vulgaris* — Height up to 75cm
Grey-green perennial with a creeping rhizome. Upright, often branched stems bear very narrow leaves. Orange-centred yellow flowers are spurred and 15–25mm long; in clusters, June–October. Grassy places. Widespread but not in hot dry areas.

IVY-LEAVED TOADFLAX *Cymbalaria muralis* — Trailing
Hairless perennial. Long-stalked, ivy-shaped leaves are 5-lobed and borne on long reddish stems. Flowers lilac and yellow, 8–10mm long; appear April–October. Shady or damp walls and rock faces. Native to Balkans, widely naturalised elsewhere.

RED BARTSIA *Odontites verna* — Height up to 40cm
Straggly, branched downy annual. Leaves narrow and toothed; borne in opposite pairs. Flowers pinkish purple and 8–10mm long; borne in spikes, June–September. Grassy, often trampled, ground. Widespread but absent from some islands.

Digitalis lanata — Height up to 1m
Upright perennial. Stems reddish and hairy. Leaves narrow lanceolate. Flowers yellowish and dark-veined, 20–30mm long; borne on tall spikes, May–August. Favours shady woodland and scrub. Confined to mainland Balkans and Turkey.

Digitalis laevigata — Height up to 1m
Upright, hairless perennial with narrow lanceolate leaves. Flowers buffish yellow with darker veins, 15–35mm long; borne on tall spikes, May–August. Favours open woodland and scrub. Confined to Balkans region.

CYMBALARIA-LEAVED SPEEDWELL *Veronica cymbalaria*　　　Height up to 5cm
Sprawling, hairy annual. Leaves ivy-like comprising 3–7 rounded lobes. Flowers white
and 4–9mm across; March–July. Widespread on shady banks. Similar ivy-leaved speedwell has blue flowers; common on cultivated and disturbed ground.

FINGERED SPEEDWELL *Veronica triphyllos*　　　Height up to 5cm
Upright, hairy annual. Leaves divided into narrow, finger-like lobes, usually 3. Flowers
blue and 5–6mm across; borne on stalks, March–May. Favours cultivated and disturbed
ground. Widespread across the region.

BLUE WATER-SPEEDWELL *Veronica anagallis-aquatica*　　　Height up to 25cm
Hairless perennial. Upright stems carry oval and pointed leaves. Pairs of pale blue flowers, arising from leaf axils, are borne in spikes, March–July. Favours marshes, river margins and other damp habitats. Widespread across the region.

YELLOW BARTSIA *Parentucellia viscosa*　　　Height up to 40cm
Stickily-hairy, unbranched annual. Leaves are lanceolate and unstalked. Flowers are
bright yellow and 15–25mm long; appear April–July. Favours damp, grassy ground, often
on coastal marshes; semi-parasitic. Widespread across the region.

✓ *Bellardia trixago*　　　Height up to 70cm
Upright, hairy annual. Leaves oblong-lanceolate with lobed-toothed margins; leaf-like
bracts appear up stem. Flowers white and pink and 20–25mm long; borne up stem,
March–June. Stony and cultivated ground; semi-parasitic. Widespread.

CISTANCHE *Cistanche phelypaea*　　　Height up to 70cm
Distinctive perennial, lacking chlorophyll. Leaves oval and scale-like. Flowers yellow and
30–40mm long; borne in tall, dense spikes, March–June. Favours dry sandy or stony
ground; parasitic on saltworts, goosefoots and their relatives. Local, S Iberia and parts of
E Mediterranean.

GREATER BROOMRAPE *Orobanche rapum-genistae*　　　Height up to 1m
Upright perennial, lacking chlorophyll. Stems yellow-brown and swollen at base. Leaves
small, oval and scale-like. Flowers yellow-brown, tinged purple-brown, 20–25mm long;
appear April–July. Plants persist as withered brown stems after flowering. Grassy areas.
Parasitic on broom and other legumes. W Mediterranean.

Orobanche crenata　　　Height up to 40cm
Perennial with reddish yellow stem; leaves scale-like. Flowers pale with violet veins,
20–30mm long; March–July. Parasite of pea and bean crops. Widespread.

THYME BROOMRAPE *Orobanche alba*　　　Height up to 35cm
Distinctive reddish perennial with scale-like leaves. Flowers 15–30mm long; appear
March–June. Parasite of thymes and relatives. Widespread across region.

BEDSTRAW BROOMRAPE *Orobanche caryophyllacea*　　　Height up to 40cm
Clove-scented perennial; yellow-brown, tinged purple. Scale-like leaves narrow and
pointed. Flowers 20–30mm long; appear May–July. Parasite of bedstraws and relatives in
grassland and garrigue. Widespread, mainly in W and C of region.

THISTLE BROOMRAPE *Orobanche reticulata*　　　Height up to 45cm
Reddish-yellow perennial with darker veins. Flowers 15–30mm long; appear May–July.
Favours grassy areas and scrub and parasitic on thistles and related composites.
Widespread from Iberia to Turkey.

PURPLE BROOMRAPE *Orobanche purpurea*　　　Height up to 35cm
Upright hairy perennial. Stem brown and swollen at base. Leaves narrow and scale-like.
Flowers purple and 20–25mm long; appear May–July. Favours grassy habitats and para-
sitic on yarrow and related composites. Widespread across the region.

OXTONGUE BROOMRAPE *Orobanche loricata*   Height up to 40cm
Upright perennial with yellow-brown stem, swollen at base. Leaves narrow-oval and scale-like. Flowers pale with purple veins, 14–20mm long; appear May–July. Parasitic on composites and umbellifers. Widespread. Common broomrape *O.minor* is similar but with flowers pale yellow and 10–16mm long; similar host plants.

BRANCHED BROOMRAPE *Orobanche ramosa*   Height up to 25cm
Perennial with stems brown, branched and swollen at base. Leaves oval, pointed and scale-like. Flowers violet and 10–20mm long; appear March–August. Grassy and cultivated ground; parasitic on legumes, nightshades in particular. Widespread.

Orobanche orientalis   Height up to 35cm
Yellow-brown perennial, tinged purple. Flowers reddish, 18–25mm long; April–June. Sandy ground; parasitic on *Medicago* and *Astragalus* species. E of region only.

COMMON PASSION FLOWER *Passiflora caerulea*   Ascending, up to 5m
Climbing assisted by coiling tendrils. Leaves divided into 5–7, narrow lobes. Flowers comprise spreading pale green sepals and petals and radiating banded filaments, the whole up to 8cm across; May–August. Widely cultivated.

SPINY BEAR'S-BREECH *Acanthus spinosus*   Height up to 80cm
Robust hairy perennial with large pinnately-lobed and spiny leaves. Flowers white with purple veins, 35–50mm long; borne in tall spikes, May–July. Favours grassy and disturbed ground. Aegean, Balkan Peninsula and S Italy only.

BEAR'S-BREECH *Acanthus mollis*   Height up to 1m
Robust hairless perennial. Leaves large and pinnately-lobed but spineless. Flowers white with purple veins, 35–50mm long; borne in tall spikes, May–July. Stony and disturbed ground. Native from Iberia to Greece; also widely planted.

GREATER PLANTAIN *Plantago major*   Height up to 20cm
Persistent low perennial. Leaves broad, oval and up to 25cm long with 3–9 veins; leaves form a basal rosette. Flowers tiny and borne in long, stalked spikes, March–October. Favours grassland and disturbed ground. Widespread.

HOARY PLANTAIN *Plantago media*   Height up to 20cm
Low perennial with narrow-oval to elliptical leaves that have 7–9 veins and are covered in hairs; leaves form a basal rosette. Flowers tiny and borne in long, stalked spikes, March–October. Mainly grassland. Widespread; absent from most islands.

BUCK'S-HORN PLANTAIN *Plantago coronopus*   Height up to 15cm
Downy, grey-green perennial. Leaves are usually deeply-cut and pinnately divided. Flowers are tiny and yellowish, borne in long spikes on curved stems, February–October. Favours loose, sandy and stony soils, mainly coastal. Widespread.

SEA PLANTAIN *Plantago maritima*   Height up to 15cm
Hardy, low perennial. Leaves strap-like, fleshy and 3–5 veined, forming a basal rosette. Flowers tiny and brownish; borne on long stalks, March–October. A characteristic coastal plant of sandy and stony ground. Widespread.

RIBWORT PLANTAIN *Plantago lanceolata*   Height up to 15cm
Hairy or hairless perennial. Leaves lanceolate, ribbed and up to 20cm long; form a basal rosette. Compact, ovoid heads of tiny flowers borne on furrowed stalks, March–October. Disturbed grassland and cultivated ground. Widespread.

DWARF ELDER OR DANEWORT *Sambucus ebulus*   Height up to 1.5m
Foetid upright perennial. Leaves deeply divided into 5–13 toothed leaflets. Flowers pinkish white; borne in umbel-like clusters, 10–15cm across, June–August. Favours grassy scrub, hedges and field margins. Widespread.

GREATER PERIWINKLE *Vinca major*   Height up to 50cm
Spreading, trailing perennial. Leaves oval and bright green with a hairy margin. Flowers 30–50mm across and bluish purple; borne on long upright stems, March–May. Woodland banks, hedgerows and scrub. Widespread native but also naturalised.

INTERMEDIATE PERIWINKLE *Vinca difformis*   Height up to 1.5m
Upright evergreen perennial, sometimes becoming a small shrub. Leaves oval and bright green, without hairy margins. Flowers 30–70mm across and pale blue; borne on long upright stems, February–May. Shady banks and woods. W of region only.

LESSER PERIWINKLE *Vinca minor*   Height up to 30cm
Spreading or trailing perennial. Leaves narrow-oval, without hairy margins. Flowers 25–30mm across and usually blue or purple; borne on long stems, February–May. Shady banks and hedgerows. Widespread native but also naturalised.

ETRUSCAN HONEYSUCKLE *Lonicera etrusca*   Climbing, up to 5m
Deciduous shrub with twining stems. Leaves oval; lower ones stalked, those below flowers fused and enclosing stem. Flowers pale yellow, tinged pink, 35–45mm long; in clusters, April–July. Berries red. Maquis, garrigue and scrub. Widespread.

FEDIA *Fedia cornucopiae*   Height up to 25cm
Branched, fleshy annual. Leaves oval to elliptical; lower ones only are stalked. Flowers pink and purple, 8–15mm long; borne in clusters, March–June. Favours cultivated and disturbed ground on sandy or stony ground. S Iberia to Greece.

RED VALERIAN *Centranthus ruber*   Height up to 75cm
Grey-green, fleshy perennial. Leaves oval, untoothed and borne in opposite pairs. Flowers pink, red or sometimes white; 9–12mm long and borne in terminal clusters, April–August. Favours rocks, broken ground and walls. Widespread.

WILD TEASEL *Dipsacus fullonum*   Height up to 2m
Upright biennial with prickly, angled stems. Basal rosette of oval, spine-coated leaves seen in first year. In second year, conical heads of purple flowers are borne on tall stems, July–August. Damp, often disturbed ground. Widespread.

FIELD SCABIOUS *Knautia arvensis*   Height up to 75cm
Robust, hairy biennial or perennial. Spoon-shaped, lobed basal leaves form a rosette; those on stem are less divided. Flowers bluish violet; borne in heads, 30–40mm across, June–September. Favours dry grassland. Widespread in W and C.

Pterocephalus perennis   Height up to 5cm
Hairy, greyish annual. Leaves oval, pinnately lobed and stalked, forming a spreading rosette. Pinkish purple flowers borne in heads, 20–30mm across, April–July; calyx has feathery bristles. Dry grassland. E Mediterranean only.

CARMEL DAISY *Scabiosa prolifera* March '06 : N. Cyprus   Height up to 40cm
Upright, hairy annual. Leaves oval to spoon-shaped. Flowers creamy yellow; borne in heads, 30–40mm across, February–May. Favours disturbed grassland and cultivated ground. E Mediterranean only.

SPREADING BELLFLOWER *Campanula patula*   Height up to 40cm
Straggly upright biennial or perennial. Lower leaves oval and stalked, upper ones narrow and stalkless. Flowers bell-shaped, bluish purple and 20–25mm long; borne upright, June–September. Grassy places. Widespread; absent from most islands and E of region.

PEACH-LEAVED BELLFLOWER *Campanula persicifolia*   Height up to 70cm
Upright hairless perennial. Lower leaves oval and stalked, upper ones narrow and unstalked. Flowers bell-shaped, blue and 30–40mm across; borne upright or horizontally, June–August. Grassy places. Widespread; absent from most islands and E.

NETTLE-LEAVED BELLFLOWER *Campanula trachelium* Height up to 75cm
Roughly-hairy perennial. Basal leaves stalked and heart-shaped; nettle-like stem leaves oval and toothed. Flowers blue-violet, 30–40mm long; in leafy spikes, June–August. Open woods and scrub. W and C Mediterranean but absent from most islands.

Campanula ramosissima Height up to 45cm
Spindly, upright and hairy annual. Lower leaves oblong, upper ones narrow. Flowers bell-shaped with spreading lobes, bluish-violet and 18–23mm long; appear April–May. Grassy, stony slopes, mainly upland areas. Mainly Balkans and Italy.

CREEPING BELLFLOWER *Campanula rapunculoides* Height up to 70cm
Straggly, upright and hairy perennial. Lower leaves narrow-oval and stalked, upper ones narrower and unstalked. Flowers bell-shaped, bluish violet and 20–30mm long; in one-sided spikes, June–August. Grassy places. W and C Mediterranean.

VENUS'S LOOKING-GLASS *Legousia hybrida* Height up to 30cm
Upright, hairy annual. Leaves oblong-oval with wavy margins. Flowers purple, 4–6mm across; borne in clusters, March–June, opening in sun. Cultivated arable fields and bare, stony ground. Widespread across Mediterranean.

LARGE VENUS'S LOOKING-GLASS *Legousia speculum-veneris* Height up to 40cm
Much-branched, upright and hairy annual. Leaves oblong and alternate. Flowers deep violet, 8–10mm across; borne in clusters, March–June, opening in sun. Cultivated arable fields and bare, stony ground. Widespread across Mediterranean.

Legousia pentagonica Height up to 30cm
Upright, hairy annual. Leaves oblong-oval with wavy margins. Flowers purple and 9–12mm across; borne in clusters, March–June, opening in sun. Cultivated arable fields and bare, stony ground. Widespread in E Mediterranean only.

SPIKED VENUS' LOOKING-GLASS *Legousia falcata* Height up to 30cm
Upright, rather straggly annual. Leaves oblong-oval with slightly wavy margins. Flowers lilac-purple, 4–6mm across, with long, narrow calyx lobes; borne in spikes, April–June. Stony ground and garrigue. Widespread across region.

PETROMARULA *Petromarula pinnata* Height up to 80cm
Robust perennial. Leaves divided into paired oval and toothed lobes; lower ones stalked, forming a basal rosette. Pale blue flowers, 10mm across, comprise 5 recurved lobes; in spike-like clusters, April–May. Rocky places, Crete only.

LAURENTIA *Laurentia gasparrinii* Height up to 12cm
Delicate annual or perennial with alternate oblong to spoon-shaped leaves with shallowly lobed margins. Flowers bluish-purple, 5–10mm long and lobelia-like; appear May–July. Damp open ground in marshes and woods. Widespread but local.

DAISY *Bellis perennis* Height up to 10cm
Familiar perennial. Spoon-shaped leaves form prostrate rosettes from which flower stalks arise, each bearing single flower heads, 15–25 across; comprise yellow disc and white ray florets; flowers all year. Short grass and lawns. Widespread.

ANNUAL DAISY *Bellis annua* Height up to 10cm
Bristly annual. Spoon-shaped leaves form prostrate rosettes from which flower stalks arise, each with single heads, 5–15mm across; disc florets yellow, ray florets white, pinkish below. Flowers February–June. Widespread on damp ground.

BLUE FLEABANE *Erigeron acer* Height up to 30cm
Grey-green hairy annual or biennial. Basal leaves stalked and spoon-shaped; stem leaves narrow and unstalked. Flower heads 12–18mm across, with yellow disc florets and blue-lilac ray florets; June–August. Widespread; absent from most islands.

SEA ASTER *Aster tripolium*   Height up to 75cm
Salt-tolerant perennial with fleshy and narrow leaves. Flower heads, 10–20mm across,
comprise yellow disc and blue-lilac ray florets; borne in clusters, June–October. Found on
saltmarshes and coastal cliffs. Widespread across the region.

GOLDILOCKS ASTER *Aster linosyris*   Height up to 70cm
Upright, hairless perennial. Leaves narrow with rough margins. Flower heads yellow and
12–18mm across; borne in flat-topped clusters, July–September. Grassy and rocky slopes,
often coastal. Iberia to Turkey; absent from most islands.

Evax pygmaea   Height up to 3cm
Low but distinctive grey-green, felted annual. Leaves oval-oblong, forming a rosette.
Flower heads yellow-brown; borne in tight clusters, April–May. Favours bare, stony
ground and often on paths. Widespread across the Mediterranean.

COMMON CUDWEED *Filago vulgaris*   Height up to 30cm
Upright, branched annual covered in greyish woolly hairs. Leaves narrow oval and alternate. Flower heads yellowish; in dense rounded clusters of 20–35, June–August. Flower
bracts pale-tipped. Disturbed ground, often on sand. Widespread.

BROAD-LEAVED CUDWEED *Filago pyramidata*   Height up to 25cm
Branched, often prostrate annual covered in greyish woolly hairs. Leaves narrow oval and
alternate. Flower heads yellowish; in dense clusters of 5–20, each overtopped by leaves,
March–July. Disturbed sandy soils. Widespread.

RED-TIPPED CUDWEED *Filago lutescens*   Height up to 25cm
Branched, upright annual covered in yellowish woolly hairs. Leaves narrow-oval to
spoon-shaped. Flowers heads yellowish; in clusters of 10–25, April–July. Flower bracts
red-tipped. Disturbed sandy soils. W Mediterranean; absent from many islands.

SMALL CUDWEED *Filago minima*   Height up to 10cm
Upright, grey-green and woolly annual, often much-branched above. Leaves narrow and
alternate. Flower heads yellowish and 3mm long, without overtopping leaves; appear
June–August. Short grassland on sandy soil. Widespread, mainly W and C.

JERSEY CUDWEED *Pseudognaphalium luteo-album*   Height up to 25cm
Upright annual, covered in white woolly hairs. Leaves alternate and narrow with wavy
margins. Flower heads yellow-orange; borne in ovoid clusters of up to 40, April–July.
Usually on damp, sandy ground. Widespread.

Helichrysum stoechas   Height up to 50cm
Much-branched, upright undershrub with narrow, alternate and aromatic leaves that are
coated with white woolly hairs. Flower heads yellow; in clusters 15–20mm across,
March–July. Stony ground, dunes and garrigue. Widespread; absent from Cyprus.

Helichrysum conglobatum   Height up to 50cm
Much-branched, upright undershrub. Narrow spoon-shaped, alternate leaves have white
woolly hairs; not aromatic. Flower heads yellow; in clusters 25–60mm across,
March–June. Stony ground and garrigue. E Mediterranean including Cyprus.

Phagnalon rupestre   Height up to 50cm
Upright undershrub, coated in white woolly hairs. Leaves narrow oval, smooth above and
woolly below. Flower heads long-stalked, solitary yellow and bell-shaped; appear
March–May. Garrigue and stony ground. Widespread.

COMMON FLEABANE *Pulicaria dysenterica*   Height up to 50cm
Upright, branched and woolly perennial. Basal leaves soon wither; stem leaves heart-
shaped and clasping. Flower heads yellow and 15–30mm across; borne in clusters,
August–October. Damp meadows and ditches. Widespread across the region.

WILD FLOWERS

Pallenis spinosa   Height up to 50cm
Upright, branched annual or biennial. Stems reddish and downy. Leaves narrow; stem leaves stalkless and clasping. Flower heads yellow and 20mm across, surrounded by spine-tipped bracts; appear March–July. Stony ground. Widespread.

GOLDEN SAMPHIRE *Inula crithmoides*   Height up to 75cm
Striking tufted perennial. Upright stems have bright green, narrow and fleshy leaves. Flower heads yellow and 15–30mm across; borne in clusters, June–September. Saltmarshes, shingle and sea cliffs. Widespread across Mediterranean.

PLOUGHMAN'S-SPIKENARD *Inula conyza*   Height up to 1m
Upright, hairy perennial. Stems red and hairy. Lower leaves oval; stem leaves narrower. Flowers yellow and rayless, 10mm across; borne in clusters, July–September. Dry grassland, often on calcareous soils. Widespread across region.

Inula oculus-christi   Height up to 50cm
Upright, branched and hairy perennial. Leaves oblong to oval; stem leaves are clasping. Flower heads yellow and 25–30mm across; appear May–July. Favours dry grassy habitats. Balkan Peninsula and Turkey only.

YELLOW SEA ASTER *Asteriscus maritimus*   Height up to 20cm
Spreading and much-branched perennial, sometimes forming compact clumps. Leaves spoon-shaped and stalked. Flowers yellow and 30–40mm across, surrounded by leafy bracts; appear March–June. Rocky coastal habitats, from Iberia to Greece.

SUNFLOWER *Helianthus annuus*   Height up to 3m
Imposing and robust upright annual. Leaves broadly oval; lower ones heart-shaped at the base. Flower heads nodding, yellow and up to 30cm across. Widely cultivated for the oil extracted from its seeds. Also grown in gardens.

COTTON LAVENDER *Santolina chamaecyparissus*   Height up to 50cm
Upright whitish woolly perennial, forming small shrubs. Leaves narrow and pinnately lobed. Flower heads yellow and 6–10mm across; appear June–August. Favours dry stony and rocky ground. Widespread, mainly in W and C.

CORN CHAMOMILE *Anthemis arvensis*   Height up to 50cm
Hairy, upright annual. Leaves deeply divided into narrow, pointed segments. Flower heads, 20–40mm across, comprise yellow disc and white ray florets; appear April–July. Favours cultivated and disturbed ground. Widespread across region.

Anthemis maritima   Height up to 60cm
Often hairless dwarf shrub. Leaves deeply divided into fleshy lobes. Flower heads, 25–40mm across, comprise yellow disc and white ray florets; appear April–June. Favours coastal sand dunes. Widespread, mainly in W Mediterranean.

RAYLESS CHAMOMILE *Anthemis rigida*   Height up to 30cm
Downy, often spreading annual. Leaves deeply divided into pointed lobes. Flower heads, 4–9mm across, comprise yellow disc florets only; appear February–May. Favours coastal sand and shingle. E Mediterranean only.

Asteriscus aquaticus   Prostrate
Distinctive annual comprising flattened clumps of radiating oblong leaves and bright yellow flowers, 10–20mm across; appear March–June. Favours bare ground, usually close to the sea. Widespread, especially in W Mediterranean.

CYPRUS WOOLLY CHAMOMILE *Anthemis tricolor*   Height up to 20cm
Spreading, often prostrate, woolly annual. Leaves deeply divided into narrow lobes. Flowers, 15–25mm across, comprise purple disc and whitish ray florets; appear February–May. Favours stony and rocky ground. Endemic to Cyprus.

300

BUTTONWEED *Cotula coronopifolia*   Height up to 30cm
Upright hairless and aromatic annual. Leaves alternate and narrow, sometimes divided. Flower heads yellow and 5–10mm across; on long stalks, June–September. Favours damp, saline ground, often coastal. Naturalised in W Mediterranean.

YARROW *Achillea millefolium*   Height up to 50cm
Strong-smelling, hairy perennial. Leaves dark green, finely divided and feathery. Flower heads, 4–6mm across, comprise yellowish disc and pinkish white ray florets; borne in flat-topped clusters, May–August. Grassy places. Widespread.

CHAMOMILE *Chamaemelum nobile*   Height up to 10cm
Creeping, strongly aromatic perennial. Leaves finely divided and feathery. Flower heads, 18–25mm across, comprise yellow disc and white ray florets; May–July. Areas of short grass on sandy soil. Native to Iberia; naturalised elsewhere.

SCENTLESS MAYWEED *Matricaria perforata*   Height up to 70cm
Upright, hairless annual. Leaves alternate, finely divided and feathery. Flower heads, 30–45mm across, comprise yellow disc and white ray florets; appear June–September. Cultivated and disturbed ground. Widespread, but absent from most islands.

SCENTED MAYWEED *Matricaria recutita*   Height up to 60cm
Upright, hairless and aromatic annual. Leaves alternate, finely divided and feathery. Flower heads, 10–25mm across, comprise yellow disc and white ray florets; disc is hollow. Flowers March–July. Cultivated ground. Widespread.

COTTONWEED *Otanthus maritimus*   Height up to 40cm
Spreading perennial covered in white woolly hairs. Leaves alternate, narrow-oval and fleshy. Flower heads yellow and compact, 7–10mm across; appear June–August. Found on coastal sand and shingle. Widespread across the Mediterranean.

CORN MARIGOLD *Chrysanthemum segetum*   Height up to 50cm
Hairless, upright annual. Leaves narrow, deeply lobed and slightly fleshy. Flower heads yellow and 30–60mm across; appear February–June. A widespread plant of arable fields on sandy soils. Common across the Mediterranean.

CROWN DAISY *Chrysanthemum coronarium*   Height up to 50cm
Upright, slightly hairy annual. Similar to corn marigold but leaves deeply divided into very narrow lobes. Flower heads yellow and 30–60mm across; appear January–September. Cultivated and disturbed ground. Widespread across the region.

TANSY *Tanacetum vulgare*   Height up to 75cm
Aromatic, downy perennial. Leaves pinnately divided into deeply cut lobes. Flower heads yellow and 7–12mm across; born in flat-topped clusters up to 1cm in diameter, July–September. Waysides and disturbed ground. Widespread, mainly in W.

FEVERFEW *Tanacetum parthenium*   Height up to 50cm
Aromatic, downy perennial. Leaves yellowish and pinnately divided. Flowers daisy-like, 1–2cm across and comprise yellow disc and white ray florets; June–August. Cultivated and disturbed ground. Native to Balkans; naturalised elsewhere.

OX-EYE DAISY *Leucanthemum vulgare*   Height up to 60cm
Upright hairless perennial. Spoon-shaped basal leaves form a rosette; smaller stem leaves are pinnately lobed. Solitary flower heads, 30–50mm across, comprise yellow disc and white ray florets; May–September. Grassy places. Widespread.

WINTER HELIOTROPE *Petasites fragrans*   Height up to 20cm
Spreading hairy perennial. Leaves rounded or kidney-shaped and 20cm across. Flowering stems appear December–March, bearing fragrant, pink-lilac flower heads. Damp, shady ground. Native to Italy, Sardinia and Sicily; naturalised elsewhere.

FIELD MARIGOLD *Calendula arvensis*   Height up to 25cm
Upright, slightly hairy annual with oval, finely toothed leaves. Flower heads 10–25mm
across and usually uniformly orange; appear March–June. Favours disturbed and cultivated, often stony, ground. Widespread across the region.

GROUNDSEL *Senecio vulgaris*   Height up to 40cm
Branched and slightly hairy annual. Leaves pinnately lobed; lower ones stalked, upper
ones clasping the stem. Open clusters of small, rayless flower heads can be found throughout the year. Cultivated and disturbed ground. Widespread.

Senecio rodriguezii   Height up to 10cm
Small, rather fleshy and sometimes slightly hairy annual with oval leaves. Flowers com-
prise pale pinkish white ray florets and lilac-purple disc florets; appear March–June.
Garrigue and stony ground. Endemic to Mallorca and Menorca.

CINERARIA *Senecio cineraria*   Height up to 1m
Much-branched, white-woolly shrub. Leaves oval and sometimes lobed; dark green above
and white-woolly below. Flower heads yellow; borne in clusters, March–June. Favours
stony and rocky ground. Naturalised locally in W and C Mediterranean.

ACANTHUS-LEAVED CARLINE THISTLE *Carlina acanthifolia*   Prostrate
Distinctive stemless perennial. Leaves oval and pinnately lobed, the margins armed with
spines. Flowers, 30–70mm across, comprise golden outer ray-like bracts and pinkish central florets; July–September. Stony ground. Iberia to Greece.

GLOBE THISTLE *Echinops ritro*   Height up to 1.2m
Upright perennial covered in soft white hairs. Leaves narrow and deeply divided into
spiny lobes. Flower heads spherical, 35–45mm across, and blue; appear July–September.
Dry grassland and stony ground. Widespread; also grown in gardens.

Echinops sphaerocephalus   Height to 1.5m
Upright perennial covered in soft white hairs. Leaves narrow-oval and deeply divided
into spiny lobes. Flower heads spherical, 30–60mm across, and whitish; appear
June–August. Dry grassland and stony ground. Iberia to Turkey.

MILK THISTLE *Silybum marianum*   Height up to 1.5m
Upright biennial, stems armed with soft spines. Leaves oblong, with spiny margins and
reticulated with white veins. Flower heads 25–40mm across and purple; borne above
spiny bracts, March–June. Grassland and cultivated ground. Widespread.

CARDOON *Cynara cardunculus*   Height up to 1m
Upright perennial with spiny leaves. Flower heads pinkish purple or blue; 40–60mm
across above bulbous array of spiny bracts; May–July. Stony and grazed ground. Similar
globe artichoke *C.scolymus* is larger; bracts not spiny. Widely grown.

GREATER BURDOCK *Arctium lappa*   Height up to 1m
Upright biennial. Leaves large, downy and heart-shaped. Flowers egg-shaped, reddish
purple and 20–30mm across; borne in open clusters, July–September. Favours woodland,
scrub and grassy places. Widespread across region.

WOOLLY THISTLE *Cirsium eriophorum*   Height up to 1.5m
Upright, branched biennial, coated in white-woolly hairs. Leaves deeply divided into
spiny lobes; green above and white-woolly below. Flower heads pinkish purple and
30–50mm across, above spherical mass of bracts and woolly fibres; appear
July–September. Favours grassy places. Widespread from Iberia to Greece.

SPEAR THISTLE *Cirsium vulgare*   Height up to 1.5m
Upright biennial with spiny stems. Leaves narrow, deeply divided into spiny lobes.
Flower heads purple, 20–40mm across; in clusters July–October. Widespread.

CREEPING THISTLE *Cirsium arvense*   Height up to 1m
Creeping perennial with upright, unwinged stems. Leaves are pinnately lobed with spiny margins. Flower heads pinkish-lilac and 10–15mm across; borne in clusters, June–August. Cultivated and disturbed ground. Widespread.

SYRIAN THISTLE *Notobasis syriaca*   Height up to 70cm
Upright, branched annual with pale-veined leaves divided into narrow, spine-tipped lobes. Flowers purple and 15–25mm across; borne in clusters, February–June. Cultivated and stony ground. Widespread across Mediterranean.

GALACTITES *Galactites tomentosa*   Height up to 1m
Upright, softly-hairy annual. Leaves, variegated dark green and whitish, divided into narrow spine-tipped lobes. Flower heads 15–20mm across, usually purple; in clusters, April–July. Stony and sandy soils. Widespread in W and C Mediterranean.

SCOTCH THISTLE *Onopordum acanthium*   Height up to 1.2m
Upright biennial, covered in white, filamentous hairs and with spiny stems. Leaves oblong with spiny margins. Flower heads purple and 40–60mm across; May–July. Disturbed and stony ground. W and C Mediterranean; naturalised elsewhere.

RED STAR-THISTLE *Centaurea calcitrapa*   Height up to 80cm
Spreading, much-branched perennial. Leaves divided into spine-tipped lobes. Flower heads reddish purple and 8–10mm across, above star-like array of spine-like bracts; June–August. Cultivated and disturbed ground. Widespread.

YELLOW STAR-THISTLE *Centaurea solsistalis*   Height up to 60cm
Upright, much-branched biennial with winged stems. Lower leaves lobed and stalked; upper ones narrow and unstalked. Flower heads yellow and 10–12mm across, above array of spine-like bracts; May–July. Stony ground. Widespread.

Centaurea aegialophila   Height up to 15cm
Low perennial. Leaves mostly at ground level forming a rosette; oval and downy. Flower heads pinkish lilac and 15–30cm across; appear March–May. Favours coastal sands. Confined to Cyprus, Crete and Turkey.

✓ 25 · 3 · 00
Centaurea pullata   Height up to 30cm
Low, hairy annual. Leaves shallowly lobed, lower ones forming a basal rosette. Flower heads pinkish purple and 30–50mm across, outer florets long and spreading; April–July. Favours stony ground. Iberian Peninsula only.

✓
CORNFLOWER *Centaurea cyanus*   Height up to 1m
Upright, branched annual with very narrow leaves. Flower heads bluish and 15–30mm across, outer florets much larger than inner ones; appear April–June. Cultivated and disturbed ground. Native to E Mediterranean, naturalised elsewhere.

CRUPINA *Crupina crupinastrum*   Height up to 30cm
Slender, upright annual. Lower leaves deeply divided into narrow lobes; upper ones oval and toothed. Flower heads purple and 18–22mm long; appear April–June. Favours stony ground and garrigue. Widespread across Mediterranean.

BLESSED THISTLE *Cnicus benedictus*   Height up to 25cm
Short, hairy annual. Leaves oblong and divided into spine-tipped lobes. Flower heads yellow and 25–30mm long; appear February–July. Favours cultivated and disturbed ground. Widespread but absent from Corsica, Sicily and Balearics.

SPANISH OYSTER-PLANT *Scolymus hispanicus*   Height up to 85cm
Upright, much-branched perennial with spiny-winged stems. Flower heads yellow and 20–30mm across; in clusters, May–September. Favours cultivated and disturbed ground. Widespread.

CHICORY *Cichorum inybus* Height up to 1m
Branched, hairy perennial. Lower leaves stalked and lobed, upper ones narrow and clasping. Flower heads sky blue and 30–40mm across; borne in clusters, May–August, opening in sunshine. Garrigue, stony and cultivated ground. Widespread.

CUPIDONE *Catananche caerulea* Height up to 1m
Branched, upright perennial. Leaves narrow, with 2–4 sharp teeth on margins. Flower heads violet-blue and 25–35mm across, above ovoid head of overlapping bracts; May–September. Garrigue and dry grassland. Spain, S France and Italy.

SMOOTH CAT'S-EAR *Hypochoeris glabra* Height up to 20cm
Upright annual. Leaves lanceolate, glossy and usually hairless; form a basal rosette. Flower heads yellow and 10–15mm across; appear March–June. Favours stony ground and garrigue. Widespread across the Mediterranean.

BRISTLY OXTONGUE *Picris echioides* Height up to 80cm
Branched, bristly-stemmed perennial. Leaves narrow and clasping, covered with swollen-based bristles and pale spots. Flower heads pale yellow and 20–25mm across; borne in clusters April–July. Dry, disturbed ground. Widespread.

HAWKWEED OXTONGUE *Picris hieracioides* Height up to 70cm
Bristly-stemmed, branched perennial. Leaves narrow and toothed, lacking swollen-based bristles. Flower heads yellow and 20–25mm across; borne in clusters, April–July. Rough grassy places. Widespread only in mainland W and C Mediterranean.

SALSIFY *Tragopogon porrifolius* Height up to 1m
Upright, hairless perennial. Leaves narrow and grass-like. Flower heads reddish purple and 35–50mm across, opening in morning sunshine; appear April–June. Favours dry grassland and cultivated ground. Widespread.

GOAT'S-BEARD *Tragopogon pratensis* Height up to 60cm
Upright, usually hairless perennial. Leaves narrow and clasping or sheathing at the base. Flower heads yellow and 30–40mm across, fringed by bracts and opening only on sunny mornings; April–June. Grassy places. Widespread, not on islands.

REICHARDIA *Reichardia tingitana* Height up to 30cm
Hairless annual or perennial with oblong, sharply-toothed or lobed leaves, and these mainly basal. Flower heads yellow, 18–25mm across; appear March–May. Favours dry grassy places. S Spain and Greece; also on some islands.

PINK HAWKSBEARD *Crepis rubra* Height up to 30cm
Hairy upright annual. Leaves oblong and toothed or lobed; mainly basal. Flower heads pink and 25–30mm across; appear April–June. Favours dry grassy places and cultivated. Confined to S Italy, Balkan region and Crete.

Crepis fraasii Height up to 30cm
Upright, slightly hairy annual or perennial. Leaves narrow and divided into lobes, the terminal one being the largest. Flower heads yellow and 25–30mm across; April–June. Rocky places in upland regions. Greece, Crete and Cyprus.

SMOOTH SOW-THISTLE *Sonchus oleraceus* Height up to 1m
Upright, hairless annual. Broken stems exude milky sap. Leaves pinnately divided with toothed margins and pointed basal lobes. Flower heads pale yellow, 20–25mm across; in clusters, March–October. Cultivated and grassy places. Widespread.

NIPPLEWORT *Lapsana communis* Height up to 1m
Upright, branched annual. Leaves divided into narrow, paired lobes and oval terminal lobe. Flower heads yellow and 10–20mm across; borne in clusters, May–October. Grassy places and disturbed ground. Widespread across the region.

LEAST LETTUCE *Lactuca saligna* — Height up to 70cm
Hairless, branched perennial. Lower leaves divided into narrow segments; stem leaves narrow and clasping. Flower heads yellow and 8–10mm across, opening only in morning sunshine; July–October. Stony ground, often near the sea. Widespread.

BLUE LETTUCE *Lactuca perennis* — Height up to 1m
Upright hairless and branched perennial. Leaves divided into narrow lobes; stem leaves clasping. Flower heads blue and 30–40mm across; borne in clusters, April–July. Dry stony uplands. Widespread in Mediterranean but absent from islands.

POSIDONIA *Posidonia oceanica* — Creeping
Submerged, marine perennial. Leaves narrow, up to 50cm long. Flowers in clusters above bracts. In deep water on sandy or muddy substrates. Generally encountered as compact balls of fibrous leaf remains, washed up on shore. Widespread.

WHITE ASPHODEL *Asphodelus albus* — Height up to 1m
Upright, hairless perennial. Leaves narrow, grey-green and basal. Flowers white, star-shaped and 30–40mm across; borne on tall flowering spikes, March–June. Stony and disturbed ground. Widespread from Iberia to Greece; absent from most islands.

YELLOW ASPHODEL *Asphodeline lutea* — Height up to 1m
Upright, hairless perennial. Leaves narrow and blue-green; basal and borne up stem. Flowers yellow, star-shaped and 30–40mm across; borne on tall flowering spikes, March–May. Stony ground and garrigue. Mainly in E Mediterranean.

✓ **COMMON ASPHODEL** *Asphodelus microcarpus* — Height up to 1m
Upright, hairless perennial. Leaves narrow and grey-green. Flowers star-shaped, white and 20–30mm across; borne in branched spikes, January–June. Favours stony ground and garrigue. Widespread throughout the Mediterranean.

✓ **ST BERNARD'S LILY** *Anthericum liliago* — Height up to 50cm
Elegant, upright and hairless perennial. Leaves narrow, grey-green and basal. Flowers white, star-shaped and 20–30mm across; borne in open spikes, April–June. Favours stony, grassy places. Widespread but absent from most islands.

Gagea fistulosa — Height up to 25cm
Bulbous, hairless perennial. Has 2 cylindrical leaves at base, 2 narrow flat leaves on stem. Flowers yellow, star-shaped and 25–35mm across; in groups of 3–5, May–June. Stony ground. W Mediterranean but absent from Balearics and Sardinia.

CYPRUS YELLOW GAGEA *Gagea juliae* — Height up to 8cm
Bulbous, slightly hairy perennial. Has 2 cylindrical basal leaves and narrow, flat stem leaves. Flowers yellow, star-shaped and 10–15mm across; in groups of 3–15, February–April. Damp, rocky slopes. Endemic to Cyprus.

Gagea graeca — Height up to 10cm
Bulbous, hairless perennial. Leaves narrow; basal and on stem. Flowers white, with purple stripes on outer surface, and 10–15mm across; in small clusters, March–May. Stony ground and garrigue. From S Greece eastwards.

MEADOW SAFFRON *Colchicum autumnale* — Height up to 10cm
Bulbous perennial. Leaves long and ovate, appearing in spring long before flowers appear and dying back by summer. Flowers pinkish purple and borne on pale stalks; appear August–October. Damp ground, often in open woodland. Iberia to Greece.

Colchicum cupanii — Height up to 7cm
Delicate bulbous perennial with 2 narrow leaves. Flowers pinkish purple, spreading and 15–20mm across; appear September–December. Favours stony and rocky ground. Widespread from S France to Greece.

WILD TULIP *Tulipa sylvestris*   Height up to 40cm
Hairless perennial. Leaves 2–3, narrow and up to 25cm long. Flowers yellow, usually solitary and 30–40cm across when petals open fully and spread; appear May–June. Favours grassy places and open woodland. Widespread but local.

Tulipa australis   Height up to 30cm
Hairless perennial. Leaves 2–3, narrow and up to 15cm long. Flowers yellow, tinged orange on the outer surface, and 20–25cm across when open fully; appear April–June. Grassy places and woodland rides. Widespread but local.

ROCK TULIP *Tulipa saxatilis*   Height up to 25cm
Hairless perennial. Leaves 2–3, narrow-oblong and shiny. Flowers pink, flushed yellow at base, and 40–50mm long, seldom opening fully; appear March–June. Favours stony and rocky ground. Native to Crete and SW Turkey.

ORANGE WILD TULIP *Tulipa orphanidea*   Height up to 30cm
Perennial, sometimes slightly hairy. Leaves 2–5, narrow and up to 15cm long. Flowers reddish orange, darkest at base, and 30–35mm long, seldom opening fully; appear March–May. Stony, grassy slopes. Balkan region.

Tulipa celsiana   Height up to 15cm
Hairless perennial. Leaves 2–3, narrow and up to 10cm long, often coiled on the ground. Flowers yellow, usually solitary and 25–50mm long; appear May–June. Favours grassy places and open woodland. Confined to S Spain.

Fritillaria persica   Height up to 1m
Distinctive, upright perennial. Leaves blue-green, narrow and alternate. Flowers bell-shaped, reddish purple and 18–25mm long; borne in tall spikes, February–April. Grassy, stony ground. Native to E Mediterranean; cultivated elsewhere.

Fritillaria obliqua   Height up to 20cm
Bulbous perennial. Leaves 8–11, grey-green and narrow. Flowers solitary and nodding, bell-shaped, deep reddish purple and 20–30mm long; appear March–April. Favours rocky slopes with scrub. Confined to S Greece.

Fritillaria pontica   Height up to 40cm
Bulbous perennial. Leaves 8, grey-green and narrow. Flowers bell-shaped, greenish and 25–45mm long; solitary and nodding, appearing May–June. Favours stony ground among woods and scrub. Confined to Balkan region and Turkey.

Fritillaria graeca   Height up to 30cm
Bulbous perennial. Leaves 5–12, grey-green and narrow; lowest pair opposite, others alternate. Flowers marbled reddish brown and green, 20–25mm long; solitary or paired and nodding, May–June. Stony ground with scrub. S and E Greece only.

Fritillaria thessala   Height up to 30cm
Sometimes treated as a subspecies of *F.graeca*. Leaves 5–12, grey-green; lowest pair opposite, upper ones whorled. Flowers marbled or chequered green and brown; nodding and solitary, May–June. Stony ground. NW Greece and former Yugoslavia.

Fritillaria messanensis   Height up to 30cm
Bulbous perennial. Leaves 7–10 and narrow. Flowers bell-shaped, marbled or chequered reddish brown and green, 25–30mm long; solitary and nodding, appearing March–May. Grassy, stony ground. Italy to the Balkan region.

Fritillaria lusitanica   Height up to 30cm
Bulbous perennial. Leaves 6–9, grey-green and alternate. Flowers bell-shaped, marbled or chequered green and reddish-orange, 20–30mm long; nodding and solitary, appearing April–May. Grassy, rocky ground. Iberian peninsula only.

SEA SQUILL *Urginea maritima*   Height up to 1.5m
Bulbous perennial. Leaves, narrow, tough and shiny; appear as a basal clump, March–June, withering before flower spike appears. Flowers star-shaped, white and 10–15mm across; July–October. Stony ground and coastal sand. Widespread.

BATH ASPARAGUS *Ornithogalum pyrenaicum*   Height up to 80cm
Upright perennial. Leaves 5–8, narrow and green. Flowers star-shaped, yellowish and 13–17mm across; borne in drooping-tipped spikes, May–July, asparagus-like when in bud. Open woodland. Widespread but local, Iberia to former Yugoslavia.

STAR-OF-BETHLEHEM *Ornithogalum umbellatum*   Height up to 30cm
Attractive perennial. Leaves 6–9, narrow and green with a pale central stripe; in basal tufts. Flowers star-shaped, white and 30–40mm cross; borne in open spikes, March–May. Rocky, sometimes disturbed, ground. Widespread across the region.

NODDING STAR-OF-BETHLEHEM *Ornithogalum nutans*   Height up to 35cm
Bulbous perennial. Leaves 4–6, narrow and green with a pale central stripe. Flowers bell-shaped, 30–45mm across, white, flushed green on outside; in one-sided spikes, March–May. Grassy slopes, open woodland. Native to E Mediterranean.

Ornithogalum narbonense   Height up to 60cm
Upright, bulbous perennial. Leaves 4–6, narrow and green. Flowers star-shaped, white and 15–25mm across; borne in tall spikes, March–May. Garrigue, stony grassland and cultivated ground. Widespread across the Mediterranean.

DIPCADI *Dipcadi serotinum*   Height up to 25cm
Bulbous perennial with extremely narrow, grey-green basal leaves. Flowers bell-shaped, reddish brown and 12–15mm long; borne in one-sided spikes, April–June. Favours stony and sandy ground. Mainly confined to Iberia and Balearics.

AUTUMN SQUILL *Scilla autumnalis*   Height up to 10cm
Bulbous perennial with 3–12 narrow, basal leaves; present in winter and spring but withered before flowering. Flowers star-shaped, blue-purple and 5–7mm across; in spikes of 6–20, September–November. Dry grassy places. Widespread.

TWO-LEAVED SQUILL *Scilla bifolia*   Height up to 15cm
Bulbous perennial, usually with just two basal leaves, these being dark green and narrow. Flowers blue-purple, star-shaped and 5–10mm across; in spikes of 1–7, January–May. Grassy places and open woodland. W and C Mediterranean.

ONE-LEAVED SQUILL *Scilla monophyllos*   Height up to 10cm
Bulbous perennial with a solitary basal leaf, this being dark green and lanceolate. Flowers blue, star-shaped and 7–9mm across; in compact spikes, March–May. Stony and sandy ground. Confined to S Iberian Peninsula.

SPANISH BLUEBELL *Scilla hispanica*   Height up to 60cm
Bulbous perennial with 4–8 narrow-lanceolate and basal leaves. Flowers bell-shaped, blue and 25mm across; in spikes, April–May. Stony ground and grassy places. Native to Iberian Peninsula; widely cultivated and naturalised elsewhere.

TASSEL HYACINTH *Muscari comosum*   Height up to 60cm
Bulbous perennial with 3–6 narrow, basal leaves. Flower spikes comprise brownish lower flowers and purple upper flowers, topmost ones erect on long stalks; appear March–June. Grassy places and disturbed ground. Widespread across the region.

COMMON GRAPE HYACINTH *Muscari neglectum*   Height up to 15cm
Bulbous perennial with 3–6 narrow, basal leaves. Flower spikes comprise upper pale blue flowers and lower ones brownish blue with white mouths; appear February–May. Stony and sometimes cultivated ground. Widespread.

COMMON ASPARAGUS *Asparagus officinalis*   Height up to 1.75m
Branched, upright perennial. Slender, leaf-like structures (cladodes) borne in clusters, giving feathery appearance. Flowers bell-like and whitish; June–August. Berries bright red. Grassy, stony places, rocky coasts and garrigue. Widespread.

BUTCHER'S-BROOM *Ruscus aculeatus*   Height up to 1m
Branched, evergreen shrub. Has dark green leaf-like structures (cladodes): oval, up to 4cm long and spine-tipped. Flowers whitish, 3mm across; borne on upper surface of cladodes, February–April. Berries red. Woods and scrub. Widespread.

COMMON SMILAX *Smilax aspera*   Climbing, up to 10m
Scrambling shrub with prickly stems. Leaves triangular with a heart-shaped base and prickly margins. Flowers whitish, 3–5mm across, divided into 6; borne in clusters, August–November. Berries dark red. Maquis and garrigue. Widespread.

ROSY GARLIC *Allium roseum*   Height up to 30cm
Bulbous perennial, smelling of garlic. Leaves 2–4, slender and keeled. Flowers pink, bell-shaped and 7–12mm long; stalked and borne in umbels, March–June, with papery sheaths below. Grassy places. Widespread across the Mediterranean.

NAPLES GARLIC *Allium neapolitanum*   Height up to 30cm
Attractive, bulbous perennial, smelling of garlic. Leaves 2–4, slender and keeled. Flowers white, star-shaped and 15mm across; stalked and borne in umbels, February–May, with papery sheaths below. Grassy places. Widespread.

CROW GARLIC *Allium vineale*   Height up to 1m
Slender, bulbous perennial. Leaves 2–4, slender and cylindrical. Umbels comprise a mixture of reddish bulbils and stalked, bell-shaped pink flowers; appear May–August. Favours dry grassland. Widespread but commonest in W and C Mediterranean.

ROUND-HEADED LEEK *Allium sphaerocephalon*   Height up to 1m
Slender, bulbous perennial. Leaves 2–6, slender, rounded in cross section but grooved. Flowers reddish purple; in dense, spherical heads, 2–4cm across, May–July. Scrub, garrigue and open woodland. Widespread across much of region.

THREE-CORNERED LEEK *Allium triquetum*   Height up to 50cm
Bulbous perennial, smelling of garlic. Leaves 2–3 and narrow grass-like. Flowers white, bell-shaped and 10–15mm long; stalked and hanging, borne in one-sided sprays, March–May. Damp grassy places and banks. Native to W Mediterranean.

AGAVE *Agave americana*   Height up to 5m when flowering
Imposing and distinctive perennial. Seen mostly as rosettes of fleshy, blue-green leaves, spine-tipped, with spiny margins. Tall spikes of yellowish flowers appear when plant is mature, after which plant dies. Stony ground. Widely naturalised.

SPANISH BAYONET *Yucca gloriosa*   Height up to 1m
Woody, branching perennial with dark green, narrow and spine-tipped leaves forming rosettes. Flowers creamy white, bell-shaped, 40–60mm long and hanging; in tall spikes, June–September. Widely cultivated; sometimes naturalised on coasts.

COMMON STERNBERGIA *Sternbergia lutea*   Height up to 20cm
Bulbous, hairless perennial. Leaves 3–9, dark green, narrow and basal. Crocus-like flowers bright yellow, 40–50mm long, divided into 6 parts; appear August–October. Stony upland slopes. Widespread but local; absent from some islands.

Galanthus ikariae   Height up to 15cm
Bulbous perennial. Leaves 2–3, broadly lanceolate and shiny. Flowers white with green marks on inner 3 structures (tepals); solitary and pendant, December–February. Andros and Tinos only. Similar species occur elsewhere in Greece.

SUMMER SNOWFLAKE *Leucojum aestivum*   Height up to 35cm
Bulbous, sometimes clump-forming perennial. Leaves, basal, narrow and fleshy. Flowers bell-shaped, white with a green spot near the tip of each segment; flowers stalked and pendant; April–June. Damp ground, mainly C Mediterranean.

AUTUMN SNOWFLAKE *Leucojum autumnale*   Height up to 30cm
Slender bulbous perennial with thread-like basal leaves; these die back before flower spike appears. Flowers 10–15mm long, bell-shaped, white but flushed pink at base; on slender stalks, August–September. Stony ground in W Mediterranean.

SEA DAFFODIL *Pancratium maritimum*   Height up to 40cm
Bulbous, sometimes clump-forming perennial. Leaves grey-green, narrow, fleshy and basal. Flowers white, 10–15cm long and daffodil-like; borne in clusters, August–October. Favours coastal sands. Widespread across the Mediterranean.

Narcissus bulbicodium   Height up to 10cm
Bulbous, sometimes clump-forming perennial. Leaves narrow, dark green and basal. Flowers yellow, cup-shaped and 20–30mm across; borne on stalks, March–June. Favours stony ground, usually in upland areas. Iberian Peninsula only.

Narcissus serotinus   Height up to 20cm
Slender, bulbous perennial. Leaves 1–2, thread-like and blue-green; these wither long before flowering occurs. Flowers 20–30mm across, white with an orange cup; appear October–December. Favours stony and rocky ground. Widespread.

Narcissus tazetta   Height up to 30cm
Bulbous perennial with grey-green, basal and narrow leaves. Flowers 20–40mm across and white with an orange cup; in clusters, November–March. Favours stony ground, cultivated fields and garrigue. Widespread but rather local.

BLACK BRYONY *Tamus communis*   Height up to 3m
Twining climber, which lacks tendrils. Leaves heart-shaped, glossy and net-veined. Flowers yellow-green, 6-petalled; male and female flowers are borne on separate plants, April–July. Berries ripen bright red; extremely poisonous. Favours scrub and open woodland. Widespread across the Mediterranean.

STINKING IRIS *Iris foetidissima*   Height up to 60cm
Tufted perennial. Leaves sword-shaped and dark green, with an unpleasant smell when crushed. Flowers purplish and 70–80mm across; appear May–July. Seeds bright orange. Favours scrub and open woodland. Mainly in W Mediterranean.

SPANISH IRIS *Iris xiphium*   Height up to 50cm
Bulbous perennial with sword-shaped, grey-green leaves. Flowers bluish purple with orange marks and 40–60mm across; appear April–May. Favours scrub, often on stony ground. Occurs from Iberian Peninsula eastwards to Italy.

YELLOW FLAG *Iris pseudacorus*   Height up to 1m
Robust perennial with grey-green, sword-shaped leaves that are often slightly wrinkled. Flowers yellow and up to 100mm across; borne in clusters, appearing May–July. Favours damp ground. Widespread across the region.

EASTERN IRIS *Iris orientalis*   Height up to 1m
Robust perennial with sword-shaped leaves. Flowers white with yellow patches and up to 100mm across; appear April–June. Turkey, N Greece and Aegean Islands.

BARBARY NUT *Gynandiris sisyrinchium*   Height up to 60cm
Perennial with 1–2 dark green, long and narrow leaves. Flowers bluish purple with yellow patches, 25–45mm across; appear February–May. Favours cultivated and disturbed ground and grassy places. Widespread across Mediterranean.

WILD FLOWERS

WILD GLADIOLUS *Gladiolus illyricus*   Height up to 70cm
Slender perennial with grey-green, grass-like leaves that are easily overlooked when not
in flower. Flowers are pinkish-purple and 30–40mm across; borne in spikes of 3–8,
appearing April–July. Favours grassy places, often in open woodland or on heaths.
Widespread across the Mediterranean.

FIELD GLADIOLUS *Gladiolus italicus*   Height up to 1m
Robust but slender perennial with green, broadly grass-like leaves. Flowers reddish-purple and 40–50 across; borne in spikes of 6–15, March–June. Favours cultivated ground
and arable fields. Widespread across the Mediterranean. The commonest gladiolus in the
region, sometimes colouring whole fields.

Gladiolus triphyllus   Height up to 15cm
Delicate perennial with 4–5 narrow and grass-like leaves. Flowers pale pink and white,
30–40mm across; borne in spikes of 1–6, March–May. Favours dry stony ground in maquis
and garrigue habitats. Endemic to Cyprus.

SAND CROCUS *Romulea columnae*   Height up to 3cm
Low perennial with 3–8 dark green and thread-like basal leaves. Flowers pale bluish lilac,
crocus-like and 10–20mm long. Favours dry sandy habitats, mostly in coastal regions.
Widespread across the Mediterranean.

Romulea bulbicodium   Height up to 5cm
Low perennial with 3–7 dark green, thread-like basal leaves. Flowers crocus-like,
20–35mm long and usually whitish; appear February to May. Favours stony ground and
areas of short grassland. Widespread across much of the Mediterranean.

Crocus chrysanthus   Height up to 5cm
Low perennial with 3–7 grey-green, narrow leaves. Flowers yellow and 15–25mm long;
appearing January–April. Stony ground. Mainly Greece and Turkey.

Crocus flavus   Height up to 7cm
Low perennial with 5–8 green, narrow leaves with pale midrib. Flowers yellow and
15–25mm long; March–April. Grassy and stony places. Mainly Greece and Turkey.

Crocus sieberi   Height up to 5cm
Low perennial with 2–7, narrow and basal green leaves. Flowers pale lilac with a yellow
throat, 8–10mm long; appear March–June. Favours stony ground, often on upland slopes.
Confined to S Balkan Peninsula and parts of the Aegean.

CYPRUS CROCUS *Crocus cypria*   Height up to 5cm
Low perennial with 2–7, narrow and basal dark green leaves. Flowers pale lilac with a yellow throat, 15–25mm long; appear March–June. Bare stony ground in areas where snow
has recently melted. Endemic to mountains in Cyprus.

COMMON DRAGON ARUM *Dracunculus vulgaris*   Height up to 1m
Perennial with deeply divided dark green leaves. Flowers tiny, borne at base of elongated
deep purple spadix, shrouded by maroon spathe up to 40cm long; April–July. Foul-
smelling when in flower. Stony ground. Widespread but local.

LARGE CUCKOO-PINT *Arum italicum*   Height up to 70cm
Perennial with autumn-appearing triangular leaves, heart-shaped at base; usually varie-
gated with pale veins. Flowers with pale green spathe and yellowish spadix; appear
April–May. Berries bright red. Scrubby areas. Widespread.

CUCKOO-PINT OR LORDS-AND-LADIES *Arum maculatum*   Height up to 50cm
Perennial with arrow-shaped leaves that appear in spring and are sometimes purple-spot-
ted. Flowers with purple, rod-like spadix shrouded by cowl-like pale green spathe; appear
April–May. Scrub and woodland. Widespread across the region.

320

MEDITERRANEAN ARUM *Arum conophalloides*   Height up to 60cm
Striking perennial when in flower. Leaves arrow-shaped and shiny, borne on long stalks. Flowers comprise purple, spike-like spadix, shrouded by greenish purple spathe, up to 50cm long; borne on long stalks, April–May. Favours stony slopes in open woodland. Local in E Mediterranean. Similar species occur locally elsewhere.

NARROW-LEAVED BIARUM *Biarum tenuifolium*   Height up to 25cm
Perennial with narrow green leaves that often have wavy margins. Flower comprises deep purple, spike-like spadix and cowl-like greenish maroon spathe that is often reflexed; spadix exceeds the spathe in length. Flowers appear July–November. Favours stony ground and garrigue. Widespread in Mediterranean.

FRIAR'S COWL *Arisarum vulgare*   Height up to 40cm
Hairless, sometimes patch-forming perennial. Leaves oval, heart-shaped at the base and green, sometimes with dark blotches. Flower comprises a narrow tubular spathe, greenish and red, curved and hooded at the tip, surrounding a spike-like spadix; borne on long stalks, October–May. Favours shady scrub. Widespread.

BROAD-LEAVED HELLEBORINE *Epipactis helleborine*   Height up to 75cm
Purple-tinged, clump-forming orchid. Downy stems bear broadly-oval, strongly-veined leaves. Flowers are greenish, tinged with purple; borne in tall, loose spikes of up to 50, May–July. Favours shady areas in woodland and scrub. Widespread across much of the region but scarce in the E.

DARK RED HELLEBORINE *Epipactis atrorubens*   Height up to 70cm
Upright, rather striking orchid with downy stems that bear oval, strongly-veined leaves. Flowers are usually deep reddish purple; borne in tall, loose spikes of up to 18, May–June. Favours dry ground among woodland and scrub, invariably on calcareous soils, often in upland areas. Widespread but local in the region.

EASTERN MARSH HELLEBORINE *Epipactis veratrifolia*   Height up to 75cm
Upright orchid with downy stems that bear narrow-oval, clasping leaves arranged spirally up stem. Flowers strikingly marked with green and maroon; borne in tall spikes of up to 40, April–May. Favours damp flushes and marshy hollows on calcareous rocks. Confined to E Mediterranean including Cyprus.

SWORD-LEAVED HELLEBORINE *Cephalanthera longifolia*   Height up to 50cm
Upright perennial with hairless stems that bear leaves that are long and narrow, largest at the base of the plant. Each flower appears with a leafy bract, is pure white and up to 20mm long; borne in spikes of up to 15, April–June. Favours shady banks and woods, usually on calcareous soils. Widespread but local.

WHITE HELLEBORINE *Cephalanthera damasonium*   Height up to 50cm
Attractive upright orchid. Leaves are broad and oval at base of plant but become smaller and narrower up stem. Flowers are creamy white and 15–20mm long, each with a leafy bract; borne in terminal spikes of up to 14, May–June. Favours shady scrub and woodland, usually on calcareous soils in upland areas. Widespread.

RED HELLEBORINE *Cephalanthera rubra*   Height up to 50cm
Distinctive, slender and upright orchid. Leaves are dark green, narrow-oval and pointed. Flowers pinkish red and 15–20mm long, each with a leafy bract; borne in spikes of up to 10, May–June. Favours dry, shady woodlands, invariably on calcareous soils. Widespread but distinctly local.

VIOLET BIRD'S-NEST ORCHID *Limodorum abortivum*   Height up to 1m
Arguably the most distinctive and attractive orchid in the region. Entire plant is purple-tinged and lacks chlorphyll. Upright stems bear scales but not leaves. Flowers violet and up to 45mm across; borne in tall spikes, April–July. Favours bare ground in pine woodlands. Widespread across Mediterranean; locally abundant.

BIRD'S-NEST ORCHID *Neottia nidus-avis*   Height up to 35cm
Yellowish brown orchid that lacks chlorophyll and is saprophytic on underground decaying organic matter; root mass resembles a bird's nest. Flowers comprise a hood and 2-lobed lip; appear May–July. Favours undisturbed and usually densely shaded woodland, often beech. Widespread across the Mediterranean but local.

COMMON TWAYBLADE *Listera ovata*   Height up to 50cm
Distinctive orchid comprising a pair of broad, oval and basal leaves that first appear well before the flowering stem, from February onwards. Flowers yellowish green and borne in a loose spike, May–July; the lower lip is deeply forked. Favours woodland and grassy areas. Widespread across the Mediterranean.

AUTUMN LADY'S-TRESSES *Spiranthes spiralis*   Height up to 15cm
Charming little orchid. Rosette of oval leaves appears in early summer and withers before flowering stems appear. Tiny white flowers are borne in a spiral row up the stem and appear August–November. Favours short dry grassland, often on calcareous soils. Widespread across the Mediterranean.

GENNARIA *Gennaria diphylla*   Height up to 40cm
Unusual and easily overlooked orchid. Has two, broadly oval to heart-shaped and conspicuously veined leaves, one low down stem, the other mid-way up. Flowers are yellowish-green; borne in a spike, February–May. Favours stony ground with scrub or open woodland. Confined to S Iberian Peninsula and Sardinia.

LESSER BUTTERFLY-ORCHID *Platanthera bifolia*   Height up to 40cm
Attractive orchid with a single pair of broad, oval leaves at the base and smaller, scale-like leaves up the stem. Flowers are greenish white with a long, narrow lip, a long spur and pollen sacs that are parallel; borne in open spikes, May–July. Undisturbed grassy places and woods. Widespread across the region.

GREATER BUTTERFLY-ORCHID *Platanthera chlorantha*   Height up to 50cm
Impressive orchid with a single pair of large, oval leaves at the base of the plant and a few smaller stem leaves. Greenish white flowers have a long, narrow lip, a long spur and pollen sacs that form an inverted V; borne in open spikes, May–July. Undisturbed grassland and woods. Widespread but local in E of region.

COMMON SPOTTED-ORCHID *Dactylorhiza maculata*   Height up to 60cm
Familiar orchid with green, glossy leaves that are dark-spotted and appear as a rosette long before the flower stalk is produced; narrower leaves sheathe the lower stalk. Flowers pale pink to pinkish purple, marked with darker streaks and spots on the 3-lobed lip; May–July. Grassland and woods. Widespread but local.

ELDER-FLOWERED ORCHID *Dactylorhiza sambucina*   Height up to 30cm
Attractive orchid with 2–5 pale green, narrow basal leaves and 2 smaller, narrower leaves up stem. Flowers usually yellow, sometimes purple, elderflower-scented, with a rounded lip and downcurved spur; in spikes, March–May. Favours grassy areas on calcareous soils. Widespread but always in mountains.

Dactylorhiza saccifera   Height up to 80cm
Imposing orchid with fresh green leaves that are oval at the base and narrow and spreading further up stem; usually unmarked. Flowers pale pink or pinkish purple, with dark streaks and spots on distinctly 3-lobed lip; borne in tall spikes, May–July. Widespread but local in W and C Mediterranean; absent from most islands.

ROMAN ORCHID *Dactylorhiza romana*   Height up to 40cm
Delicate-looking and attractive orchid with pale green, unmarked and narrow-oval leaves, mostly in a basal rosette. Flowers usually pale yellow, sometimes pinkish purple, with a rounded and unspotted 3-lobed lip; borne in dense spikes, March–May. Favours maquis, open woodland and scrub. Widespread across Mediterranean.

MAN ORCHID *Aceras anthopophorum*   Height up to 25cm
Distinctive orchid with oval, fresh green leaves that form a basal rosette and sheathe the lower part of the flowering stem. The unusual flowers have a pronounced green hood, comprising sepals and upper petals, and an elongated, 4-lobed yellow lower lip, the whole fancifully resembling a man. Flowers borne in tall spikes, March–May. Garrigue and calcareous grassland. Widespread.

ANATOLIAN ORCHID *Orchis anatolica*   Height up to 25cm
Elegant and slender orchid with a reddish stem. Leaves are lanceolate and green blotched with purple spots; grouped at base with smaller leaves sheathing lower part of the flowering stem. Flowers pink, white or purple; the lip is usually conspicuously spotted and the spur is long and upcurved or horizontal. Flowers appear March–May. Grassy slopes, maquis and garrigue. E Mediterranean only.

BUG ORCHID *Orchis coriophora*   Height up to 35cm
Distinctive orchid. Leaves are narrow and fresh green; most form a basal rosette but a few sheathe the stem. Flowers have a conspicuous hood and are mostly pinkish brown; the lip is usually dark-spotted and sometimes tinged greenish. Flowers are borne in a dense spike, March–May, and smell musky. Favours grassy places and maquis. Widespread across the Mediterranean.

NAKED MAN ORCHID *Orchis italica*   Height up to 50cm
Attractive orchid with narrow-oval leaves that are sometimes purple-spotted; form a basal rosette with smaller leaves sheathing the flowering stem. Flowers usually pale pink, the hood with darker veins; lip is divided into segments fancifully resembling arms and legs. Flowers appear March–May; borne in dense heads, flowers opening from bottom upwards. Favours maquis, garrigue and grassy slopes; often forms extensive colonies. Widespread across the Mediterranean.

MILKY ORCHID *Orchis lactea*   Height up to 25cm
Delicate-looking orchid. Leaves fresh green and narrow-oval; larger leaves appear as basal rosette with smaller ones sheathing flowering stem. Flowers pale pink to white, the divided lip sometimes dark-spotted; shows a conspicuous hood. Flowers March–May. Favours grassy places and maquis. Widespread but local.

LAX-FLOWERED ORCHID *Orchis laxiflora*   Height up to 50cm
Distinctive and elegant orchid with a reddish stem. Leaves lanceolate and borne up stem. Flowers pinkish purple and proportionately large and with an upward-pointing spur; lip is often folded back on itself down the middle. Flowers borne in open spikes, March–May. Favours marshes and other damp, grassy places. Widespread across the Mediterranean but rather local.

LONG-SPURRED ORCHID *Orchis longicornu*   Height up to 25cm
Attractive orchid with narrow-oval, green and unspotted leaves; appear as a basal rosette with smaller ones sheathing flowering stem. Flowers comprise pale, dark-veined hood, a purple reflexed lip and a long pinkish purple, upward-pointing spur; in open spikes, March–April. Maquis and garrigue. W of region only.

PINK BUTTERFLY ORCHID *Orchis papilionacea*   Height up to 35cm
Distinctive and attractive orchid with narrow green leaves forming a basal rosette and a few sheathing the flowering stem. Flowers proportionately large and usually pink with a small hood and a large, rounded lip; in spikes, March–April. Maquis, garrigue and stony ground. Widespread across the Mediterranean.

PROVENCE ORCHID *Orchis provincialis*   Height up to 35cm
Attractive orchid with narrow oval green, dark-spotted, leaves; these form a basal rosette and sheathe the lower part of the flowering stem. Flowers yellow with a hood and a rounded, 3-lobed lip; in dense spikes, March–May. Maquis, garrigue and stony ground. Widespread in W and C Mediterranean.

FOUR-SPOTTED ORCHID *Orchis quadripunctata*   Height up to 25cm
Elegant and delicate-looking orchid. Leaves are narrow-oval to lanceolate and green, sometimes with dark spots; appear at base of plant and sheathing lower part of flowering stem. Flowers pinkish purple with a spur; lip is 3-lobed, usually with 4 dark spots in centre. Flowers borne in open spikes, April–May. Favours maquis, garrigue and grassy places. Mainly in E Mediterranean.

FAN-LIPPED ORCHID *Orchis colina*   Height up to 20cm
Distinctive orchid. Basal leaves oval and green; stem leaves and bracts are often flushed with brownish purple. Flowers comprise green-purple petals and sepals and a fan-shaped to oval, purple lip. Flowers borne in spikes, February–April. Favours maquis, garrigue and stony ground, most on calcareous soil. Widespread across the Mediterranean but distinctly local.

SPITZEL'S ORCHID *Orchis spitzelii*   Height up to 35cm
Elegant orchid with oval, green and unspotted leaves; these mostly form a basal rosette but some sheathe the lower part of the stem. Flowers comprise a greenish hood and a 3-lobed, pinkish purple, dark spotted lip. Flowers borne in dense spikes, March–May. Favours grassy slopes in upland areas. Widespread across the Mediterranean but absent from many islands.

EARLY-PURPLE ORCHID *Orchis mascula*   Height up to 40cm
Distinctive orchid. Rosettes of glossy, dark green leaves with dark spots, appear from December onwards, from which the flower stalk arises later in spring. The flowers are pinkish purple with a long spur and 3-lobed lip; borne in tall spikes, April–May. Favours open woodland, short grassland and garrigue, often in upland areas. Mainly confined to W Mediterranean, including Balearics.

GREEN-WINGED ORCHID *Orchis morio*   Height up to 40cm
Variable orchid with narrow-oval, unmarked glossy green leaves that form a basal rosette and sheathe the lower part of the flowering stem. The flowers vary from pinkish purple to almost white on different plants. The upper petals in particular are marked with dark veins and often suffused green; the lip has a red-dotted, pale central patch. Favours undisturbed grassland. Widespread.

MONKEY ORCHID *Orchis simia*   Height up to 40cm
Showy orchid with oval, glossy green basal leaves and smaller, narrower leaves sheathing lower part of flowering stem. Flowers are pinkish purple and comprise a hood and a lip deeply divided into narrow lobes resembling arms and legs; borne in dense heads, opening uppermost first, April–May. Garrigue and stony ground. Widespread in Mediterranean but absent from Corsica, Sardinia and Balearics.

LADY ORCHID *Orchis purpurea*   Height up to 75cm
Impressive orchid with broad, oval leaves that form a basal rosette and loosely sheathe the flowering stem. Flowers have a dark red hood and a pale pink, red-spotted lip; borne in 10–15cm tall, cylindrical flower spikes with flowers opening from the bottom. Flowers appear April–June. Favours woodland and grassland with scrub, on calcareous soils. W and C Mediterranean but absent from most islands.

TOOTHED ORCHID *Orchis tridentata*   Height up to 35cm
Attractive orchid with oval, green basal leaves and narrower, smaller leaves sheathing lower part of flowering stem. Flowers are pinkish with darker spots; comprise hood and lip divided into 2 'arms' and 2 'legs' with a small 'tooth' between the latter. Borne in a dense, inverted spike, March–May. Widespread.

HOLY ORCHID *Orchis sancta*   Height up to 35cm
Has narrow leaves at base and sheathing lower part of flowering stem. Flowers large and reddish pink, comprising hood and elongate oval, sharply lobed lip; borne in spikes, April–May. Garrigue and stony ground. E Mediterranean only.

MIRROR ORCHID *Ophrys speculum*   Height up to 20cm
Basal leaves oval; narrower leaves sheathe lower part of stem. Flowers comprise oval greenish sepals with maroon veins, and narrow purple upper petals; lip 3-lobed and 10–13mm long, with metallic blue speculum edged by yellow and fringed with hairs. Flowers in spikes, March–May. Maquis and garrigue. Widespread.

YELLOW OPHRYS *Ophrys lutea*   Height up to 25cm
Distinctive orchid with oval basal leaves; narrow leaves sheathe lower part of stem. Flowers comprise greenish oval sepals and yellowish narrow upper petals; lip is broadly oval, 14–18mm long, 3-lobed and yellow with maroon centre. In spikes, March–May. Garrigue and stony maquis. Widespread in W and C of region.

EASTERN YELLOW OPHRYS *Ophrys sicula*   Height up to 25cm
Distinctive orchid with oval basal leaves; narrow leaves sheathe lower part of stem. Flowers similar to those of *O.lutea* but 3-lobed lip is narrower, 10–15mm long and often with more extensive maroon and lilac central area. In spikes, March–May. Garrigue and stony ground. E Mediterranean only.

SOMBRE BEE ORCHID *Ophrys fusca*   Height up to 35cm
Slender orchid with narrow-oval basal leaves; lanceolate leaves sheath lower part of stem. Flowers comprise fresh green sepals and greenish upper petals; lip is oblong, 3-lobed and 10–15mm long, maroon-purple with lilac, 2-lobed speculum. Spikes of 4–10, February–May. Maquis, garrigue and open woodland. Widespread.

Ophrys iricolor   Height up to 30cm
Slender orchid with oval basal leaves; narrower leaves sheathe lower part of stem. Flowers similar to *O.fusca* but lip is 15–24mm long and 2-lobed, lilac-blue speculum is proportionately large. In spikes of 1–4, February–May. Favours maquis, garrigue and open woodland. C and E Mediterranean only.

FUNEREAL ORCHID *Ophrys funerea*   Height up to 25cm
Slender orchid with oval basal leaves; narrower leaves sheathe lower part of stem. Flowers similar to *O.fusca* with yellow-green sepals and upper petals; lip is 3-lobed and 7–12mm long, mainly maroon but with a blue-lilac speculum and yellowish border; in spikes of 4–9, March–May. Stony ground. E Mediterranean.

BORNMUELLER'S ORCHID *Ophrys bornmuelleri*   Height up to 25cm
Attractive orchid with oval basal leaves and narrower sheathing stem leaves. Flowers comprise oval whitish green sepals and short, hairy upper petals; lip is broadly square-shaped, 7–12mm long, velvety maroon with lilac, H-shaped speculum; in spikes of 4–15, March–May. Garrigue and open woodland. E Mediterranean.

EARLY SPIDER ORCHID *Ophrys sphegodes*   Height up to 30cm
Has blunt, oval basal leaves and narrower, pointed stem leaves. Flowers comprise oblong, yellowish green sepals and greenish upper petals, sometimes tinged pink; lip is broadly oval, 10–15mm long, velvety maroon with H-shaped violet speculum. In spikes of 3–9, March–May. Garrigue and short grassland. C Mediterranean only.

Ophrys lapethica   Height up to 25cm
Has oval basal leaves and narrower, pointed stem leaves. Flowers comprise large, oval and pink sepals and much shorter, narrower pink upper petals. Lip is oval, 9–12mm long and 3-lobed at base; complex reddish speculum defined by pale lines. Garrigue and stony ground. Endemic to Cyprus.

Ophrys herae   Height up to 35cm
Slender orchid with oval basal leaves and narrow stem leaves. Flowers comprise oval-tri-angular sepals, greenish but tinged red on lower half; upper sepals green, tinged red. Lip is rounded-square and 3-lobed at base; velvety maroon with H-shaped blue-lilac speculum. Garrigue and maquis. Aegean to Cyprus.

Ophrys mammosa   Height up to 40cm
Attractive orchid with oval basal leaves; narrower, pointed leaves sheathe the lower part of the stem. Flowers comprise relatively large, triangular-oval sepals that are usually striped green and pinkish-red; upper petals narrow and greenish pink. Lip is 10–15mm long and velvety maroon, with 2 basal lumps and lilac speculum comprising 2 parallel bars joined at top. Flowers in spikes of 5–10, March–May. Favours maquis and garrigue. E Mediterranean only.

BERTOLONI'S BEE ORCHID *Ophrys bertolonii*   Height up to 40cm
Slender orchid with narrow leaves, those at the base larger than those sheathing the lower part of the stem. Flowers comprise oval pinkish sepals and smaller pinkish-red upper petals; lip is square to rounded, velvety deep maroon with a shiny, bow-shaped lilac speculum. Flowers April–May. Favours stony ground, including garrigue. Widespread in W and C Mediterranean but distinctly local.

BUMBLEBEE ORCHID *Ophrys bombylifera*   Height up to 25cm
Upright perennial with a rosette of narrow-oval basal leaves and smaller stem leaves. Flowers comprise relatively large, oval and green sepals and smaller greenish upper petals; lip is 3-lobed, 7–8mm long and dark maroon with a bluish speculum. Flowers March–May. Widespread but local and absent from Cyprus.

CRETAN BEE ORCHID *Ophrys cretica*   Height up to 20cm
Distinctive orchid with oval, pointed basal leaves and smaller, narrower stem leaves. Flowers comprise triangular-oval sepals and shorter, narrower upper petals, all green flushed with red; lip is 3-lobed and deep purple with a white-bordered lilac speculum. Flowers in spikes of 3–8, March–April. Favours stony ground, including garrigue. Crete, Aegean Islands and S Greece only.

LATE SPIDER ORCHID *Ophrys fuciflora*   Height up to 50cm
Attractive orchid with oval basal leaves and narrower pointed leaves up stem. Flowers comprise broadly oval pink sepals and smaller, narrower pink upper petals. Lip is rounded to square-shaped with a reflexed tip, velvety maroon in colour; lilac speculum is variable but sometimes star-shaped with a central circle. Flowers April–May. Short grassland and garrigue. Widespread in W and C.

REINHOLD'S BEE ORCHID *Ophrys reinholdii*   Height up to 30cm
Unobtrusive little orchid with narrow leaves, those at base larger than those on stem. Flowers comprise relatively large, triangular-oval sepals that are pinkish green, and shorter, narrower reddish maroon upper petals; lip is oval and velvety deep maroon with a white-bordered, blue-lilac and often bow-shaped speculum. Flowers in spikes of 4–8, March–April. Grassy places. S Greece to W Turkey.

WOODCOCK ORCHID *Ophrys scolopax*   Height up to 40cm
Attractive orchid with narrow leaves, those at base larger than those on the stem. Flowers comprise triangular-oval pink sepals and smaller, narrower pink upper petals. Lip is 3-lobed and velvety maroon; speculum markings are variably H-shaped, enclosing a round central area. Appear March–May. Favours maquis, garrigue and open woodland. Widespread in W and C Mediterranean.

SAWFLY ORCHID *Ophrys tenthredinifera*   Height up to 40cm
Attractive orchid with oval basal leaves and smaller, narrower stem leaves. Flowers comprise deep pink, oval sepals and smaller, narrower pink upper petals; lip is hairy and maroon-brown with a yellow margin. Flowers appear March–May. Favours maquis and garrigue. Widespread in W and C Mediterranean.

BEE ORCHID *Ophrys apifera*   Height up to 30cm
Has basal rosette of oval leaves and two narrower sheathing leaves on stem. Flowers, 12mm across, comprise pink sepals and green upper petals; lip is furry and maroon with yellow markings. Appear March–May. Grassy places. Widespread.

LIZARD ORCHID *Himantoglossum hircinum* Height up to 1m
Tall with a reddish green stem. Oval basal leaves soon wither but smaller, narrower stem leaves persist. Flowers comprise grey-green, reddish streaked sepals and upper petals that form a hood; lip is reddish, very long and twisted with 2 short projections at base. Flowers in tall spikes, April–June, and smell of goats. Grassy places and open scrub. Widespread in W and C Mediterranean.

GIANT ORCHID *Barlia robertiana* Height up to 60cm
Robust and impressive orchid with a reddish stem. Has large oval leaves at base of plant; stem leaves smaller and narrower. Flowers comprise reddish green sepals and upper petals that form a hood; lip is purple and elongate, divided into 2 'arms' and 2 'legs'. Flowers borne in dense spikes, February–April. Favours grassy slopes, garrigue and maquis. Widespread across the Mediterranean.

PYRAMIDAL ORCHID *Anacamptis pyramidalis* Height up to 30cm
Attractive orchid with grey-green lanceolate leaves that are usually carried upright, partially sheathing the flowering stem. Flowers are deep pink and comprise spreading sepals, upper petals that form a small hood, a 3-lobed lip and a long spur; borne in dense, conical or domed heads, March–May. Dry grassland on calcareous soils, maquis and garrigue. Widespread but local.

TONGUE ORCHID *Serapias lingua* Height up to 25cm
Intriguing and distinctive orchid with reddish streaked stems. Leaves narrow and grey-green and bracts purplish and as long as flowers. Flowers comprise reddish green sepals and upper petals; lip is 25–30mm long, oval and pointed, fancifully resembling a tongue. Flowers are borne in spikes of 3–9, appearing March–May. Favours grassy slopes, maquis and garrigue. Widespread in W and C Mediterranean, sometimes locally common where conditions suit it.

HEART-FLOWERED SERAPIAS *Serapias cordigera* Height up to 25cm
Distinctive orchid with reddish stems and narrow, pointed leaves that partly sheathe the flowering stem. Flowers comprise reddish sepals and upper petals; lip is 20–35mm long, deep purple, and broadly heart-shaped with 2 basal dark lumps. Flowers borne in spikes of 3–10, April–May. Favours grassy places, maquis and garrigue. Widespread across Mediterranean but local or absent from parts of E.

SMALL-FLOWERED SERAPIAS *Serapias parviflora* Height up to 30cm
Slender and distinctive orchid with a reddish stem and narrow reddish green leaves that partly sheathe the flowering stem. Flowers comprise reddish sepals and upper petals; lip is dark red, 15–18mm long, narrow-oval and pointed. Flowers are borne in spikes of 3–8, March–May. Favours grassy places on sandy soils and garrigue. Widespread from Iberia to Turkey but absent from many islands.

LONG-LIPPED SERAPIAS *Serapias vomeracea* Height up to 25cm
Upright perennial with a reddish stem and narrow grey-green leaves that sheathe the flowering stem at the base; bracts longer than flowers. Flowers comprise reddish purple sepals and upper petals; lip is deep red and 30–40mm long. Flowers borne in spikes of 4–10, March–May. Favours grassy slopes and garrigue, usually on damp flushes. Widespread across most of the Mediterranean.

DENSE-FLOWERED ORCHID *Neotinea maculata* Height up to 25cm
Stem often flushed with reddish yellow. Basal leaves broadly oval; stem leaves smaller and narrower. Flowers vanilla-scented and whitish or pink, comprising sepals and upper petals that form a hood; lip is distinctly lobed. Flowers borne in dense spikes, March–May. Favours open woodland and maquis. Widespread.

KOMPER'S ORCHID *Comperia comperiana* Height up to 40cm
Flowers comprise pinkish brown hood and large lip with lower margin divided into 4 long threads. Under conifers and sweet chestnut. Lesvos, Samos and Turkey only.

LARGE QUAKING GRASS *Briza maxima*   Height up to 60cm
Distinctive grass when in flower with upright stems and flat leaves. Narrow, wiry stalks carry the inflorescence of flowers, March–June; this comprises dangling spikelets resembling miniature hops. Cultivated ground and maquis. Widespread.

HARE'S-TAIL *Lagurus ovatus*   Height up to 40cm
Downy annual that is distinctive in flower. Leaves flat and grey-green. Inflorescence comprises an egg-shaped mass of densely packed spikelets; appear March–July. Favours dry, stony ground. Widespread across the Mediterranean.

FERN-GRASS *Catapodium rigidum*   Height up to 10cm
Tufted hairless annual with narrow, usually flat leaves. Inflorescence comprises a spreading and superficially fern-like array of spikelets, and appears April–September. Favours cultivated and disturbed ground. Widespread across the region.

MARRAM GRASS *Ammophila arenaria*   Height up to 1m
Colonises and stabilises shifting sands by means of its underground stems. Leaves are tough, grey-green and rolled. Flower spikes are dense, comprising 1-flowered spikelets; May–July. Coastal sand dunes. Widespread native; widely planted.

Aegilops geniculata   Height up to 25cm
Distinctive upright annual with narrow flat leaves. Inflorescence comprises a compact head of spikelets, fertile ones of which have long, spine-like awns; these catch in clothing; March–June. Cultivated and disturbed ground. Widespread.

SEA BARLEY *Hordeum marinum*   Height up to 10cm
Short tufted annual with narrow grey-green leaves. Inflorescence comprises a compact and slender head of spikelets each with long spine-like awns; March–July. Favours bare grassy places, usually by the sea. Widespread.

BERMUDA GRASS *Cynodon dactylis*   Height up to 10cm
Creeping perennial with narrow flat leaves. Inflorescence comprises 3–6 finger-like spikes bearing small spikelets; spikes spread in full flower, March–October. Cultivated and disturbed ground, often coastal. Widespread.

Ampelodesmus mauritanicus   Height up to 2.5m
Imposing tufted grass with rough leaves up to 1m long. Inflorescence is branched and mostly 1-sided, the branches bearing flattened spikelets, March–July. Favours maquis and garrigue. Widespread in W Mediterranean only.

GIANT REED *Arundo donax*   Height up to 5m
Bamboo-like grass with woody stems and long, broad green leaves. Inflorescence terminal and up to 70cm long. Favours damp ground beside rivers and in marshes, sometimes forming extensive single-species stands. Widespread and common.

GOLDEN DOG'S-TAIL *Lamarckia aurea*   Height up to 12cm
Tufted, upright grass with very narrow leaves. Distinctive inflorescence is one-sided, usually overtopped by bare stalk. Flowers March–June, green at first but soon turning golden brown. Cultivated and stony bare ground. Widespread.

ROUGH DOG'S-TAIL *Cynosurus echinatus*   Height up to 25cm, often much shorter
Tufted, upright annual grass. Inflorescence is dense and oval or rounded with long projecting hair-like awns; flowers March–June. Favours stony and cultivated ground. Widespread and generally common.

WINTER WILD OAT *Avena sterilis*   Height up to 1.5m
Upright annual with long blue-green leaves. Inflorescence comprises a loose array of drooping, stalked spikelets; flowers March–May. Favours cultivated ground, grassy roadside verges and fallow fields. Widespread and common.

SHARP RUSH *Juncus acutus*   Height up to 1.5m
Robust, clump-forming rush with tall, narrow and cylindrical leaves ending in a sharp spine. Clusters of reddish brown flowers are also topped by a sharp spine and appear March–May. Sandy ground, usually coastal. Widespread.

SOFT RUSH *Juncus effusus*   Height up to 1.5m
Clump-forming rush with green, smooth-looking stems. Leaves are soft-tipped. Pale brown flowers are borne in a loose, rounded cluster topped by a narrow bract and appear April–July. Damp grassland, often indicative of overgrazing. Widespread.

BULBOUS RUSH *Juncus bulbosus*   Height up to 60cm
Tufted delicate-looking rush, bulbous at base; stems sometimes trail or float depending on habitat. Inflorescence comprises branched array of up to 20 clusters of green or brown flowers, May–August. Damp ground. W and C Mediterranean.

HARD RUSH *Juncus inflexus*   Height up to 1m
Densely tufted perennial with grey-green stems that are leafless and ridged. The brown flowers are borne in a loose cluster, topped by a narrow, pointed bract, and appear April–July. Favours damp ground. Widespread but local.

TOAD RUSH *Juncus bufonis*   Height up to 40cm
Tufted annual with narrow leaves that arise at the base of the plant. The flowers are borne in branched clusters and appear April–June. Favours damp, bare ground including wheel ruts and pond margins. Widespread across the region.

DWARF RUSH *Juncus capitatus*   Height up to 5cm
Tufted annual with wiry basal leaves and leafless stems. The greenish flowers are borne in terminal clusters, topped by 2 bracts. Favours damp, bare ground often along tracks or trampled pond margins. Widespread but local.

COMMON REED *Phragmites communis*   Height up to 2m
Perennial of marshes and freshwater margins, often forming vast single-species stands. Can be confused with giant reed but is appreciably shorter. Robust stems carry terminal clusters of flowers. Plant turns brown in winter. Widespread.

Stipa offneri   Height up to 1.5m
Tough, tufted grass with grey-green leaves. Inflorescence comprises an open succession of spikelets with long awns; appear April–June. Favours stony and sometimes disturbed ground. Widespread in W.

DROOPING BROME *Bromus tectorum*   Height up to 50cm
Tufted, upright annual grass with flat, hairy leaves. Inflorescence is drooping and comprises long-stalked spikelets; appear April–June. Favours dry sandy or stony ground. Widespread.

SWEET VERNAL-GRASS *Anthoxanthum odoratum*   Height up to 40cm
Tufted perennial grass with leaves 2–4mm wide; smell of new-mown hay when dry. Inflorescence a spike-like panicle. Favours grassy habitats but absent from hot dry areas. Widespread.

Secale montanum   Height up to 2m
Tufted, upright barley-like grass with narrow leaves 2–4mm wide. Inflorescence borne on a tall stem and comprises a two-sided spike with long awns. Favours rocky and stony ground; absent from dry, low-lying areas. E of region only.

LESSER REEDMACE *Typha angustifolia*   Height up to 1.5m
Clump-forming plant with long leaves, up to 5mm wide. Sausage-shaped male and female flower heads are separated by a gap. Damp ground and pond margins. Widespread. Similar *T.latifolia* has contiguous male and female flower heads.

GALINGALE *Cyperus longus* Height up to 1.5m
Creeping perennial with upright, 3-sided stems. Leaves glossy green, up to 10mm wide and rough-edged. Inflorescence comprises an umbel of up to 10 rays, each bearing clusters of brown spikelets; June–August. Damp ground. Widespread.

BROWN GALINGALE *Cyperus fuscus* Height up to 30cm
Tufted annual with upright, 3-sided stems and leaves up to 7mm wide. Inflorescence comprises tight clusters of reddish brown spikelets with 2 long bracts; June–August. Damp muddy ground, often in drying ponds. Widespread.

GREAT FEN SEDGE *Cladium mariscus* Height up to 2.5m
Creeping perennial with upright, cylindrical and hollow stems. Leaves up to 2m long, rough-edged and usually bent in the middle. Inflorescence comprises clusters of brown spikelets; June–August. Marshy ground. Widespread.

BRANCHED BUR-REED *Sparganium erectum* Height up to 1m
Sedge-like perennial with bright green linear leaves that are keeled and triangular in cross-section. The spherical flower heads are borne in branched spikes, May–July. Still and slow-flowing water. Widespread but local.

COMMON SPIKE-RUSH *Eleocharis palustris* Height up to 50cm
Creeping perennial. The green, leafless stems arise in tufts and are topped by brown, egg-shaped spikelets, which contain the flowers; appear April–June. Favours marshes and pond margins. Widespread across the region.

BLACK BOG-RUSH *Schoenus nigricans* Height up to 50cm
Tufted perennial. Long green leaves arise at base of stems, which carry flower heads comprising black spikelets flanked by a long bract; April–June. Favours marshes and dune slacks, usually on base-rich soils. Widespread but local.

PENDULOUS SEDGE *Carex pendula* Height up to 1.5m
Clump-forming sedge with long, yellowish leaves that are up to 20mm wide. Tall, 3-sided and often arched stems carry inflorescence comprising 1–2 male spikes above 4–5 long, drooping female spikes. Damp wooded areas. Widespread.

FALSE FOX SEDGE *Carex otrubae* Height up to 80cm
Tufted sedge with stiff, upright leaves that are 5–10mm wide. Robust stems are rough and 3-sided. Inflorescence comprises a dense head of greenish brown spikes and a long bract. Favours grassy places on damp ground. Widespread.

GLAUCOUS SEDGE *Carex flacca* Height up to 50cm
Tufted sedge with upright glaucous leaves. Inflorescence comprises a single male spike above 1–3 female spikes. Found in grassland on calcareous soils, both dry and wet. Widespread.

ROUND-HEADED CLUB-RUSH *Scirpus holoschoenus* Height up to 1.5m
Tufted perennial with cylindrical, smooth stems. Leaves short and basal. Inflorescence comprises an open array of globular clusters of spikelets, appearing May–August. Damp ground, often on coastal sandy soil. Widespread.

SEA CLUB-RUSH *Scirpus maritimus* Height up to 1.25m
Creeping perennial with rough, keeled leaves. The tall stems are rough and 3-sided, topped by clusters of brown spikelets and flanked by leaf-like bracts. Found along the margins of brackish water near the sea. Widespread.

SMALL CLUB-RUSH *Scirpus cernuus* Height up to 20cm
Low, tufted annual with wiry, basal leaves. Inflorescence comprises an egg-shaped cluster of greenish brown spikelets, appearing April–July. Favours areas of damp ground with short grass, usually coastal. Widespread but local.

SAND QUILLWORT *Isoetes histrix*   Height up to 8cm
Easily overlooked tufted plant comprising radiating narrow and flat leaves that are fresh green; often slightly recurved, the tips touching the ground. Favours winter-wet hollows on bare, sandy and usually base-rich soils. Widespread.

MARSH HORSETAIL *Equisetum palustre*   Height up to 40cm
Distinctive perennial. The upright stems are grooved, brittle and sometimes branched. Spores are borne in cone-like structures, up to 30mm long. Favours damp ground and marshy habitats. Widespread and locally common across the region.

FIELD HORSETAIL *Equisetum arvense*   Height up to 75cm
Spreading, patch-forming perennial. Produces sterile shoots with ridged stems carrying whorls of branches. Fertile stems, bearing cones, appear in early spring and ripen by April. Favours dry and damp grassy places. Widespread.

MAIDENHAIR FERN *Adiantum capillus-veneris*   Frond length up to 50cm
Attractive and distinctive tufted fern. Spreading, hair-like stems carry green leaflets that are broadly triangular and 2–3 lobed. Favours humid settings, often among rocks dampened by seepage or splashed by water. Widespread but local.

MAIDENHAIR SPLEENWORT *Asplenium trichomanes*   Frond length up to 15cm
Charming and distinctive fern. Grows in tufts, fronds comprising a black, thread-like midrib bearing numerous pairs of small, oval leaflets. Favours walls and rock faces. Widespread across the Mediterranean but local.

SEA SPLEENWORT *Asplenium maritimum*   Frond length up to 25cm
Distinctive fern that grows in tufts. The fronds comprise a reddish brown midrib bearing pairs of oval, glossy green leaflets. Favours shady, humid crevices among coastal rocks and stone walls. Widespread in W and C Mediterranean.

WALL-RUE *Asplenium ruta-muraria*   Frond length up to 12cm
Delicate little fern with evergreen fronds that are dull green and 2-times pinnately divided into oval lobes with spores beneath. Favours stone walls and rocks, often in limestone areas. Widespread across the Mediterranean.

HART'S-TONGUE FERN *Phyllitis scolopendrium*   Frond length up to 60cm
Evergreen fern with fresh green, undivided fronds that are strap-like and form clumps. Dark brown spore cases are borne in rows on underside of fronds. Favours damp, shady woods and banks. Widespread but local in W and C Mediterranean.

BROAD BUCKLER FERN *Dryopteris dilatata*   Frond length up to 1m
Robust fern with fronds that are dark green and 3-times pinnately divided, the stalks with dark-centred scales; grow in a shuttlecock-like array. Favours damp wooded areas and upland slopes. Widespread but local in W Mediterranean.

MEDITERRANEAN CLUBMOSS *Selaginella denticulata*   Mat-forming
Low, spreading moss-like plant. Much-branched stems bear oval, scale-like leaves, each about 2mm long. Found on shaded, damp rocks, often under overhangs with trickling water. Appears fresh green in spring. Thereafter turns red and withers.

LICHEN *Xanthoria sp*   Encrusting
Forms conspicuous bright orange patches on rocks, even in surprisingly arid, sun-baked locations. Often commonest near the sea. Surface encrustation comprises wrinkled, leafy scales. Widespread and common throughout.

LICHEN *Cladonia sp*   Encrusting
A genus of greyish lichens, most of which comprise flattened branches that tufted and much-divided. Some species form carpets on bare ground or among low vegetation in maquis. Others grow attached to branches of trees and shrubs.

GLOSSARY

Aestivation: dormancy observed in an animal during summer

Abdomen: hind section of an insect's body; usually appears segmented

Alien: species that is not native to a particular region but which has been introduced by man and has become naturalised

Annelid: a type of worm (see plant and animal groups)

Annual: a plant that lives for a single growing season

Antennae: slender, paired sensory organs on the head of an insect

Anther: pollen-containing structure in a flower, located on the end of the male reproductive structure, the stamen

Arboreal: tree-dwelling

Awn: bristle found in flowers of many grasses

Axil: angle where upper surface of a leaf meets the stem on a plant

Berry: fleshy fruit containing several seeds

Biennial: a plant that takes two years to complete its life cycle

Bivalve: mollusc whose shell comprises two halves

Bract: a small leaf- or scale-like structure beneath a flower

Bulb: fleshy, underground structure found in certain plants and comprising leaf bases and next years bud

Bulbil: small, bulb-like structure

Capsule: structure within which seeds are formed in flowering plants and spores develop in mosses and liverworts

Carapace: hard, upper surface of a crustacean's shell

Carpal: area on a bird's wing corresponding to the 'wrist' joint

Caterpillar: larval stage of butterfly or moth

Catkin: flowering structure of certain trees and shrubs

Cephalothorax: fused head and thorax found in spiders

Cerci: paired appendages at hind end of an insect's body

Chlorophyll: green pigment found in plant tissue and essential for photosynthesis

Compound eye: eye structure typical of insects and some other invertebrates comprising numerous cells and lenses not a single lens

Cone: structure bearing reproductive elements of conifers

Conifer: tree which bears its reproductive structures in cones

Deciduous: woody plant which sheds its leaves in winter

Disc florets: small flowers found at centre of inflorescence of members of daisy family

Dorsal: upper surface

Diurnal: active during daylight

Elytra: hardened forewings of a beetle

Endemic: confined to a geographical area such as an island or a country

Evergreen: plant which retains its leaves throughout the year

Feral: having returned to the wild

Floret: small flower

Frond: leaf-like structure found in some lower plants

Fruit: seeds together with their surrounding tissues

Gall: plant growth induced by another organism, often a gall wasp

Garrigue: see introductory section on Mediterranean habitats

Glume: stiffened bract found on a grass flower

Haemoglobin: red pigment in blood which absorbs oxygen

Holdfast: root-like structure which anchors seaweeds to rocks

Hybrid: offspring from different parent species

Inflorescence: combination of a flower, its bracts and flowering stems

Insectivore: an organism which feeds on insects

Juvenile: newly fledged bird which has not yet acquired adult plumage

Lanceolate: lance-shaped

Larva: soft-bodied, pre-adult stage in the life-cycle of certain insect species

Leaflet: small, separate segment of a leaf

Lek: communal display area used by certain bird species

Ligule: membranous leaf sheath found in grasses

Maquis: see introductory section on Mediterranean habitats

Melanic: showing dark pigmentation

Migrant: bird which spends the summer and winter in different areas

Moult: process seen in birds during which old feathers are lost and replaced by new ones

Mucus: slimy, viscous fluid secretion

Nocturnal: active after dark

Node: part of stem at which leaves arise

Nut: dry and often hard fruit containing a single seed

Nymph: immature stage in the life cycle of certain insects groups, notably dragonflies and bugs

Operculum: plate found in some molluscs and used to seal off entrance to shell

Ovate: roughly oval in outline

Ovoid: egg-shaped

Ovipositor: egg-laying structure found at the tail-end of some female insects

Needle: narrow leaves found in conifers

Nymph: pre-adult stage in certain insects, notably bugs, which has some characters in common with its adult stage

Palps: sensory appendages found around the mouth in insects and crustaceans

Palmate: leaf divided into lobes which fancifully resemble a hand

Parasite: organism which lives on or in another organism, relying on it entirely for its nutrition

Passage migrant: bird species seen mostly on migration and which does not necessarily breed in Britain

Perennial: plant which lives for more than two years

Petal: often colourful inner row of structures surrounding reproductive part of a flower

Pinnate: leaf divided into more than three leaflets, these being arranged in pairs on either side of stem

Planarian: a flatworm (see section on plant and animal groups)

Pollen: minute grains produced by anthers and containing male sex cells

Pronotum: hardened dorsal plate covering the thorax of an insect

Pupa: stage in an insect's life-cycle between the larva and adult; also called the chrysalis

Ray florets: small flowers found on the outer fringe of the inflorescence in flowers of the daisy family

Recurved: turned backwards in a curve

Rhizome: underground stem

Rosette: radiating arrangement of leaves

Runner: creeping stem which occurs above ground and may root at nodes or tip

Saprophyte: a plant that lacks chlorophyll and which gains its nutrition from decaying organic matter such as leaf mould

Secondaries: flight feathers located on the inner half of the wing

Sepal: outer row of structures surrounding the reproductive part of a flower

Sole: underside of the foot in molluscs

Spadix: upright spike of florets, found in arums

Spathe: large bract surrounding spadix in arums

Species: unit of classification defining animals or plants which are able to breed with one another and produce viable offspring

Speculum: species-specific patch of colour seen on ducks' wings

Spike: simple, branched inflorescence

Spikelet: inflorescence arrangement in grasses and sedges etc

Spore: tiny reproductive body that disperses and gives rise to a new organism

Stamen: male reproductive structure of a flower

Steppe: see introductory section on Mediterranean habitats

Stigma: receptive tip of female part of flower, the style

Stipule: leaf-like or scale-like structure at base of leaf stalk

Style: female reproductive structure of a flower

Subspecies: sub-division of a species, members of which are able to breed with other subspecies but seldom do so because of geographical isolation

Tendril: slender, modified leaf or stem structure which assists climbing in some plants

Thallus: unspecialised vegetative body of a lower plant

Thorax: middle section of an insect's body

Tragus: pointed inner ear out-growth in some bat species

Trifoliate: leaf divided into three sections

Umbel: umbrella-like inflorescence

Ventral: lower surface

FURTHER READING

MAMMALS
David MacDonald and Priscilla Barrett, Collins Field Guide *Mammals of Britain and Europe*. HarperCollins*Publishers*.

BIRDS
Lars Svensson, Killian Mullarney, Dan Zetterström, Peter Grant, *Collins Bird Guide*. HarperCollins*Publishers*.

Hermann Heinzel, Richard Fitter and John Parslow, *Pocket Guide Birds of Britain and Europe*. HarperCollins*Publishers*.

Paul Sterry, *Field Guide to the Birds of Britain and Europe*. The Crowood Press.

Richard Brooks, *Birding on the Greek Island of Lesvos*. Brookside Publishing.

OTHER VERTEBRATES
Nicholas Arnold and John Burton, *Field Guide Reptiles and Amphibians of Britain and Europe*. HarperCollins*Publishers*.

Peter Miller and Mick Loates, *Pocket Guide Fish of Britain and Europe*. HarperCollins*Publishers*.

BUTTERFLIES AND MOTHS
Tom Toman and Richard Lewington, *Field Guide Butterflies of Britain and Europe*. HarperCollins*Publishers*.

Paul Sterry, *A Photographic Guide to the Butterflies of Britain and Europe*. New Holland.

OTHER INVERTEBRATES
Michael Chinery, *Field Guide Insects of Britain and Western Europe*. HarperCollins*Publishers*.

THE SEASHORE
Peter Hayward, Tony Nelson-Smith and Chris Shields, *Pocket Guide Sea Shore*. HarperCollins*Publishers*.

A.C. Campbell, Roger Gorringe and James Nicholls, *The Hamlyn Guide to the Flora and Fauna of the Mediterranean Sea*. Hamlyn.

TREES
Andrew Cleave, *Field Guide to the Trees of Britain, Europe and North America*. The Crowood Press.

Keith Rushforth, *Wildlife Trust Guide Trees of Britain and Europe*. HarperCollins*Publishers*.

Paul Sterry and Bob Press, *A Photographic Guide to the Trees of Britain and Europe*. New Holland.

WILD FLOWERS
Paul Sterry and Bob Press, *A Photographic Guide to the Wild Flowers of Britain and Europe*. New Holland.

Marjorie Blamey and Christopher Grey-Wilson, *Mediterranean Wild Flowers*. HarperCollins*Publishers*.

LOWER PLANTS
Hans Martin Jahns, *Photoguide Ferns, Mosses and Lichens of Britain and Northern and Central Europe*. HarperCollinsPublishers.

PICTURE CREDITS

t = top, l = left, r = right, up = upper, c = centre, lw = lower, b = bottom

All pictures by Paul Sterry apart from the following:
Supplied by FLPA: Frank W. Lane 209 upcr. Linda Lewis 209 bl. Panda Photo 55 br. Silvestris 49 br, 209 lwcr. D.P. Wilson 209 cl, cr, lwcl.
Supplied by Nature Photographers: S.C. Bisserot 49 cl, 51 all, 53 tl, 125 cr, lwcl, 127 upcl, cr, lwcr, bl, 129 tr, upcl, lwcl, bc, 131 tr, upcl, lwcr, bl, 135 upcl, 137 tl, 139 lwc, bl, 141 tl, tr, 143 tl, 145 tc, 153 tr, upcl, lwcl, 155 tr, 165 tl, 167 tl, 169 lwcl, 171 tr, lwcr, 177 tr, lwcr, bl, 179 tc, bc, br, 181 tc, lwc, 185 tc, 187 bl, 189 bl, 199 tc, 201 lwcr, bl, 205 tl, cl, lwcr, bl, 207 lwcl, upbl, br, 247 upcl, 259 bc, 297 tr. Frank B. Blackburn 71 lwcl, 93 bl, 95 tr, 107 upc, lwcl, 121 br, 167 upcl, 235 lwcr, 303 lwcr. Ken Blamire 133 lwcl, 135 lwcr, 137 upcl, lwcr, 141 lwc, bl, bc, br, 143 tr, upcr, lwc, lwcr, bc, 145 tl, tr, br, 147 tl, upcl, upc, lwcl, 149 upcr, 153 bl, 161 tl, 171 lwcl, 173 upcl, 181 upcl, 183 upcr, 319 tr. Mark Bolton 42 t, 57 upc, upcr, lwcl, 81 tl, 83 bl, 97 c, upcr, cr, lwcl, 101 upcr, 107 tl, 109 tr, 113 tl. Derek Bonsall 145 bc, 177 upcr, 247 br. Nicholas Phelps Brown 125 lwcr, 167 upc, 169 upcr, 177 upcl. Brinsley Burbidge 127 upcr, 129 tl, bl, 217 upcl, lwcr, 219 lwc, bc, lwc, bc, 223 tr, upcr, 225 bl, 227 tl, 231 upcl, upc, br, 233 upcl, lwc, br, 235 tl, tc, lwcl, 237 upc, upcr, lwcr, 239 upc, bc, 241 upcl, upc, upcr, lwc, bl, br, 243 tl, bl, 247 tl, 249 lwcl, 251 lwc, 255 tc, 257 upcl, 259 tc, upcl, lwcr, 261 tl, upcl, upc, upcr, lwcl, 263 tr, bc, 267 lwcl, 269 br, 275 upc, 281 bc, 283 bl, 287 br, 289 tl, tc, bc, br, 291 lwc, 293 upc, 295 tr, upcl, lwcr, 297 tc, lwc, lwcr, bc, 301 lwcl, bl, 303 tc, 305 upcr, bl, 307 tr, bc, 309 tc, 311 tc, upcl, lwcl, lwc, 313 tr, upc, upcr, lwcl, lwcr, bc, 315 lwc, br, 317 bc, br, 319 lwc (top), 321 upcr, lwc, br, 323 tc, 325 bc, 327 lwcl, 329 tl, tc, tr, 331 upcr, 333 tr. Robin Bush 22, 23 t, b, 34 t, 55 upcl, 63 upcr, 133 upcl, 135 lwcl, br, 137 tc, upcr, 139 tl, tr, upcl, cr, lwcr, bc, 143 upc, 147 tr, upcr, lwc, bl, br, 149 tl, upcl, upc, 171 upcr, 213 tl, 225 bc, 237 bc, 239 tl (both), 243 lwcr, 255 lwcl, 257 tc, upcr, 265 br, 269 lwc, 271 br, 275 lwcl, 277 lwc, 283 tc, 289 upc, 291 bc, 293 tl, 305 bc, 309 bc, 317 upcr, 323 c, bl, bc, 333 lwcl, lwc, 343 upcl. N.A. Callow 37, 145 lwcr, bl, 147 lwcr, 149 lwcl, 167 upcr, lwcl, 169 tl, tr, upcl, bc, 179 tr, upcl, bl, 181 tr, 183 tl, 185 tr, upc, upcr (both), lwc, bl, br, 191 tl, 221 upcr, 225 br, 245, bc, 253 tl, 259 tr, 285 tl, 287 lwcr, 291 lwcl, 295 upc, 301 upcl, 305 upc, 313 bl, 317 tl, 321 bl. Kevin Carlson 73 br, 87 bl, 97 bl, 99 bl, 105 tl, tr, 109 br, 111 upcr, 113 br, 123 lwcl, 127 tl, 129 lwcr, 135 tl, bc, 137 lwcl, 139 lwcl, 141 lwcl, 153 tl, 163 br, 173 tr, 233 tl, 243 upc, 245 lwcr, 263 upc, br, 265 tl, lwcl, lwc, lwcr, 267 upcl, 273 upcl, 275 upcl, 283 lwcl, 299 lwcr, 311 br, 313 tc, br, 319 upc, lwcr, 327 bc. Colin Carver 49 upcl, 105 upcl, 107 bc, 123 br, 127 tr, 129 upcr, 143 br, 155 lwc. Bob Chapman 157 lwcl. Hugh Clark 55 tl, 85 lwc, 171 br, 215 br, 217 tr. Andrew Cleave 4, 16, 19, 21, 28, 32, 41, 43, 44, 59 tl, 69 lwcl, 147 tc, 155 upcr, 169 tc, 189 tr, upcl, br, 191 upc, 195 tl, 199 bl, 201 br, 203 upc, br, 205 br, 211 tl, tc, upcr, lwcl, lwcr, bl, bc, br, 213 tc, tr, upcl, lwcl. lwc, lwcr, bl, bc, br, 215 tl, tc, tr, upcl, upc, upcr, bl, 217 tl, tc, upcr, lwc, bl, bc, br, 219 tl, upcl, upc, upcr, lwcl, lwcr, bl, br, 221 tl, upcl, upc, lwcl, lwcr, bl, 223 tl, upcl, upc, lwcl, lwc, lwcr, bl, bc, br, 225 tl, tc, tr, upcl, lwcl, lwc, 227 tc, 229 upc, lwc, lwcr, 231 lwcr, bc, 233 tr, 235 br, 237 tl, lwc, 239 br, 241 tc, lwcl, 243 lwcl, 247 tc, 249 br, 251 bc, br, 255 tr, 257 bl, 259 lwc, bl, br, 263 lwc, 267 tl, upc, upcr, 269 lwcr, 271 lwcl, 273 bl, 277 tr, upc, bl, 279 lwcr, 281 br, 283 tc, 287 tr, lwcl, lwc, 289 upcl, 293 lwc, 299 tc, 301 upc, 303 upc, upcr, bc, 305 tr, lwcl, 311 tr, upc, 315 lwcl, bl, 317 upcl, lwcr, bl, 319 tc, upcr, 321 upcl, bc, 323 lwcl, 329 lwcl, lwc, 335 tc, 337 lwc, 339 tl, tr, upcl, upc, lwcl, 341 tl, tr, upc, lwcr, bc, 343 upcr, lwc. Peter Craig-Cooper 61 br, 67 upcl, 75 upcl, 85 upcr. Ron Croucher 163 upcr, 343 tr. R.S. Daniell 61 bl. Martin Edge 207 tl. Geoff du Feu 47 cr, 53 br, 77 lwcl, 171 lwcl, 177 tl, br, 181 upcr, 215 lwcr, 259 tl, 297 upc, 301 lwcr. Michael Gore 49 lwcl, 67 upcr, 71 lwc, 73 upcl, 315 tl, 335 c. Christopher Grey-Wilson 215 bc, 237 upcl, 239 lwcr, 241 lwcr, 245 upcl, 247 lwcr, 253, bc, 263, upcr, lwcl, 279 upcl, upcr, 283 upcr, 293 upcr, 295 tc, 301 lwcr, 307 lwc. Jean Hall 211 tr, 239 lwcl, lwc, 257 lwcr, 267 bl, 279 bl, 289 tr, 293 br, 317 lwcl, 341 lwcl. Michael J. Hammet 191 tc, tr, 201 lwc, 203 tl, 205 upcr, 207 tr, lwtl, lwtr, lwcr, 209 upcl. James Hancock 189 lwcr, 309 bl. Dr Michael Hill 157 lwc, 227 upcr. Barry R. Hughes 81 lwcl, 83 upcr, 93 tr, 107 upcl, 109 upcl. J. Hyett 315 tr. E.A. Janes 30, 47 bl, 53 tc, lwcr, 55 cl, 69 upc, 77 br, 87 tr, lwcl, 89 tr, upcl, 109 cl, 135 upc, 141 upc, 143 tc, upcl, 167 lwcr, bc, 187 upbl, 233 upc, 301 lwc, 343 tc. Len Jessup 131 lwcl, 149 tc, 157 lwcr, 271 tc, 289 upcr. Lee Morgan 24, 83 lwcr, 159 lwc, 205 tr, 231 tl, 339 br. H. Wolmuth (and M. Muller) 69 tr. Owen Newman 47 tl, cl, 49 tl. Philip Newman 57 tr, 67 bl, 69 tl, upcl, 71 tl, 79 cr, 95 tl, 99 lwcr, 103 tl, 109 upcr, 113 tc. David Osborn 55 upcr, 73 upcr, 229 lwcl, 231 tr, 243 tr, 255 upcr, 257 bc, 281 tr, 293 bc, 311 upcr. W.S. Paton 47 lwcr, br, 49 upcr, cr, lwcr, 77 tr, 89 tl, 117 br, 211 upcl, 221 tc. David Rae 233 bc, 271 tl. Don Smith 71 bl, 189 upcr, 191 upcr, 199 upc, 203 tc, upcr, 207 upcl. R.T. Smith 57 upcl. James Sutherland 29, 125 tl, 203 bl, 211 lwc. E.K. Thompson 137 bl, 174 cl, 187 upbr. Roger Tidman 57 lwcr, 65 tr, br, 67 cl, cr, lwcl, lwcr, 69 tc, upcr, lwc, lwcr, br, bc, 71 tr, br, 73 tl, tr, 85 tl, upcl, tc, tcr, lwcl, lwcr, 87 tl, br, 89 lwcr, 95 br, 99 tl, 107 lwcr, 109 tl, bl, 111 tl, tr, 117 upcl, 119 tl, 121 tl, 153 upcr, 171 upcr, 261 lwcr, 291 br. Baron Hugo Van Lawick 49 tr. Derek Washington 325 tl. Tony Wharton 149 tr. K.D. Wilson 177 lwc.
Supplied by Planet Earth Pictures: Marty Snyderman 209 br

INDEX

Index: Mediterranean Wildlife

This index uses one tab position

A

purple, 278
ground-pine, 280
groundsel, 304
Gryllotalpa gryllotalpa, 162
Gryllus campestris, 162
gull, Audouin's, 18, 24, 82
  black-headed, 82
  lesser black-backed, 82
  little, 82
  Mediterranean, 82
  slender-billed, 82
  yellow-legged, 18, 82
gum, blue, 216
  ribbon, 216
gurnard, grey, 206
Gynandiris sisyrinchium, 318
Gypaetus barbatus, 66
Gyps fulvus, 66

H

habitat, agricultural land, 35-6
  arid grassland, 34
  cliff, 17-18
  coastal, 16-21
  freshwater, 25-6
  garrigue, 28, 32-3, 40, 44
  grassland, 30-3
  maquis, 12-13, 15, 27, 28, 30-2,
40, 44
  open sea, 24
  saltmarsh, 22-3
  saltpan, 22-3
  shrub, 30-3
  steppe, 34
  urban, 37
hairstreak, black, 144
  blue-spot, 144
  brown, 144
  false ilex, 144
  green, 144
  ilex, 144
  purple, 144
  white-letter, 144
Halcyon smyrnensis, 90
Halichondria panicea, 188
Halimione portulacoides, 226

Halimium halimifolium, 264
  lasianthum, 264
Haliotis lamellosa, 190
Halocynthia papillosa, 204
Hamearis lucina, 140
hare, brown, 46
hare's-ear, shrubby, 270
  sickle-leaved, 270
  slender, 270
hare's-tail, 336
harrier, hen, 66
  marsh, 26, 66
  Montagu's, 66
hawfinch, 120
hawker, brown, 172
  migrant, 172
  southern, 172
hawkmoth spp., 37
  bedstraw, 152
  convolvulus, 150
  death's-head, 150
  elephant, 152
  eyed, 150
  hummingbird, 152
  oleander, 152
  privet, 150
  silver-striped, 152
  spurge, 152
  striped, 152
  willowherb, 152
hawksbeard, pink, 308
hawthorn, 216
  eastern, 216
heart and dart, 154
heath, Corsican, 142
  dusky, 142
  Portuguese, 272
  small, 142
  tree, 31, 272
heather, bell, 272
  tree, 27
Hebrew character, 156
hedge-parsley, knotted, 270
hedgehog, 46
Hedysarum coronarium, 252
  spinosissimum, 252

Modiolus barbatus, 196
Mogoplistes squamiger, 162
mole, 46
Monarchus monarchus, 54
Monticola saxatilis, 104
  solitarius, 104
moorhen, 74
Morus alba, 214
  bassanus, 56
Motacilla alba, 98
  cinerea, 98
  flava, 98
  f. cinereocapilla, 98
  f. feldegg, 98
  f. flava, 98
  f. flavissima, 98
  f. iberiae, 98
  f. thunbergi, 98
moths, 150-60
mouflon, 54
mouse, harvest, 52
  house, 52
  wood, 52
mouse-ear, Cretan, 230
  sticky, 230
mulberry, white, 214
mullein, grey, 288
mullet, red, 208
  thick-lipped grey, 206
Mullus surmeletus, 208
Muraena helena, 208
murex, 194
Murex brandaris, 194
  trunculus, 194
Mus musculus, 52
Musa cavendishii, 222
Musca domestica, 178
Muscardinus avellanarius, 52
Muscari comosum, 314
  neglectum, 314
Muscicapa striata, 110
muslin moth, 160
mussel, common, 196
  fan, 198
mustard, white, 242
Mustela nivalis, 48

putorius, 48
Myotis bechsteinii, 50
  capaccinii, 50
  daubentonii, 50
  myotis, 50
  nattereri, 50
Myrmeleon formicarius, 170
myrtle, common, 31, 216
Myrtus communis, 216
Mythimna L-album, 160
Mytilus edulis, 196

N
Narcissus bulbicodium, 318
  serotinus, 318
  tazetta, 318
Nassarius incrassatus, 194
  reticulatus, 194
Natica alderi, 194
Natrix natrix, 128
natterjack, 132
navelwort, 242
necklace shell, 194
needle shell, 192
Nemobius sylvestris, 162
Nemoptera bipennis, 170
Neomys fodiens, 46
Neophron percnopterus, 66
Neotinea maculata, 334
Neottia nidus-avis, 324
Nepeta cataris, 282
Nereis diversicolor, 190
Nerium oleander, 276
Netta rufina, 64
nettle, common, 226
  membranous, 226
nettle tree, 29
  southern, 214
newt, great crested, 130
  marbled, 130
  smooth, 130
Nicotiana glauca, 288
Nigella damascene, 234
nightingale, 100
nightjar, 88
  red-necked, 88

sea, 292
Platalea leucorodia, 60
Platanthera bifolia, 324
  chlorantha, 324
Platanus orientalis, 214
  x *hispanica*, 214
Platichthys flesus, 208
Platycleis denticulata, 162
Platycnemis pennipes, 176
Plebejus argus, 146
Plecotus auritus, 50
Plegadis falcinellus, 60
Pleurodeles waltl, 130
ploughman's-spikenard, 300
plover, grey, 76
  Kentish, 22, 76
  little ringed, 76
  ringed, 76
  spur-winged, 76
Plusia gamma, 158
Pluvialis apricaria, 76
  squatarola, 76
pochard, 64
  red-crested, 64
Podalonia viatica, 178
Podarcis muralis, 126
  taurica, 126
Podiceps cristatus, 56
  nigricollis, 56
poinsettia, 258
polecat, 48
Polistes gallicus, 178
Pollachius pollachius, 206
pollack, 206
Polycera quadrilineata, 200
Polygala nicaeensis, 260
  vulgaris, 260
Polygonia c-album, 136
Polygonum maritimum, 226
Polyommatus icarus, 146
Pomatias elegans, 186
Pomatoschistus minutus, 206
pomegranate, 216
Pontia daplidice, 134
poppy, common, 36, 236
  long-headed, 236

Mediterranean, 238
  opium, 236
  prickly, 236
  rough, 238
  small, 238
Porcellana platycheles, 202
Porcellio sp., 182
porcupine, crested, 52
Porphyrio porphyrio, 74
Portugal, Cape St Vincent, 17, 18
Portuguese man-o'-war, 188
Porzana parva, 72
  porzana, 72
  pusilla, 72
posidonia, 310
Posidonia oceanica, 310
pratincole spp., 22
  black-winged, 76
  collared, 76
prawn, common, 202
prickly pear, 266
Prionace glauca, 208
processionary moth, pine, 154
prominent, pale, 154
Prosperinus prosperina, 152
Prunella collaris, 100
  grandiflora, 282
  modularis, 100
  vulgaris, 282
Prunus dulcis, 216
  lusitanica, 216
  prostrata, 216
  spinosa, 216
psammodromus, large, 126
Psammodromus algirus, 126
Pseudognaphalium luteo-album,
298
pseudorlaya, 272
Pseudorlaya pumila, 272
Pseudotergumia fidia, 140
Psoralea bituminosa, 246
Pterocephalus perennis, 294
Pterostoma palpina, 154
Ptyonoprogne rupestris, 96
Puffinus yelkouan, 56
Pulicaria dysenterica, 298